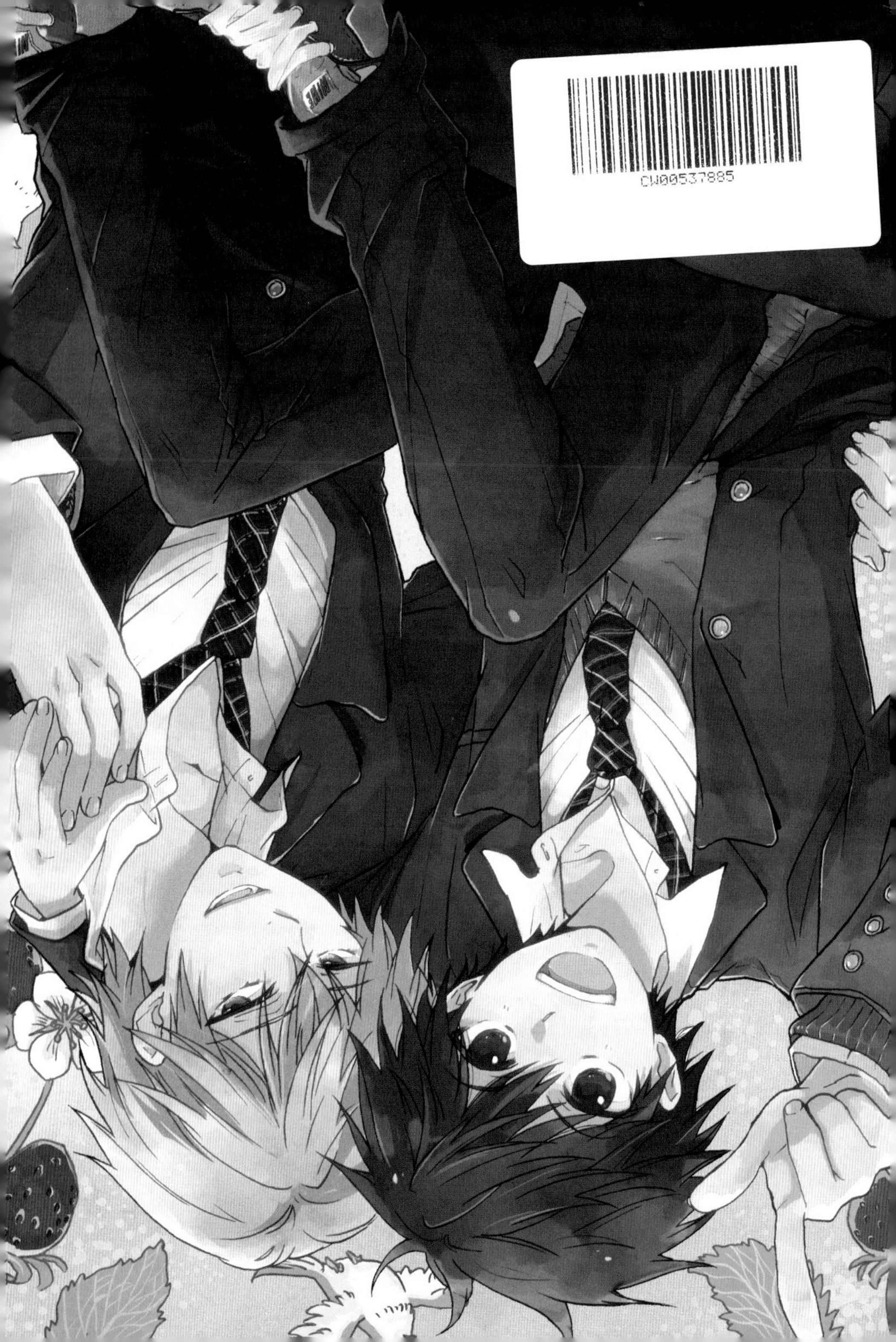

Hitorijime boyFRIEND

CONTENTS

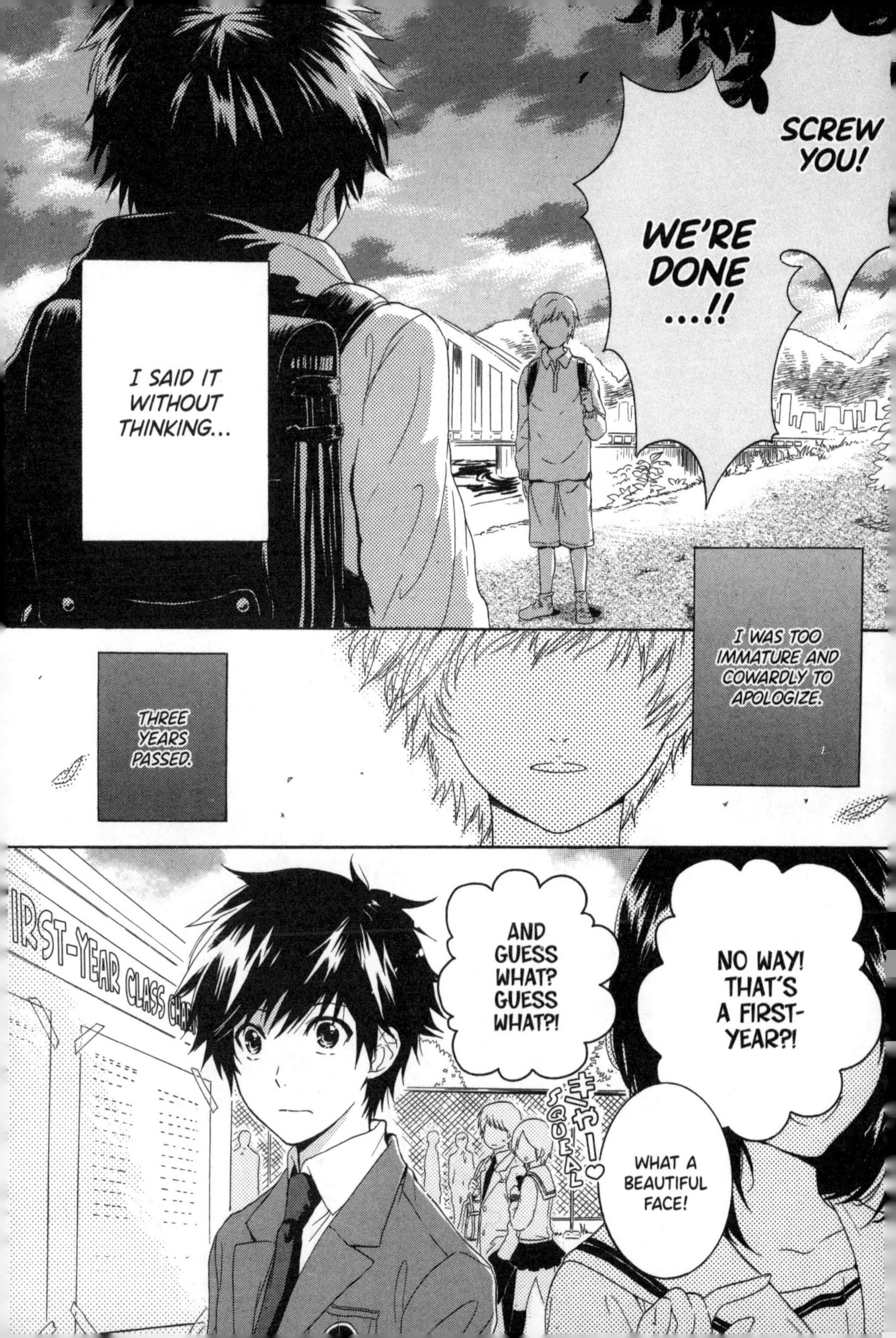

SCREW YOU!
WE'RE DONE ...!!
I SAID IT WITHOUT THINKING...
I WAS TOO IMMATURE AND COWARDLY TO APOLOGIZE.
THREE YEARS PASSED.
NO WAY! THAT'S A FIRST-YEAR?!
WHAT A BEAUTIFUL FACE!
キャー♥ SQUEAL
AND GUESS WHAT? GUESS WHAT?!

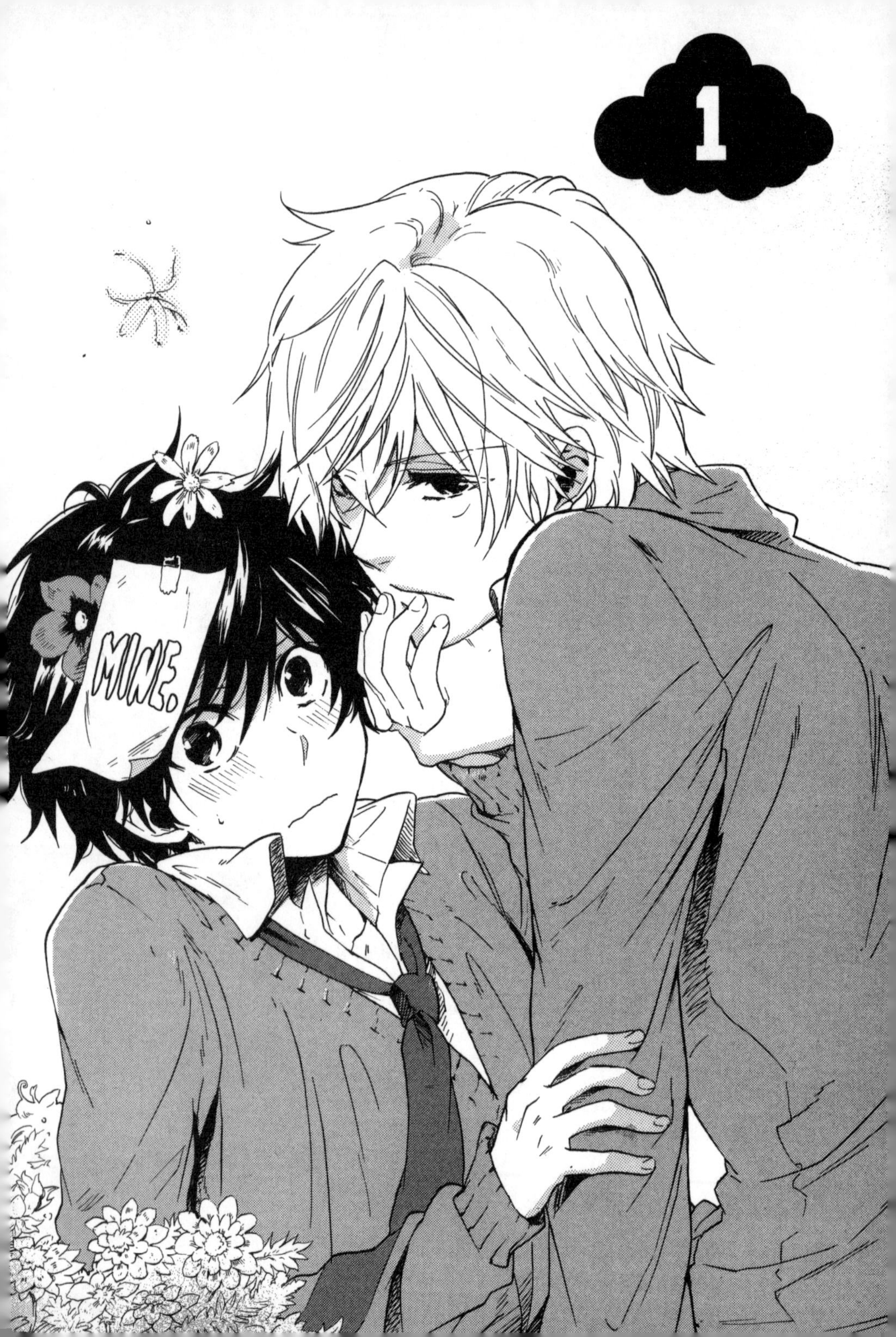
1
MINE.

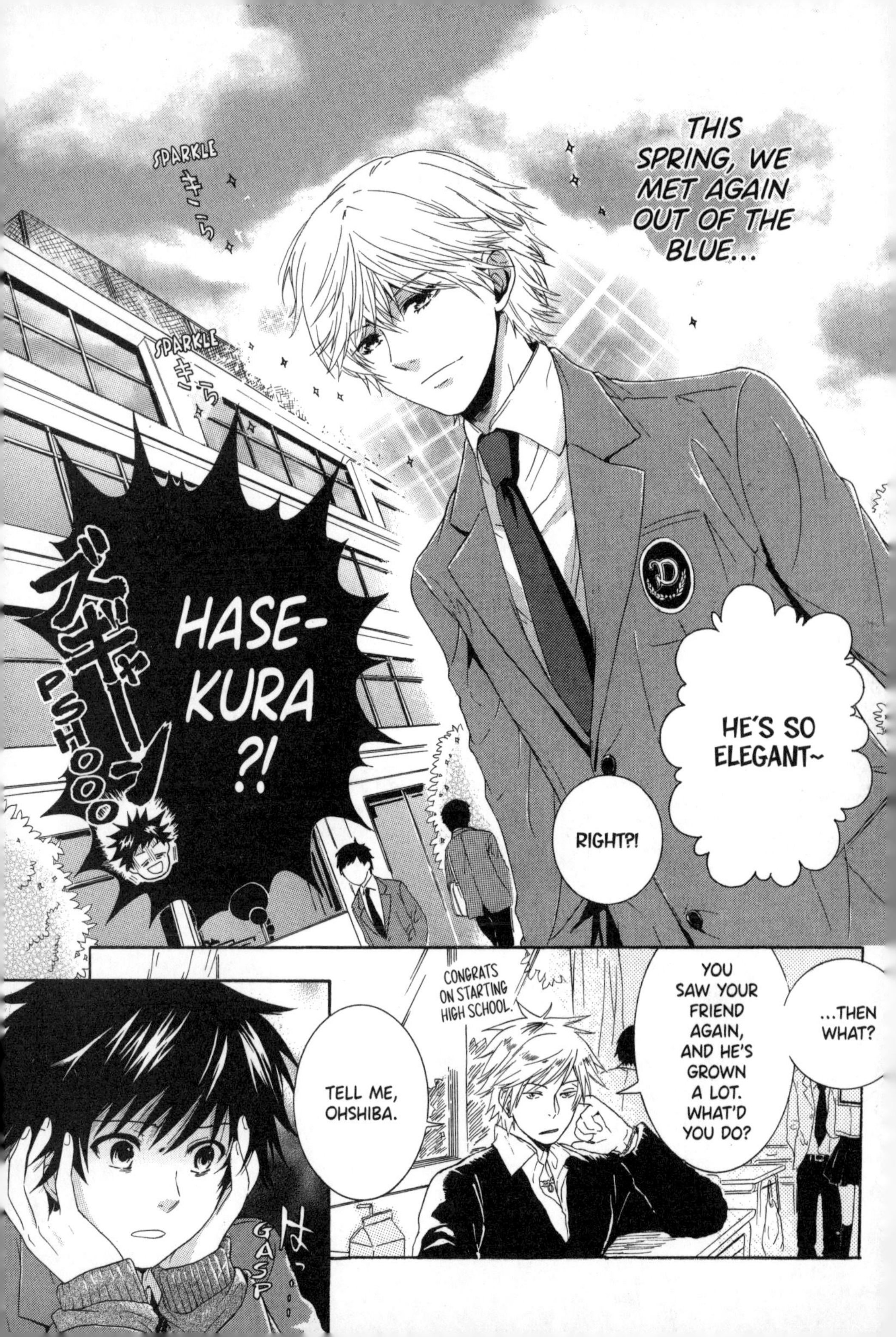
THIS SPRING, WE MET AGAIN OUT OF THE BLUE...
SPARKLE
SPARKLE
HE'S SO ELEGANT~
RIGHT?!
HASE-KURA ?!
PSHOOO
...THEN WHAT?
YOU SAW YOUR FRIEND AGAIN, AND HE'S GROWN A LOT. WHAT'D YOU DO?
CONGRATS ON STARTING HIGH SCHOOL.
TELL ME, OHSHIBA.
GASP

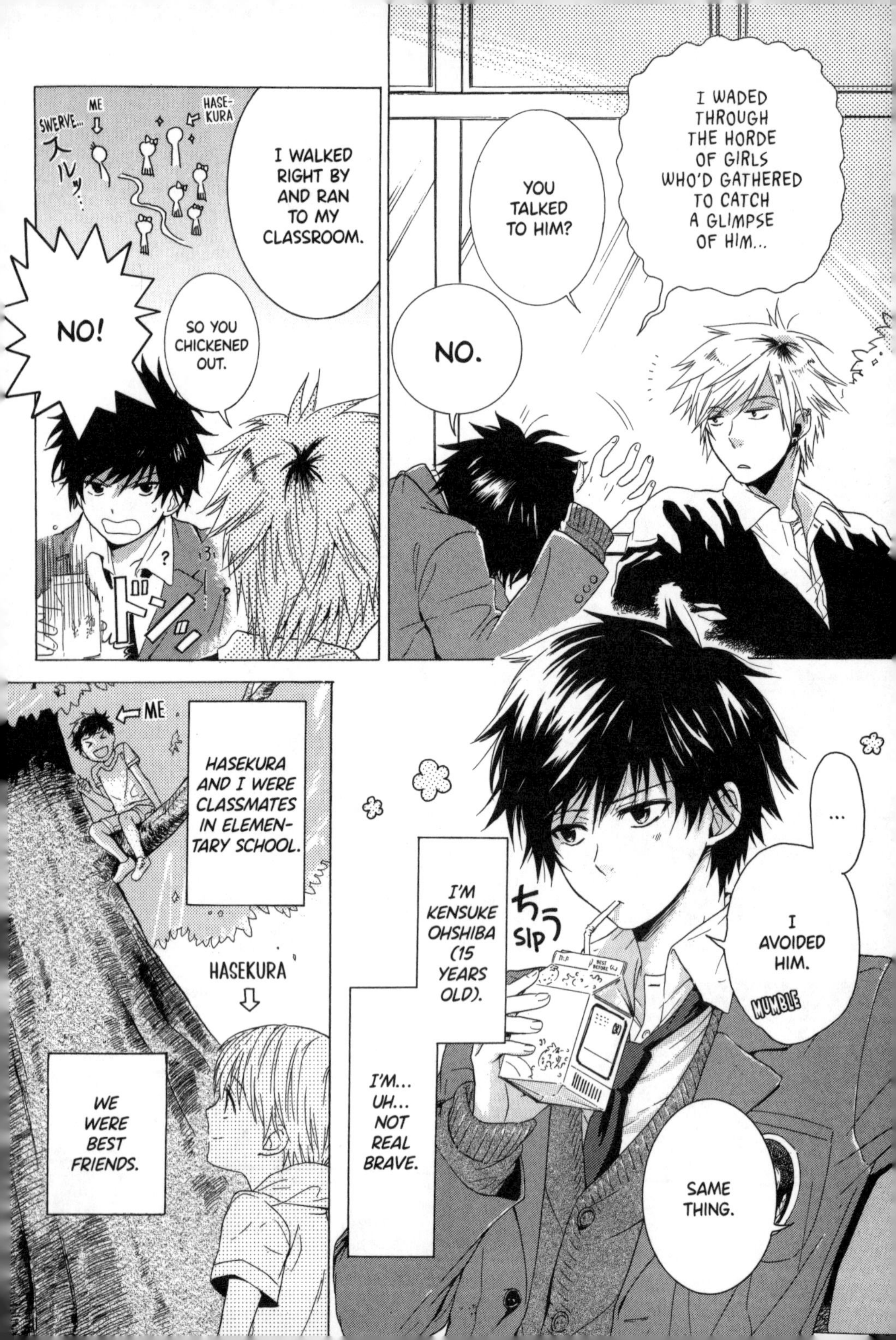
I WADED THROUGH THE HORDE OF GIRLS WHO'D GATHERED TO CATCH A GLIMPSE OF HIM...
YOU TALKED TO HIM?
NO.
I WALKED RIGHT BY AND RAN TO MY CLASSROOM.
HASE-KURA
ME
SWERVE...
SO YOU CHICKENED OUT.
NO!
...
I AVOIDED HIM.
MUMBLE
I'M KENSUKE OHSHIBA (15 YEARS OLD).
SIP
SAME THING.
I'M... UH... NOT REAL BRAVE.
ME
HASEKURA AND I WERE CLASSMATES IN ELEMENTARY SCHOOL.
HASEKURA
WE WERE BEST FRIENDS.

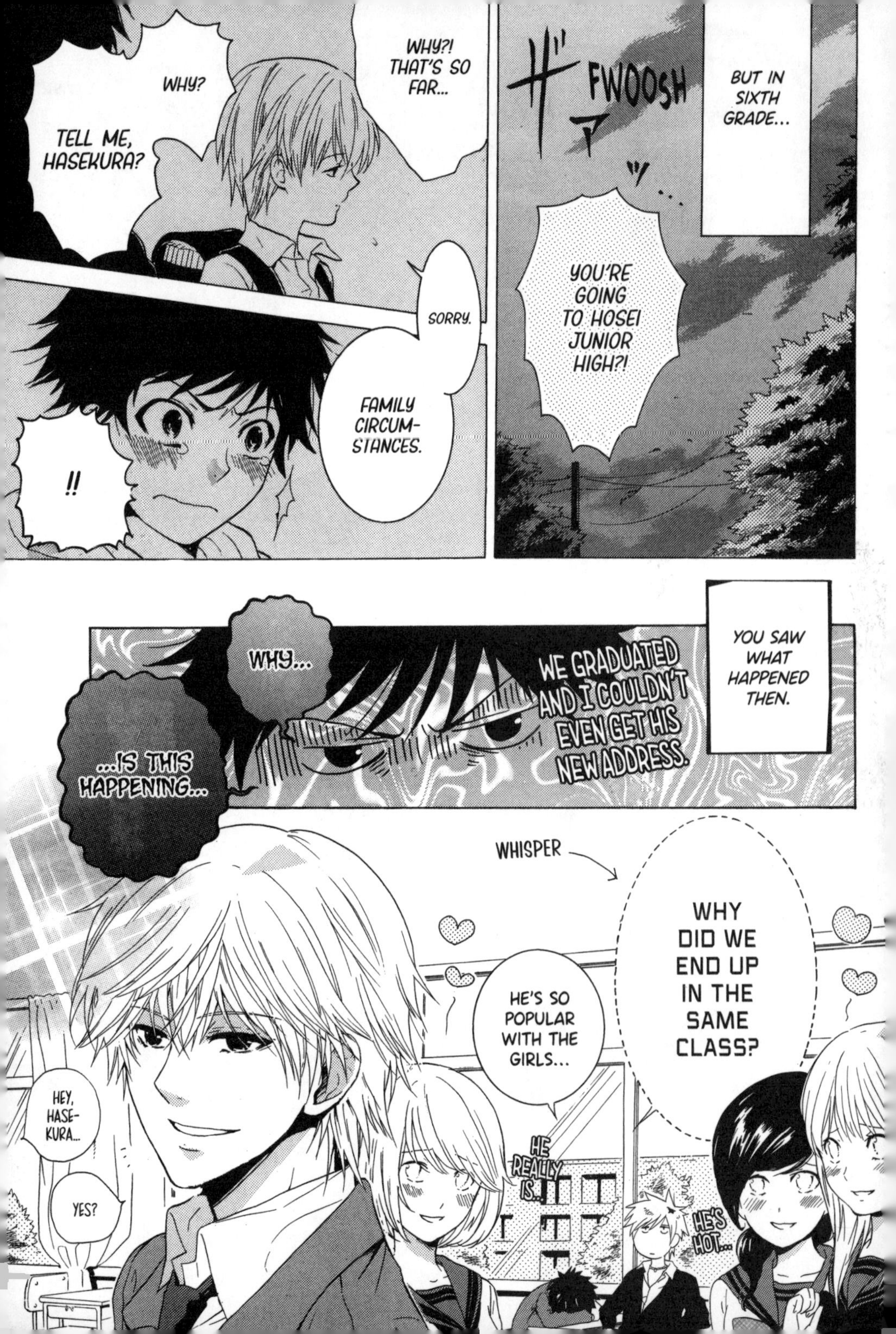
BUT IN SIXTH GRADE...
ザァッ
FWOOSH
YOU'RE GOING TO HOSEI JUNIOR HIGH?!
WHY?! THAT'S SO FAR...
WHY?
TELL ME, HASEKURA?
SORRY.
FAMILY CIRCUMSTANCES.
!!
YOU SAW WHAT HAPPENED THEN.
WE GRADUATED AND I COULDN'T EVEN GET HIS NEW ADDRESS.
WHY...
...IS THIS HAPPENING...
WHISPER
WHY DID WE END UP IN THE SAME CLASS?
HE'S HOT...
HE'S SO POPULAR WITH THE GIRLS...
HE REALLY IS...
HEY, HASEKURA...
YES?

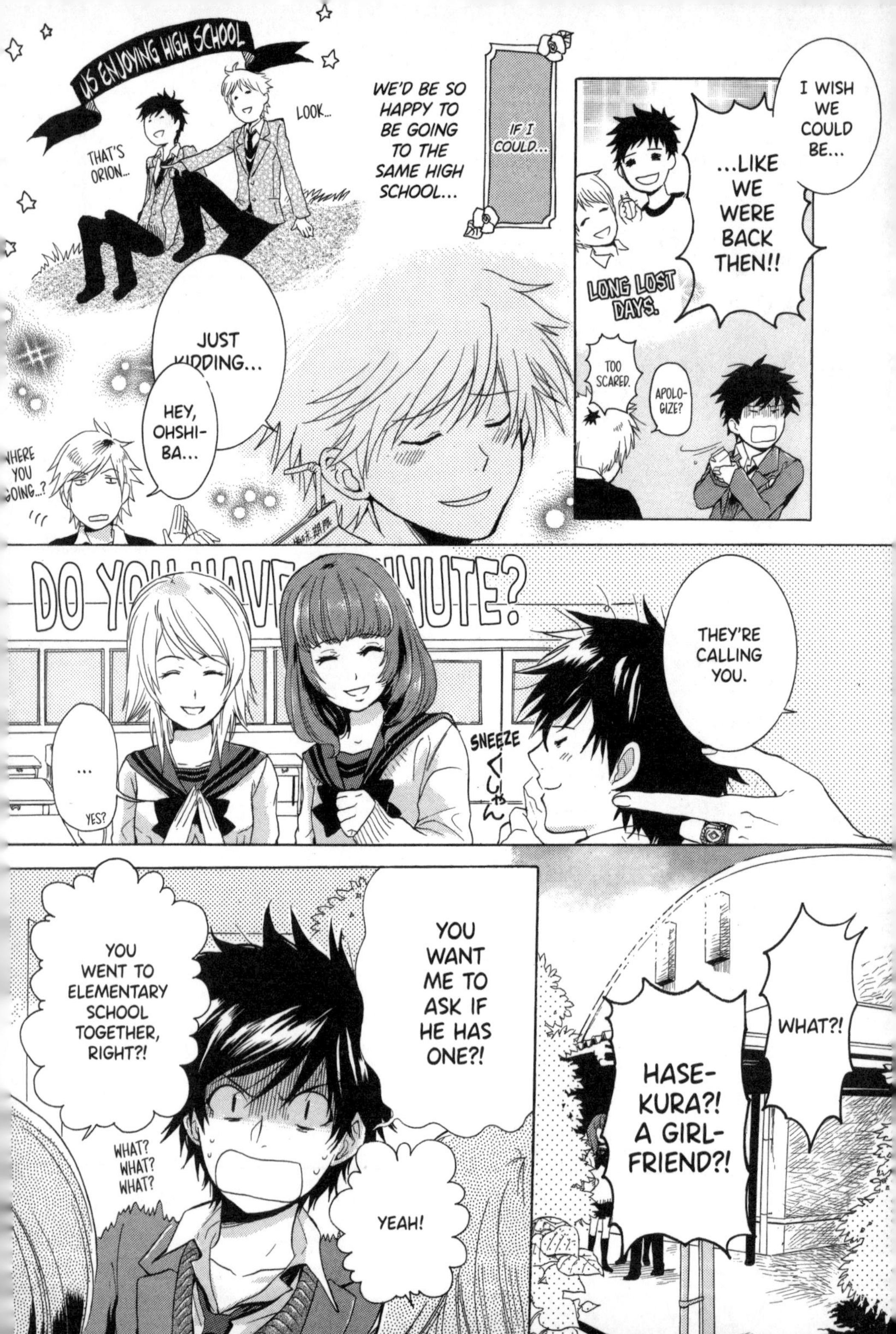
I WISH WE COULD BE...
...LIKE WE WERE BACK THEN!!
LONG LOST DAYS.
APOLO-GIZE?
TOO SCARED.
IF I COULD...
WE'D BE SO HAPPY TO BE GOING TO THE SAME HIGH SCHOOL...
US ENJOYING HIGH SCHOOL
LOOK...
THAT'S ORION...
JUST KIDDING...
HEY, OHSHI-BA...
THEY'RE CALLING YOU.
SNEEZE
...
YES?
WHAT?!
HASE-KURA?! A GIRL-FRIEND?!
YOU WANT ME TO ASK IF HE HAS ONE?!
YOU WENT TO ELEMENTARY SCHOOL TOGETHER, RIGHT?!
YEAH!
WHAT? WHAT? WHAT?

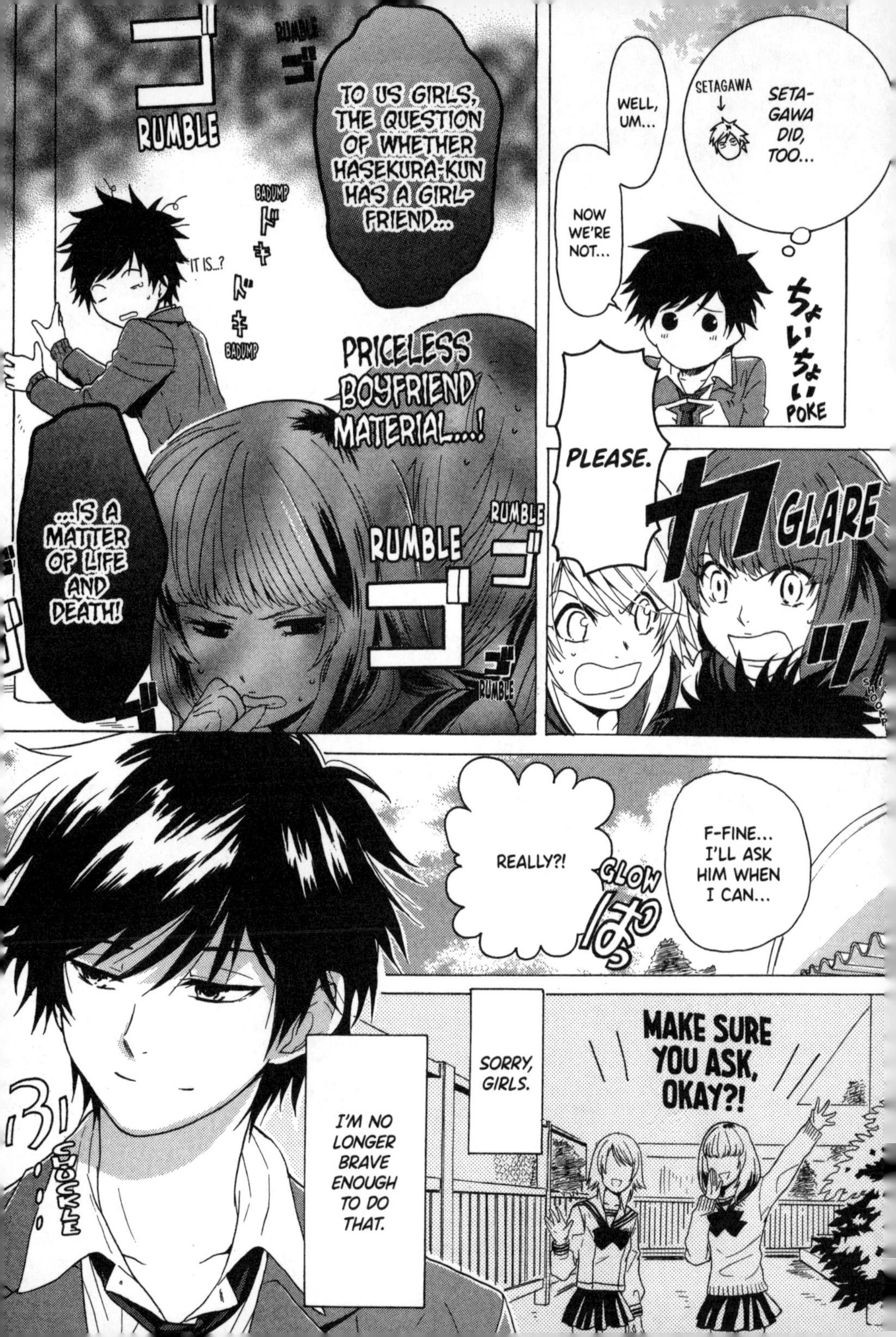
SETAGAWA
SETA-GAWA DID, TOO...
WELL, UM...
NOW WE'RE NOT...
POKE
PLEASE.
GLARE
SHOOMP
RUMBLE
RUMBLE
TO US GIRLS, THE QUESTION OF WHETHER HASEKURA-KUN HAS A GIRL-FRIEND...
BADUMP
IT IS...?
BADUMP
PRICELESS BOYFRIEND MATERIAL...!
...IS A MATTER OF LIFE AND DEATH!
RUMBLE
RUMBLE
RUMBLE
F-FINE... I'LL ASK HIM WHEN I CAN...
GLOW
REALLY?!
MAKE SURE YOU ASK, OKAY?!
SORRY, GIRLS.
I'M NO LONGER BRAVE ENOUGH TO DO THAT.
CHUCKLE

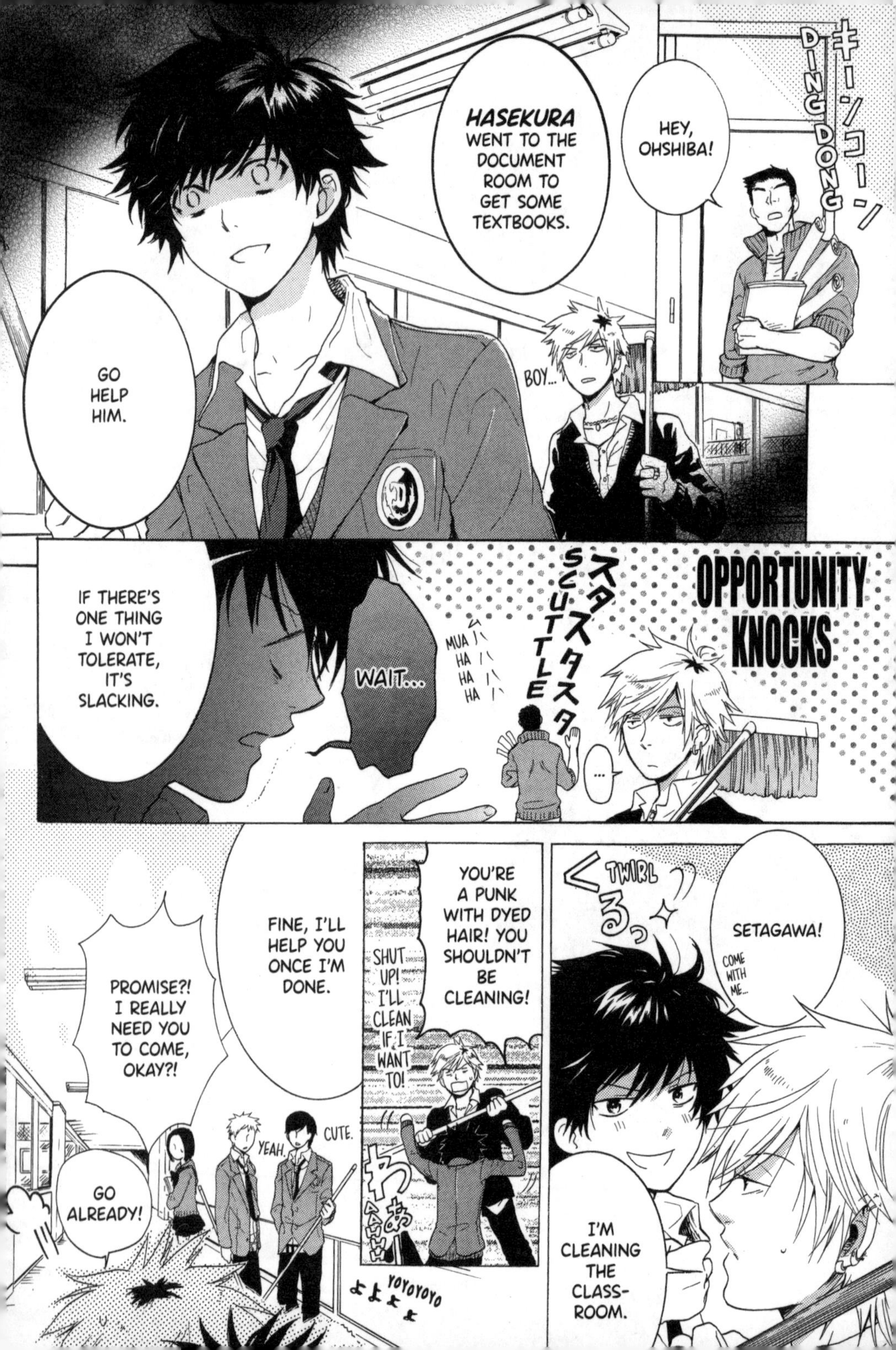
キーンコーン
DING DONG
HEY, OHSHIBA!
HASEKURA WENT TO THE DOCUMENT ROOM TO GET SOME TEXTBOOKS.
BOY...
GO HELP HIM.
OPPORTUNITY KNOCKS
スタスタスタ
SCUTTLE
...
ムハハハ
MUA HA HA HA
WAIT...
IF THERE'S ONE THING I WON'T TOLERATE, IT'S SLACKING.
SETAGAWA!
くるっ
TWIRL
COME WITH ME...
I'M CLEANING THE CLASS-ROOM.
YOU'RE A PUNK WITH DYED HAIR! YOU SHOULDN'T BE CLEANING!
SHUT UP! I'LL CLEAN IF I WANT TO!
わあ
AAUGH
FINE, I'LL HELP YOU ONCE I'M DONE.
PROMISE?! I REALLY NEED YOU TO COME, OKAY?!
CUTE.
YEAH.
GO ALREADY!
よよよよ
YOYOYOYO

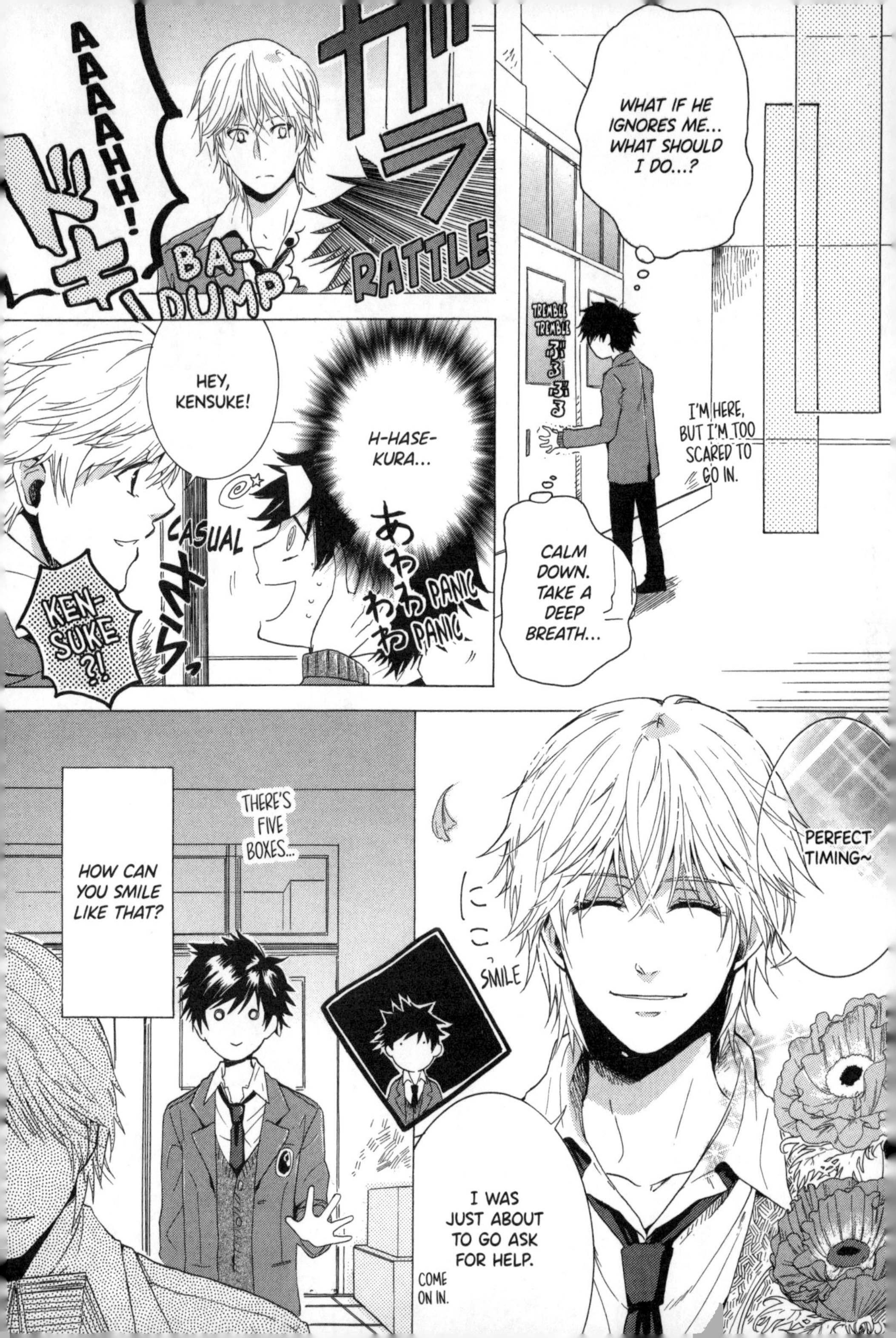
WHAT IF HE IGNORES ME... WHAT SHOULD I DO...?
TREMBLE TREMBLE
ぶるぶる
I'M HERE, BUT I'M TOO SCARED TO GO IN.
CALM DOWN. TAKE A DEEP BREATH...
ガラ
RATTLE
ドキ
BA-DUMP
AAAAAHH!
HEY, KENSUKE!
H-HASE-KURA...
あわわわ
PANIC PANIC
すらっ
CASUAL
KEN-SUKE?!
PERFECT TIMING~
にこっ
SMILE
I WAS JUST ABOUT TO GO ASK FOR HELP.
COME ON IN.
THERE'S FIVE BOXES...
HOW CAN YOU SMILE LIKE THAT?

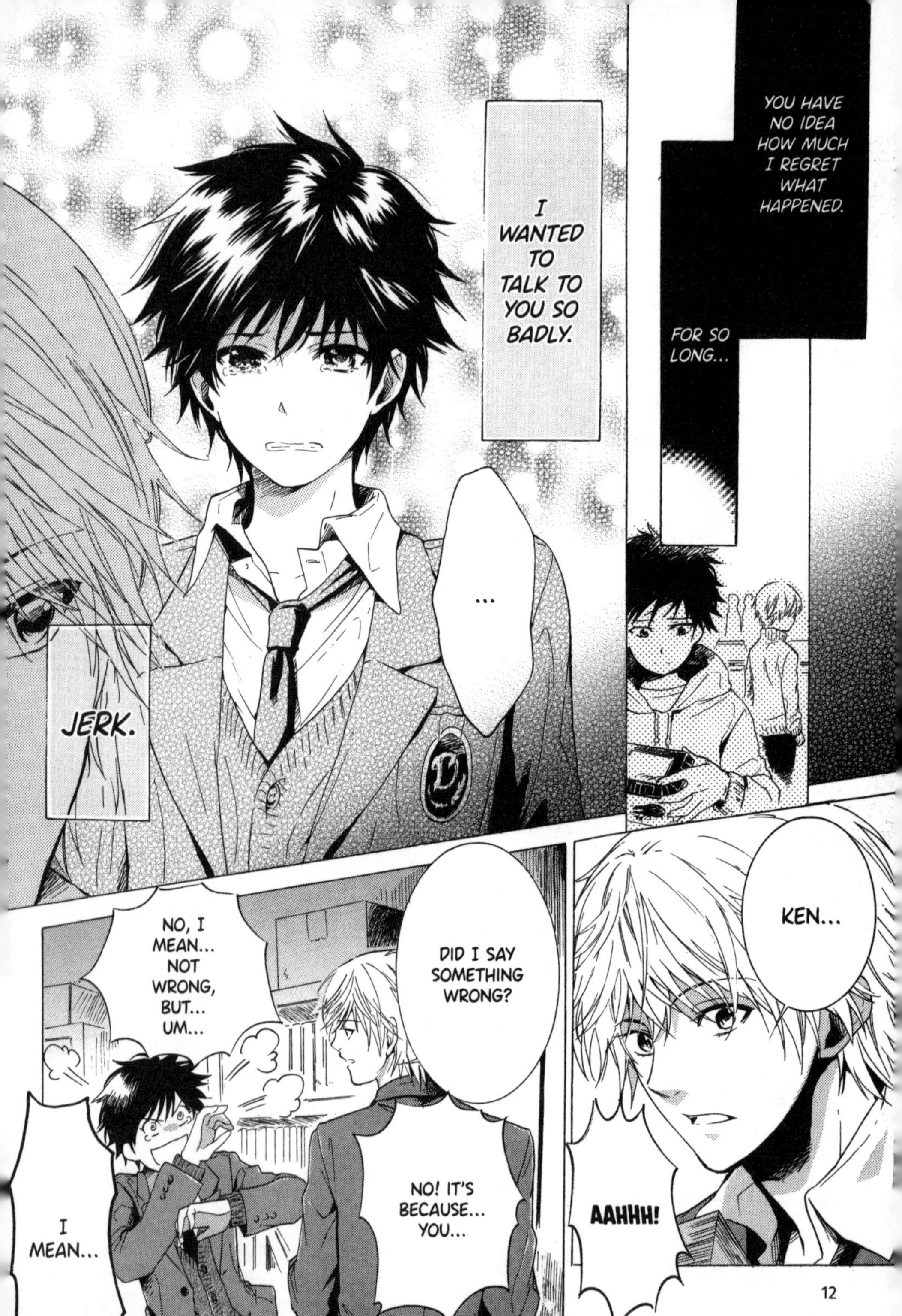
YOU HAVE NO IDEA HOW MUCH I REGRET WHAT HAPPENED.
FOR SO LONG...
I WANTED TO TALK TO YOU SO BADLY.
...
JERK.
KEN...
AAHHH!
DID I SAY SOMETHING WRONG?
NO, I MEAN... NOT WRONG, BUT... UM...
NO! IT'S BECAUSE... YOU...
I MEAN...

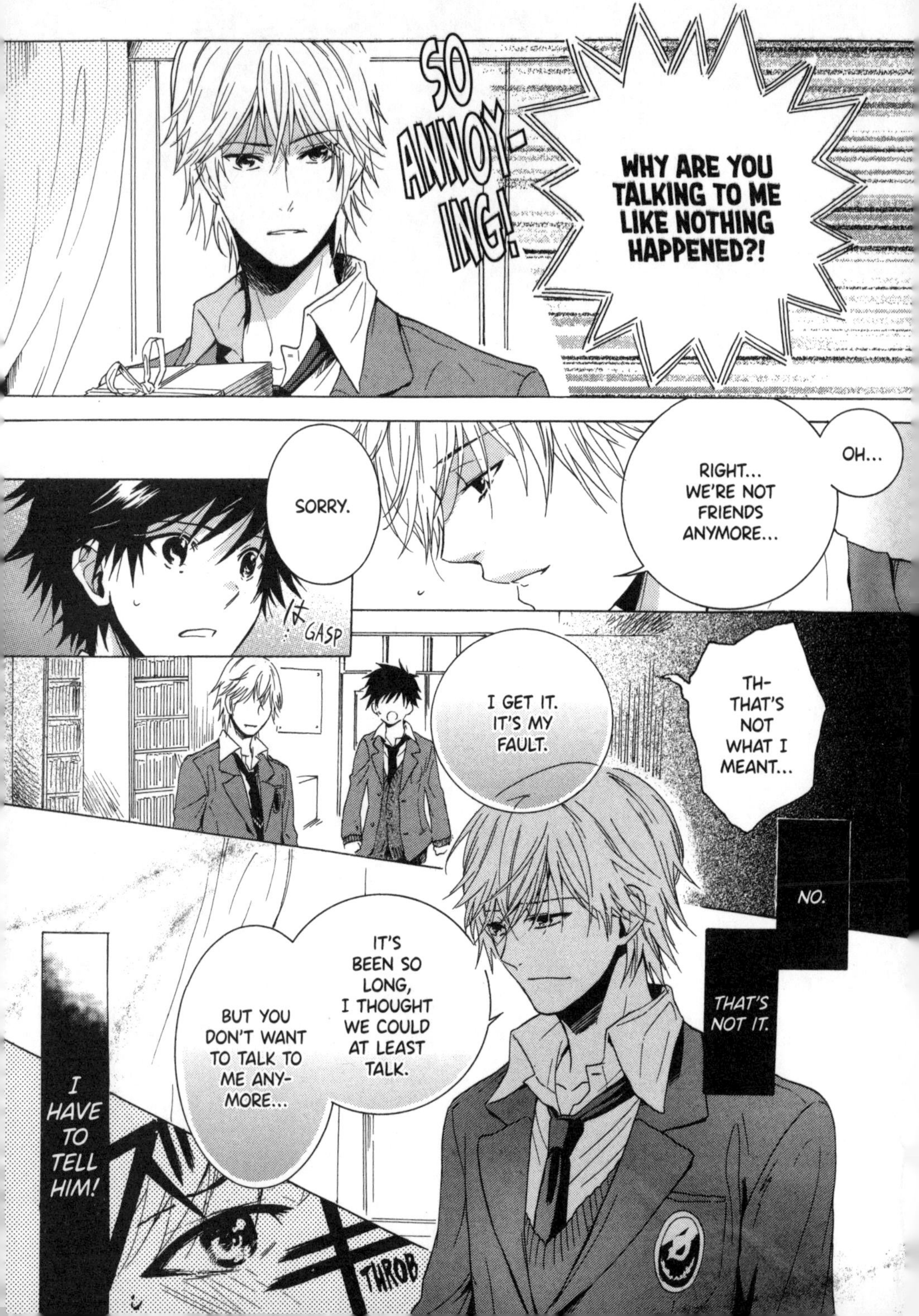
WHY ARE YOU TALKING TO ME LIKE NOTHING HAPPENED?!
SO ANNOY-ING!
OH...
RIGHT... WE'RE NOT FRIENDS ANYMORE...
SORRY.
は GASP
TH- THAT'S NOT WHAT I MEANT...
I GET IT. IT'S MY FAULT.
NO.
THAT'S NOT IT.
IT'S BEEN SO LONG, I THOUGHT WE COULD AT LEAST TALK.
BUT YOU DON'T WANT TO TALK TO ME ANY-MORE...
I HAVE TO TELL HIM!
THROB

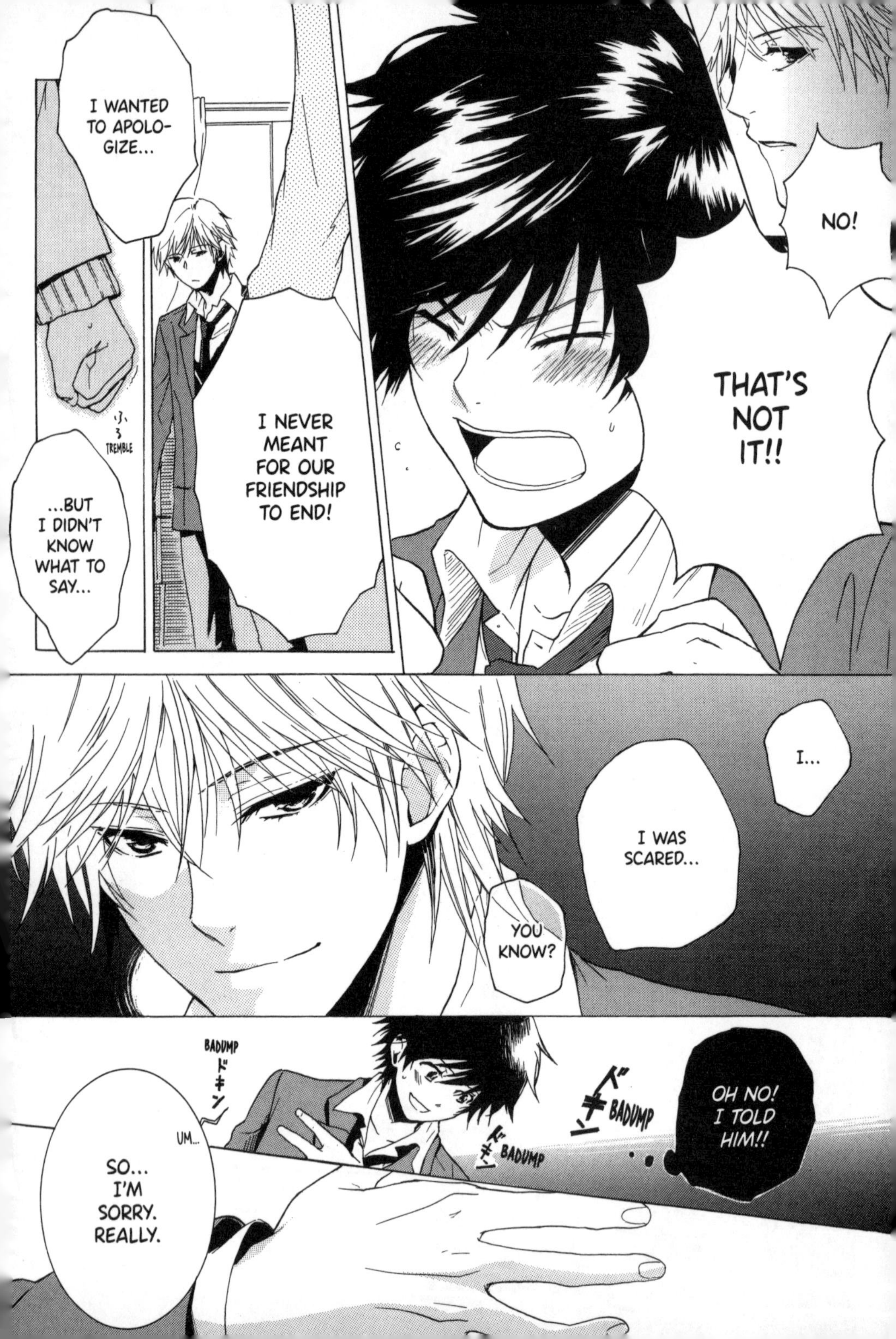
NO!
THAT'S NOT IT!!
I NEVER MEANT FOR OUR FRIENDSHIP TO END!
I WANTED TO APOLO-GIZE...
ふる
TREMBLE
...BUT I DIDN'T KNOW WHAT TO SAY...
I...
I WAS SCARED...
YOU KNOW?
OH NO! I TOLD HIM!!
ドキン BADUMP
ドキン BADUMP
ドキン BADUMP
UM...
SO... I'M SORRY. REALLY.

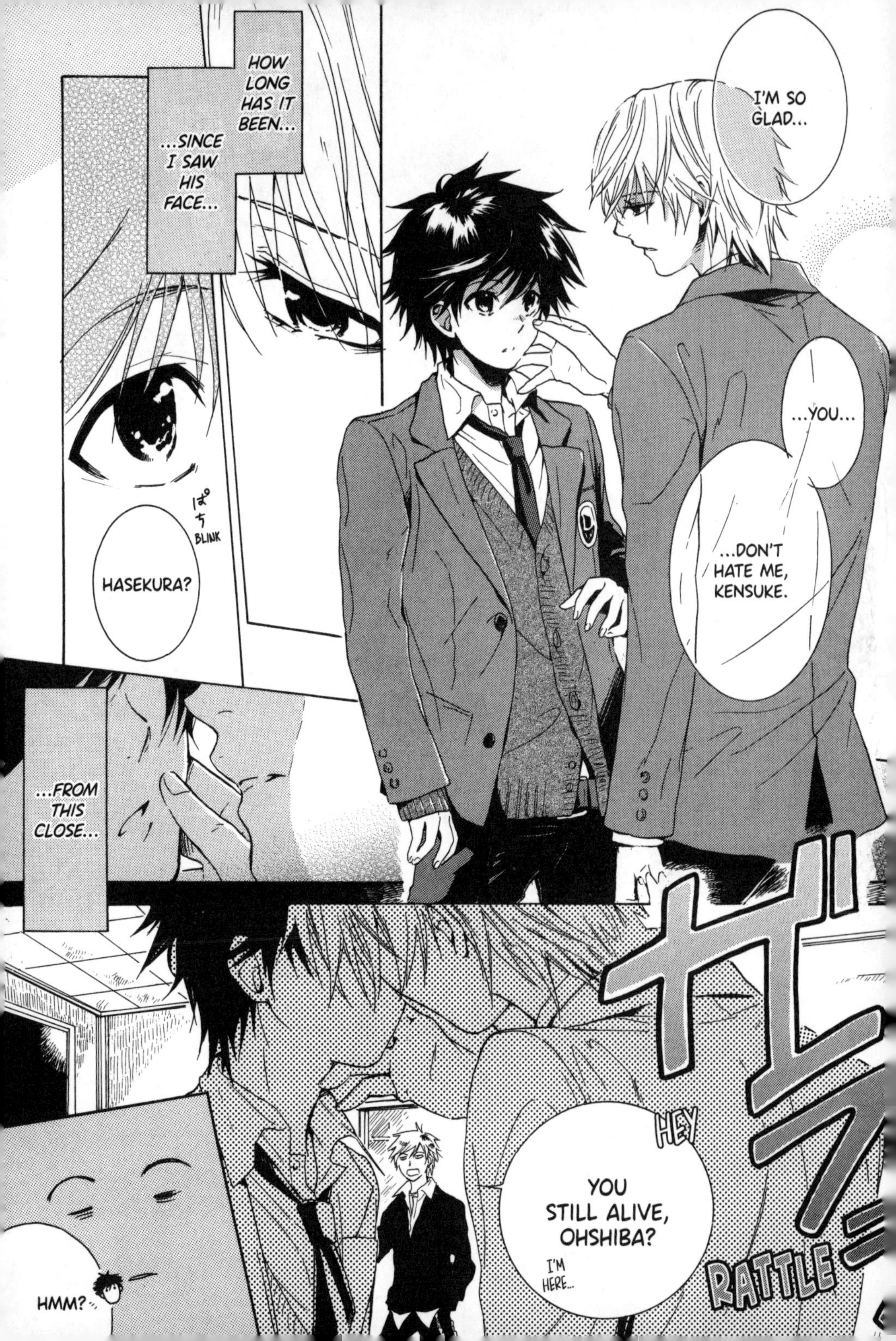
I'M SO GLAD...
...YOU...
...DON'T HATE ME, KENSUKE.
HOW LONG HAS IT BEEN...
...SINCE I SAW HIS FACE...
ぱち
BLINK
HASEKURA?
...FROM THIS CLOSE...
ガラ
RATTLE
HEY
YOU STILL ALIVE, OHSHIBA?
I'M HERE...
HMM?

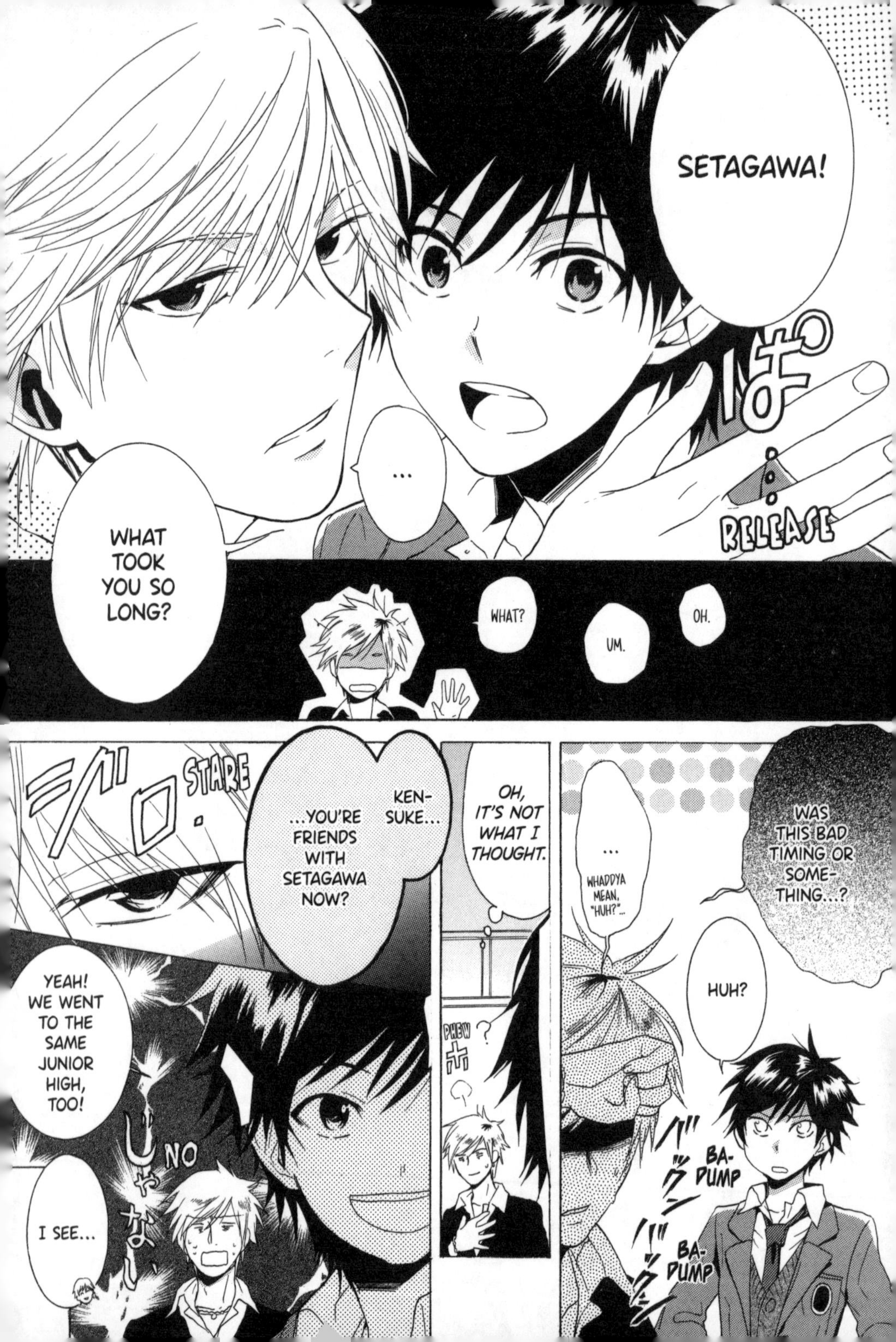
SETAGAWA!
RELEASE
...
WHAT TOOK YOU SO LONG?
OH.
UM.
WHAT?
WAS THIS BAD TIMING OR SOME-THING...?
HUH?
BA-DUMP
BA-DUMP
...
WHADDYA MEAN, "HUH?"...
OH, IT'S NOT WHAT I THOUGHT.
PHEW
?
STARE
KEN-SUKE...
...YOU'RE FRIENDS WITH SETAGAWA NOW?
YEAH! WE WENT TO THE SAME JUNIOR HIGH, TOO!
NO
I SEE...

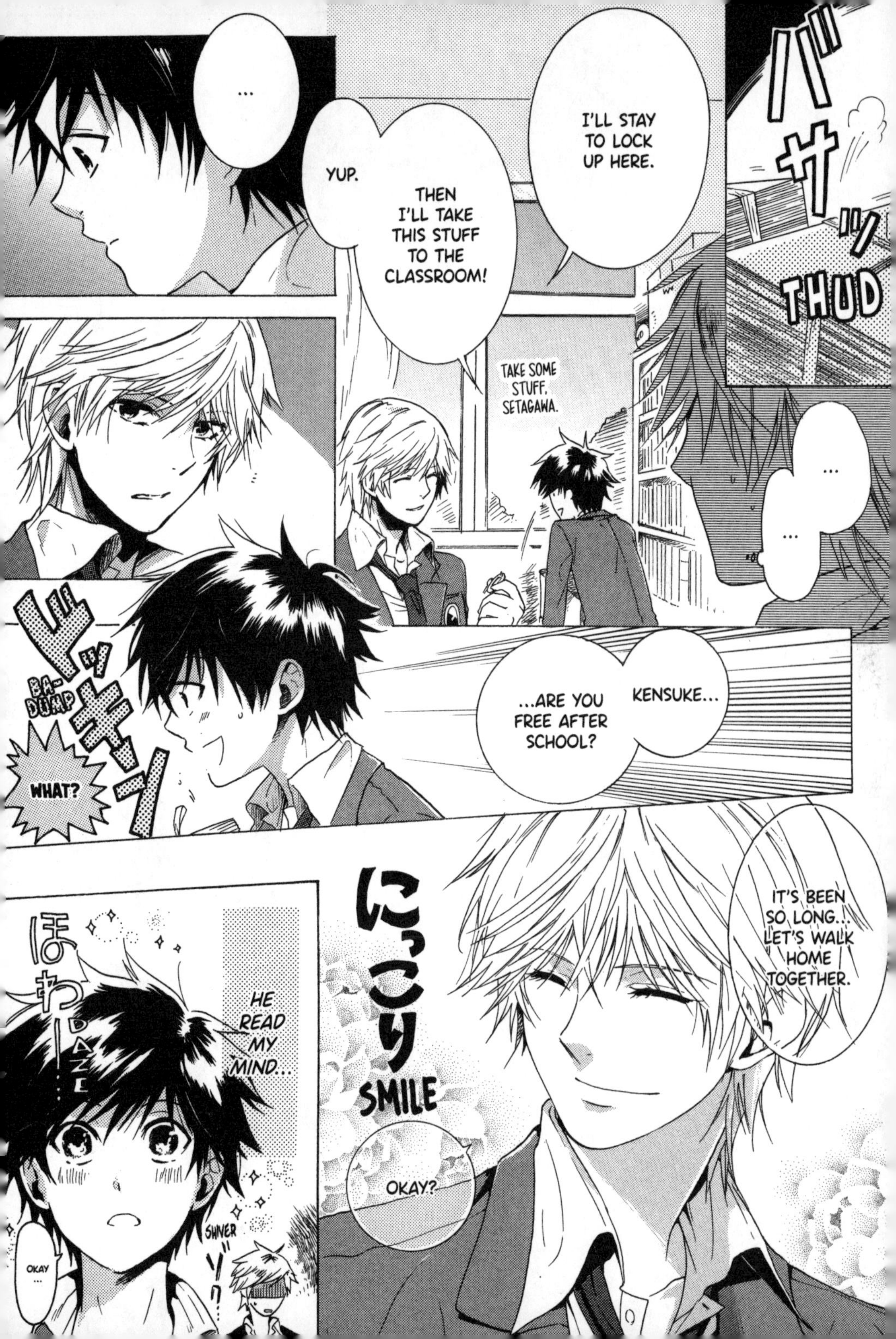
バサッ
THUD
I'LL STAY TO LOCK UP HERE.
YUP.
THEN I'LL TAKE THIS STUFF TO THE CLASSROOM!
...
...
...
TAKE SOME STUFF, SETAGAWA.
KENSUKE...
...ARE YOU FREE AFTER SCHOOL?
ドキッ
BA-DUMP
WHAT?
IT'S BEEN SO LONG... LET'S WALK HOME TOGETHER.
にっこり
SMILE
OKAY?
ほわ
DAZE
HE READ MY MIND...
SHIVER
ゾクッ
OKAY ...

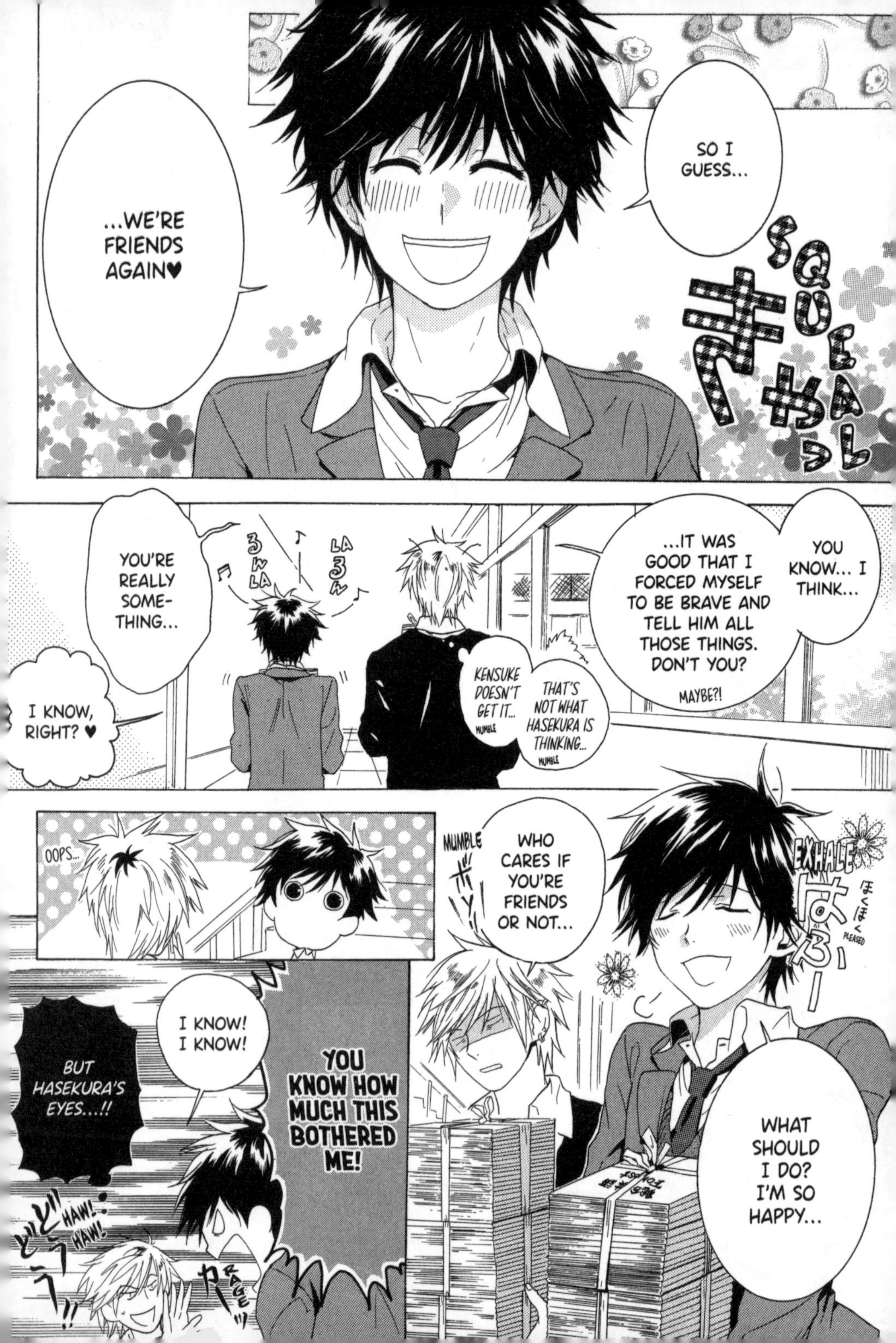
SO I GUESS...
SQUEAL
...WE'RE FRIENDS AGAIN♥
YOU KNOW... I THINK...
...IT WAS GOOD THAT I FORCED MYSELF TO BE BRAVE AND TELL HIM ALL THOSE THINGS. DON'T YOU?
MAYBE?!
THAT'S NOT WHAT HASEKURA IS THINKING... MUMBLE
KENSUKE DOESN'T GET IT... MUMBLE
LA LA
YOU'RE REALLY SOMETHING...
I KNOW, RIGHT? ♥
EXHALE
PLEASED
WHAT SHOULD I DO? I'M SO HAPPY...
MUMBLE
WHO CARES IF YOU'RE FRIENDS OR NOT...
OOPS...
I KNOW! I KNOW!
YOU KNOW HOW MUCH THIS BOTHERED ME!
RAGE
BUT HASEKURA'S EYES...!!
HAW! HAW!

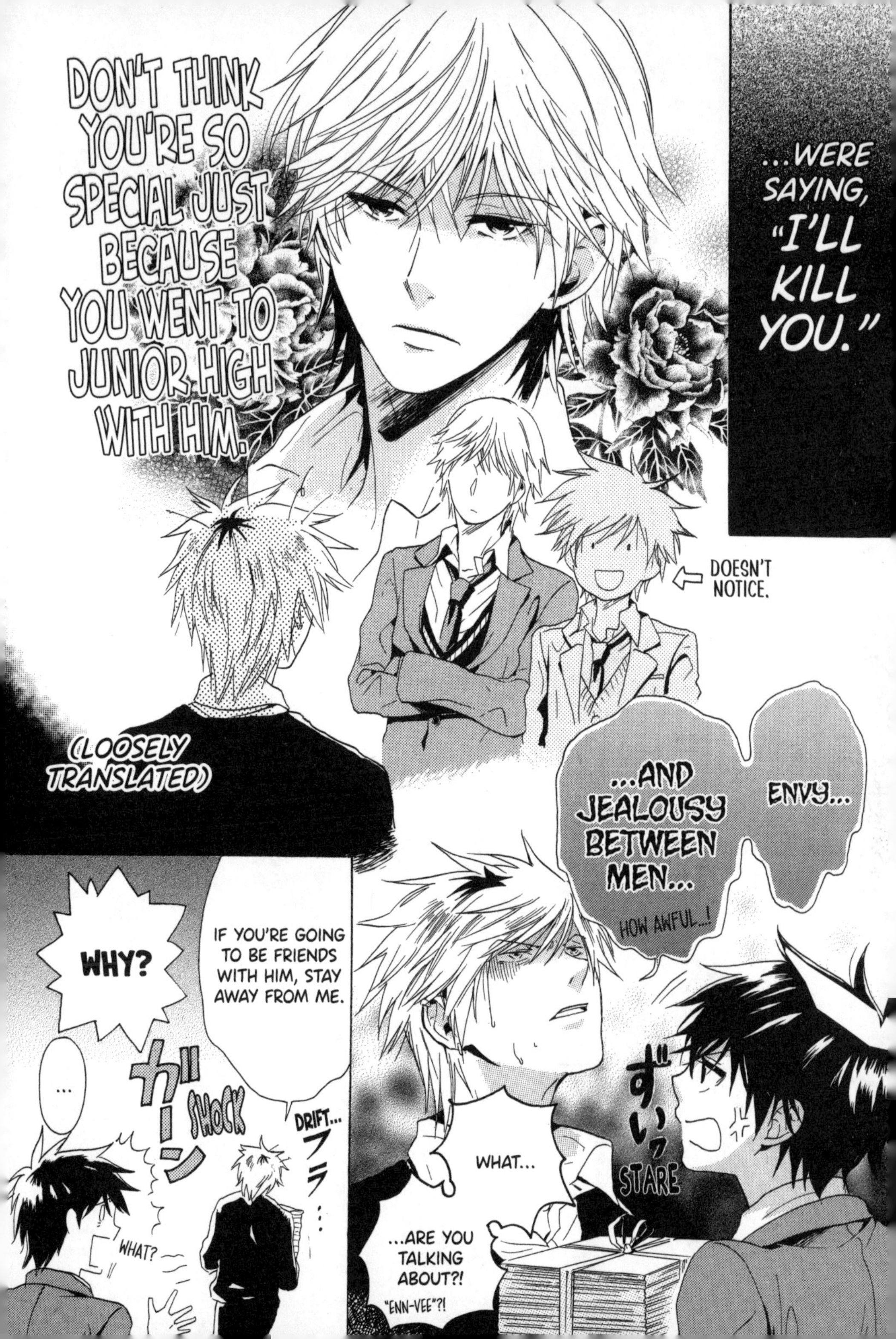

...WERE SAYING, "I'LL KILL YOU."
DON'T THINK YOU'RE SO SPECIAL JUST BECAUSE YOU WENT TO JUNIOR HIGH WITH HIM.
DOESN'T NOTICE.
(LOOSELY TRANSLATED)
ENVY...
...AND JEALOUSY BETWEEN MEN...
HOW AWFUL..!
ずいっ
STARE
WHAT...
...ARE YOU TALKING ABOUT?!
"ENN-VEE"?!
IF YOU'RE GOING TO BE FRIENDS WITH HIM, STAY AWAY FROM ME.
WHY?
DRIFT...
フラ…
ガーン
SHOCK
...
WHAT?

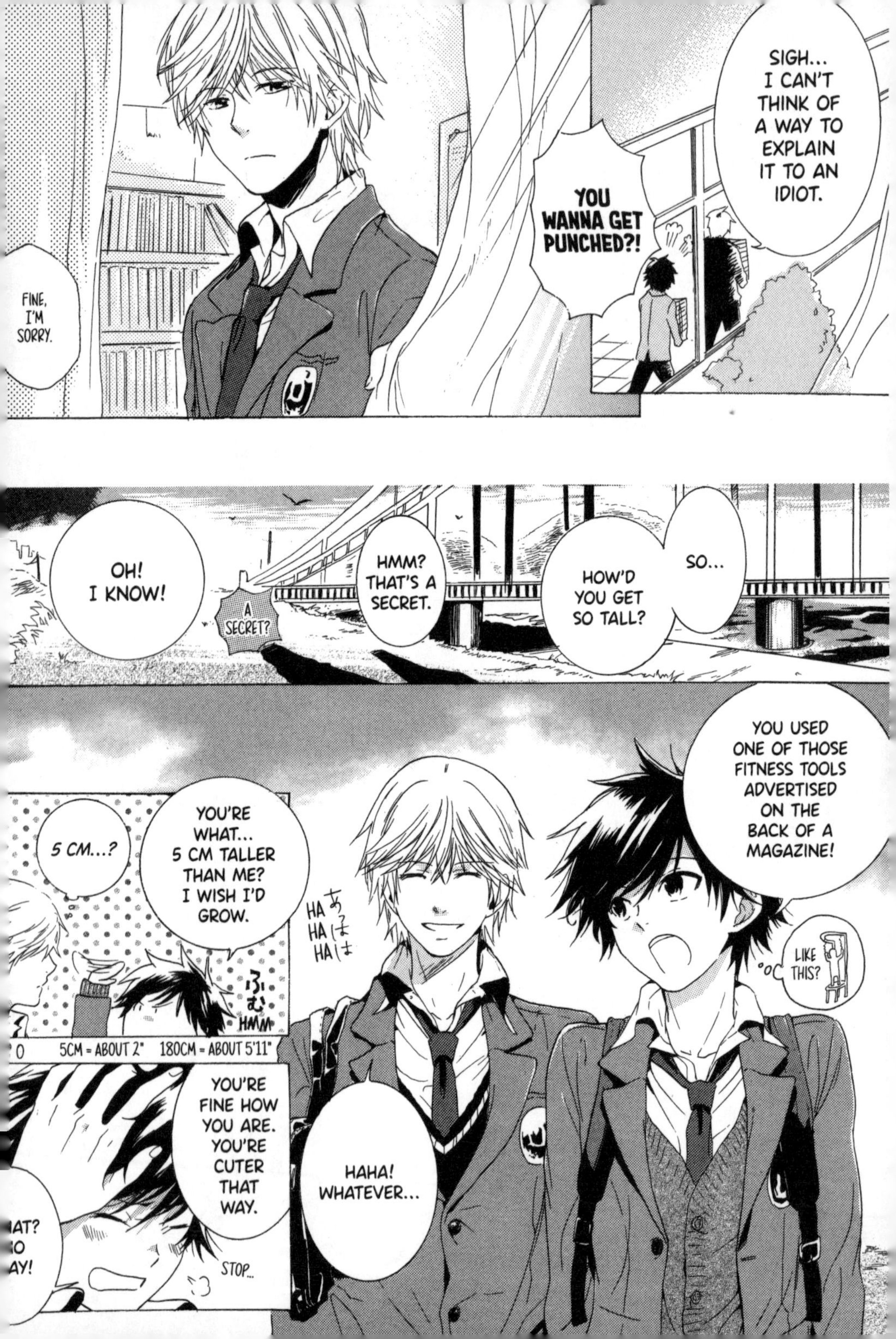
SIGH... I CAN'T THINK OF A WAY TO EXPLAIN IT TO AN IDIOT.
YOU WANNA GET PUNCHED?!
FINE, I'M SORRY.
SO...
HOW'D YOU GET SO TALL?
HMM? THAT'S A SECRET.
A SECRET?
OH! I KNOW!
YOU USED ONE OF THOSE FITNESS TOOLS ADVERTISED ON THE BACK OF A MAGAZINE!
LIKE THIS?
HA HA HA あはは
HAHA! WHATEVER...
YOU'RE WHAT... 5 CM TALLER THAN ME? I WISH I'D GROW.
5 CM...?
ふむ HMM
5CM = ABOUT 2" 180CM = ABOUT 5'11"
YOU'RE FINE HOW YOU ARE. YOU'RE CUTER THAT WAY.
STOP...

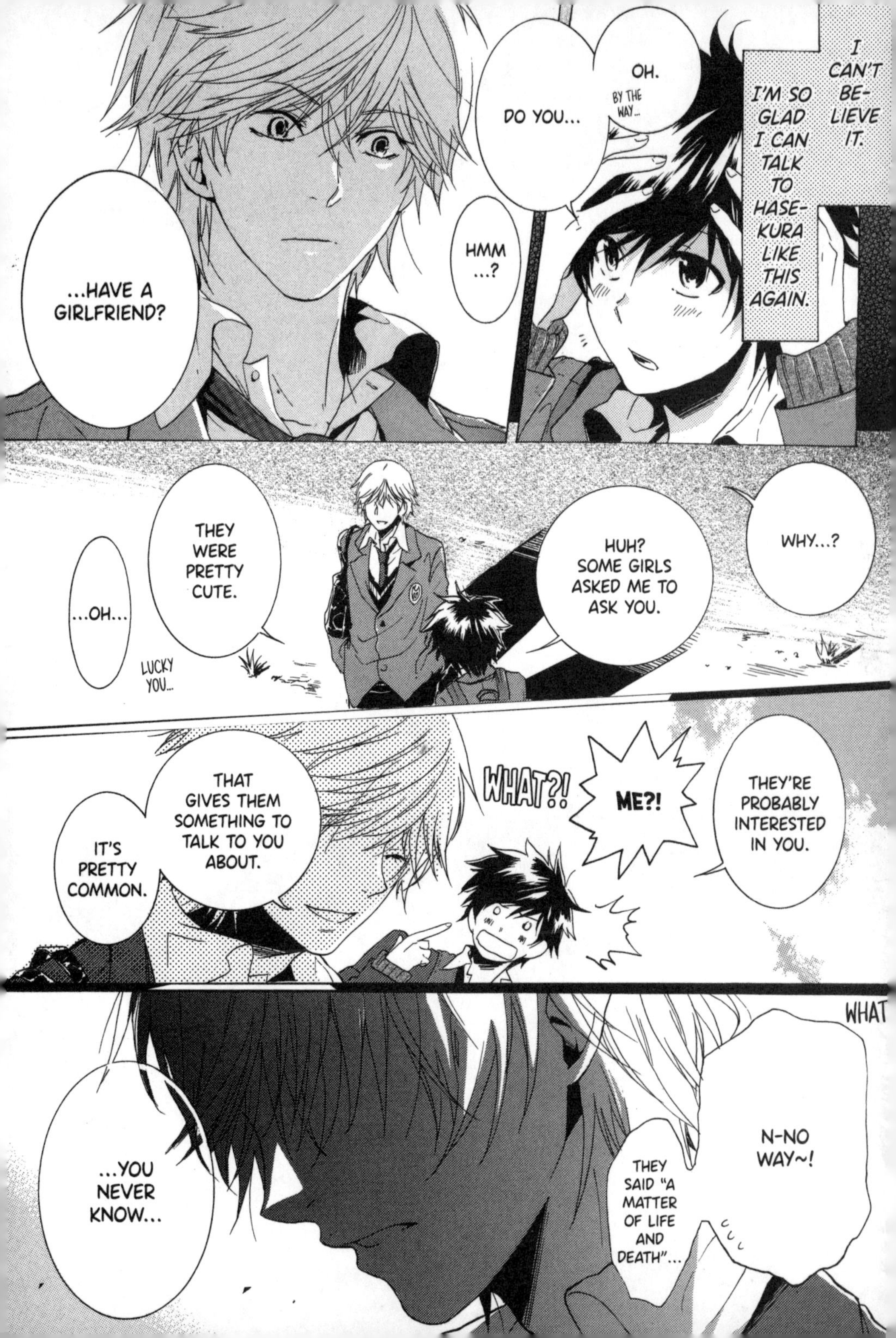

I CAN'T BE-LIEVE IT.
I'M SO GLAD I CAN TALK TO HASE-KURA LIKE THIS AGAIN.
OH.
BY THE WAY...
DO YOU...
HMM ...?
...HAVE A GIRLFRIEND?
WHY...?
HUH? SOME GIRLS ASKED ME TO ASK YOU.
THEY WERE PRETTY CUTE.
LUCKY YOU...
...OH...
THEY'RE PROBABLY INTERESTED IN YOU.
ME?!
WHAT?!
THAT GIVES THEM SOMETHING TO TALK TO YOU ABOUT.
IT'S PRETTY COMMON.
WHAT
N-NO WAY~!
THEY SAID "A MATTER OF LIFE AND DEATH"...
...YOU NEVER KNOW...

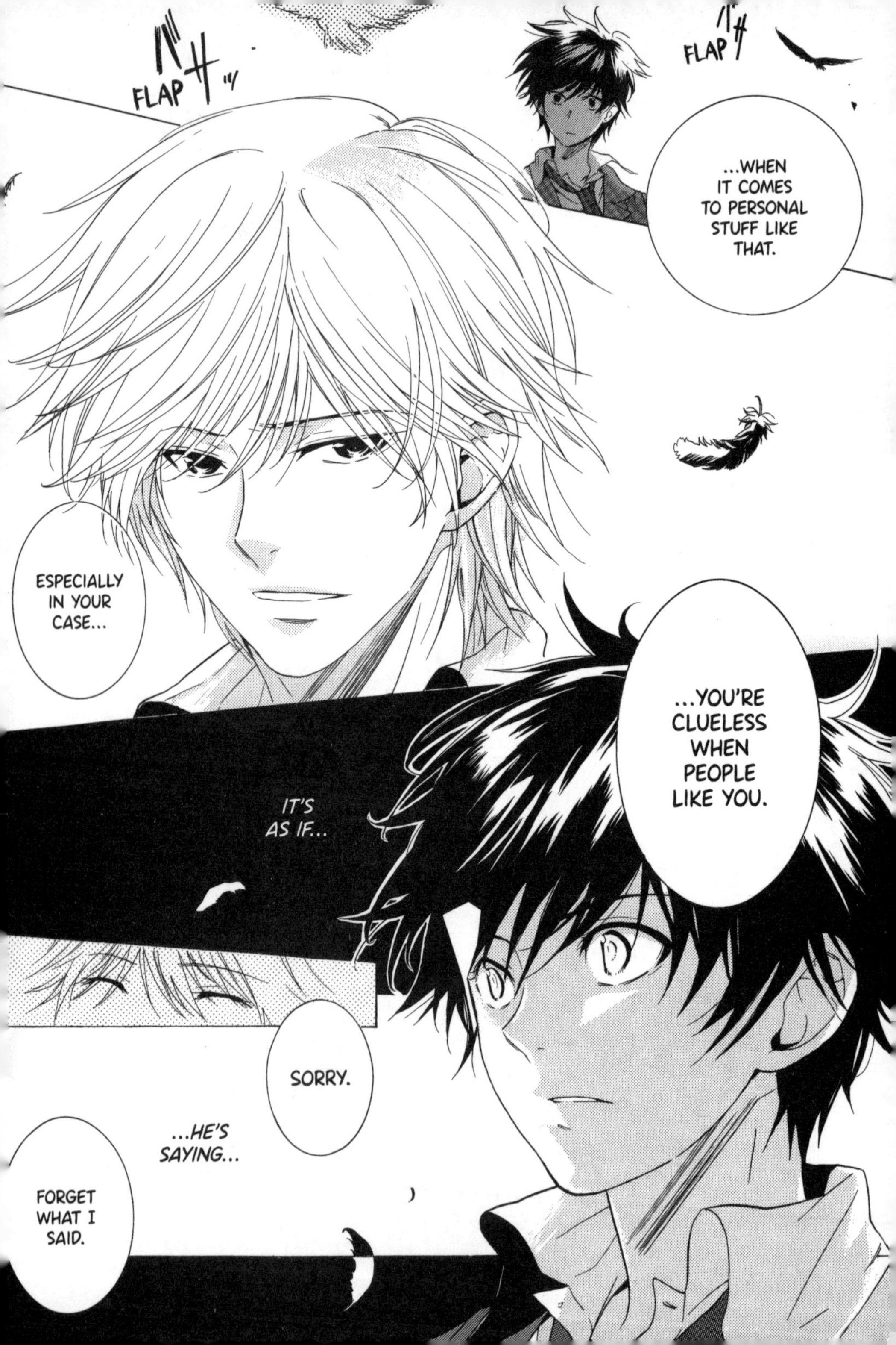
バサ FLAP
...WHEN IT COMES TO PERSONAL STUFF LIKE THAT.
バサッ FLAP
ESPECIALLY IN YOUR CASE...
...YOU'RE CLUELESS WHEN PEOPLE LIKE YOU.
IT'S AS IF...
SORRY.
...HE'S SAYING...
FORGET WHAT I SAID.

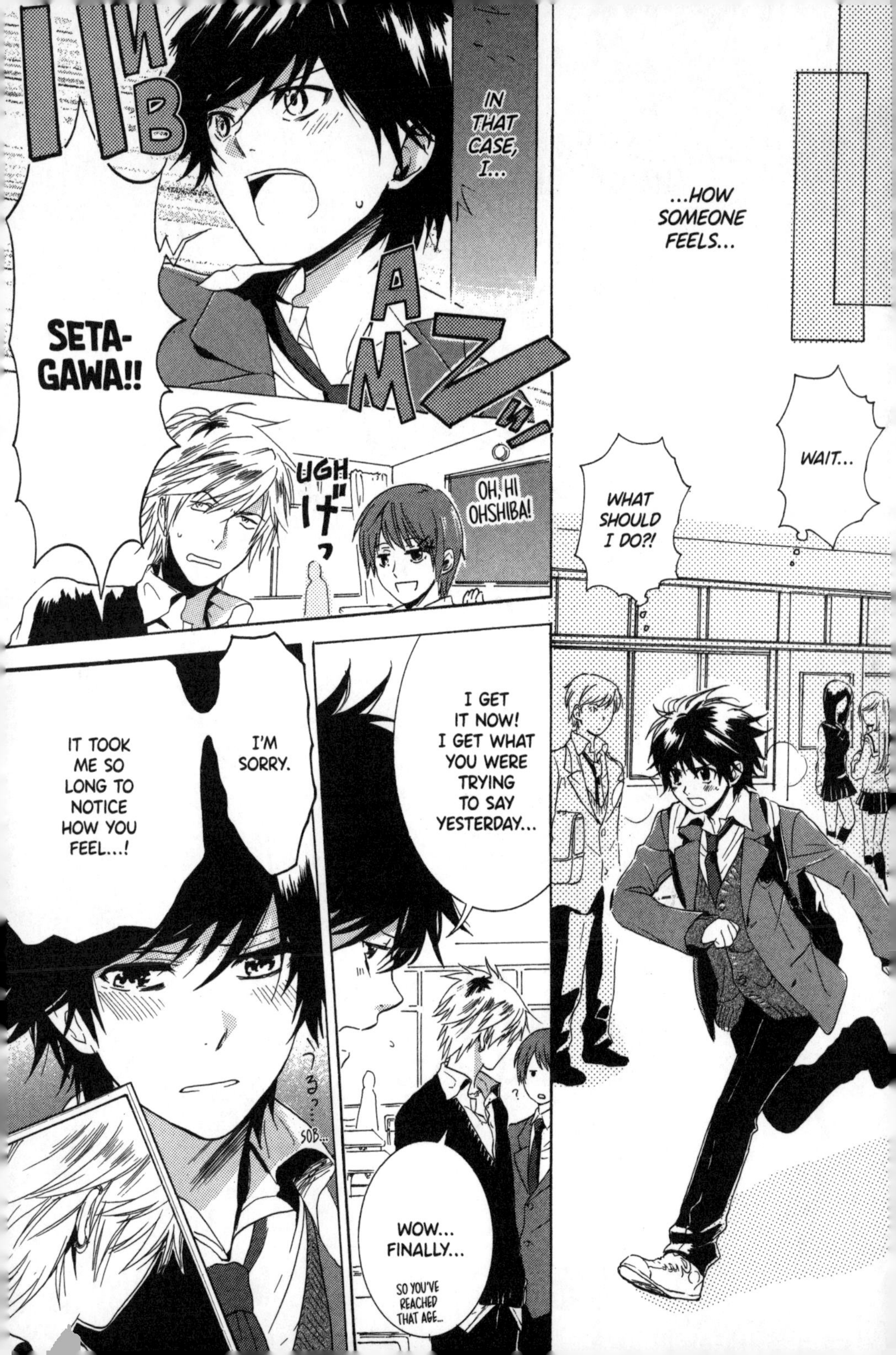
...HOW SOMEONE FEELS...
WAIT...
WHAT SHOULD I DO?!
IN THAT CASE, I...
SETA-GAWA!!
UGH
げっ
OH, HI OHSHIBA!
I GET IT NOW! I GET WHAT YOU WERE TRYING TO SAY YESTERDAY...
WOW... FINALLY...
SO YOU'VE REACHED THAT AGE...
SOB...
I'M SORRY.
IT TOOK ME SO LONG TO NOTICE HOW YOU FEEL...!

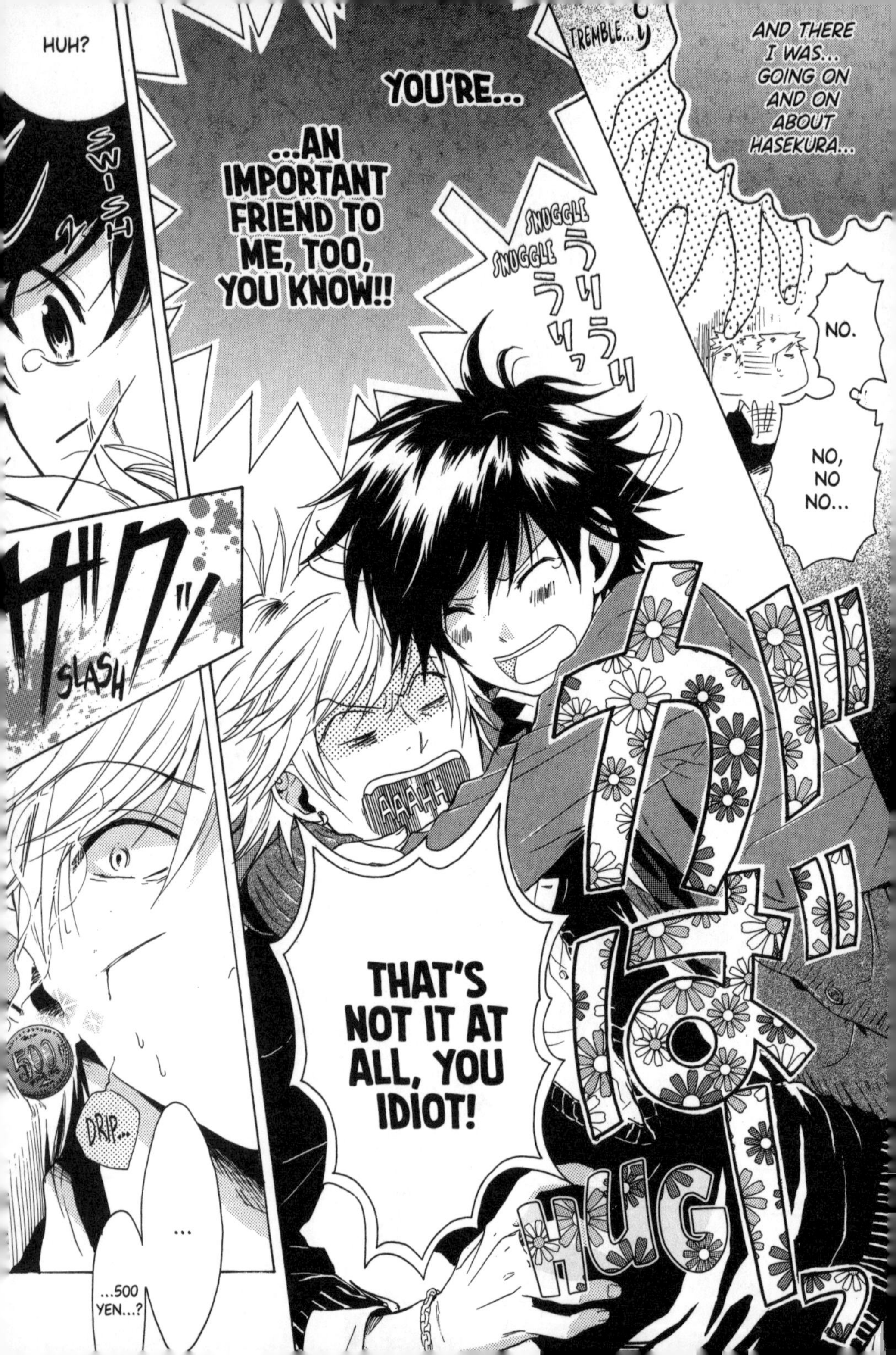
AND THERE I WAS... GOING ON AND ON ABOUT HASEKURA...
TREMBLE...
NO.
NO, NO NO...
YOU'RE...
...AN IMPORTANT FRIEND TO ME, TOO, YOU KNOW!!
SNUGGLE SNUGGLE
AAAH
THAT'S NOT IT AT ALL, YOU IDIOT!
HUG
HUH?
SWISH
SLASH
DRIP...
...
...500 YEN...?

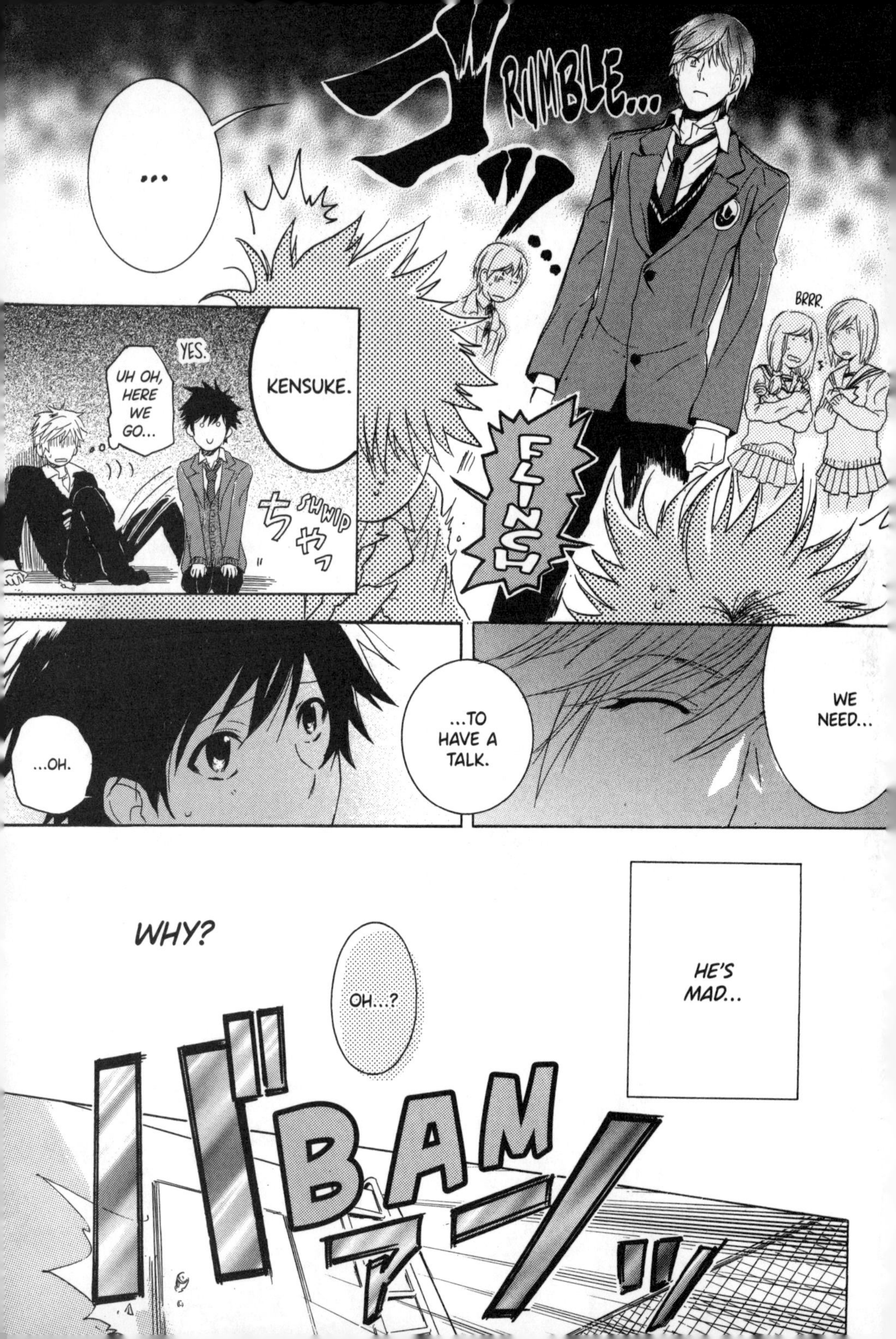
RUMBLE...
...
...
BRRR.
KENSUKE.
FLINCH
YES.
UH OH, HERE WE GO...
SHWIP
WE NEED...
...TO HAVE A TALK.
...OH.
HE'S MAD...
OH...?
WHY?
BAM

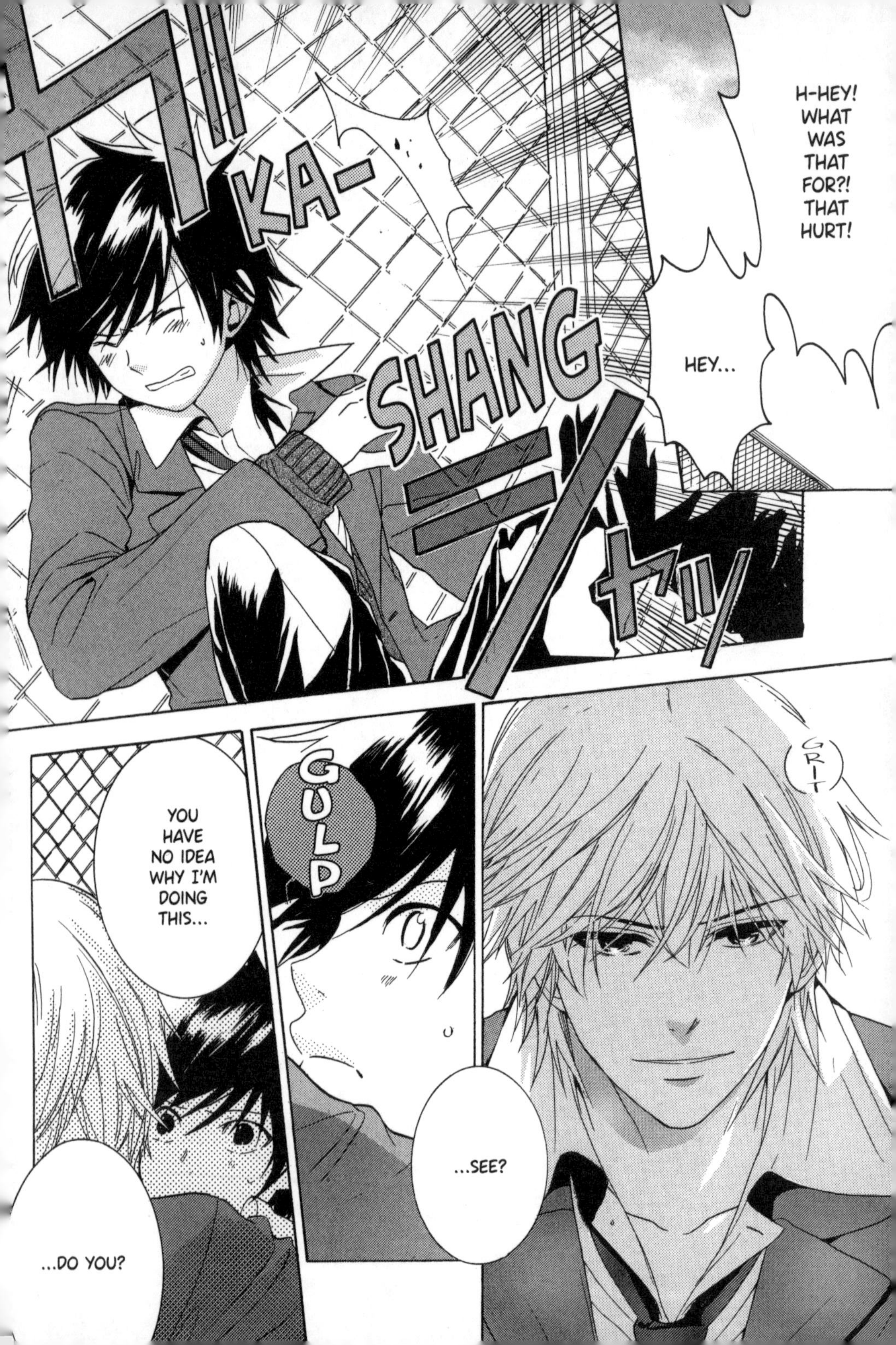
H-HEY! WHAT WAS THAT FOR?! THAT HURT!
HEY...
KA-SHANG
GRIT
...SEE?
GULP
YOU HAVE NO IDEA WHY I'M DOING THIS...
...DO YOU?

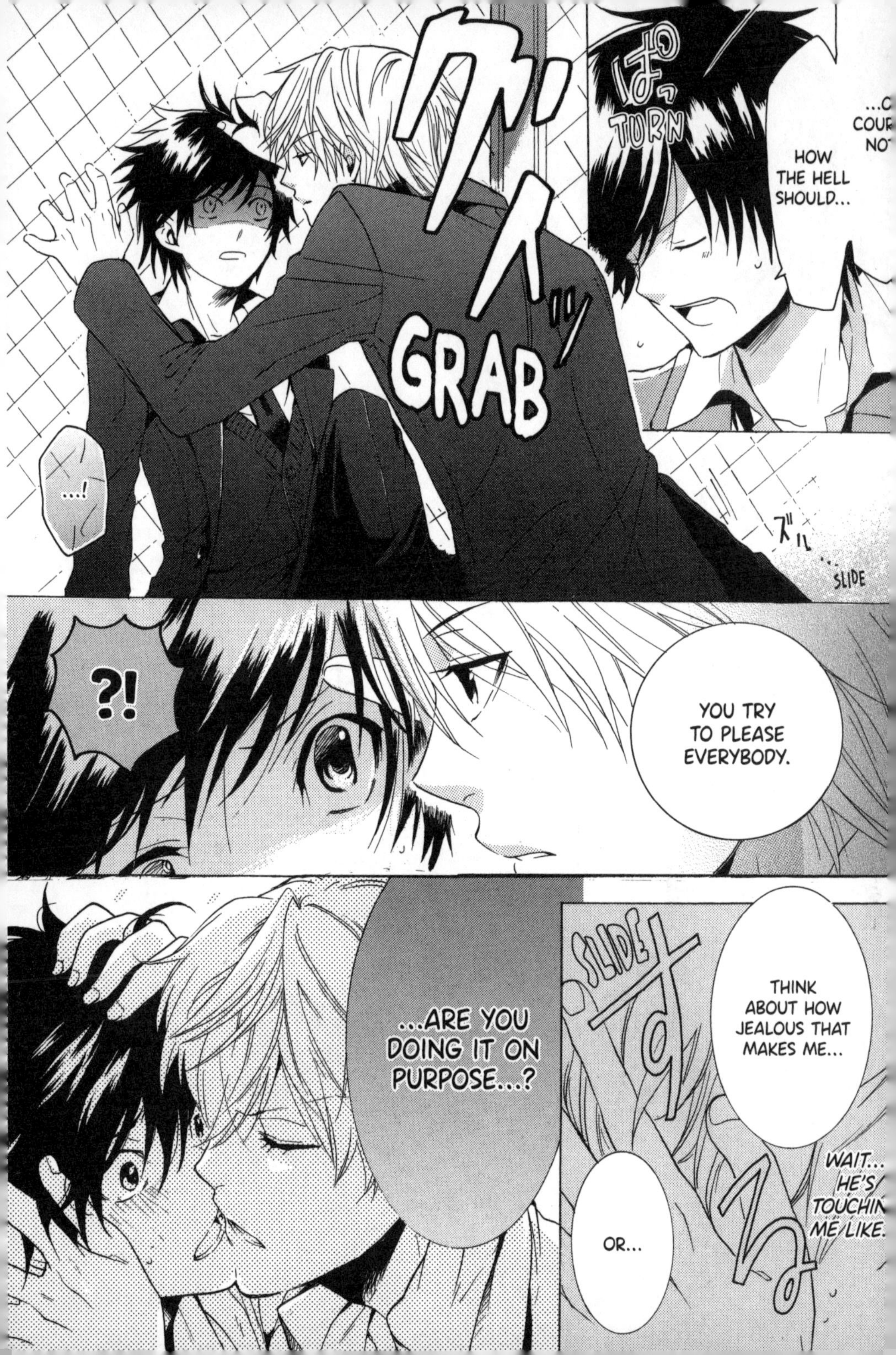

...C
COUR
NO
ぱっ
TURN
HOW THE HELL SHOULD...
グイッ
GRAB
...!
ズル..
SLIDE
YOU TRY TO PLEASE EVERYBODY.
?!
THINK ABOUT HOW JEALOUS THAT MAKES ME...
SLIDE
WAIT... HE'S TOUCHIN ME LIKE.
OR...
...ARE YOU DOING IT ON PURPOSE...?

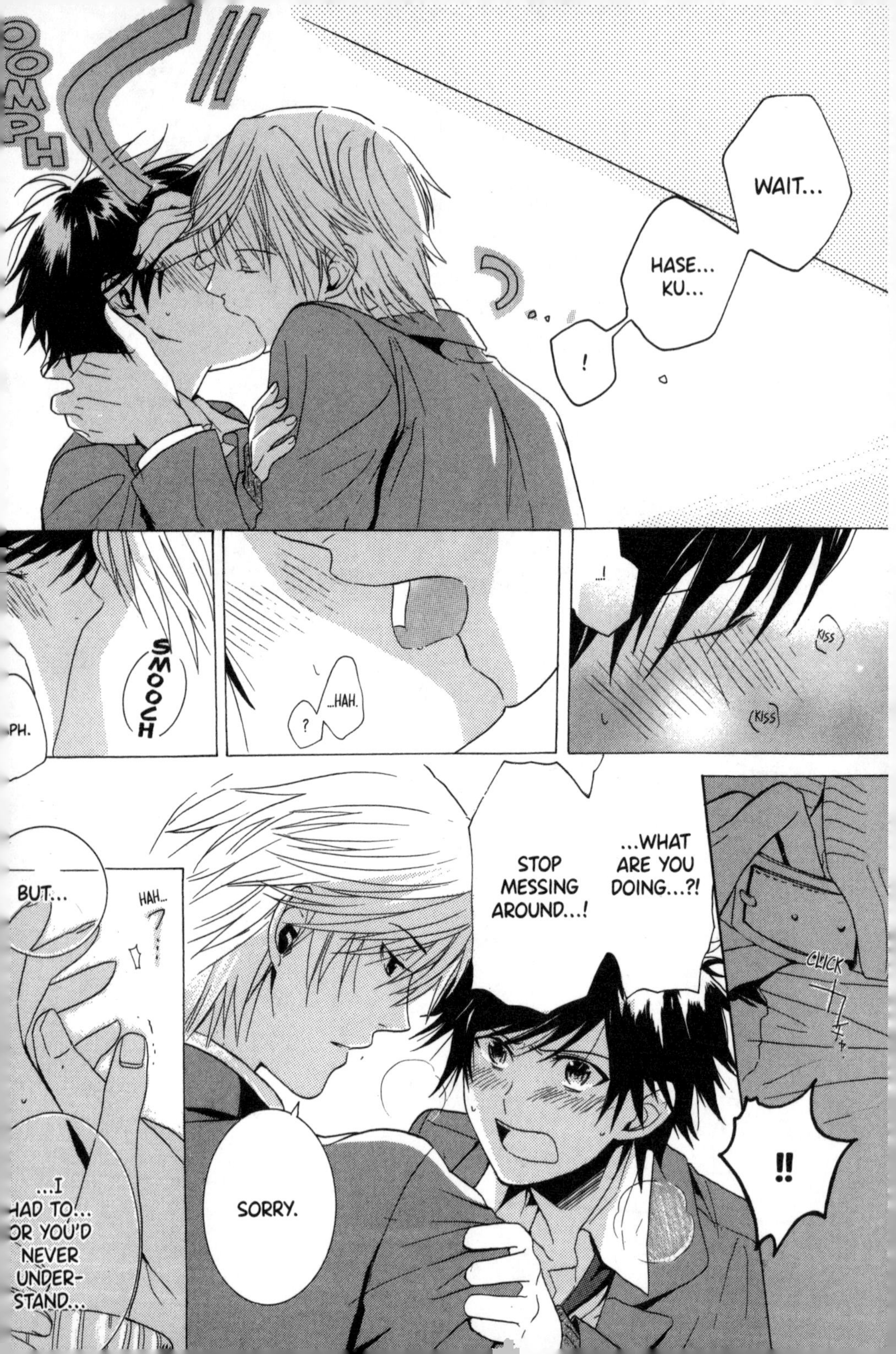
WAIT...
HASE... KU...
!
OOMPH
...!
KISS
KISS
...HAH.
?
SMOOCH
PH.
CLICK
!!
...WHAT ARE YOU DOING...?!
STOP MESSING AROUND...!
SORRY.
BUT...
HAH...
?
...I HAD TO... OR YOU'D NEVER UNDER-STAND...

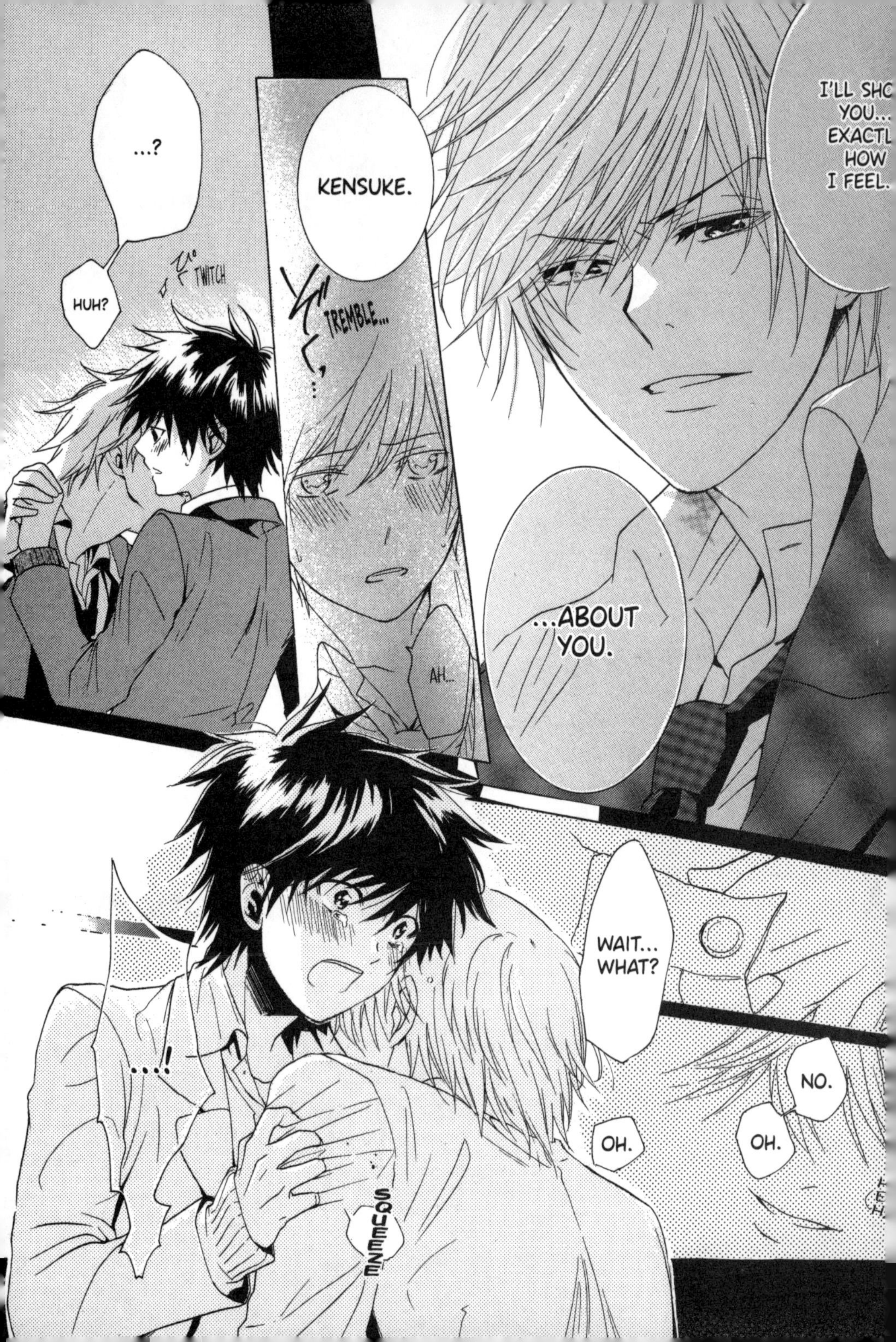

I'LL SHO YOU... EXACTL HOW I FEEL.
...ABOUT YOU.
KENSUKE.
TREMBLE...
AH...
...?
TWITCH
HUH?
WAIT... WHAT?
NO.
OH.
OH.
...!
SQUEEZE

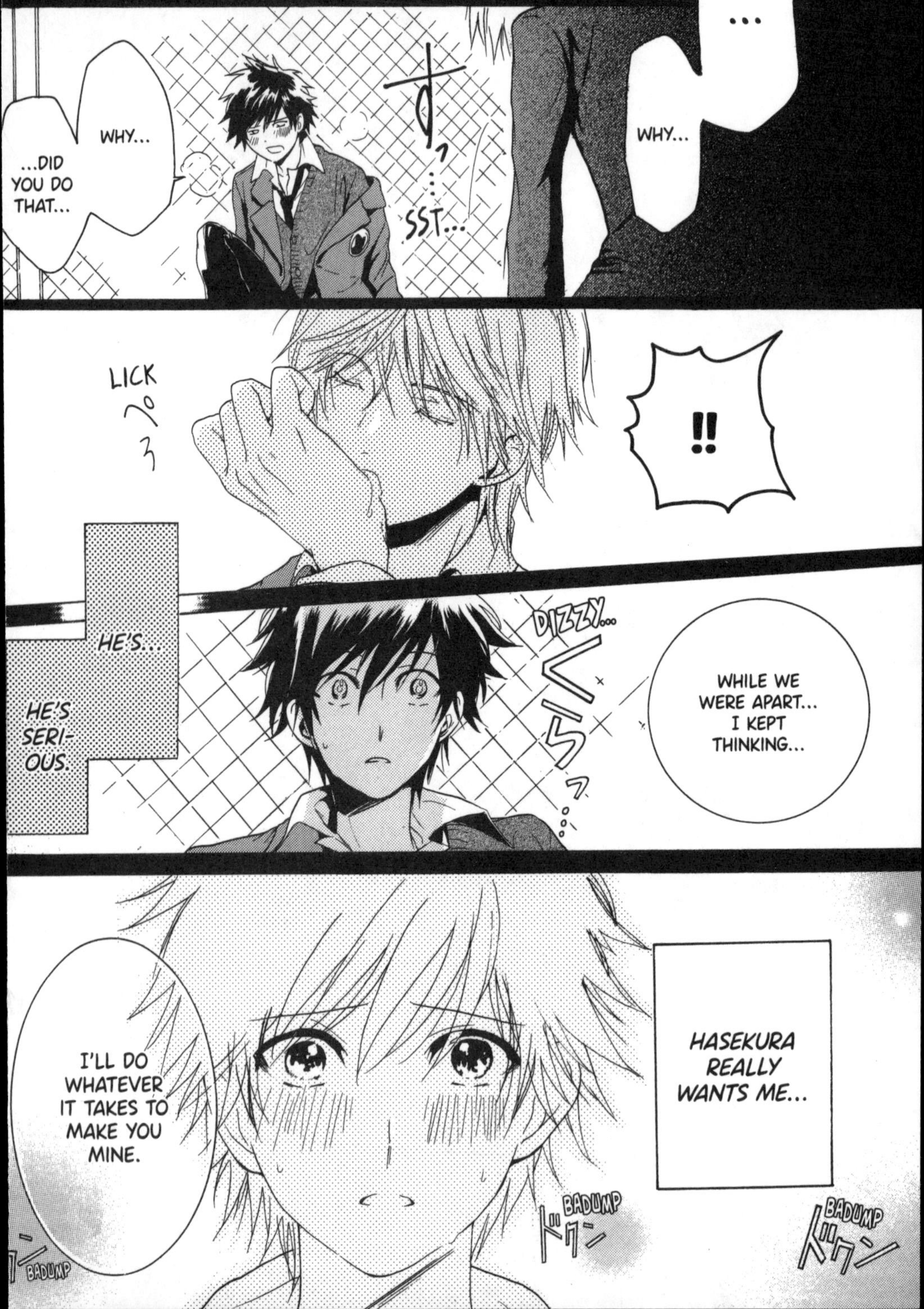

...
WHY...
すっ…
SST...
WHY...
...DID YOU DO THAT...
!!
LICK
ぺろ
DIZZY...
くらっ…
WHILE WE WERE APART... I KEPT THINKING...
HE'S...
HE'S SERIOUS.
HASEKURA REALLY WANTS ME...
BADUMP
ドクン
BADUMP
ドクン
I'LL DO WHATEVER IT TAKES TO MAKE YOU MINE.
BADUMP

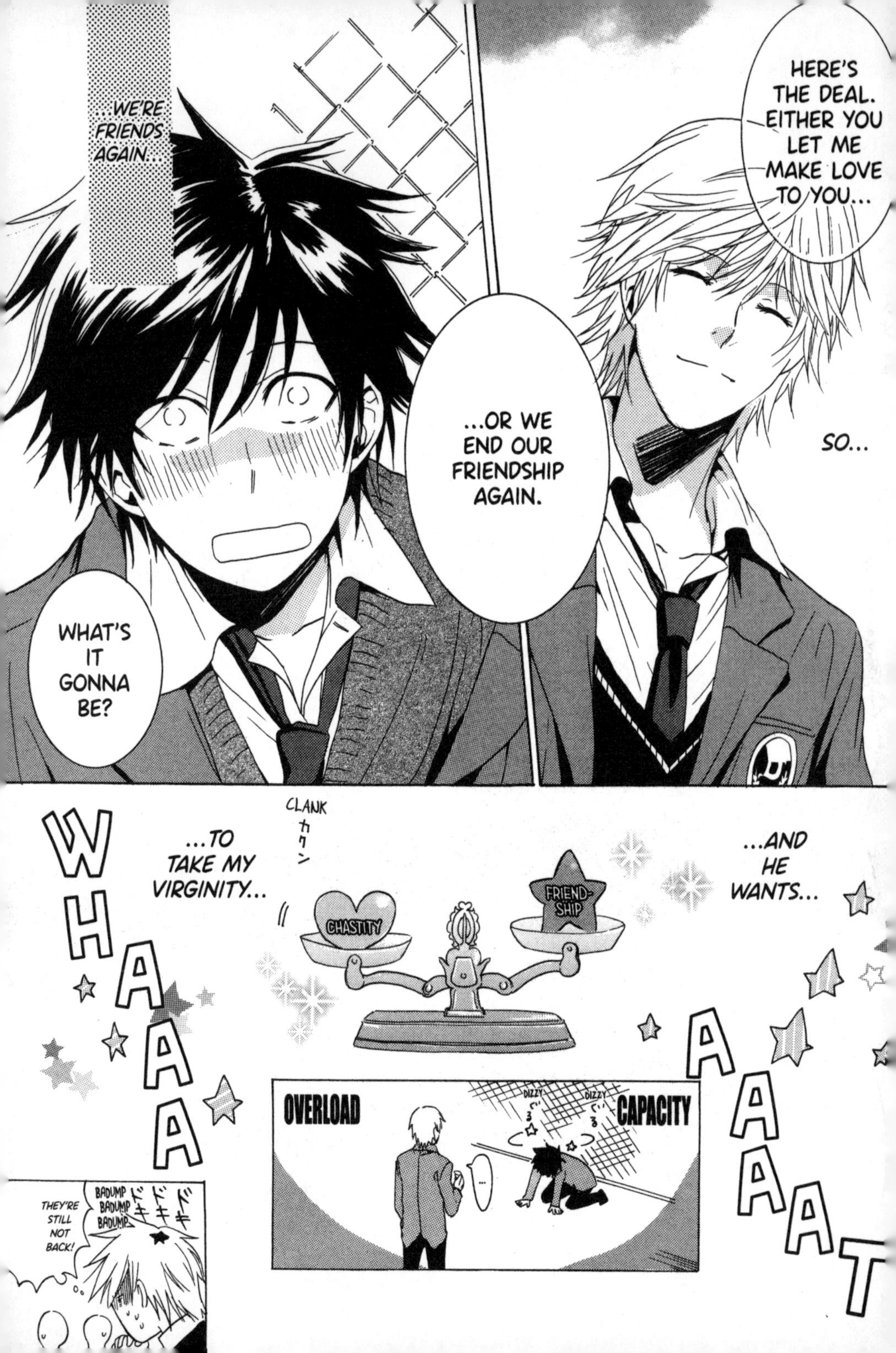
HERE'S THE DEAL. EITHER YOU LET ME MAKE LOVE TO YOU...
...OR WE END OUR FRIENDSHIP AGAIN.
SO...
WHAT'S IT GONNA BE?
...WE'RE FRIENDS AGAIN...
...AND HE WANTS...
FRIEND-SHIP
CHASTITY
CLANK
カクン
...TO TAKE MY VIRGINITY...
WHAAAA
AAAAT
CAPACITY
DIZZY
DIZZY
OVERLOAD
...
BADUMP BADUMP BADUMP
ドキドキドキ
THEY'RE STILL NOT BACK!

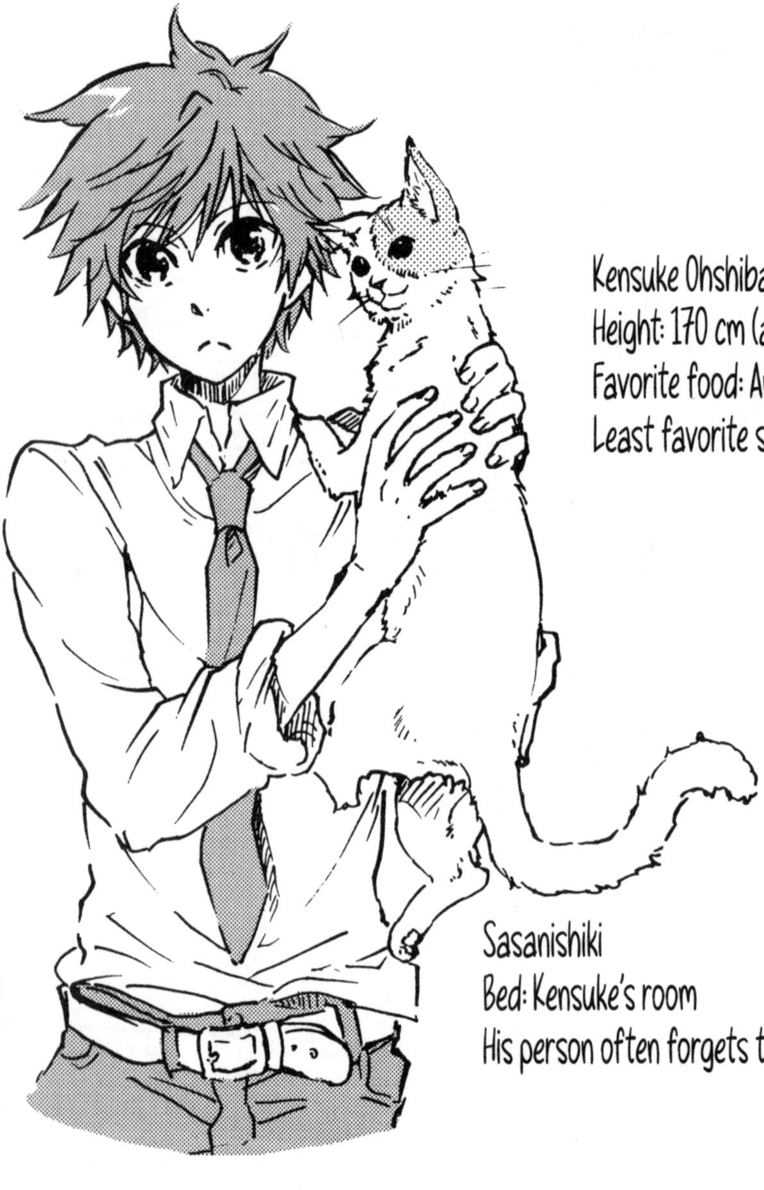

Kensuke Ohshiba
Height: 170 cm (according to him)
Favorite food: Anything
Least favorite subject: Math

Sasanishiki
Bed: Kensuke's room
His person often forgets to feed him

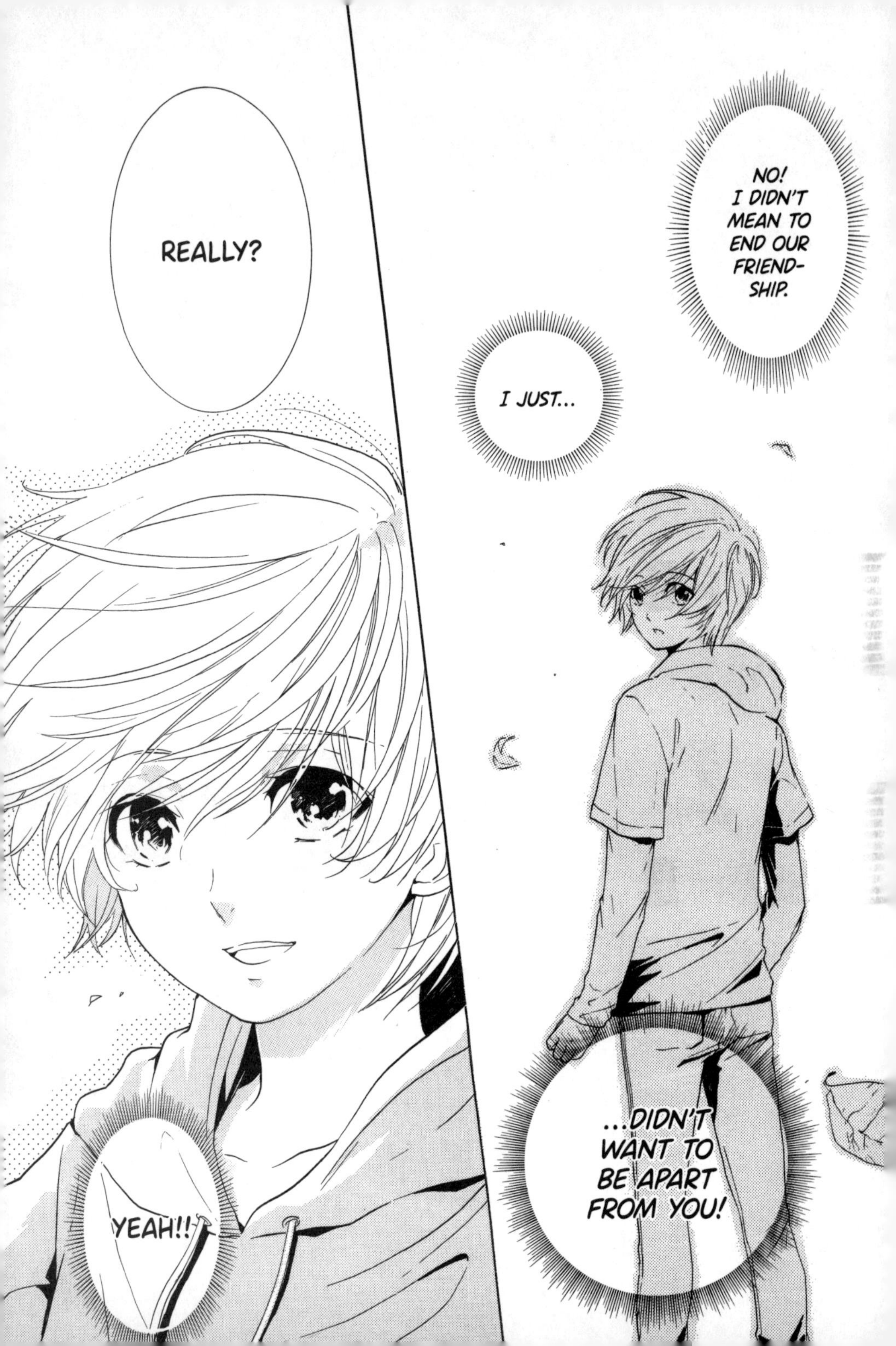
NO! I DIDN'T MEAN TO END OUR FRIEND-SHIP.
I JUST...
...DIDN'T WANT TO BE APART FROM YOU!
REALLY?
YEAH!!

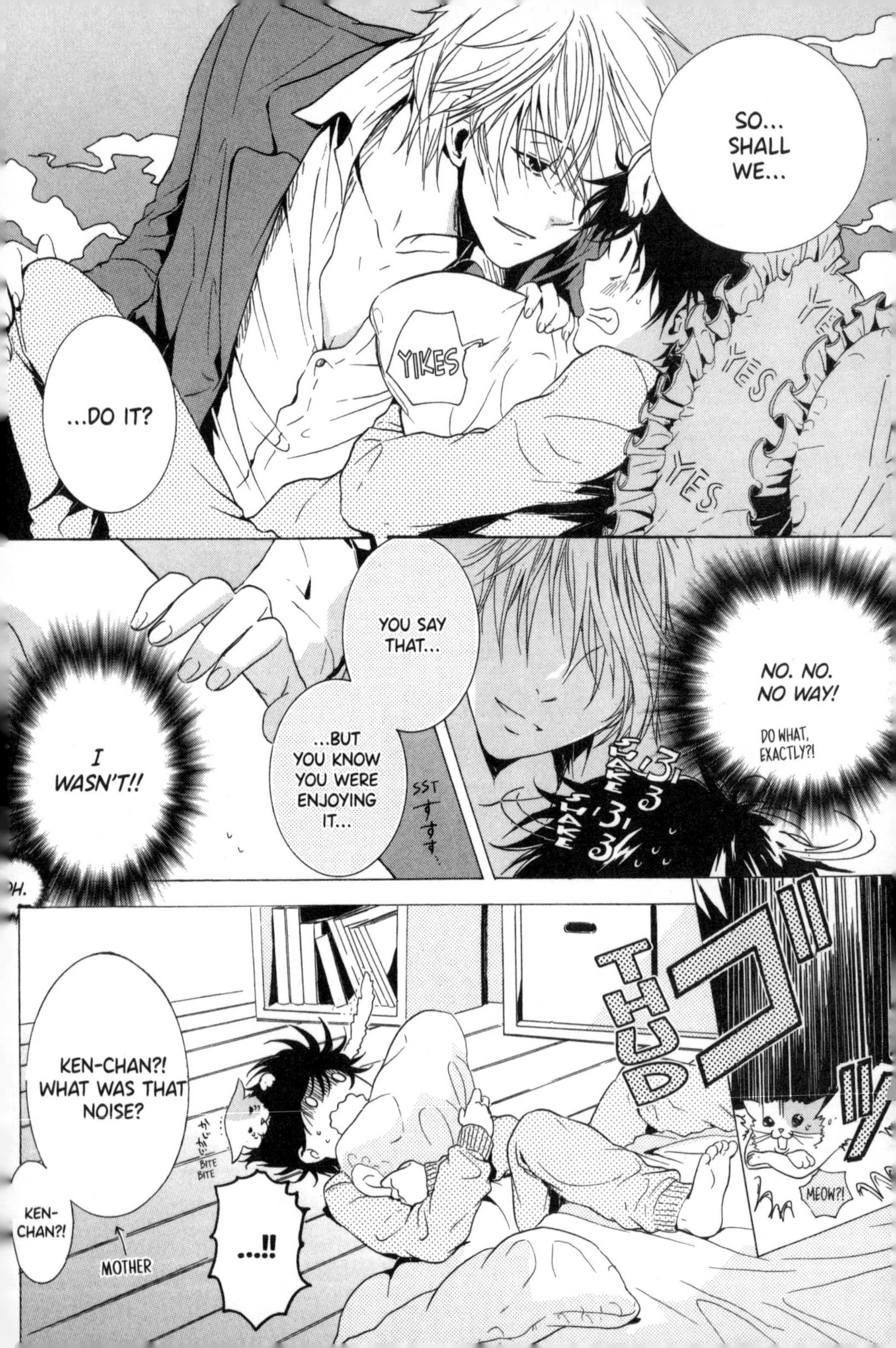
SO... SHALL WE...
YIKES
YES YES YES
...DO IT?
NO. NO. NO WAY!
DO WHAT, EXACTLY?!
SHAKE SHAKE
YOU SAY THAT...
...BUT YOU KNOW YOU WERE ENJOYING IT...
SST すすす
I WASN'T!!
THUD
MEOW?!
...!!
KEN-CHAN?! WHAT WAS THAT NOISE?
BITE BITE
KEN-CHAN?!
MOTHER

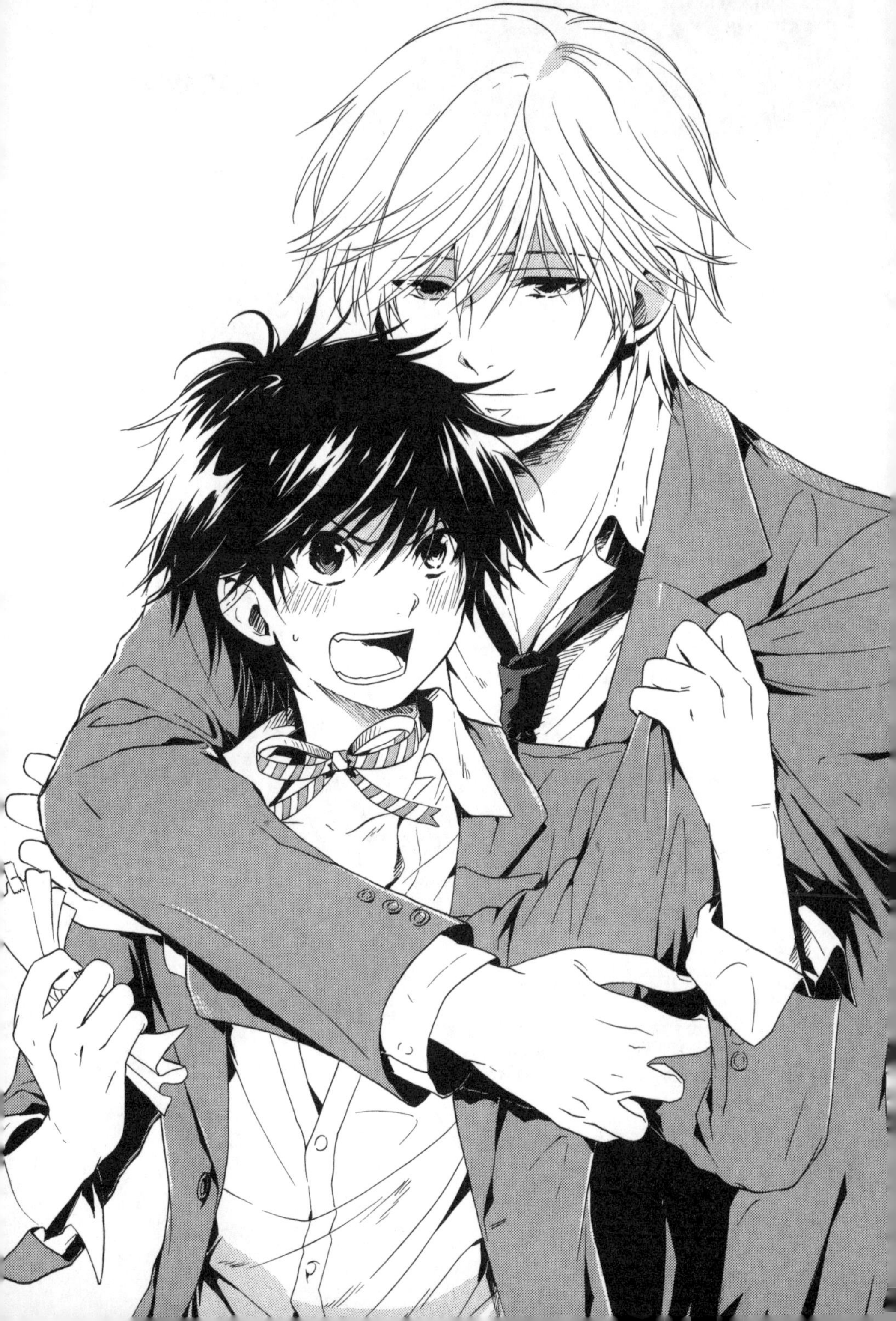

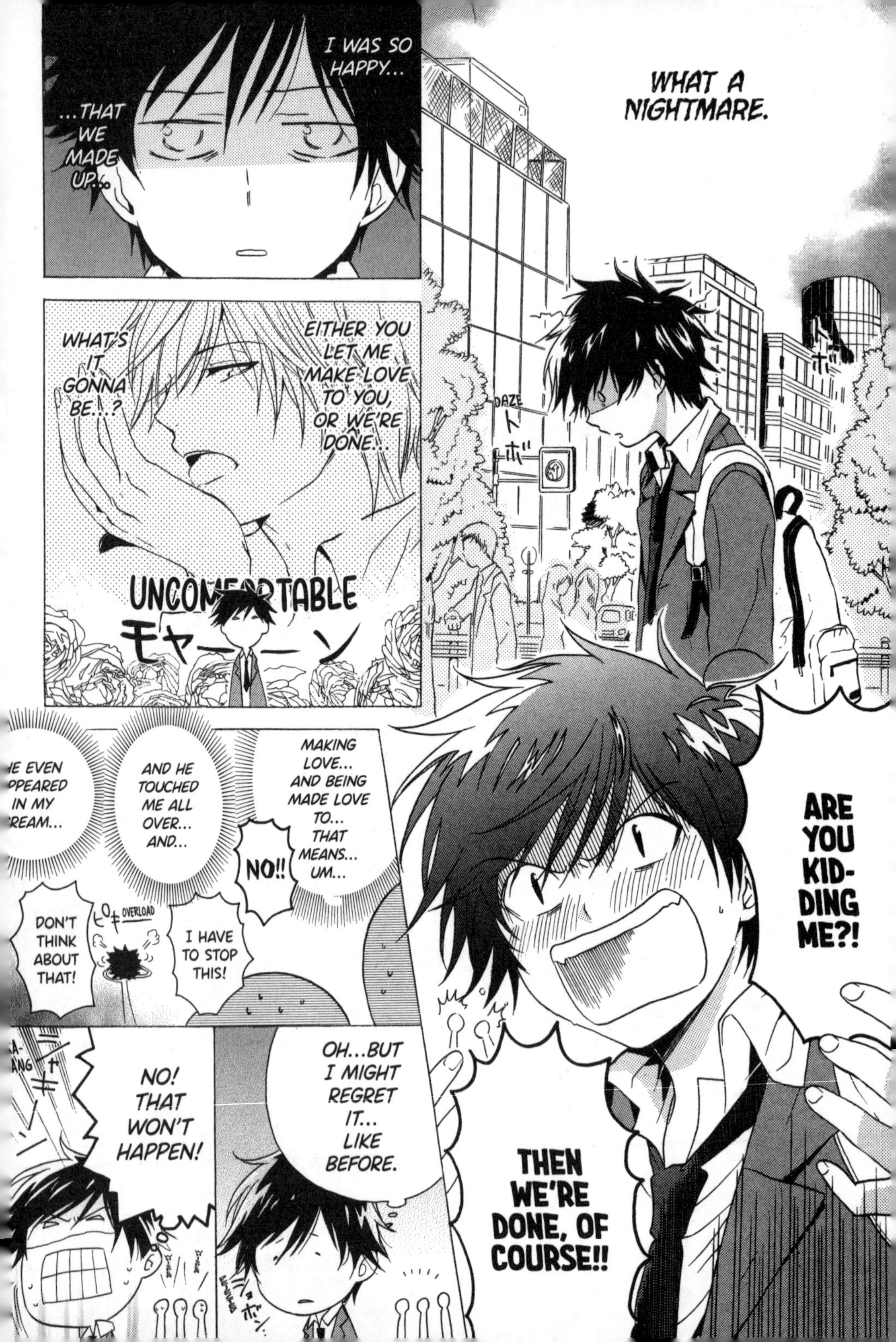
WHAT A NIGHTMARE.
DAZE
I WAS SO HAPPY...
...THAT WE MADE UP...
EITHER YOU LET ME MAKE LOVE TO YOU, OR WE'RE DONE...
WHAT'S IT GONNA BE...?
UNCOMFORTABLE
モヤーーン
ARE YOU KID-DING ME?!
THEN WE'RE DONE, OF COURSE!!
MAKING LOVE... AND BEING MADE LOVE TO... THAT MEANS... UM...
NO!!
AND HE TOUCHED ME ALL OVER... AND...
HE EVEN PPEARED IN MY REAM...
I HAVE TO STOP THIS!
OVERLOAD
DON'T THINK ABOUT THAT!
OH...BUT I MIGHT REGRET IT... LIKE BEFORE.
NO! THAT WON'T HAPPEN!

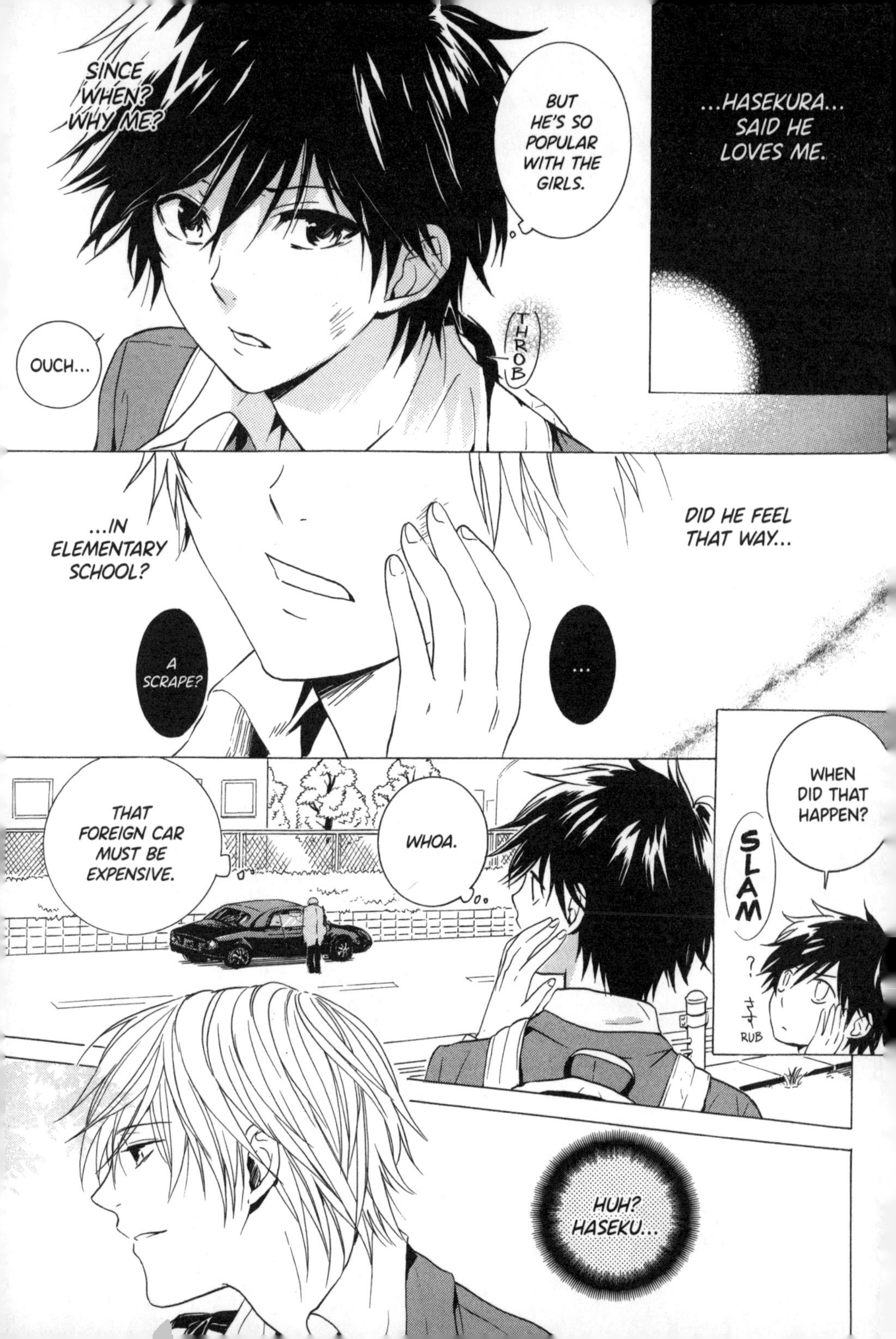
...HASEKURA... SAID HE LOVES ME.
BUT HE'S SO POPULAR WITH THE GIRLS.
SINCE WHEN? WHY ME?
THROB
OUCH...
DID HE FEEL THAT WAY...
...
...IN ELEMENTARY SCHOOL?
A SCRAPE?
WHEN DID THAT HAPPEN?
SLAM
?
RUB
WHOA.
THAT FOREIGN CAR MUST BE EXPENSIVE.
HUH? HASEKU...

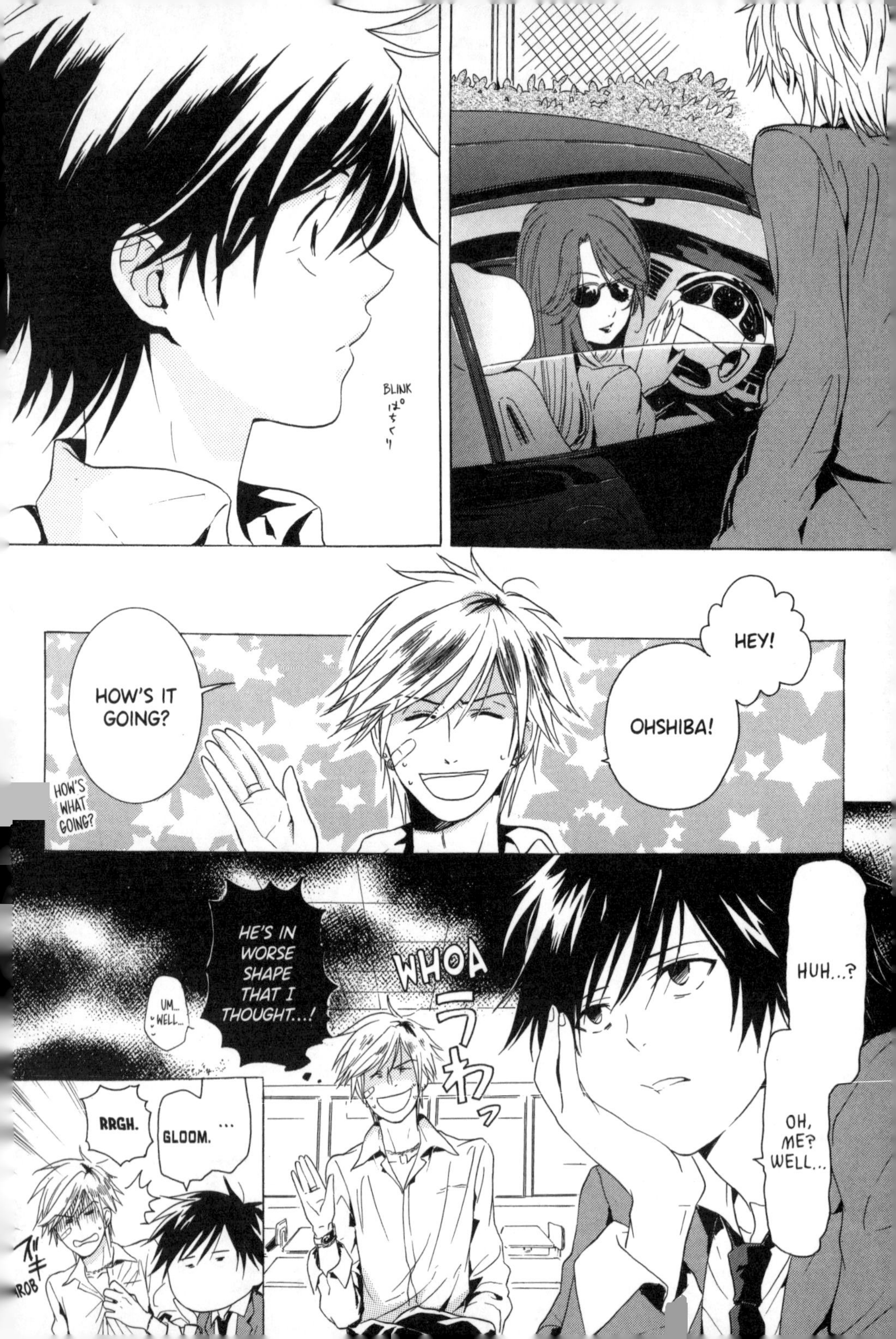
BLINK
ぱちくり
HEY!
OHSHIBA!
HOW'S IT GOING?
HOW'S WHAT GOING?
HUH...?
OH, ME? WELL...
WHOA
うわっ
HE'S IN WORSE SHAPE THAT I THOUGHT...!
UM... WELL...
...
GLOOM.
RRGH.
ズキ

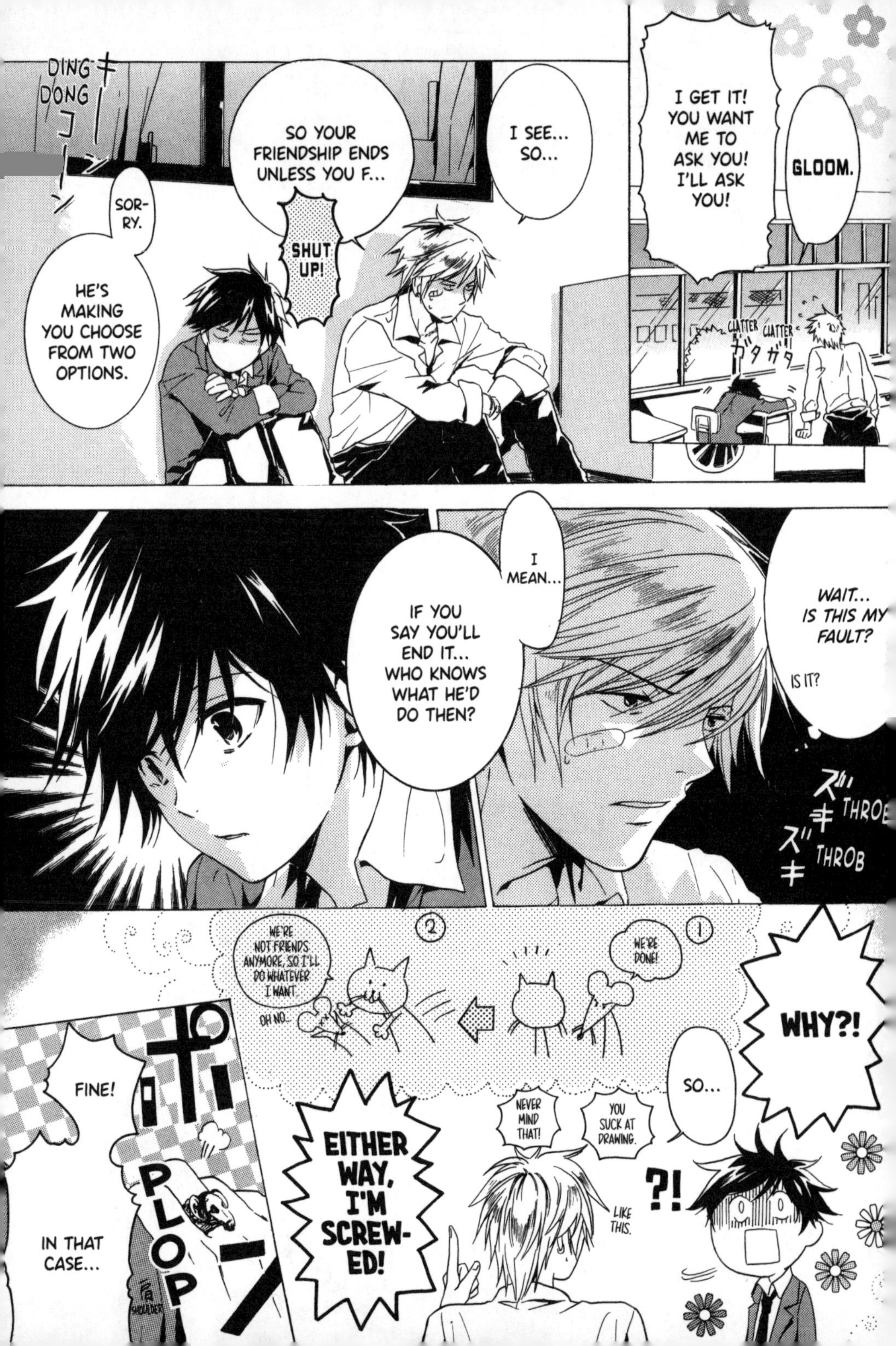
I GET IT! YOU WANT ME TO ASK YOU! I'LL ASK YOU!
GLOOM.
CLATTER CLATTER
I SEE... SO...
SO YOUR FRIENDSHIP ENDS UNLESS YOU F...
SHUT UP!
DING DONG
SOR-RY.
HE'S MAKING YOU CHOOSE FROM TWO OPTIONS.
WAIT... IS THIS MY FAULT?
IS IT?
THROB
THROB
I MEAN...
IF YOU SAY YOU'LL END IT... WHO KNOWS WHAT HE'D DO THEN?
WHY?!
1
WE'RE DONE!
2
WE'RE NOT FRIENDS ANYMORE, SO I'LL DO WHATEVER I WANT.
OH NO...
SO...
YOU SUCK AT DRAWING.
NEVER MIND THAT!
LIKE THIS.
?!
EITHER WAY, I'M SCREW-ED!
FINE!
PLOP
SHOULDER
IN THAT CASE...

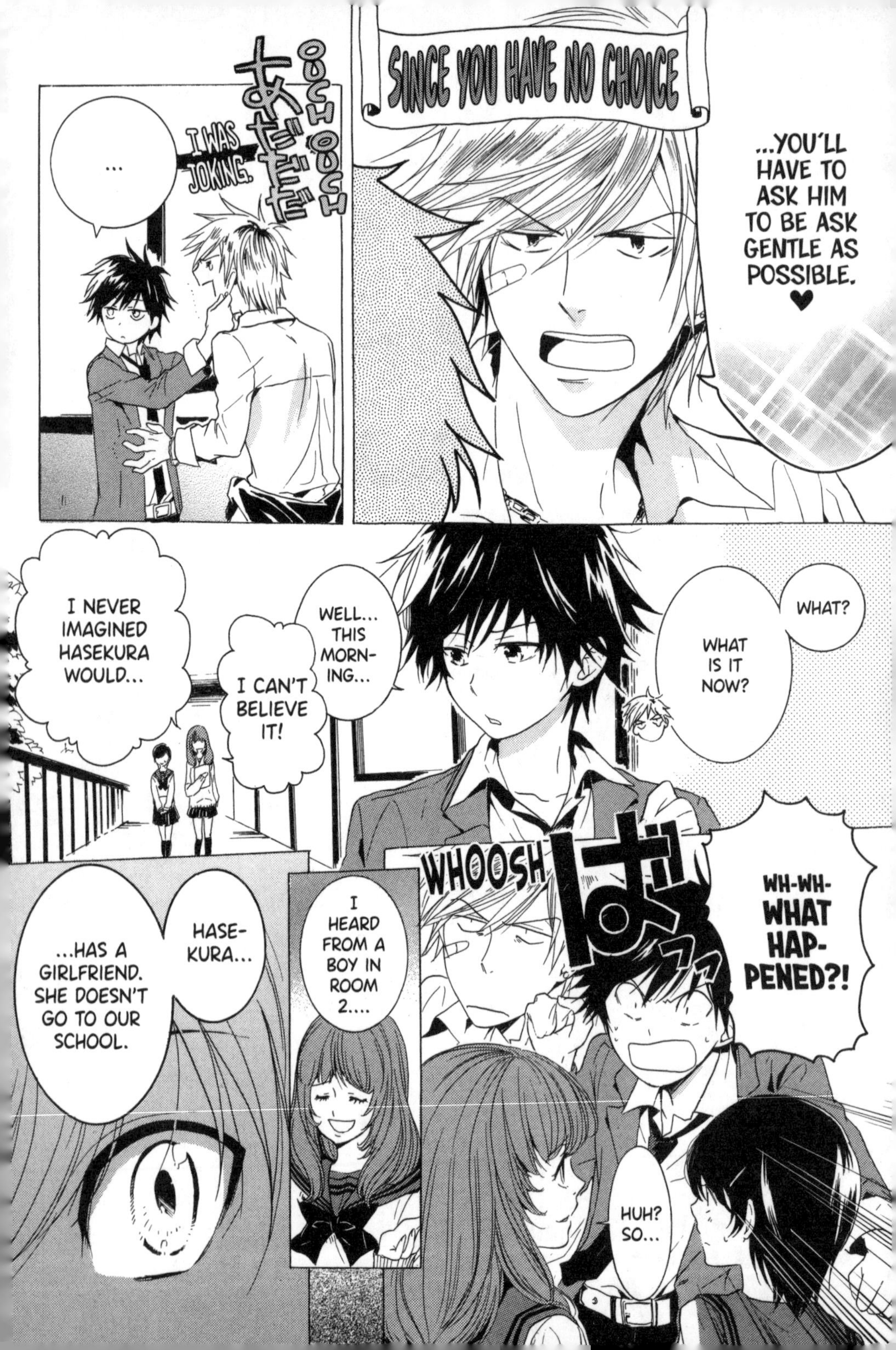
SINCE YOU HAVE NO CHOICE
...YOU'LL HAVE TO ASK HIM TO BE ASK GENTLE AS POSSIBLE. ♥
OUCH OUCH
あだだだ
I WAS JOKING.
...
WHAT?
WHAT IS IT NOW?
WELL... THIS MORN-ING...
I CAN'T BELIEVE IT!
I NEVER IMAGINED HASEKURA WOULD...
WHOOSH
ばっ
WH-WH-WHAT HAP-PENED?!
HUH? SO...
I HEARD FROM A BOY IN ROOM 2....
HASE-KURA...
...HAS A GIRLFRIEND. SHE DOESN'T GO TO OUR SCHOOL.

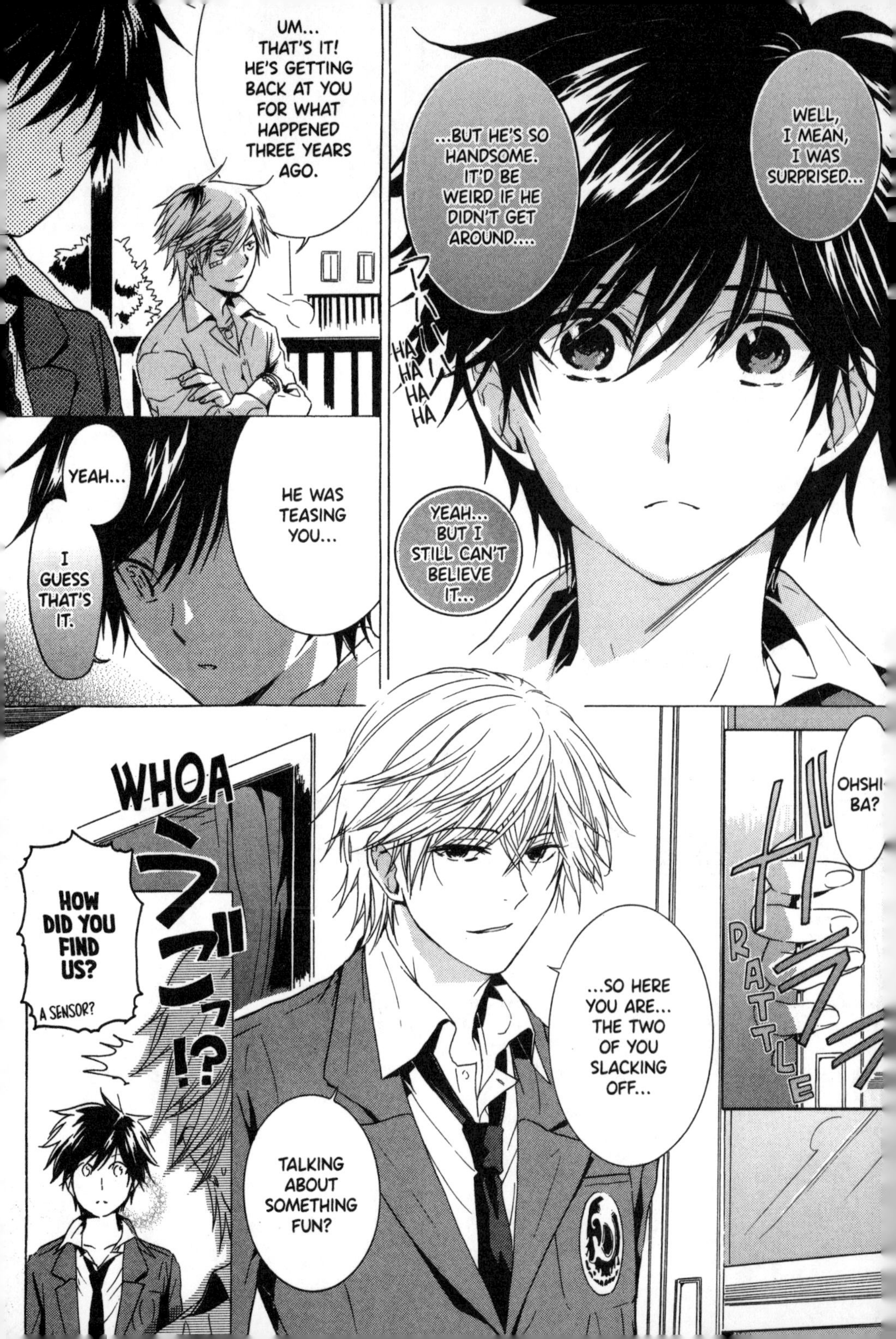
WELL, I MEAN, I WAS SURPRISED...
...BUT HE'S SO HANDSOME. IT'D BE WEIRD IF HE DIDN'T GET AROUND....
HA HA HA HA HA
YEAH... BUT I STILL CAN'T BELIEVE IT...
UM... THAT'S IT! HE'S GETTING BACK AT YOU FOR WHAT HAPPENED THREE YEARS AGO.
HE WAS TEASING YOU...
YEAH...
I GUESS THAT'S IT.
OHSHIBA?
RATTLE
...SO HERE YOU ARE... THE TWO OF YOU SLACKING OFF...
TALKING ABOUT SOMETHING FUN?
WHOA
HOW DID YOU FIND US?
A SENSOR?

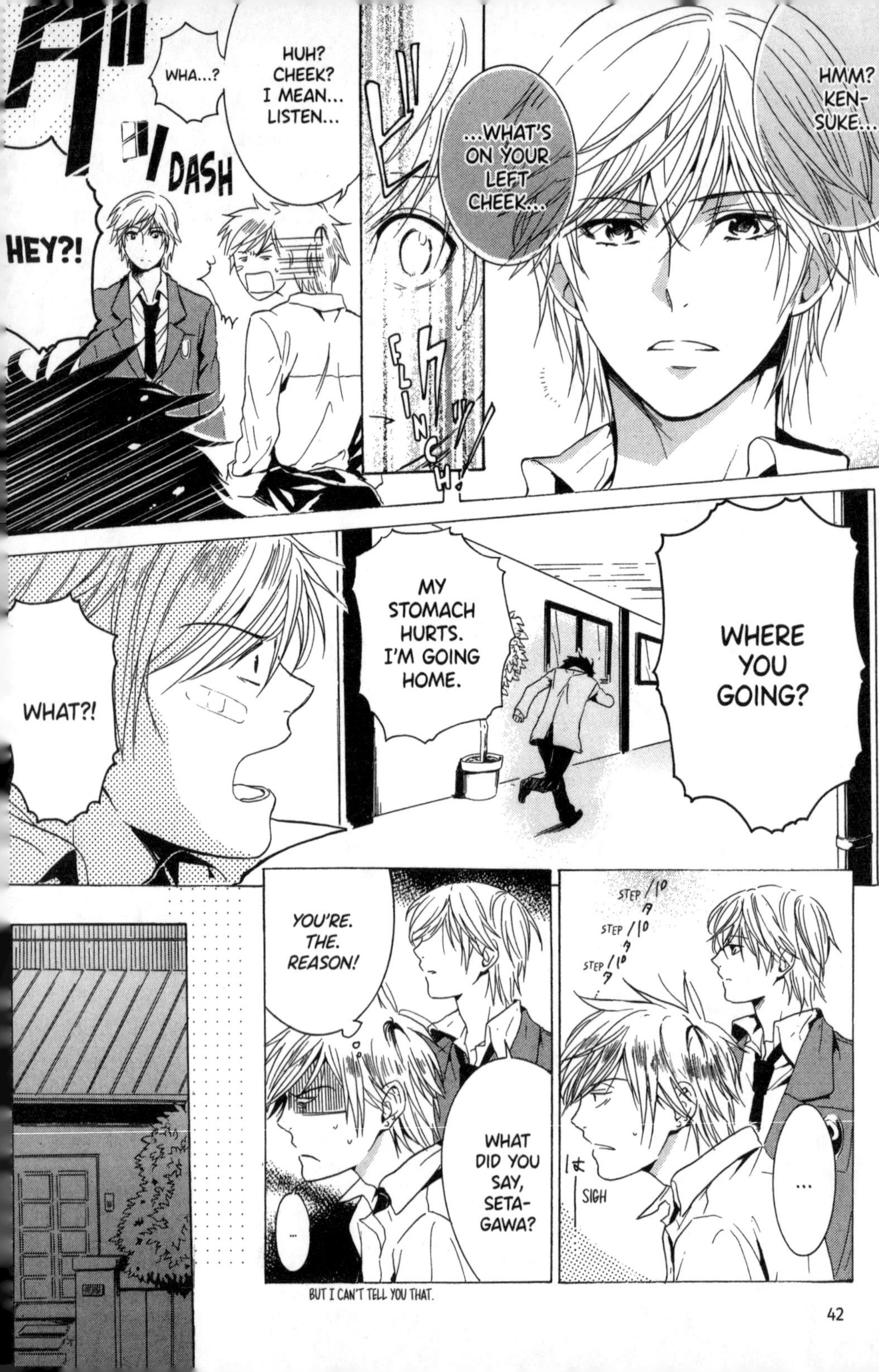
HMM? KEN-SUKE...
...WHAT'S ON YOUR LEFT CHEEK...
FLINCH
HUH? CHEEK? I MEAN... LISTEN...
WHA...?
DASH
HEY?!
WHERE YOU GOING?
MY STOMACH HURTS. I'M GOING HOME.
WHAT?!
STEP
STEP
STEP
SIGH
...
YOU'RE. THE. REASON!
WHAT DID YOU SAY, SETA-GAWA?
...
BUT I CAN'T TELL YOU THAT.

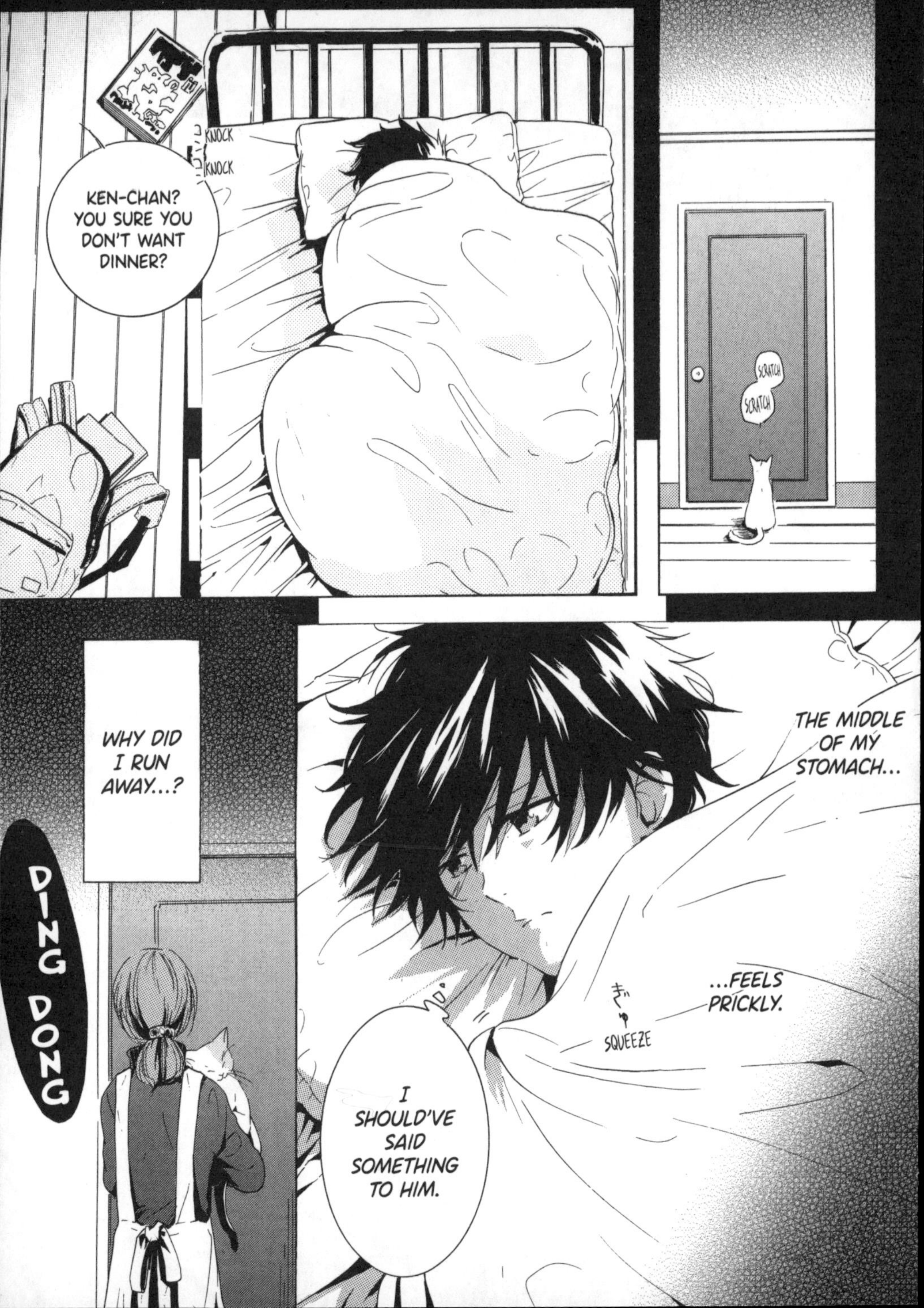
SCRATCH
SCRATCH
KNOCK
KNOCK
KEN-CHAN? YOU SURE YOU DON'T WANT DINNER?
THE MIDDLE OF MY STOMACH...
...FEELS PRICKLY.
SQUEEZE
I SHOULD'VE SAID SOMETHING TO HIM.
WHY DID I RUN AWAY...?
DING DONG

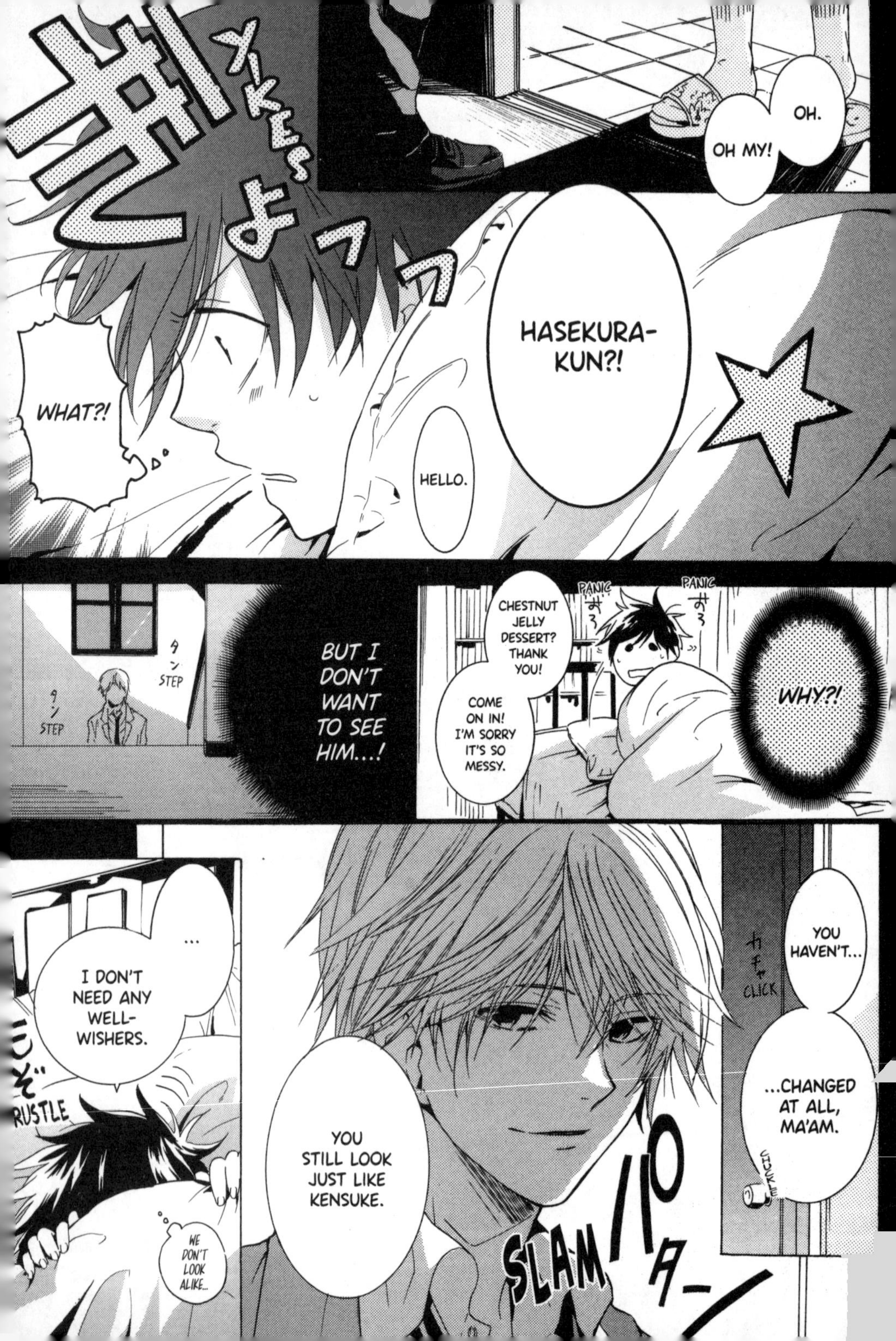
OH.
OH MY!
HASEKURA-KUN?!
HELLO.
YIKES
WHAT?!
PANIC
PANIC
WHY?!
CHESTNUT JELLY DESSERT? THANK YOU!
COME ON IN! I'M SORRY IT'S SO MESSY.
BUT I DON'T WANT TO SEE HIM...!
STEP
STEP
CLICK
YOU HAVEN'T...
...CHANGED AT ALL, MA'AM.
YOU STILL LOOK JUST LIKE KENSUKE.
SLAM
...
I DON'T NEED ANY WELL-WISHERS.
RUSTLE
WE DON'T LOOK ALIKE...

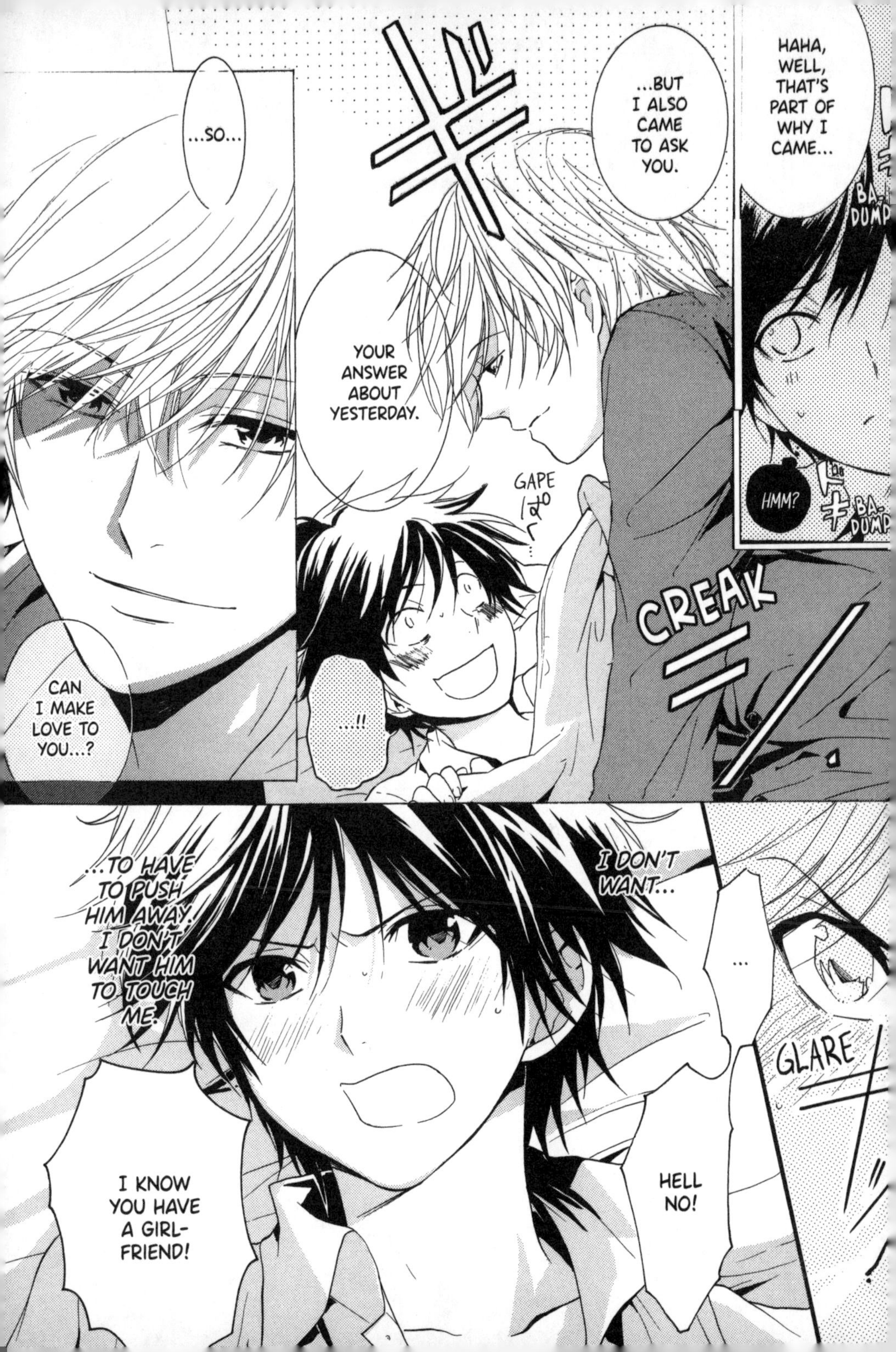
HAHA, WELL, THAT'S PART OF WHY I CAME...
BA-DUMP
HMM?
BA-DUMP
...BUT I ALSO CAME TO ASK YOU.
YOUR ANSWER ABOUT YESTERDAY.
GAPE
CREAK
...!!
...SO...
CAN I MAKE LOVE TO YOU...?
...
GLARE
I DON'T WANT...
...TO HAVE TO PUSH HIM AWAY. I DON'T WANT HIM TO TOUCH ME.
HELL NO!
I KNOW YOU HAVE A GIRL-FRIEND!

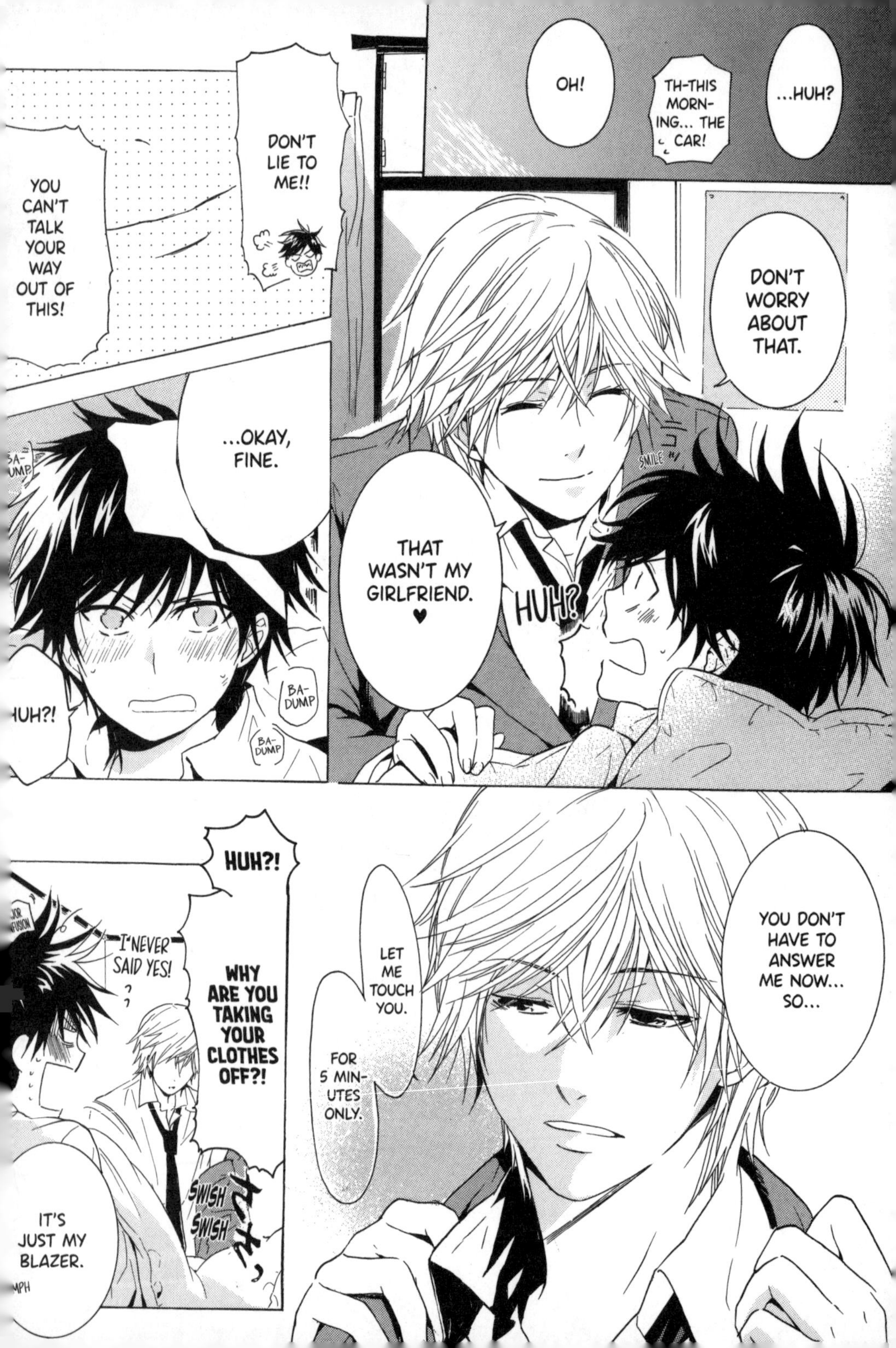
...HUH?
TH-THIS MORNING... THE CAR!
OH!
DON'T WORRY ABOUT THAT.
SMILE
THAT WASN'T MY GIRLFRIEND. ♥
HUH?
DON'T LIE TO ME!!
YOU CAN'T TALK YOUR WAY OUT OF THIS!
...OKAY, FINE.
BA-DUMP
HUH?!
BA-DUMP
BA-DUMP
YOU DON'T HAVE TO ANSWER ME NOW... SO...
LET ME TOUCH YOU.
FOR 5 MINUTES ONLY.
HUH?!
WHY ARE YOU TAKING YOUR CLOTHES OFF?!
I NEVER SAID YES!
SWISH SWISH
IT'S JUST MY BLAZER.

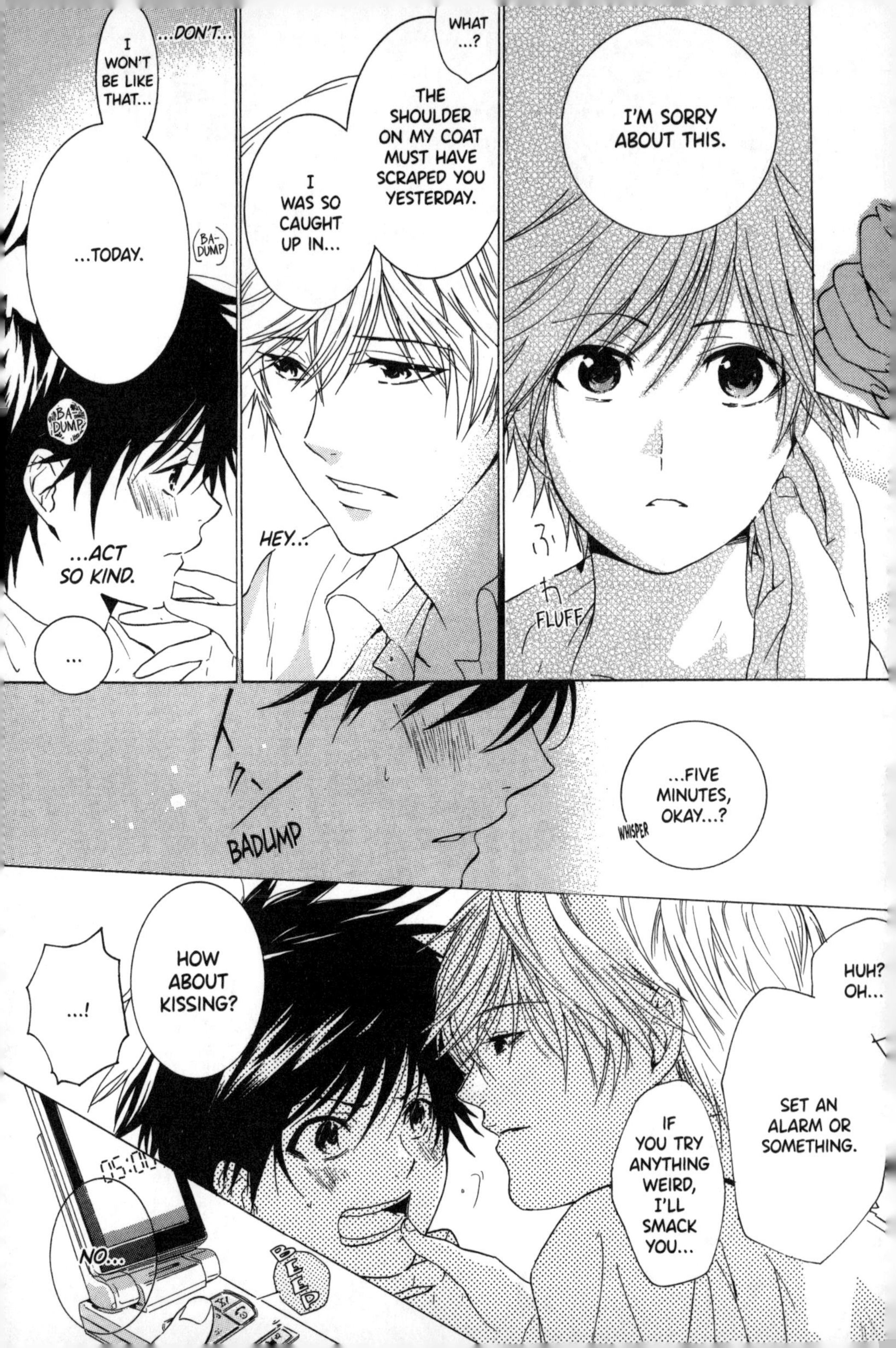

I'M SORRY ABOUT THIS.
ふわ
FLUFF
WHAT ...?
THE SHOULDER ON MY COAT MUST HAVE SCRAPED YOU YESTERDAY.
I WAS SO CAUGHT UP IN...
HEY...
...DON'T...
I WON'T BE LIKE THAT...
...TODAY.
BA-DUMP
BA-DUMP
...ACT SO KIND.
...
...FIVE MINUTES, OKAY...?
WHISPER
BADUMP
HUH? OH...
SET AN ALARM OR SOMETHING.
IF YOU TRY ANYTHING WEIRD, I'LL SMACK YOU...
HOW ABOUT KISSING?
...!
05:00
NO...
BEEP

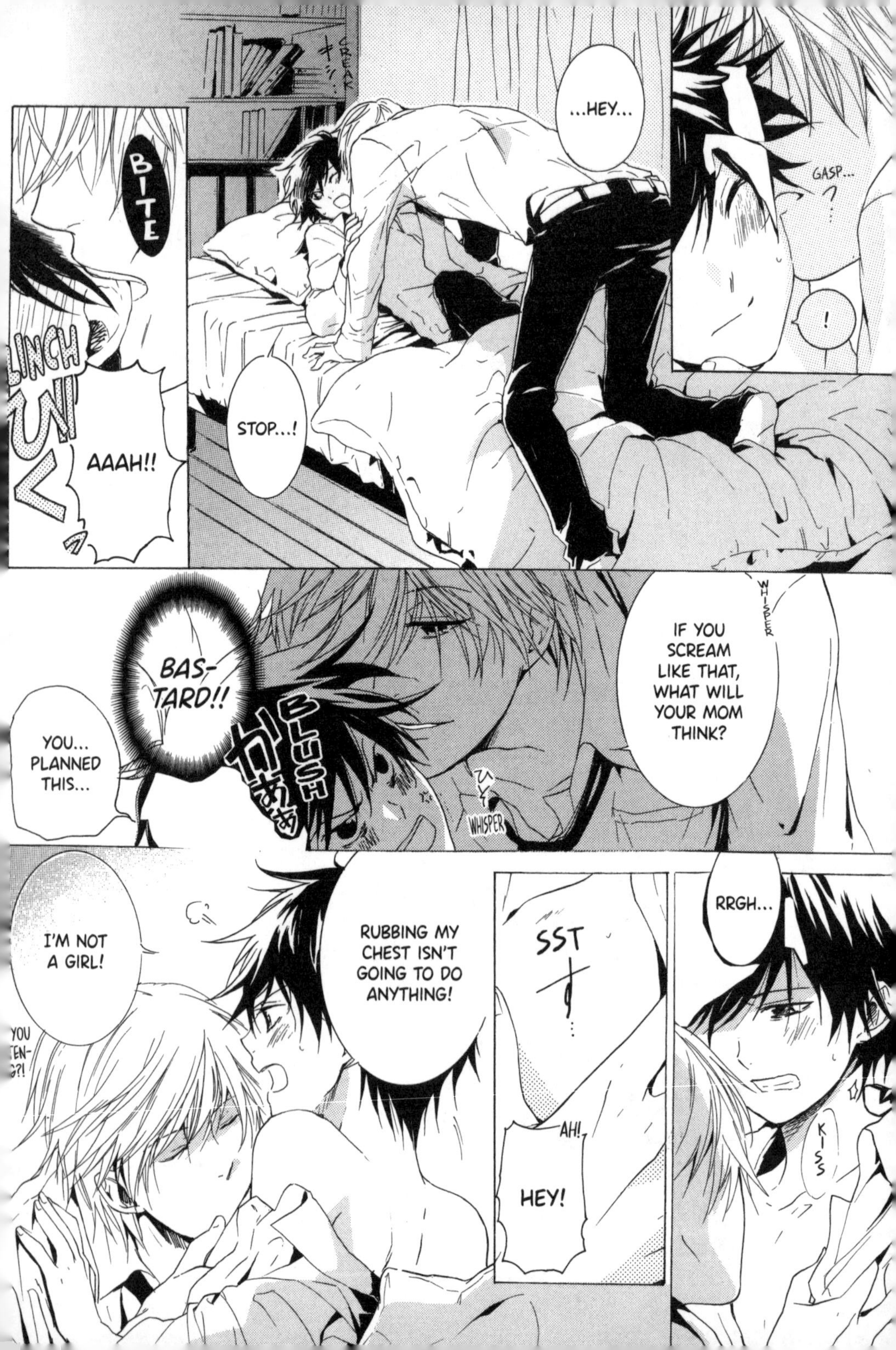
GASP...
?
!
...HEY...
CREAK
STOP...!
BITE
LINCH
AAAH!!
WHISPER
IF YOU SCREAM LIKE THAT, WHAT WILL YOUR MOM THINK?
WHISPER
BLUSH
BAS-TARD!!
YOU... PLANNED THIS...
RRGH...
KISS
SST
AH!
HEY!
RUBBING MY CHEST ISN'T GOING TO DO ANYTHING!
I'M NOT A GIRL!

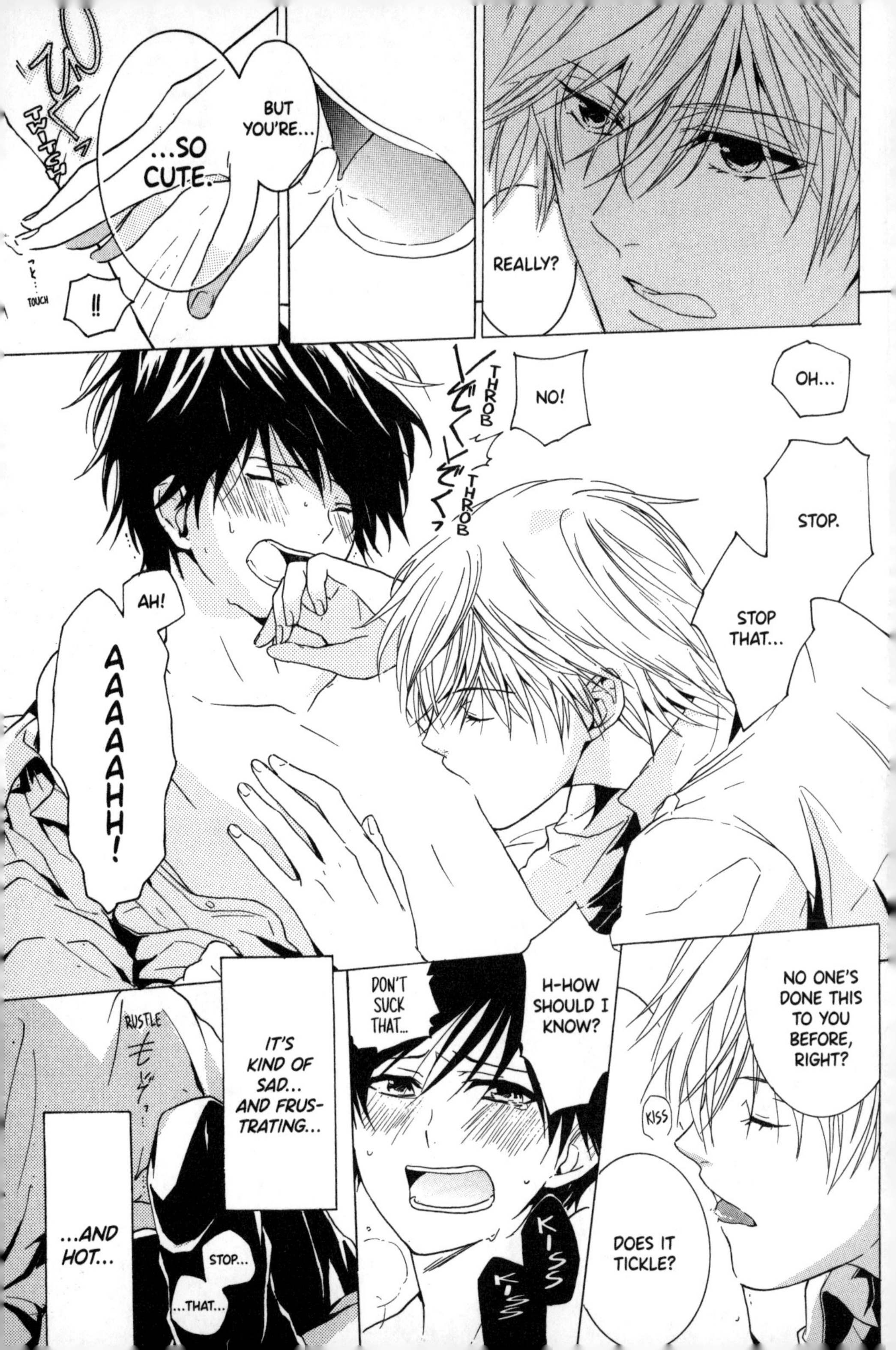
REALLY?
BUT YOU'RE...
...SO CUTE.
TWITCH
TOUCH
!!
OH...
STOP.
STOP THAT...
NO!
THROB
THROB
AH!
AAAAAAAH!
NO ONE'S DONE THIS TO YOU BEFORE, RIGHT?
KISS
DOES IT TICKLE?
H-HOW SHOULD I KNOW?
DON'T SUCK THAT...
KISS
KISS
IT'S KIND OF SAD... AND FRUS-TRATING...
RUSTLE
...AND HOT...
STOP...
...THAT...

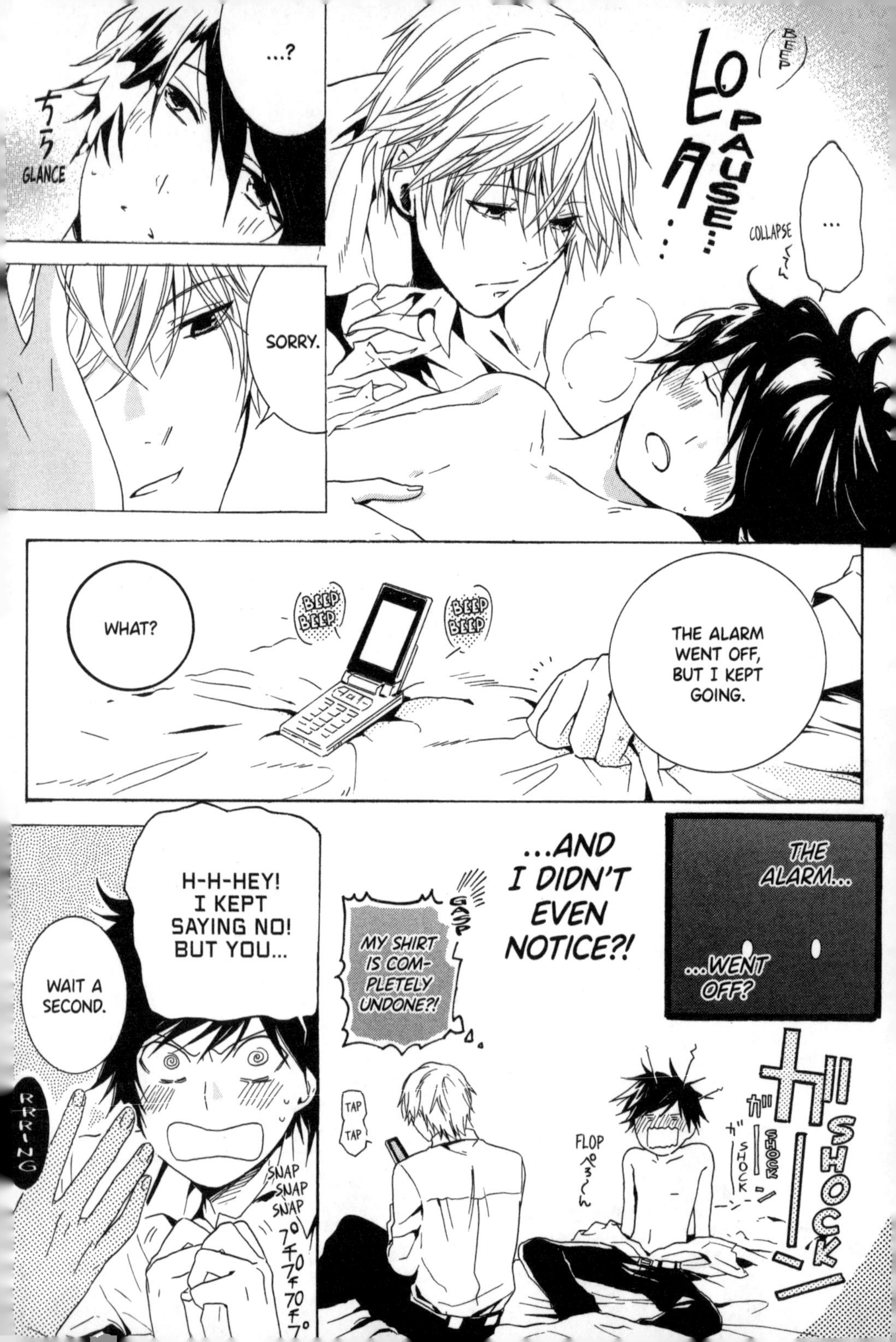
BEEP
PAUSE...
COLLAPSE
...
...?
GLANCE
SORRY.
THE ALARM WENT OFF, BUT I KEPT GOING.
BEEP BEEP
BEEP BEEP
WHAT?
THE ALARM...
...WENT OFF?
SHOCK
SHOCK
SHOCK
...AND I DIDN'T EVEN NOTICE?!
FLOP
TAP TAP
MY SHIRT IS COMPLETELY UNDONE?!
GASP
H-H-HEY! I KEPT SAYING NO! BUT YOU...
WAIT A SECOND.
SNAP SNAP SNAP
RRRING

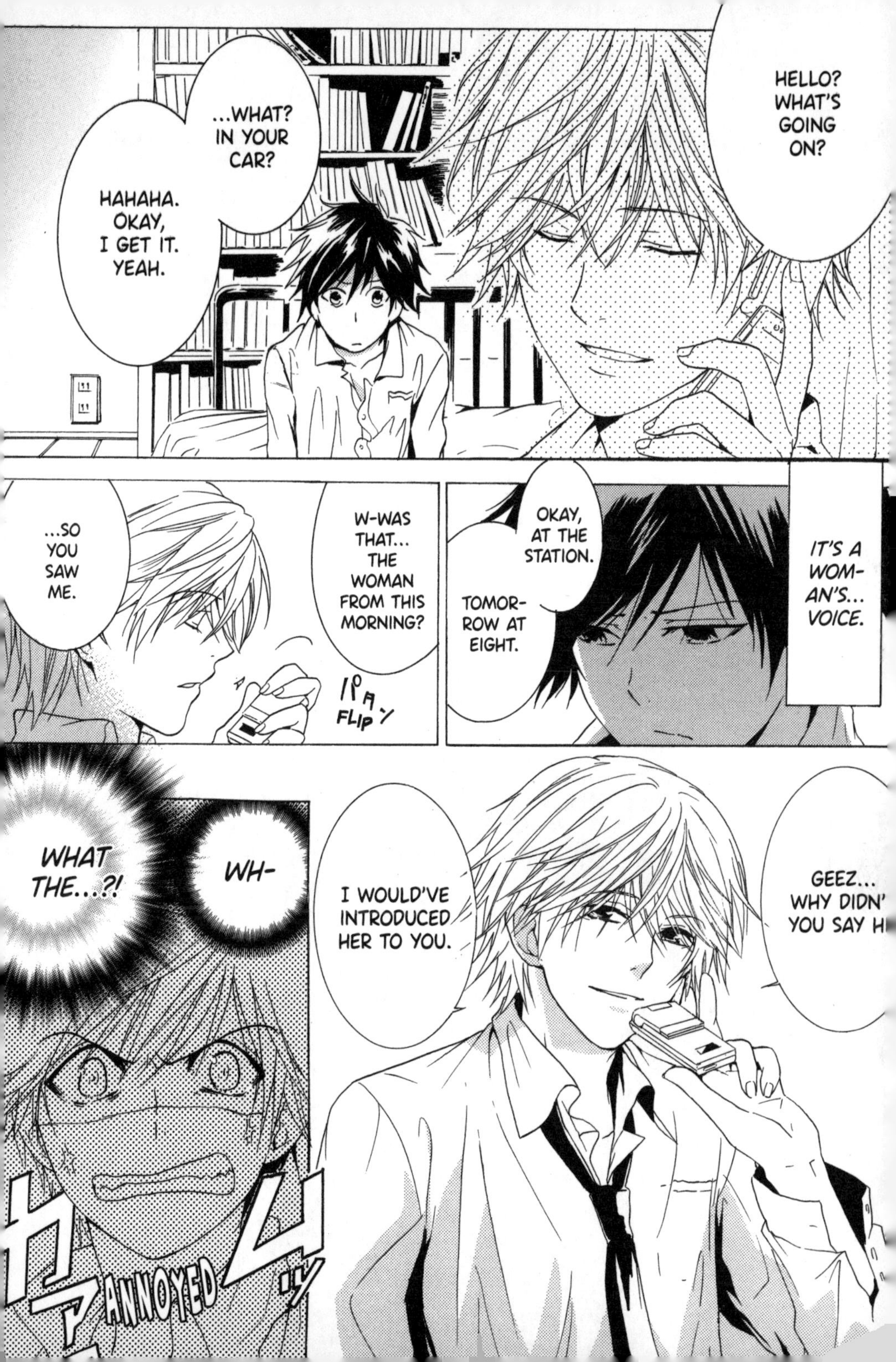

HELLO? WHAT'S GOING ON?
...WHAT? IN YOUR CAR?
HAHAHA. OKAY, I GET IT. YEAH.
IT'S A WOM-AN'S... VOICE.
OKAY, AT THE STATION.
TOMOR-ROW AT EIGHT.
W-WAS THAT... THE WOMAN FROM THIS MORNING?
...SO YOU SAW ME.
FLIP
GEEZ... WHY DIDN' YOU SAY H
I WOULD'VE INTRODUCED HER TO YOU.
WH-
WHAT THE...?!
ANNOYED

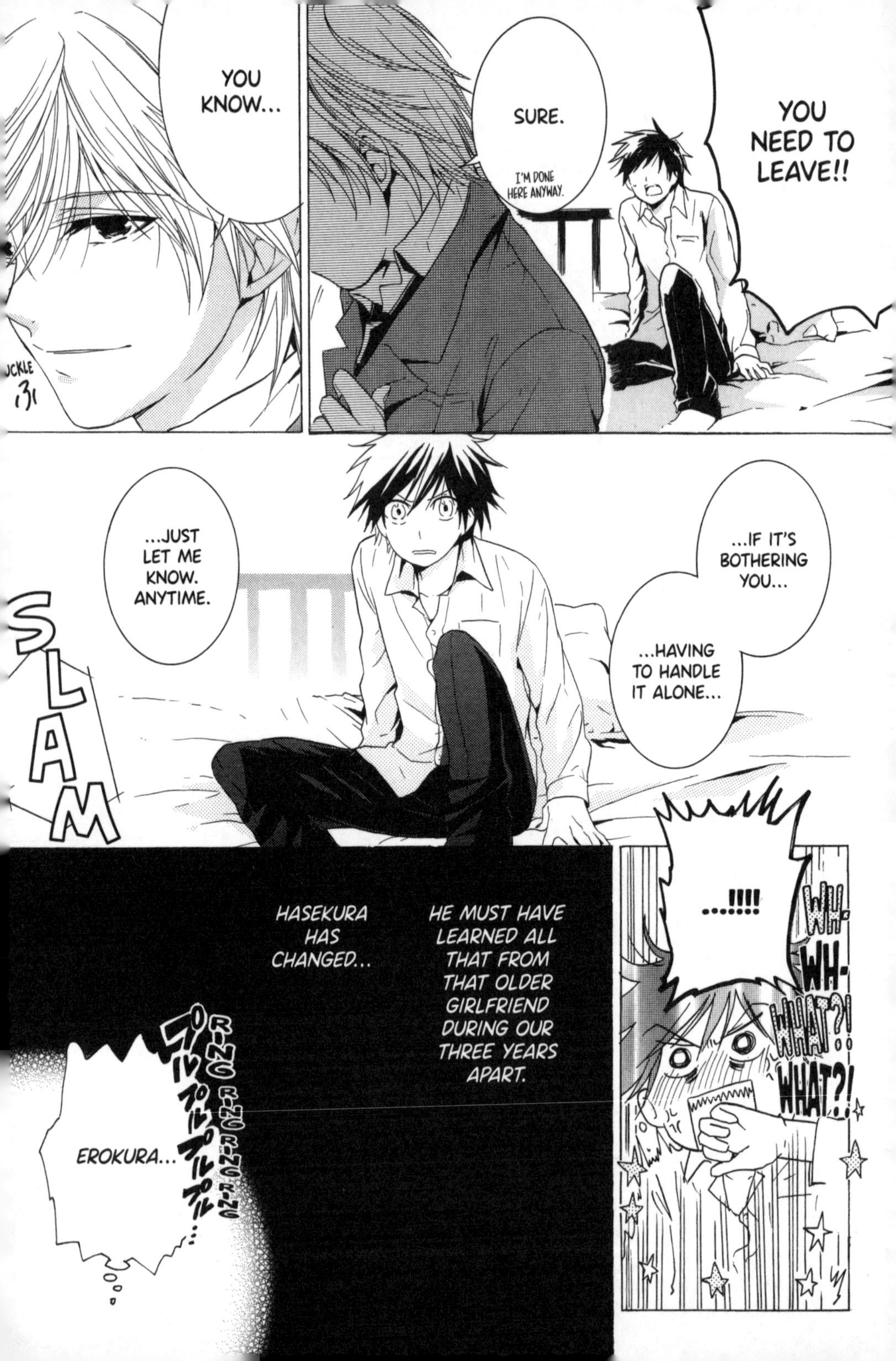
YOU NEED TO LEAVE!!
SURE.
I'M DONE HERE ANYWAY.
YOU KNOW...
...IF IT'S BOTHERING YOU...
...HAVING TO HANDLE IT ALONE...
...JUST LET ME KNOW. ANYTIME.
SLAM
...!!!!
WH-WH-WHAT?! WHAT?! WHAT?!
HE MUST HAVE LEARNED ALL THAT FROM THAT OLDER GIRLFRIEND DURING OUR THREE YEARS APART.
HASEKURA HAS CHANGED...
RING RING RING RING
EROKURA...

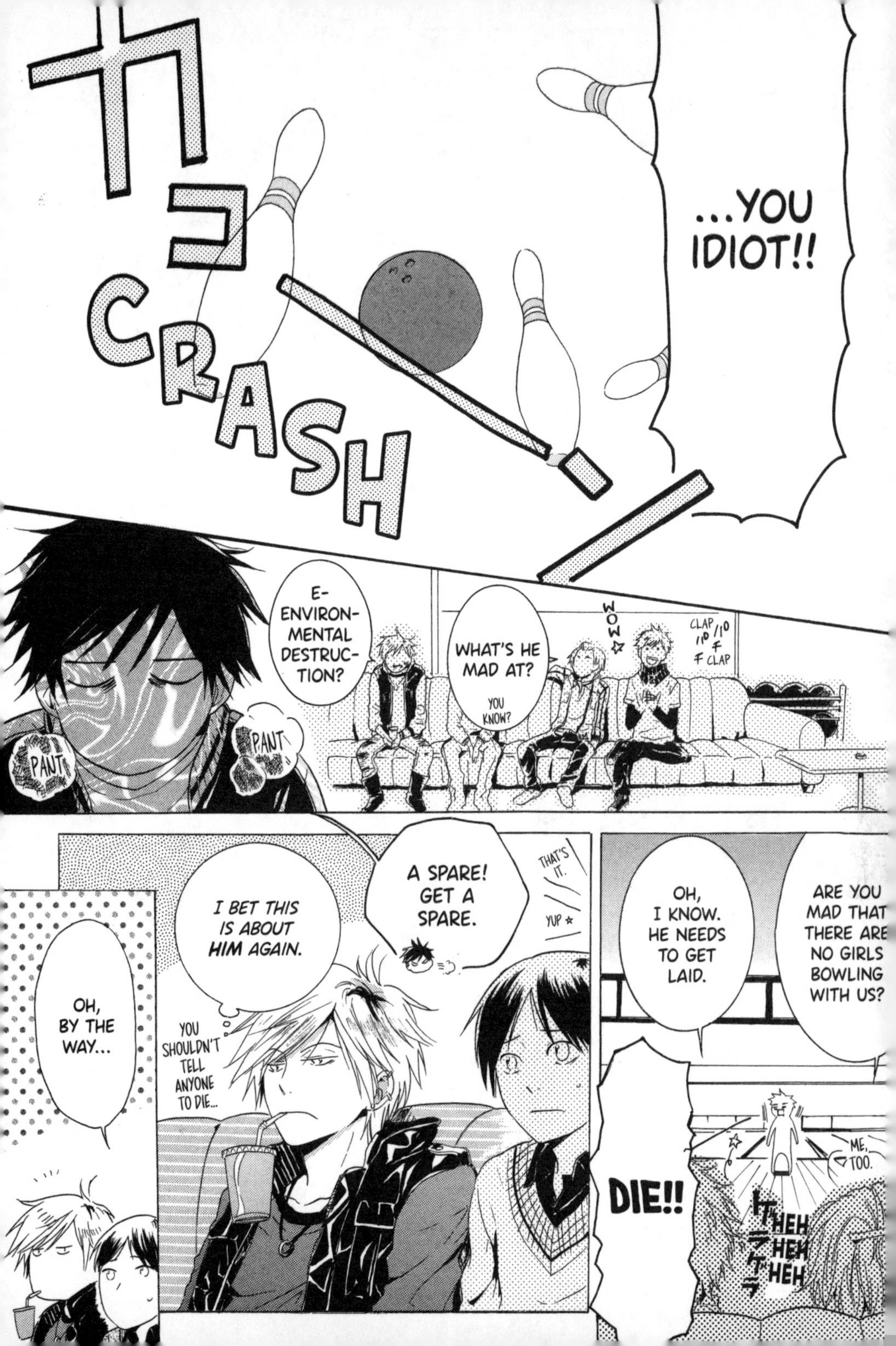
...YOU IDIOT!!
CRASH
CLAP CLAP
WOW
WHAT'S HE MAD AT?
YOU KNOW?
E-ENVIRONMENTAL DESTRUCTION?
PANT
PANT
ARE YOU MAD THAT THERE ARE NO GIRLS BOWLING WITH US?
OH, I KNOW. HE NEEDS TO GET LAID.
ME, TOO.
HEH HEH HEH
DIE!!
THAT'S IT.
YUP
A SPARE! GET A SPARE.
I BET THIS IS ABOUT HIM AGAIN.
YOU SHOULDN'T TELL ANYONE TO DIE...
OH, BY THE WAY...

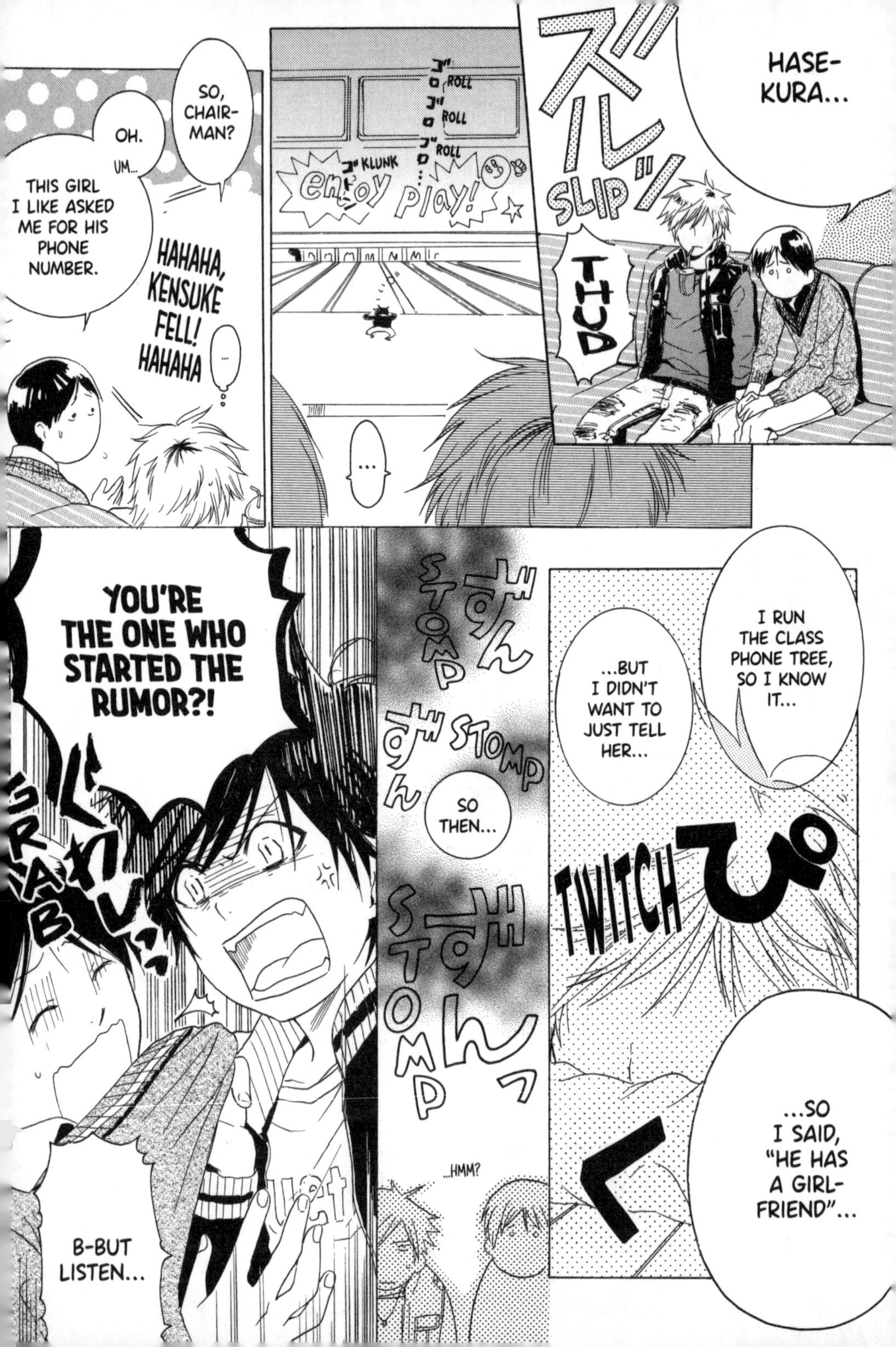

HASE-KURA...
SLIP
THUD
ROLL
ROLL
ROLL
KLUNK
enjoy play!
...
SO, CHAIR-MAN?
OH.
UM...
THIS GIRL I LIKE ASKED ME FOR HIS PHONE NUMBER.
HAHAHA, KENSUKE FELL! HAHAHA
...
I RUN THE CLASS PHONE TREE, SO I KNOW IT...
...BUT I DIDN'T WANT TO JUST TELL HER...
TWITCH
...SO I SAID, "HE HAS A GIRL-FRIEND"...
STOMP
STOMP
SO THEN...
STOMP
...HMM?
YOU'RE THE ONE WHO STARTED THE RUMOR?!
GRAB
B-BUT LISTEN...

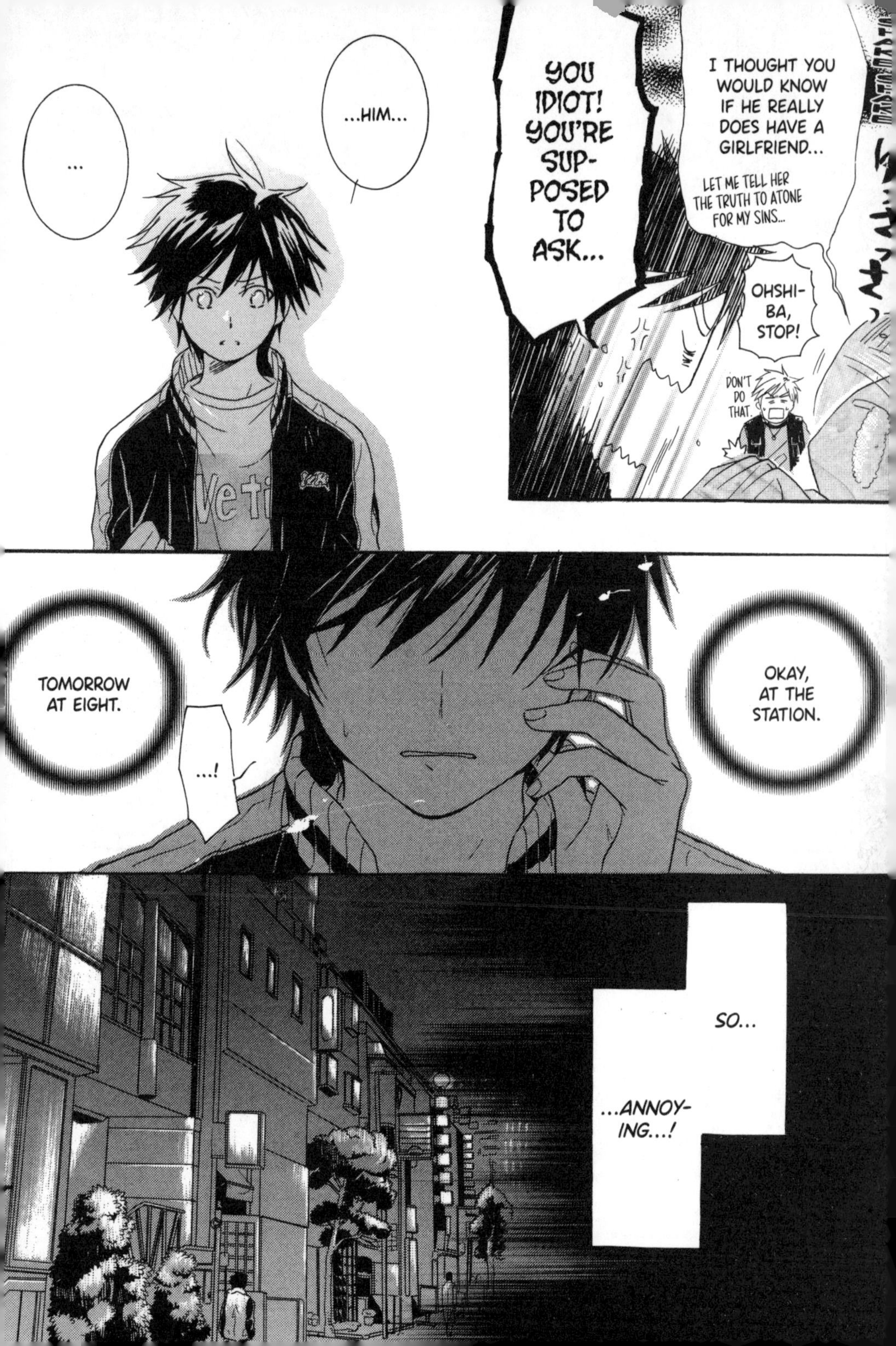
I THOUGHT YOU WOULD KNOW IF HE REALLY DOES HAVE A GIRLFRIEND...
LET ME TELL HER THE TRUTH TO ATONE FOR MY SINS...
OHSHI-BA, STOP!
DON'T DO THAT.
YOU IDIOT! YOU'RE SUP-POSED TO ASK...
...HIM...
...
OKAY, AT THE STATION.
...!
TOMORROW AT EIGHT.
SO...
...ANNOY-ING...!

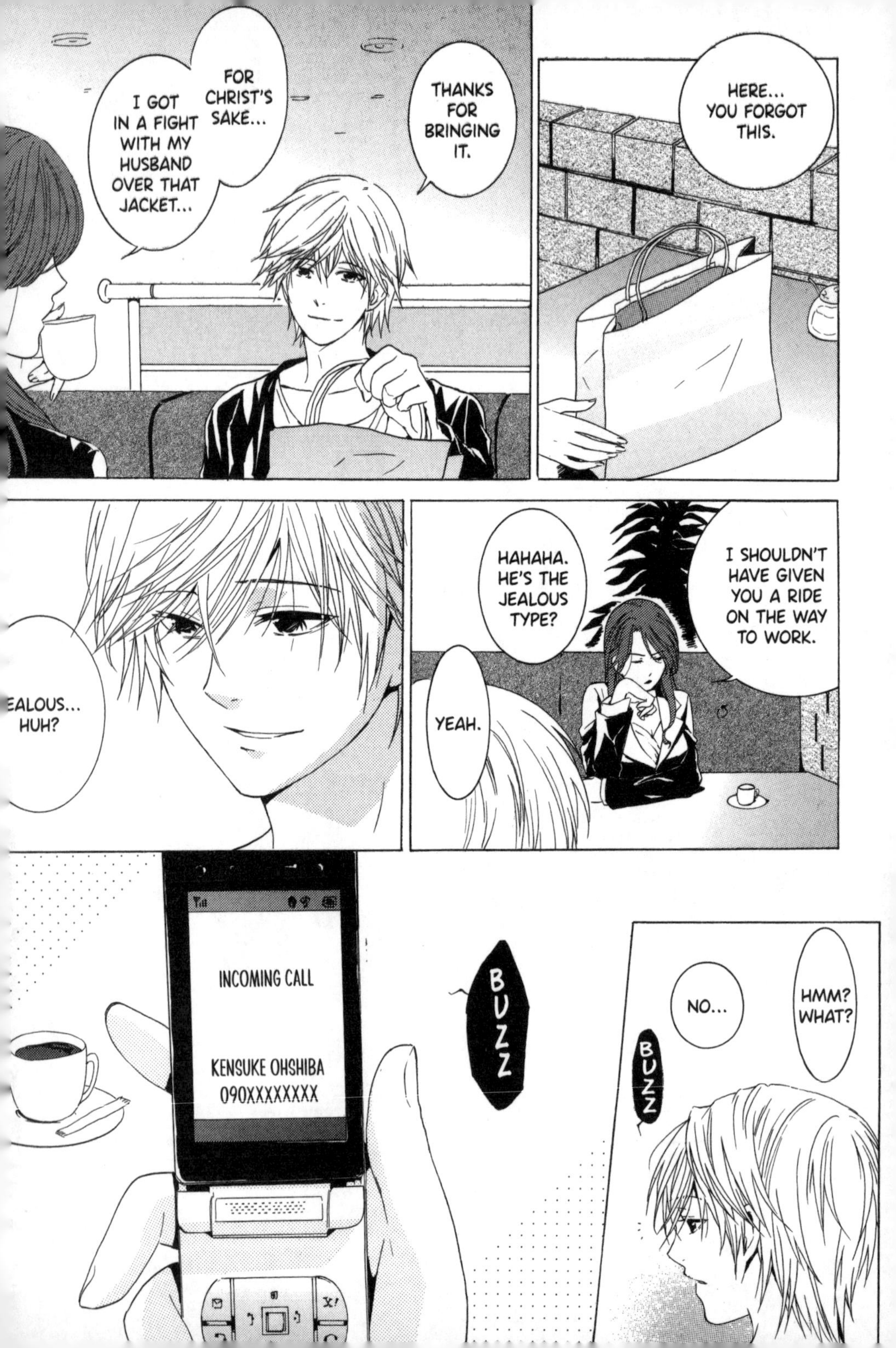
HERE... YOU FORGOT THIS.
THANKS FOR BRINGING IT.
FOR CHRIST'S SAKE...
I GOT IN A FIGHT WITH MY HUSBAND OVER THAT JACKET...
I SHOULDN'T HAVE GIVEN YOU A RIDE ON THE WAY TO WORK.
HAHAHA. HE'S THE JEALOUS TYPE?
YEAH.
EALOUS... HUH?
HMM? WHAT?
NO...
BUZZ
BUZZ
INCOMING CALL
KENSUKE OHSHIBA
090XXXXXXXX

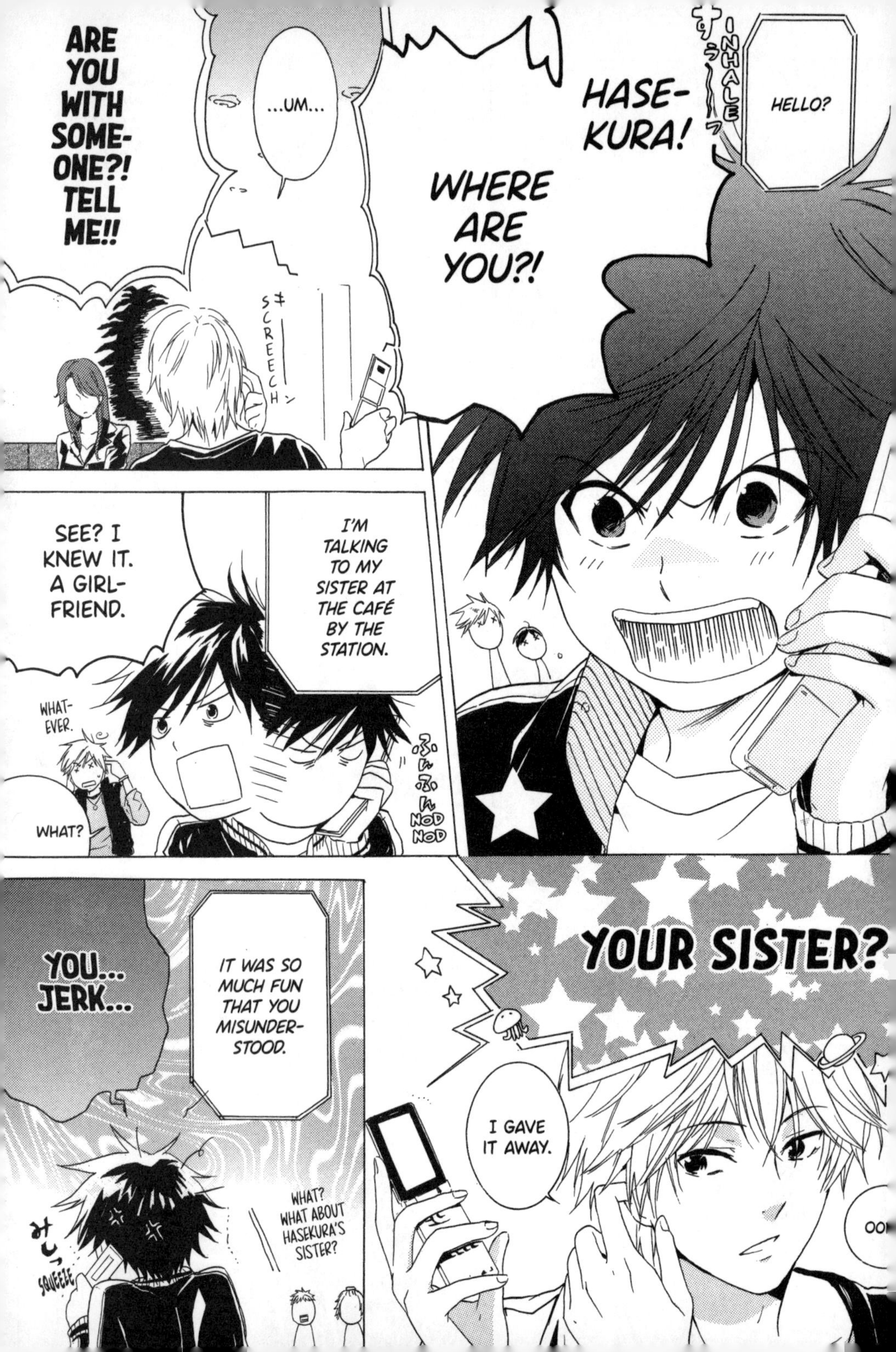
HELLO?
INHALE
HASE-KURA!
WHERE ARE YOU?!
...UM...
ARE YOU WITH SOME-ONE?! TELL ME!!
SCREECH
I'M TALKING TO MY SISTER AT THE CAFÉ BY THE STATION.
NOD NOD
SEE? I KNEW IT. A GIRL-FRIEND.
WHAT-EVER.
WHAT?
YOUR SISTER?
I GAVE IT AWAY.
IT WAS SO MUCH FUN THAT YOU MISUNDER-STOOD.
YOU... JERK...
WHAT? WHAT ABOUT HASEKURA'S SISTER?
SQUEEEZE

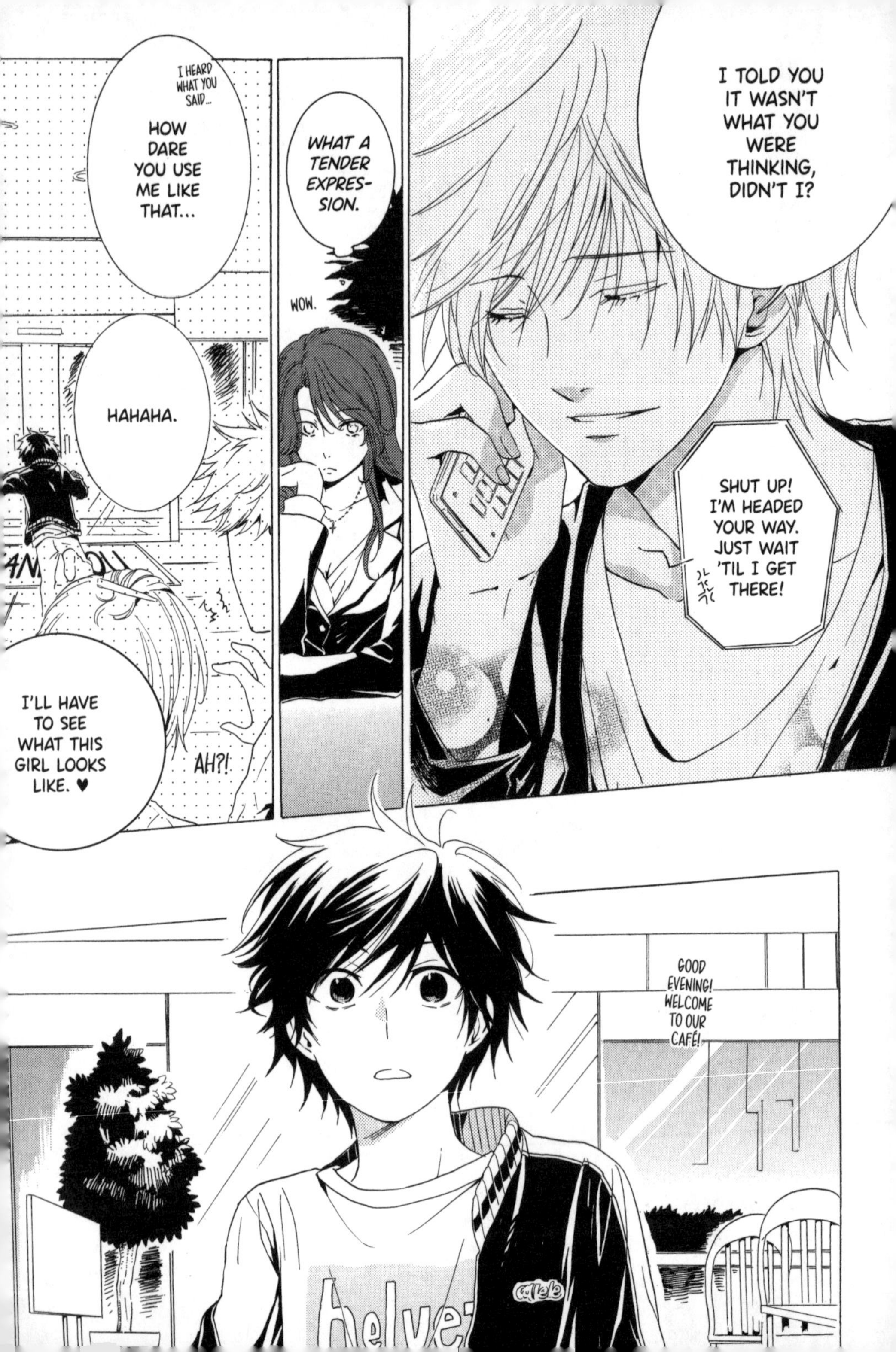
I TOLD YOU IT WASN'T WHAT YOU WERE THINKING, DIDN'T I?
SHUT UP! I'M HEADED YOUR WAY. JUST WAIT 'TIL I GET THERE!
WHAT A TENDER EXPRESSION.
WOW.
I HEARD WHAT YOU SAID...
HOW DARE YOU USE ME LIKE THAT...
HAHAHA.
AH?!
I'LL HAVE TO SEE WHAT THIS GIRL LOOKS LIKE. ♥
GOOD EVENING! WELCOME TO OUR CAFÉ!

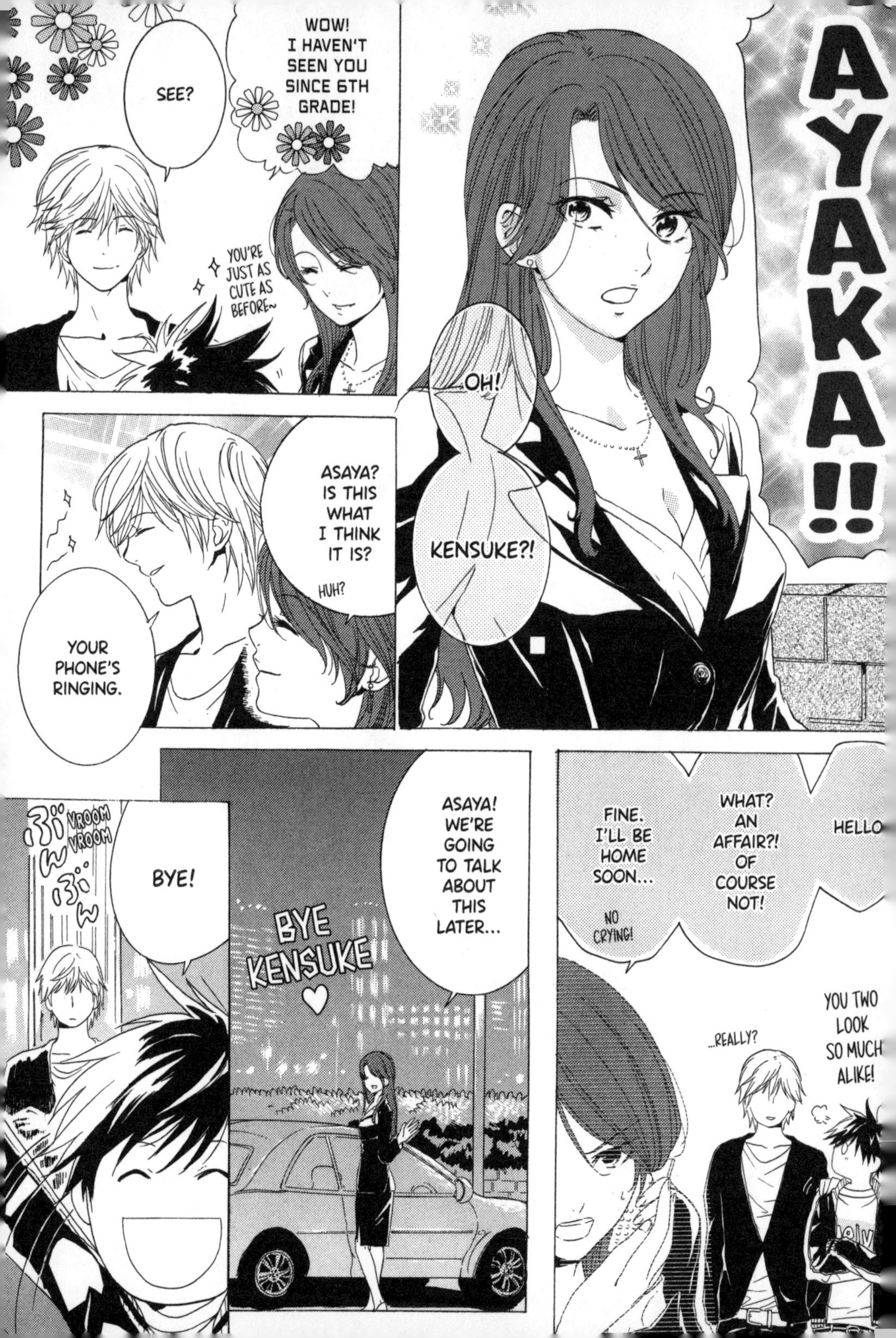
AYAKA!!
OH!
KENSUKE?!
WOW! I HAVEN'T SEEN YOU SINCE 6TH GRADE!
SEE?
YOU'RE JUST AS CUTE AS BEFORE~
ASAYA? IS THIS WHAT I THINK IT IS?
HUH?
YOUR PHONE'S RINGING.
HELLO
WHAT? AN AFFAIR?! OF COURSE NOT!
FINE. I'LL BE HOME SOON...
NO CRYING!
YOU TWO LOOK SO MUCH ALIKE!
...REALLY?
ASAYA! WE'RE GOING TO TALK ABOUT THIS LATER...
BYE KENSUKE
BYE!
VROOM VROOM

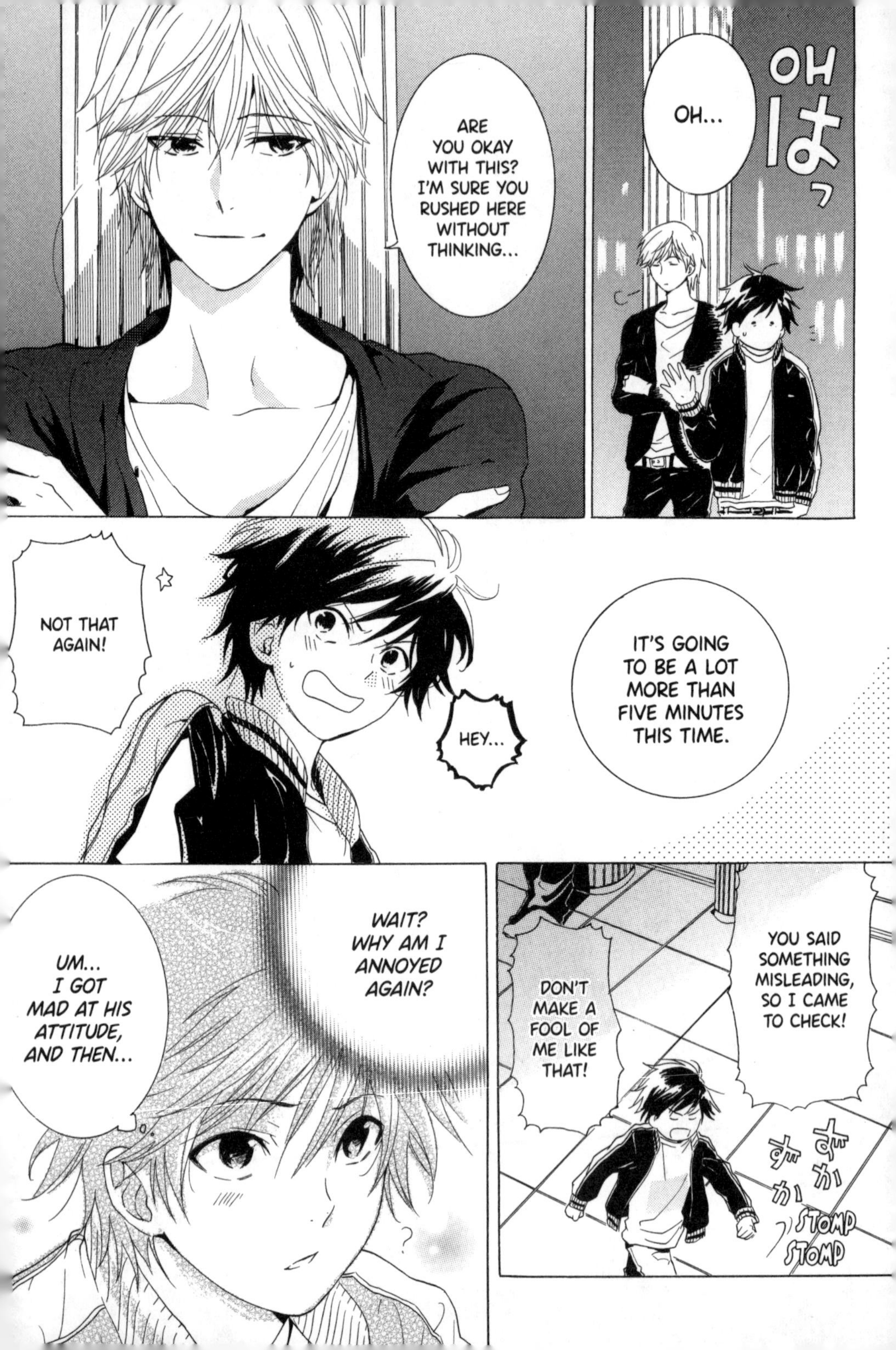
OH はっ
OH...
ARE YOU OKAY WITH THIS? I'M SURE YOU RUSHED HERE WITHOUT THINKING...
IT'S GOING TO BE A LOT MORE THAN FIVE MINUTES THIS TIME.
HEY...
NOT THAT AGAIN!
YOU SAID SOMETHING MISLEADING, SO I CAME TO CHECK!
DON'T MAKE A FOOL OF ME LIKE THAT!
ずかずか STOMP STOMP
WAIT? WHY AM I ANNOYED AGAIN?
UM... I GOT MAD AT HIS ATTITUDE, AND THEN...

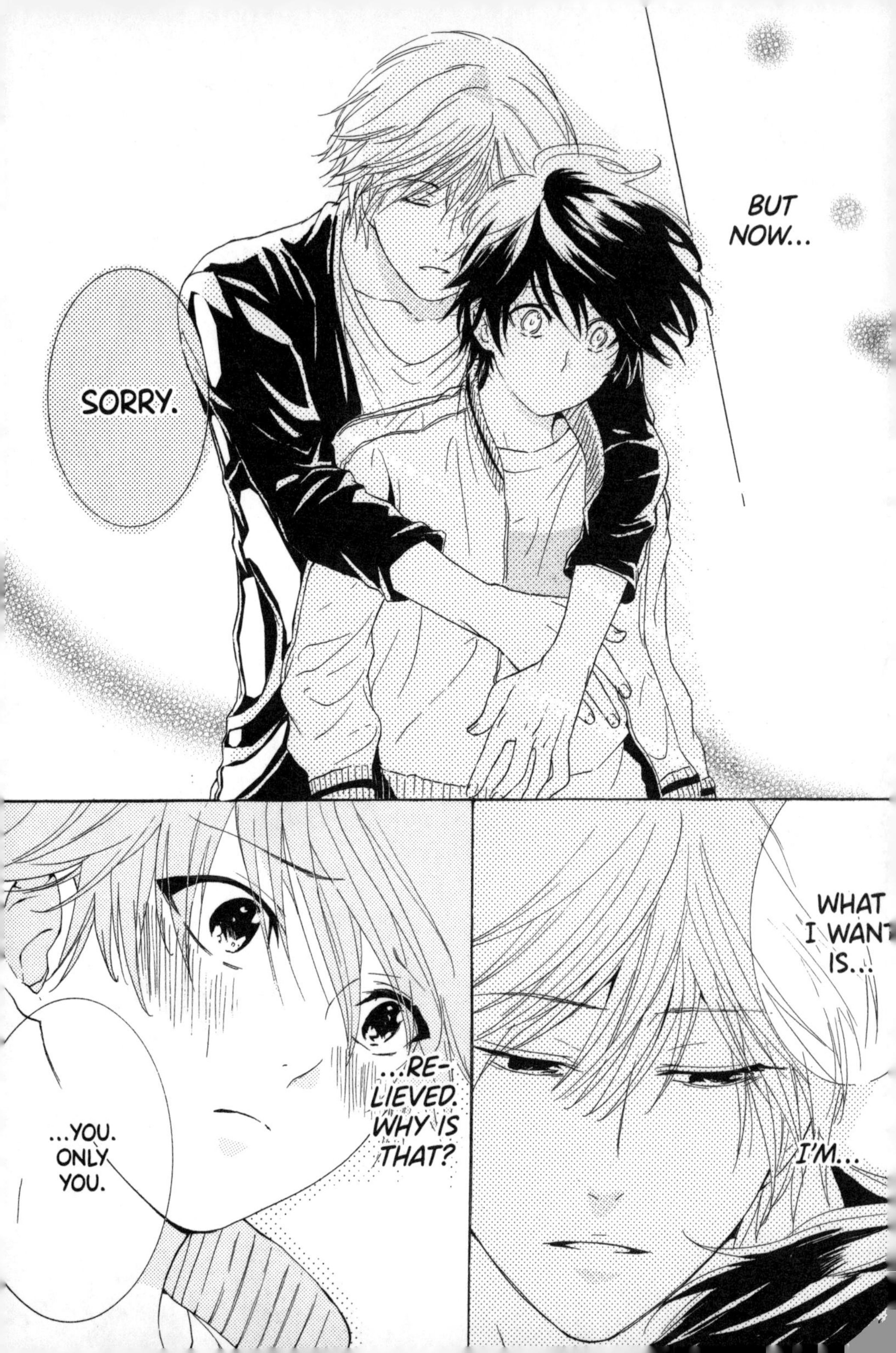
BUT NOW...
SORRY.
WHAT I WANT IS...
I'M...
...RE-LIEVED. WHY IS THAT?
...YOU. ONLY YOU.

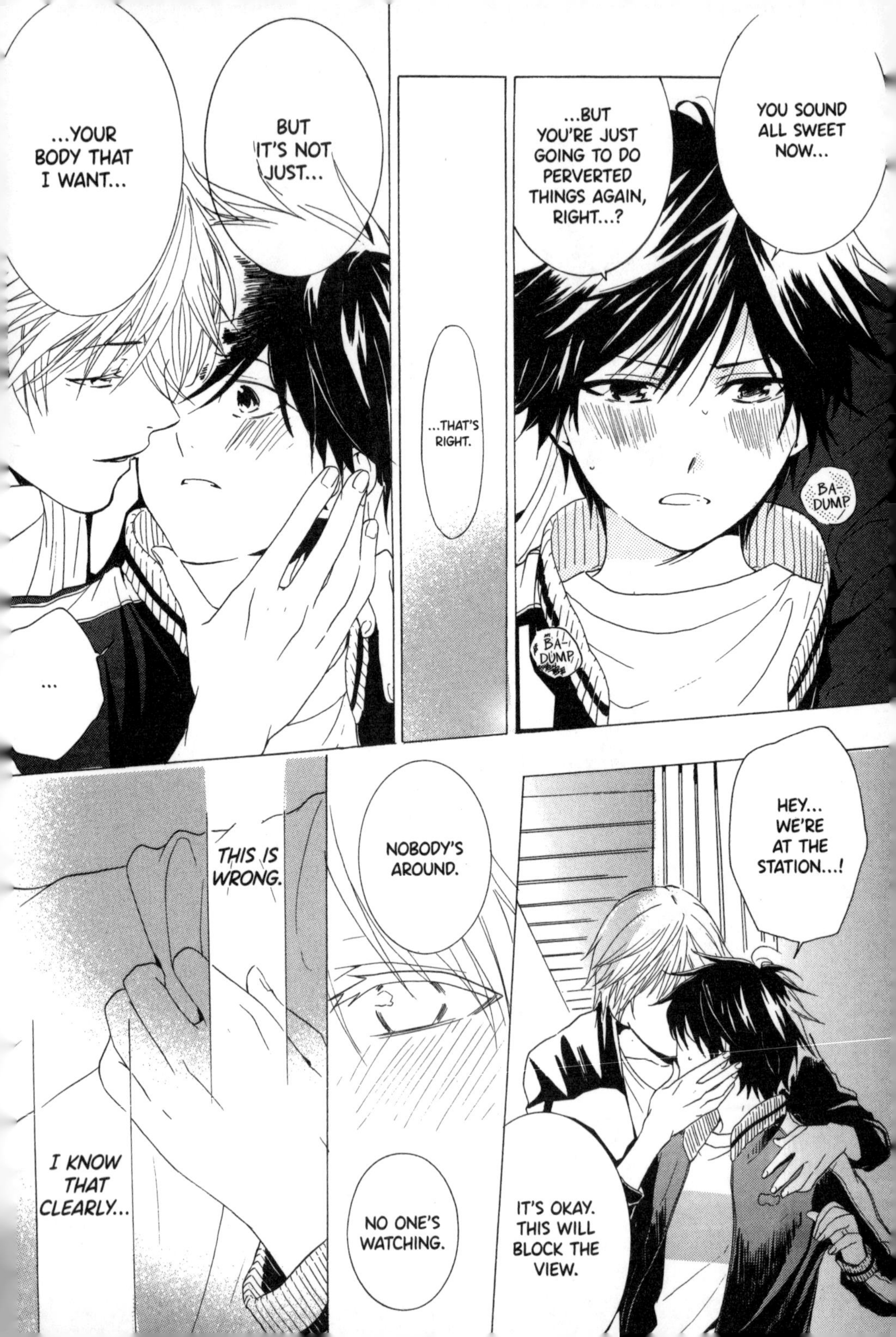
YOU SOUND ALL SWEET NOW...
...BUT YOU'RE JUST GOING TO DO PERVERTED THINGS AGAIN, RIGHT...?
BA-DUMP
BA-DUMP
...THAT'S RIGHT.
BUT IT'S NOT JUST...
...YOUR BODY THAT I WANT...
...
HEY... WE'RE AT THE STATION...!
IT'S OKAY. THIS WILL BLOCK THE VIEW.
NOBODY'S AROUND.
NO ONE'S WATCHING.
THIS IS WRONG.
I KNOW THAT CLEARLY...

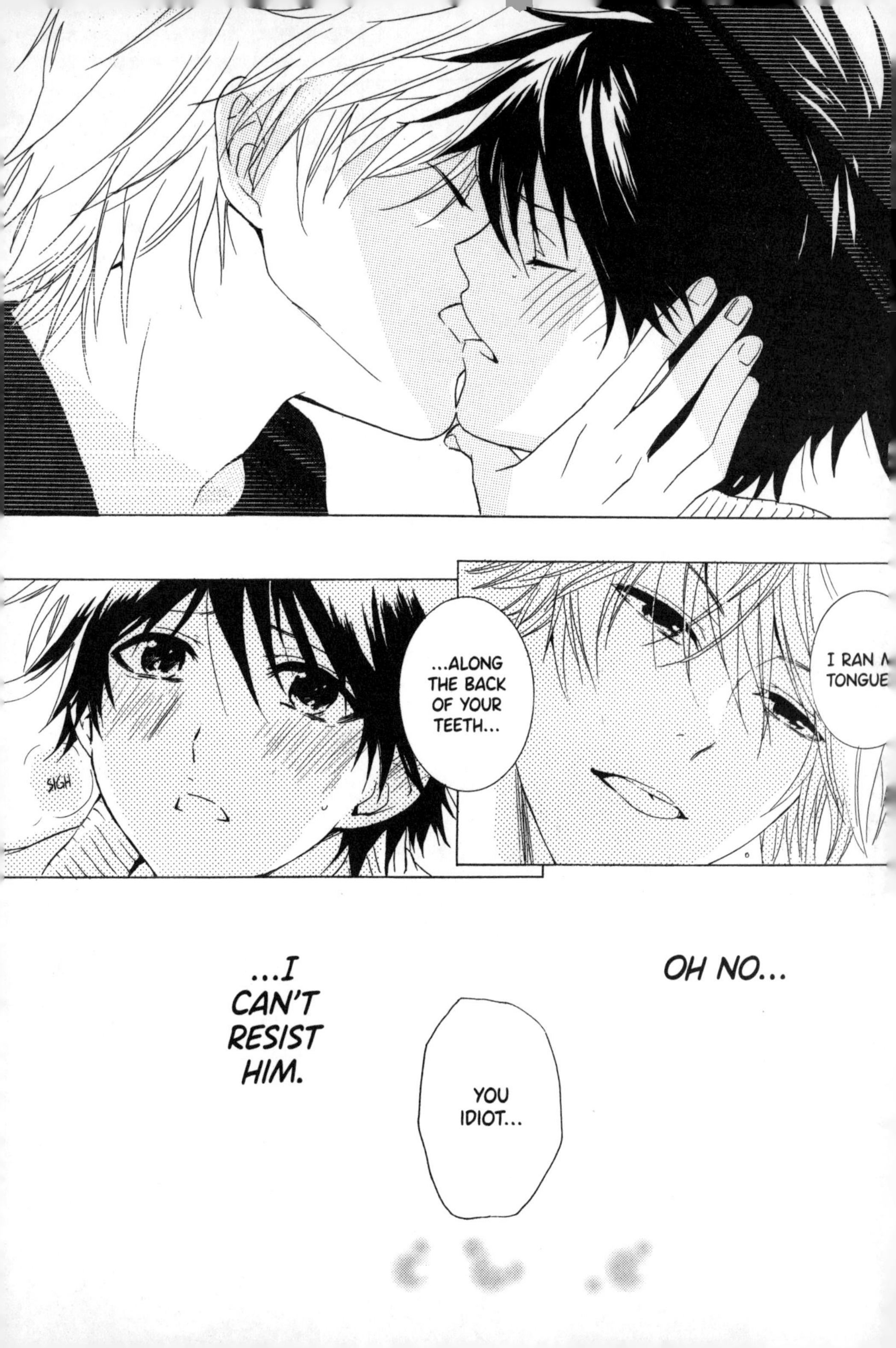
I RAN M TONGUE
...ALONG THE BACK OF YOUR TEETH...
SIGH
OH NO...
YOU IDIOT...
...I CAN'T RESIST HIM.

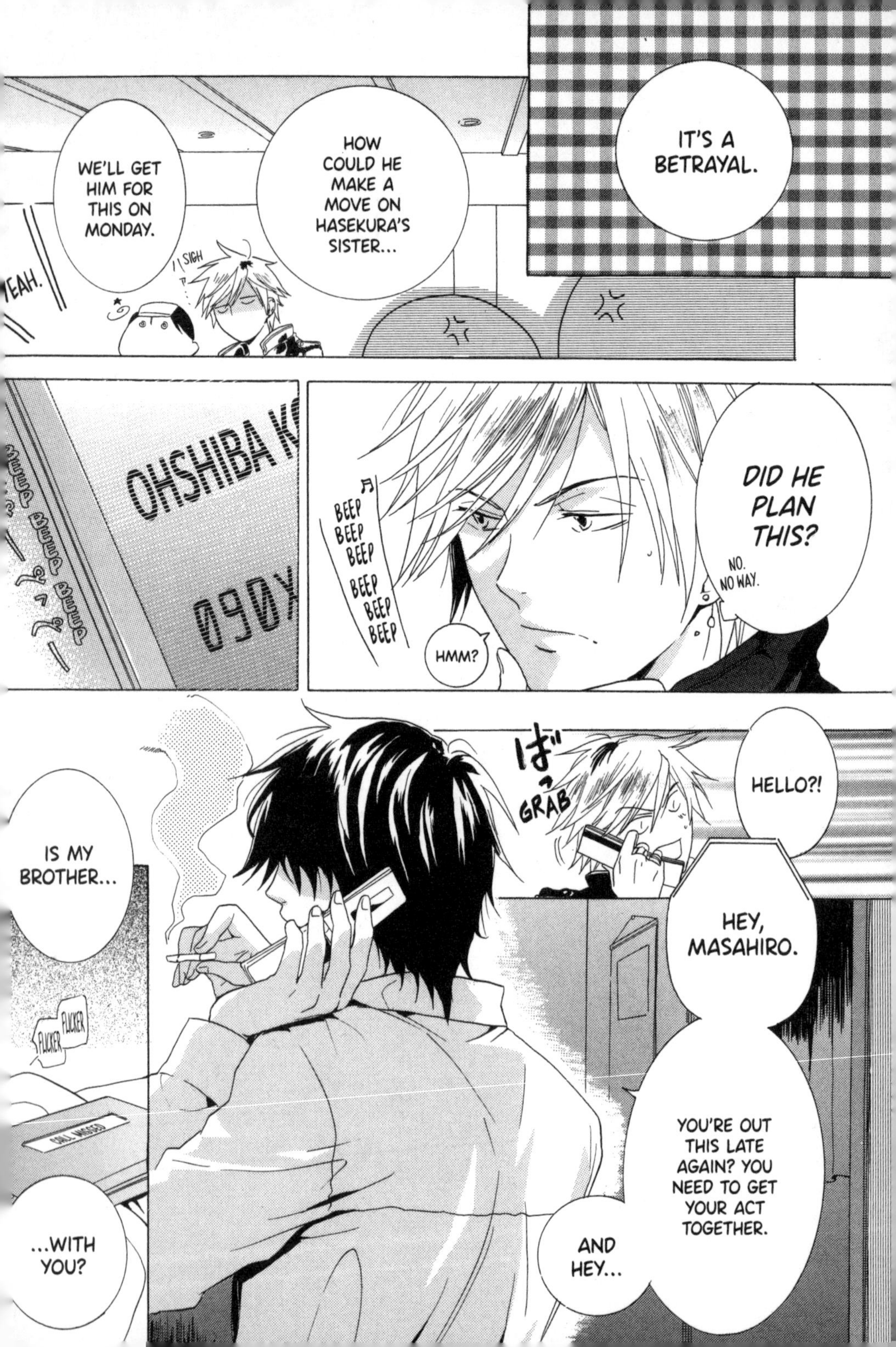
IT'S A BETRAYAL.
HOW COULD HE MAKE A MOVE ON HASEKURA'S SISTER...
WE'LL GET HIM FOR THIS ON MONDAY.
SIGH
DID HE PLAN THIS?
NO. NO WAY.
BEEP BEEP BEEP BEEP BEEP BEEP
HMM?
HELLO?!
ばっ
GRAB
HEY, MASAHIRO.
YOU'RE OUT THIS LATE AGAIN? YOU NEED TO GET YOUR ACT TOGETHER.
AND HEY...
IS MY BROTHER...
...WITH YOU?
FLICKER FLICKER

Masahiro Setagawa
Height: 176 cm
Types of girls he likes: Quiet girls
Current concerns: Social security and Japan's aging population

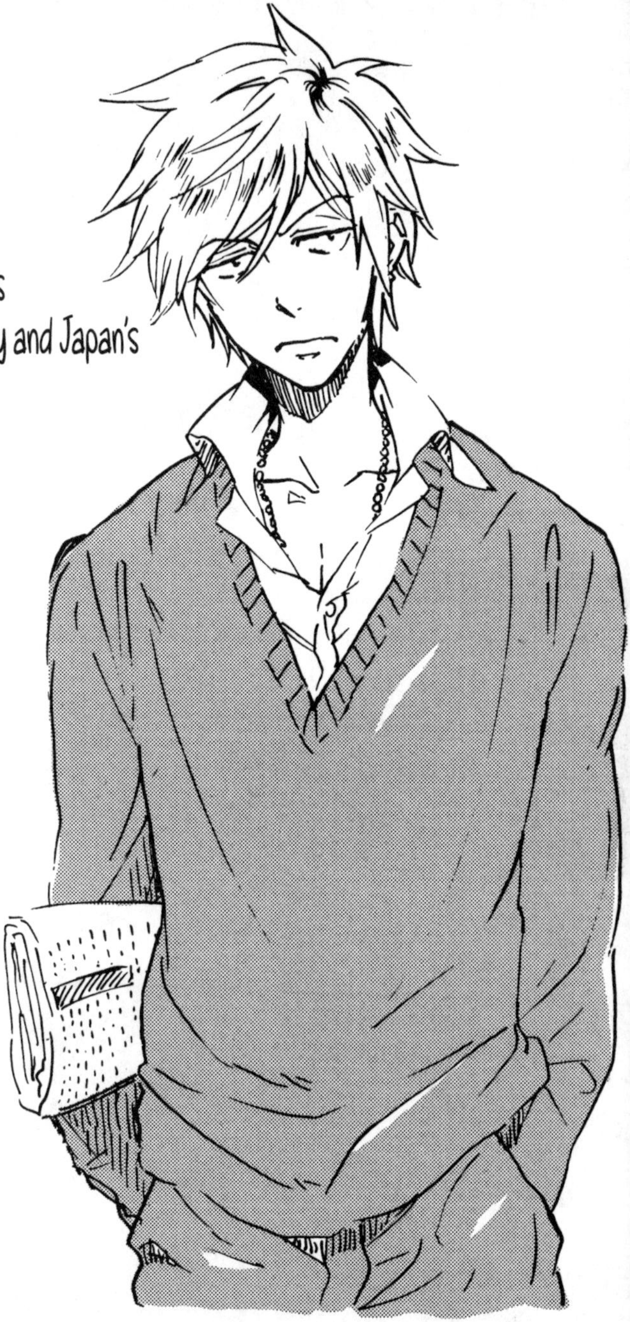

HITORIJIME BOYFRIEND

PRESENTED BY MEMECO ARII

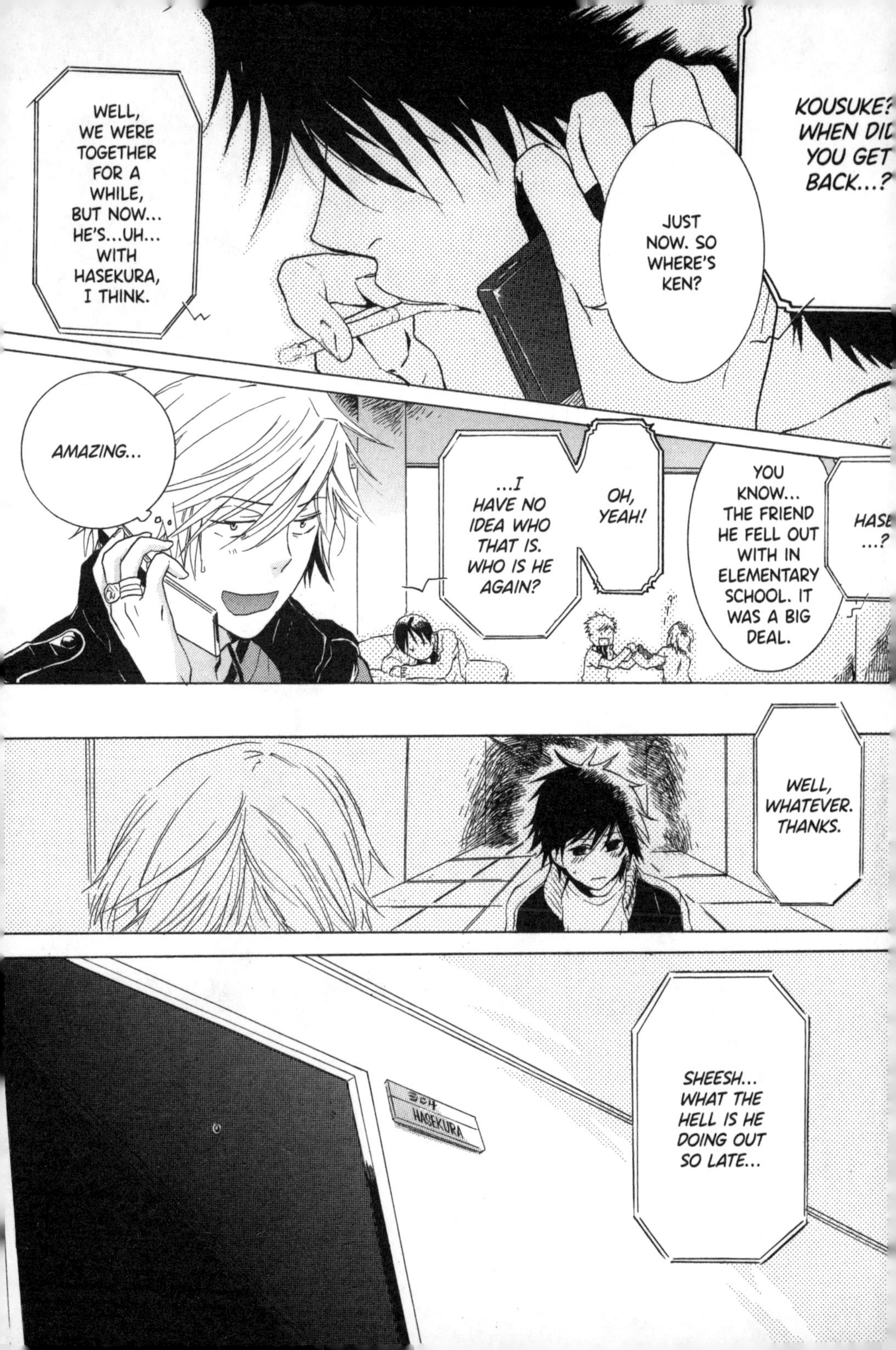
KOUSUKE? WHEN DI YOU GET BACK...?
JUST NOW. SO WHERE'S KEN?
WELL, WE WERE TOGETHER FOR A WHILE, BUT NOW... HE'S...UH... WITH HASEKURA, I THINK.
HASE ...?
YOU KNOW... THE FRIEND HE FELL OUT WITH IN ELEMENTARY SCHOOL. IT WAS A BIG DEAL.
OH, YEAH!
...I HAVE NO IDEA WHO THAT IS. WHO IS HE AGAIN?
AMAZING...
WELL, WHATEVER. THANKS.
SHEESH... WHAT THE HELL IS HE DOING OUT SO LATE...
HASEKURA

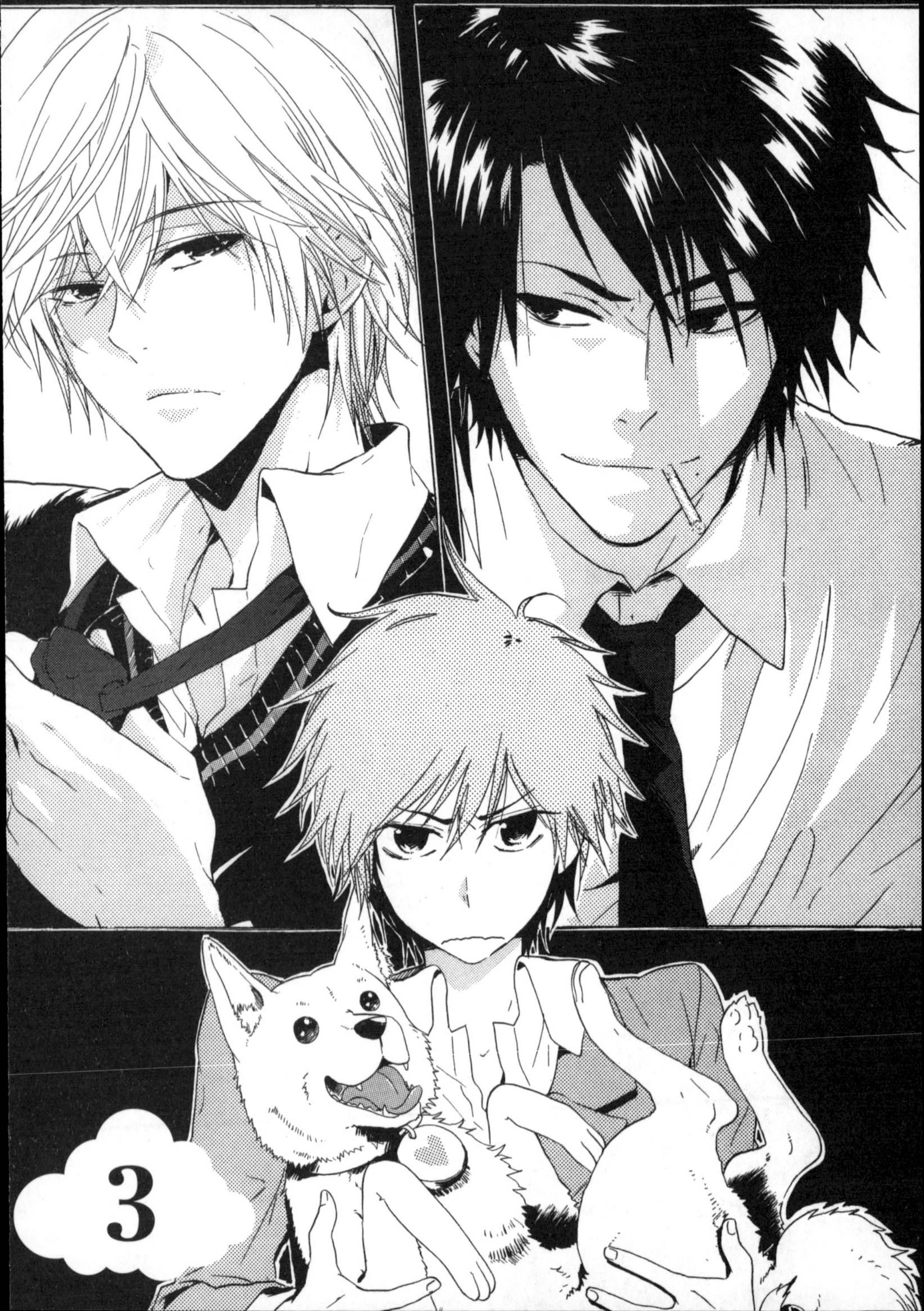
3

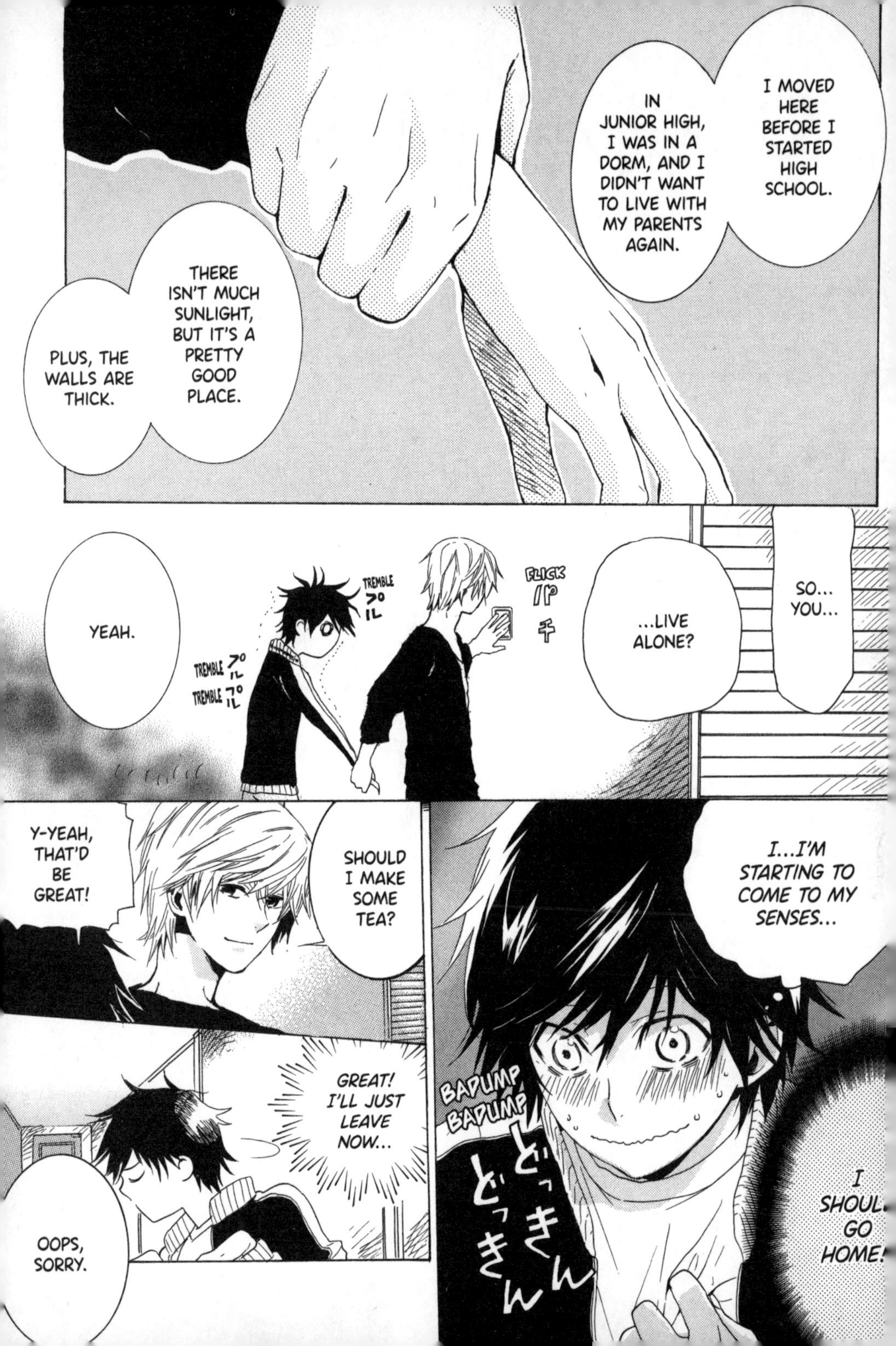
I MOVED HERE BEFORE I STARTED HIGH SCHOOL.
IN JUNIOR HIGH, I WAS IN A DORM, AND I DIDN'T WANT TO LIVE WITH MY PARENTS AGAIN.
THERE ISN'T MUCH SUNLIGHT, BUT IT'S A PRETTY GOOD PLACE.
PLUS, THE WALLS ARE THICK.
SO... YOU...
...LIVE ALONE?
FLICK
TREMBLE
YEAH.
TREMBLE
TREMBLE
I...I'M STARTING TO COME TO MY SENSES...
BADUMP BADUMP
どっきん どっきん
I SHOUL GO HOME!
SHOULD I MAKE SOME TEA?
Y-YEAH, THAT'D BE GREAT!
GREAT! I'LL JUST LEAVE NOW...
OOPS, SORRY.

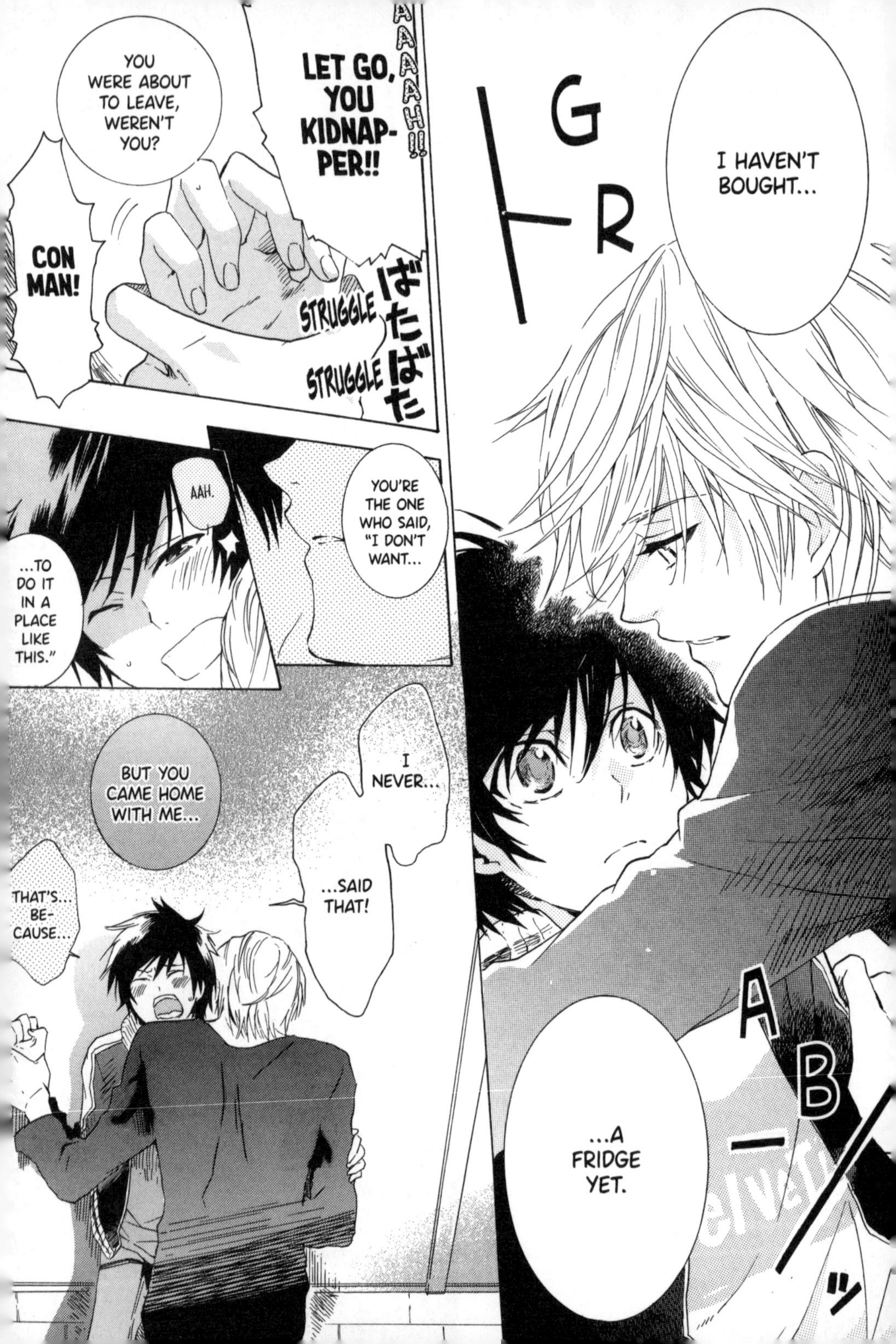
I HAVEN'T BOUGHT...
GR
AB
...A FRIDGE YET.
AAAAAH!!
LET GO, YOU KIDNAP-PER!!
YOU WERE ABOUT TO LEAVE, WEREN'T YOU?
ばたばた
STRUGGLE STRUGGLE
CON MAN!
YOU'RE THE ONE WHO SAID, "I DON'T WANT...
AAH.
...TO DO IT IN A PLACE LIKE THIS."
I NEVER...
...SAID THAT!
BUT YOU CAME HOME WITH ME...
THAT'S... BE-CAUSE...

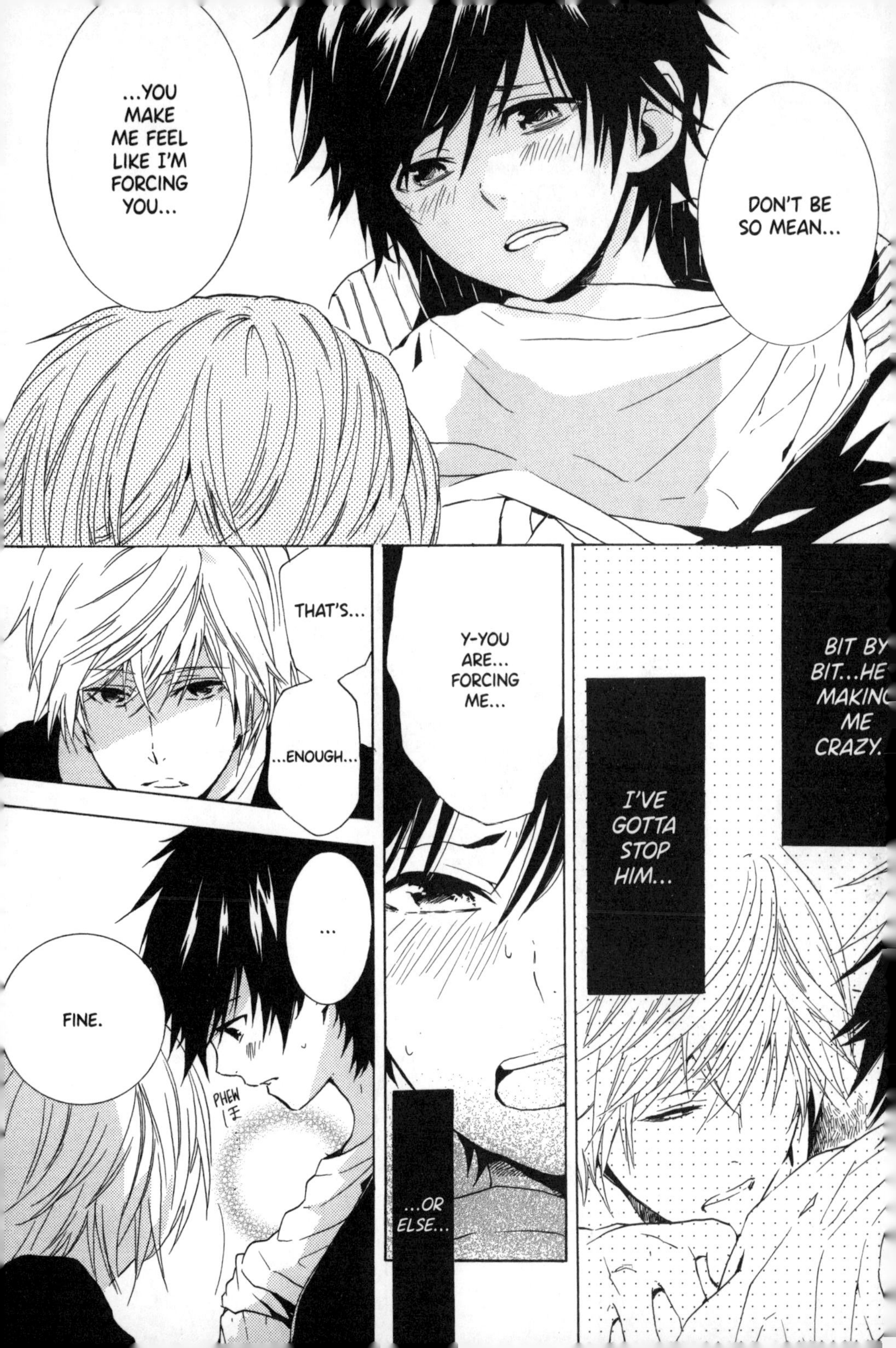
DON'T BE SO MEAN...
...YOU MAKE ME FEEL LIKE I'M FORCING YOU...
BIT BY BIT...HE MAKING ME CRAZY.
I'VE GOTTA STOP HIM...
...OR ELSE...
Y-YOU ARE... FORCING ME...
THAT'S...
...ENOUGH...
...
FINE.
PHEW

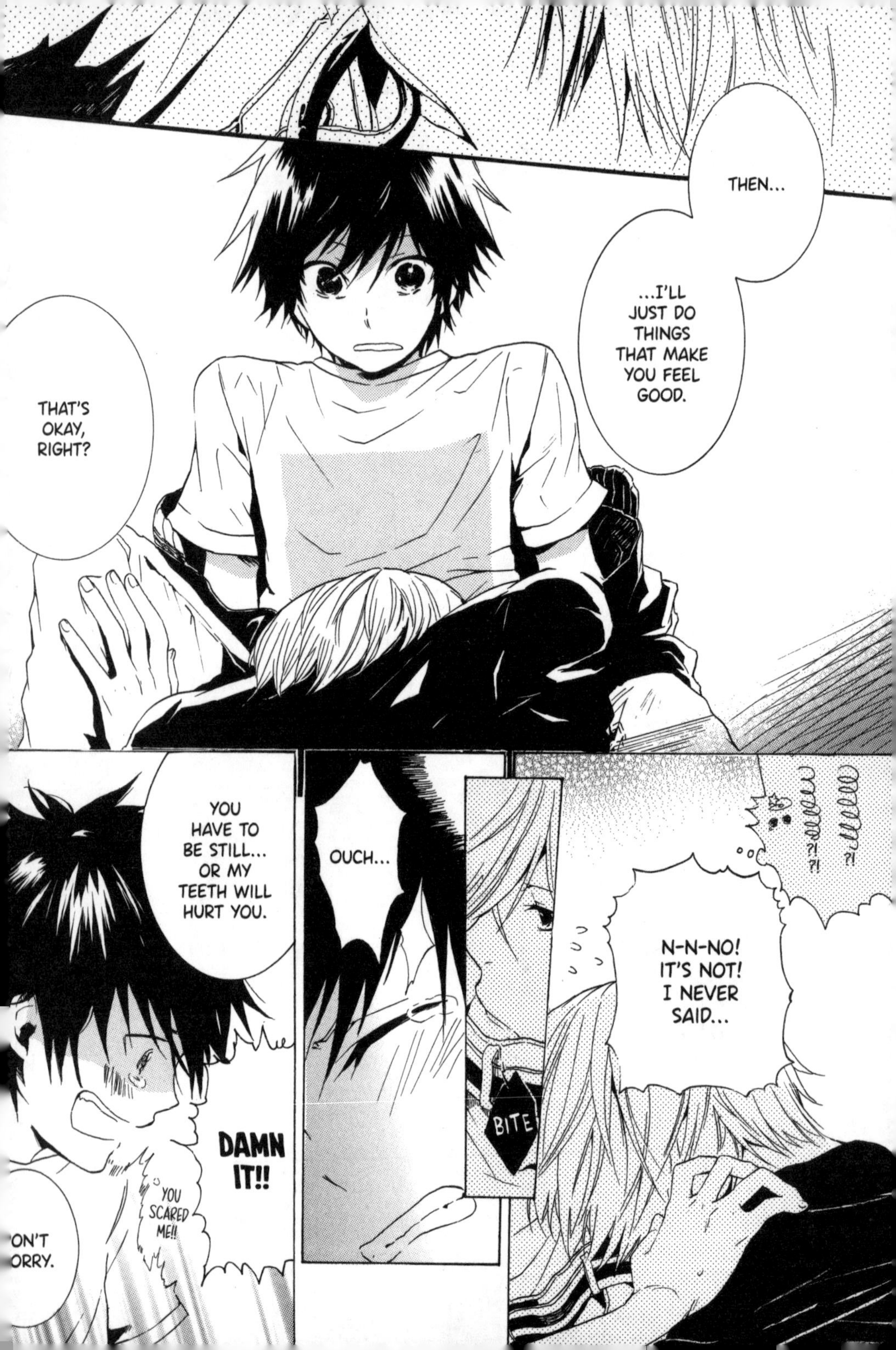
THEN...
...I'LL JUST DO THINGS THAT MAKE YOU FEEL GOOD.
THAT'S OKAY, RIGHT?
?!
?!
N-N-NO! IT'S NOT! I NEVER SAID...
BITE
OUCH...
YOU HAVE TO BE STILL... OR MY TEETH WILL HURT YOU.
DAMN IT!!
YOU SCARED ME!!
ON'T ORRY.

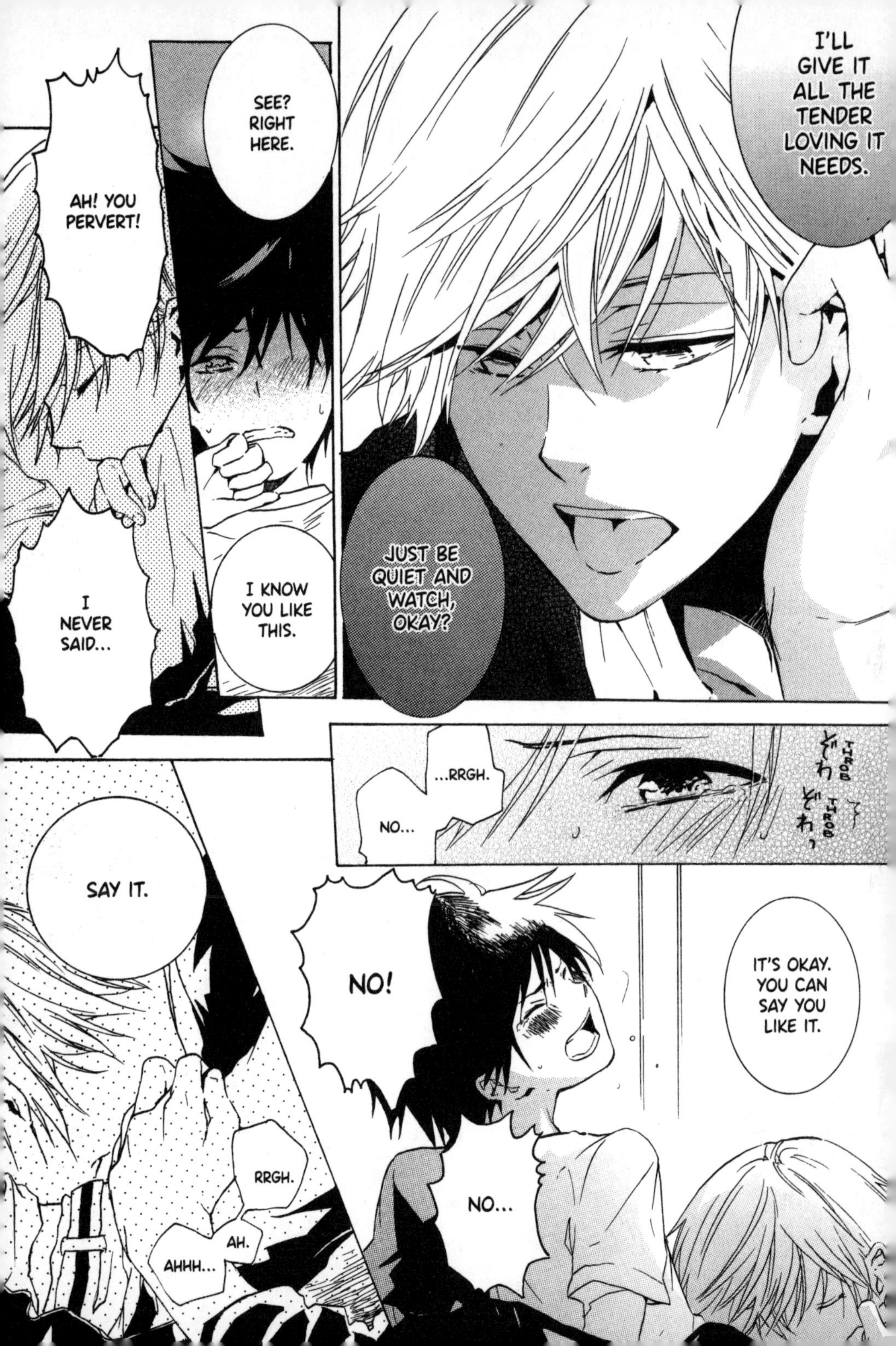
I'LL GIVE IT ALL THE TENDER LOVING IT NEEDS.
JUST BE QUIET AND WATCH, OKAY?
SEE? RIGHT HERE.
I KNOW YOU LIKE THIS.
AH! YOU PERVERT!
I NEVER SAID...
THROB THROB
...RRGH.
NO...
IT'S OKAY. YOU CAN SAY YOU LIKE IT.
NO!
NO...
SAY IT.
RRGH.
AH.
AHHH...

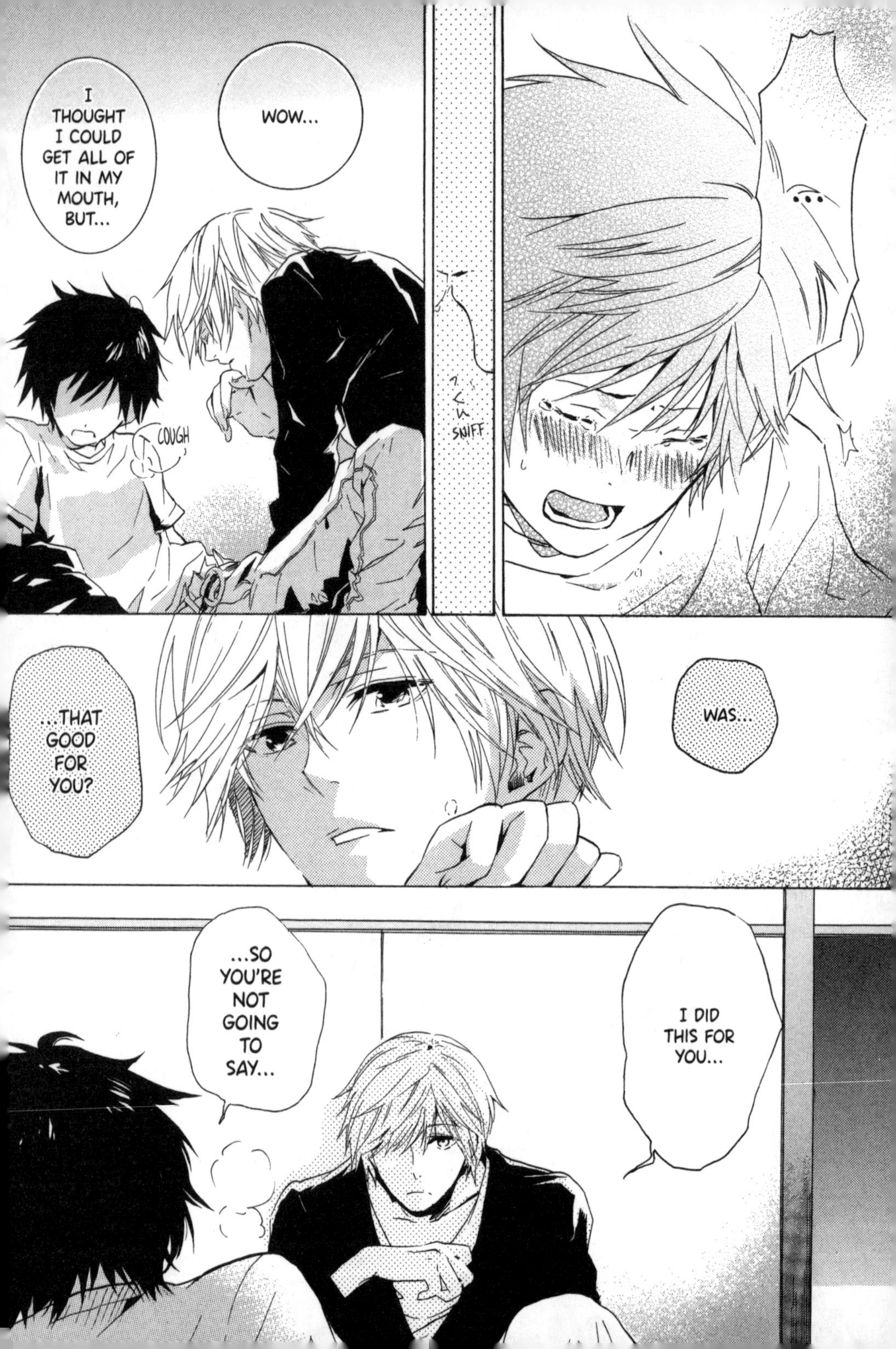
...
SNIFF
WOW...
I THOUGHT I COULD GET ALL OF IT IN MY MOUTH, BUT...
COUGH
WAS...
...THAT GOOD FOR YOU?
I DID THIS FOR YOU...
...SO YOU'RE NOT GOING TO SAY...

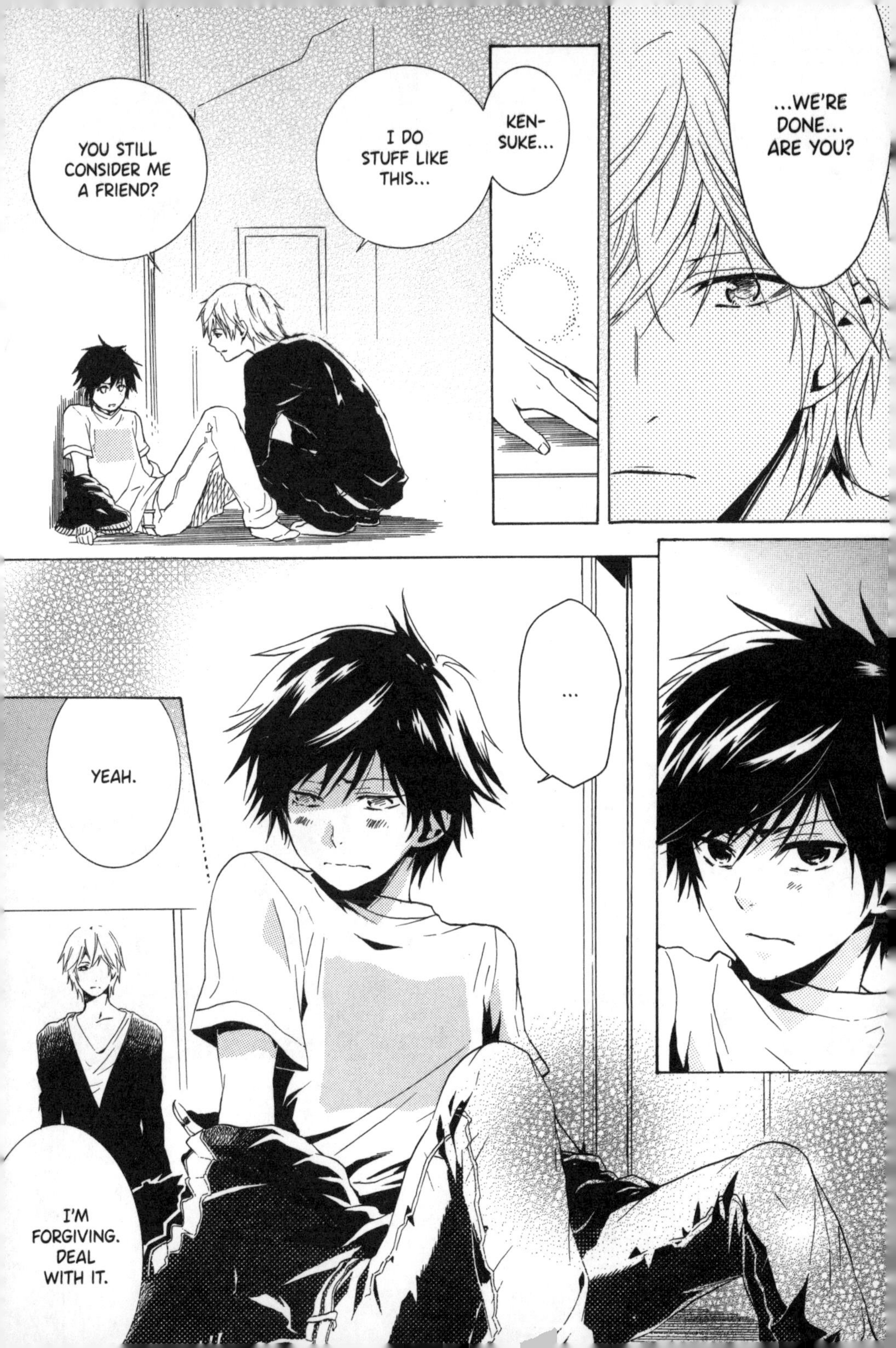

...WE'RE DONE... ARE YOU?
KEN-SUKE...
I DO STUFF LIKE THIS...
YOU STILL CONSIDER ME A FRIEND?
...
YEAH.
I'M FORGIVING. DEAL WITH IT.

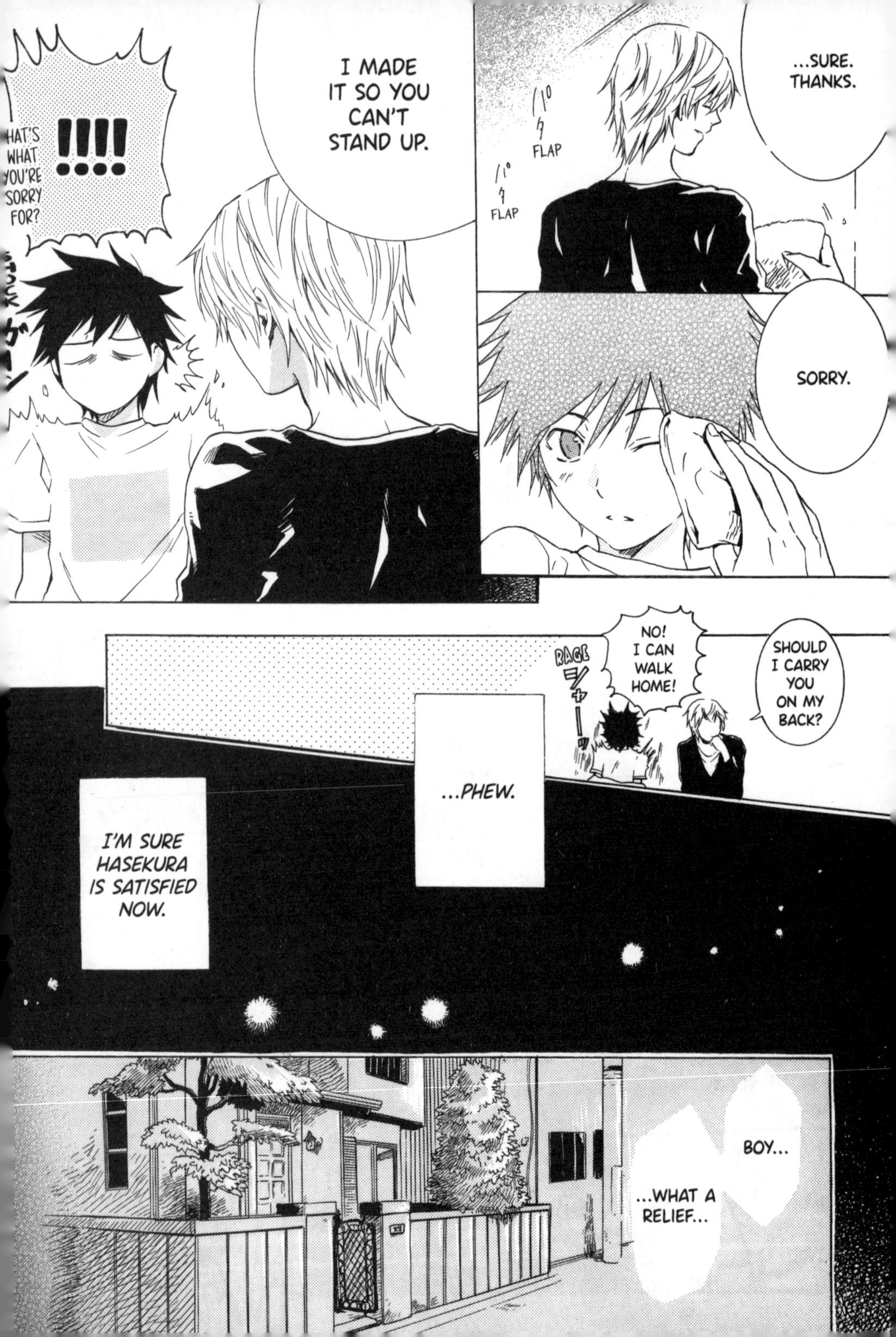

...SURE. THANKS.
FLAP
FLAP
SORRY.
I MADE IT SO YOU CAN'T STAND UP.
!!!!
HAT'S WHAT YOU'RE SORRY FOR?
SHOULD I CARRY YOU ON MY BACK?
NO! I CAN WALK HOME!
RAGE
...PHEW.
I'M SURE HASEKURA IS SATISFIED NOW.
BOY...
...WHAT A RELIEF...

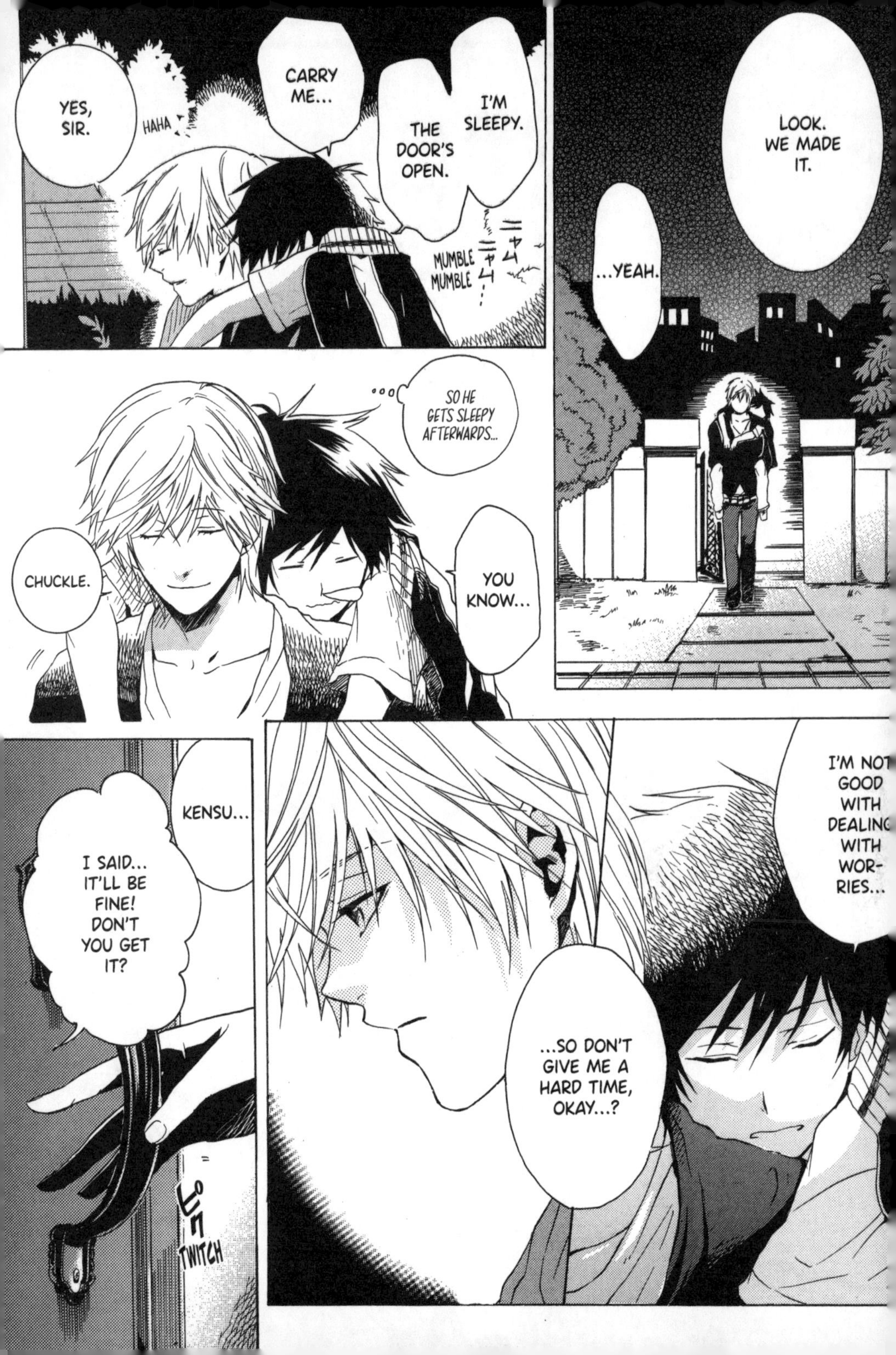
LOOK. WE MADE IT.
...YEAH.
I'M SLEEPY.
CARRY ME...
THE DOOR'S OPEN.
HAHA
YES, SIR.
MUMBLE MUMBLE
SO HE GETS SLEEPY AFTERWARDS...
YOU KNOW...
CHUCKLE.
I'M NOT GOOD WITH DEALING WITH WOR-RIES...
...SO DON'T GIVE ME A HARD TIME, OKAY...?
KENSU...
I SAID... IT'LL BE FINE! DON'T YOU GET IT?
TWITCH

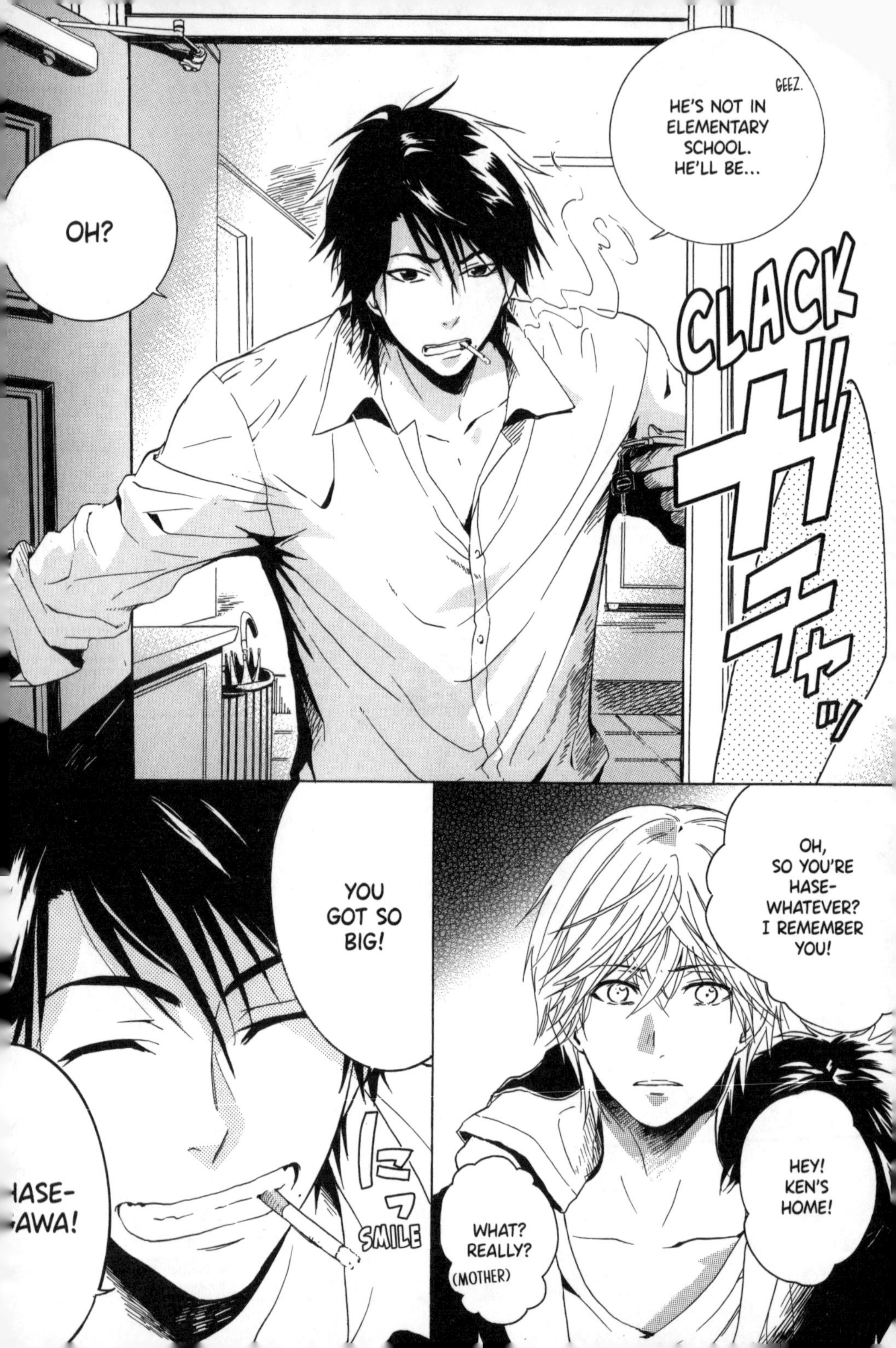
GEEZ.
HE'S NOT IN ELEMENTARY SCHOOL. HE'LL BE...
CLACK
ガチャッ
OH?
OH, SO YOU'RE HASE-WHATEVER? I REMEMBER YOU!
HEY! KEN'S HOME!
WHAT? REALLY?
(MOTHER)
YOU GOT SO BIG!
ニコッ
SMILE
HASE-
AWA!

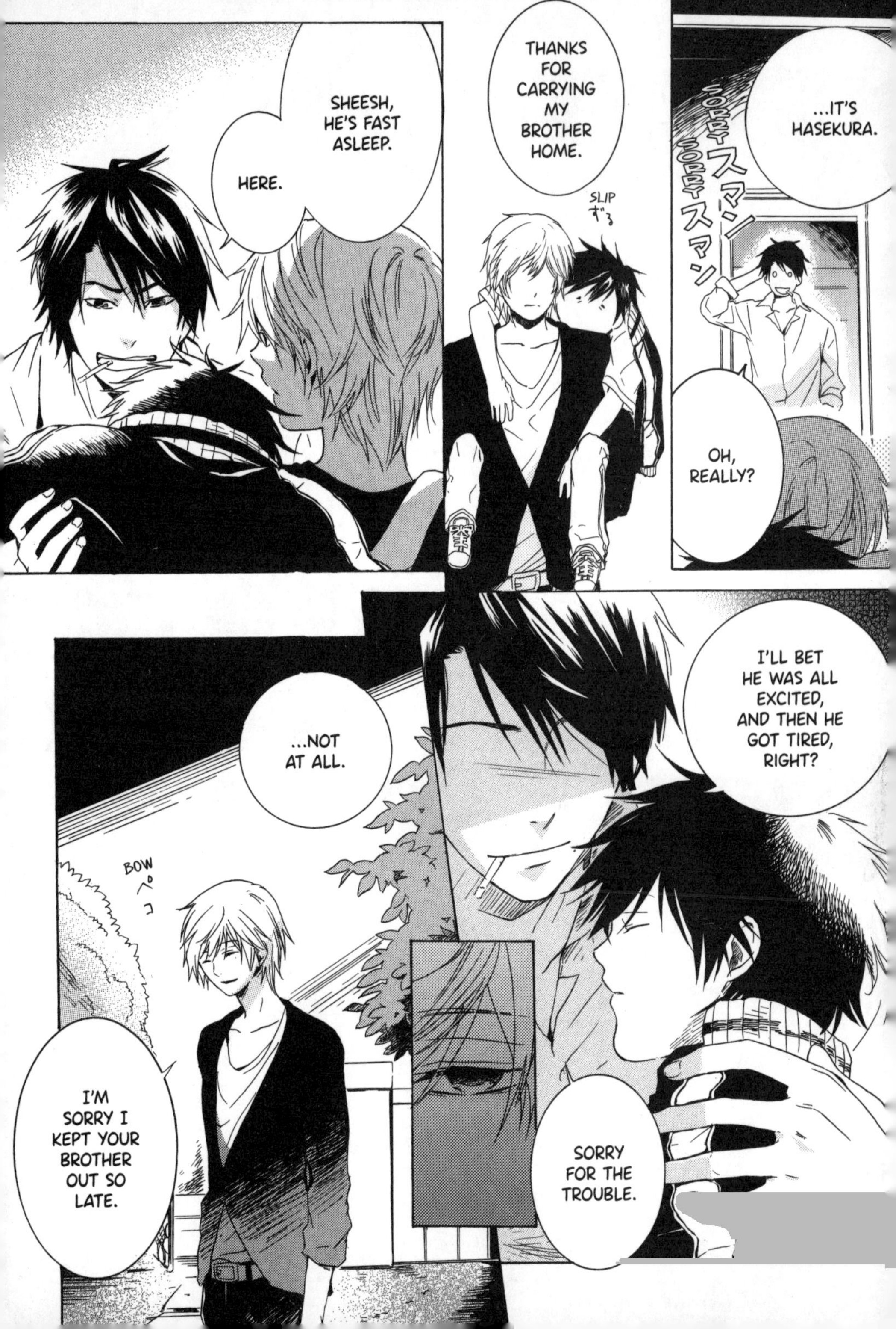
...IT'S HASEKURA.
SORRY スマン SORRY スマン
OH, REALLY?
THANKS FOR CARRYING MY BROTHER HOME.
SLIP ずる
SHEESH, HE'S FAST ASLEEP.
HERE.
I'LL BET HE WAS ALL EXCITED, AND THEN HE GOT TIRED, RIGHT?
...NOT AT ALL.
SORRY FOR THE TROUBLE.
BOW ペコ
I'M SORRY I KEPT YOUR BROTHER OUT SO LATE.

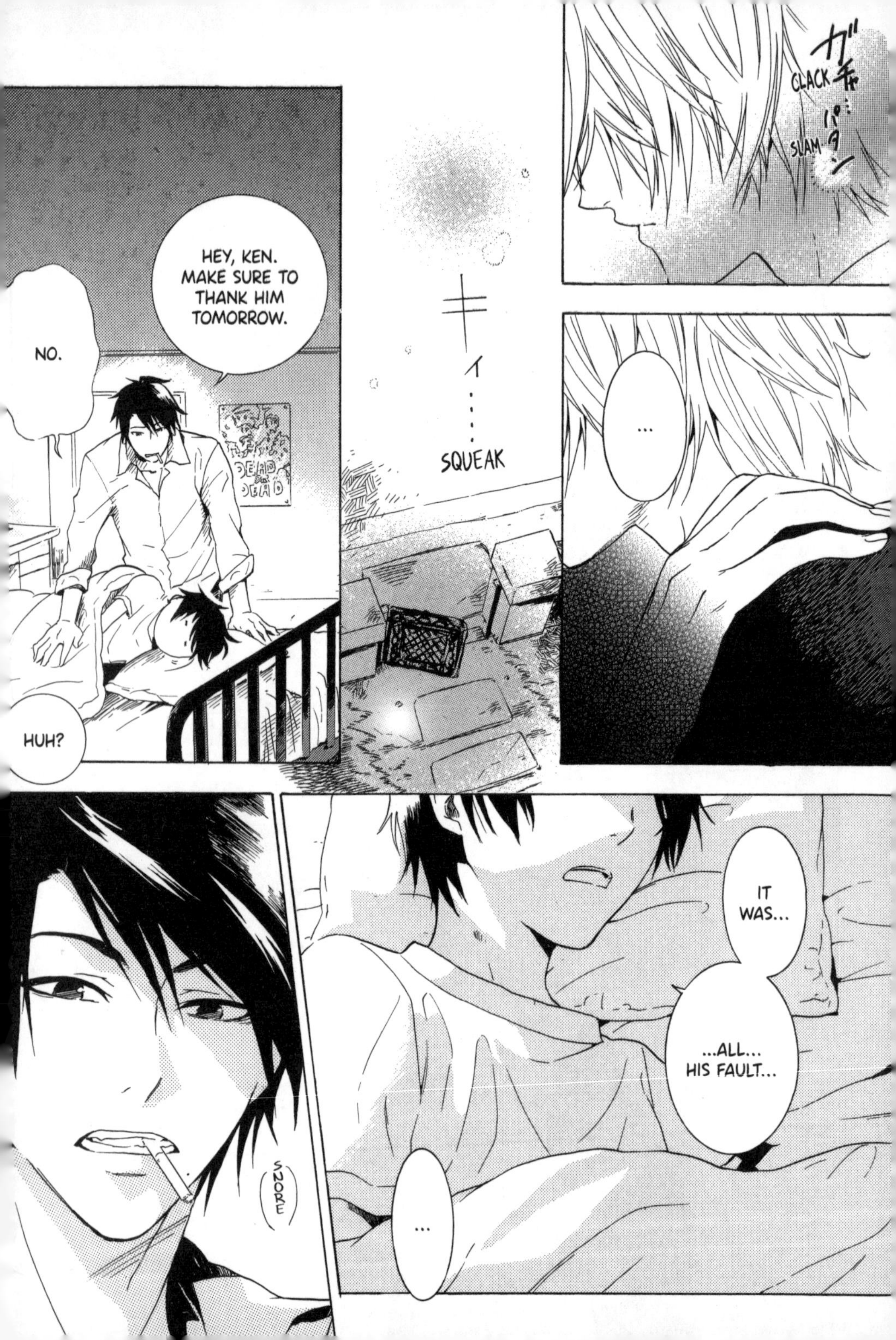

ガチャ
CLACK
パタン
SLAM
...
キィ…
SQUEAK
HEY, KEN. MAKE SURE TO THANK HIM TOMORROW.
NO.
HUH?
IT WAS...
...ALL... HIS FAULT...
...
SNORE

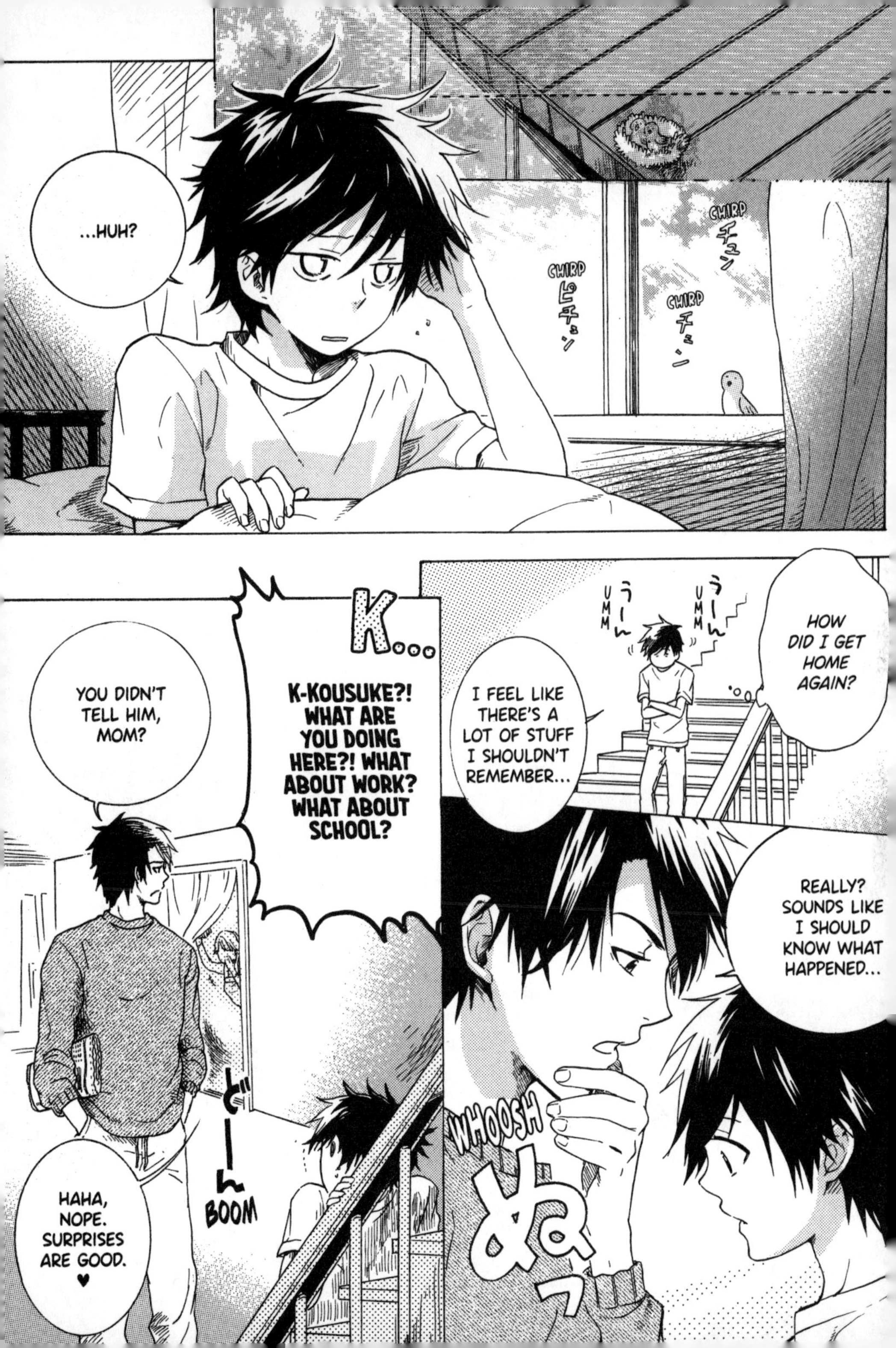
CHIRP チュン
CHIRP チュン
CHIRP ピチュン
...HUH?
HOW DID I GET HOME AGAIN?
UMM うーん
UMM うーん
I FEEL LIKE THERE'S A LOT OF STUFF I SHOULDN'T REMEMBER...
REALLY? SOUNDS LIKE I SHOULD KNOW WHAT HAPPENED...
WHOOSH ぬっ
K...
K-KOUSUKE?! WHAT ARE YOU DOING HERE?! WHAT ABOUT WORK? WHAT ABOUT SCHOOL?
YOU DIDN'T TELL HIM, MOM?
BOOM どーん
HAHA, NOPE. SURPRISES ARE GOOD. ♥

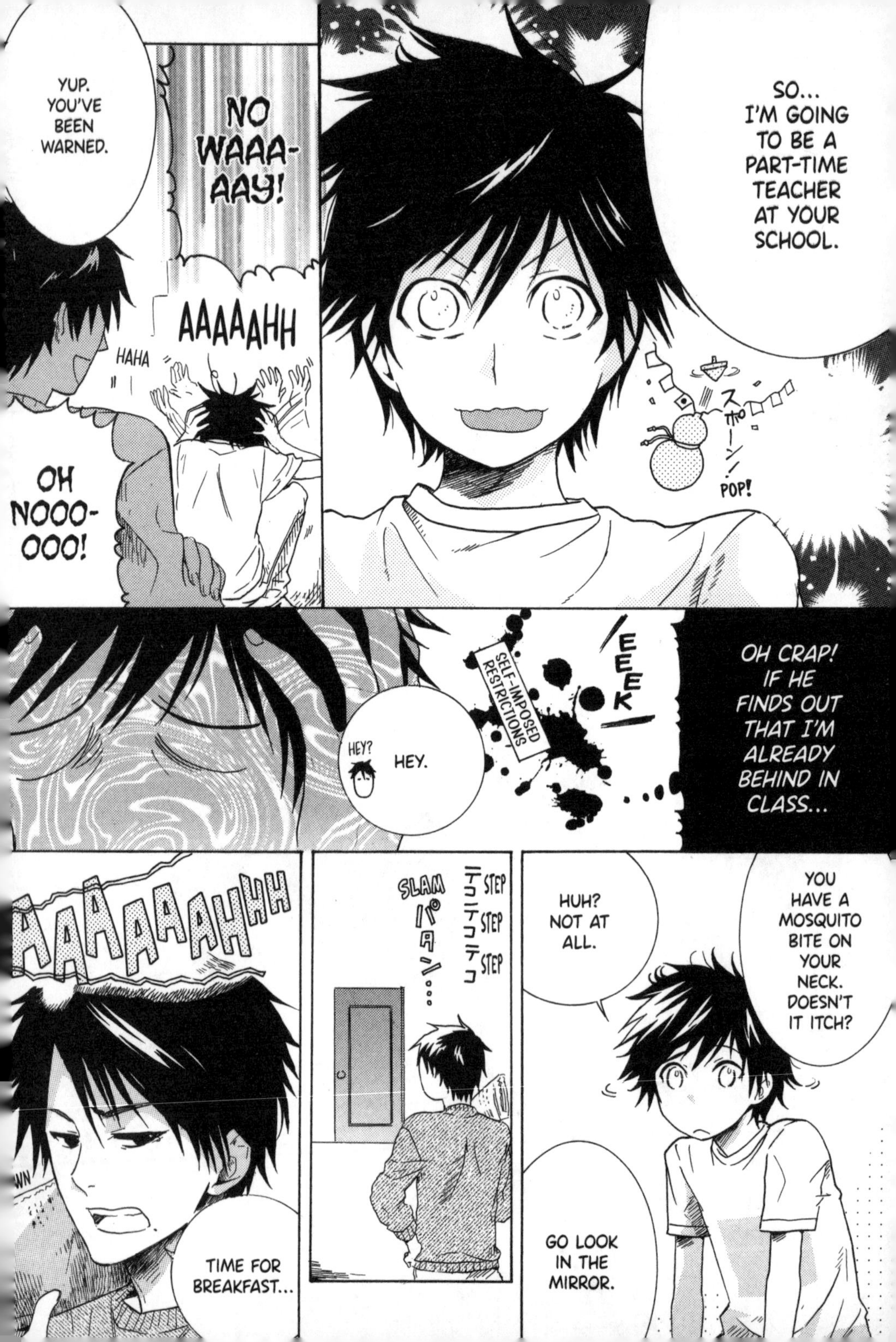
SO... I'M GOING TO BE A PART-TIME TEACHER AT YOUR SCHOOL.
スポーン
POP!
YUP. YOU'VE BEEN WARNED.
NO WAAA-AAY!
AAAAAHH
HAHA
OH NOOO-OOO!
OH CRAP! IF HE FINDS OUT THAT I'M ALREADY BEHIND IN CLASS...
EEEK
SELF-IMPOSED RESTRICTIONS
HEY.
HEY?
YOU HAVE A MOSQUITO BITE ON YOUR NECK. DOESN'T IT ITCH?
HUH? NOT AT ALL.
GO LOOK IN THE MIRROR.
テコテコテコ
STEP STEP STEP
パタン…
SLAM
AAAAAAAHHH
TIME FOR BREAKFAST...

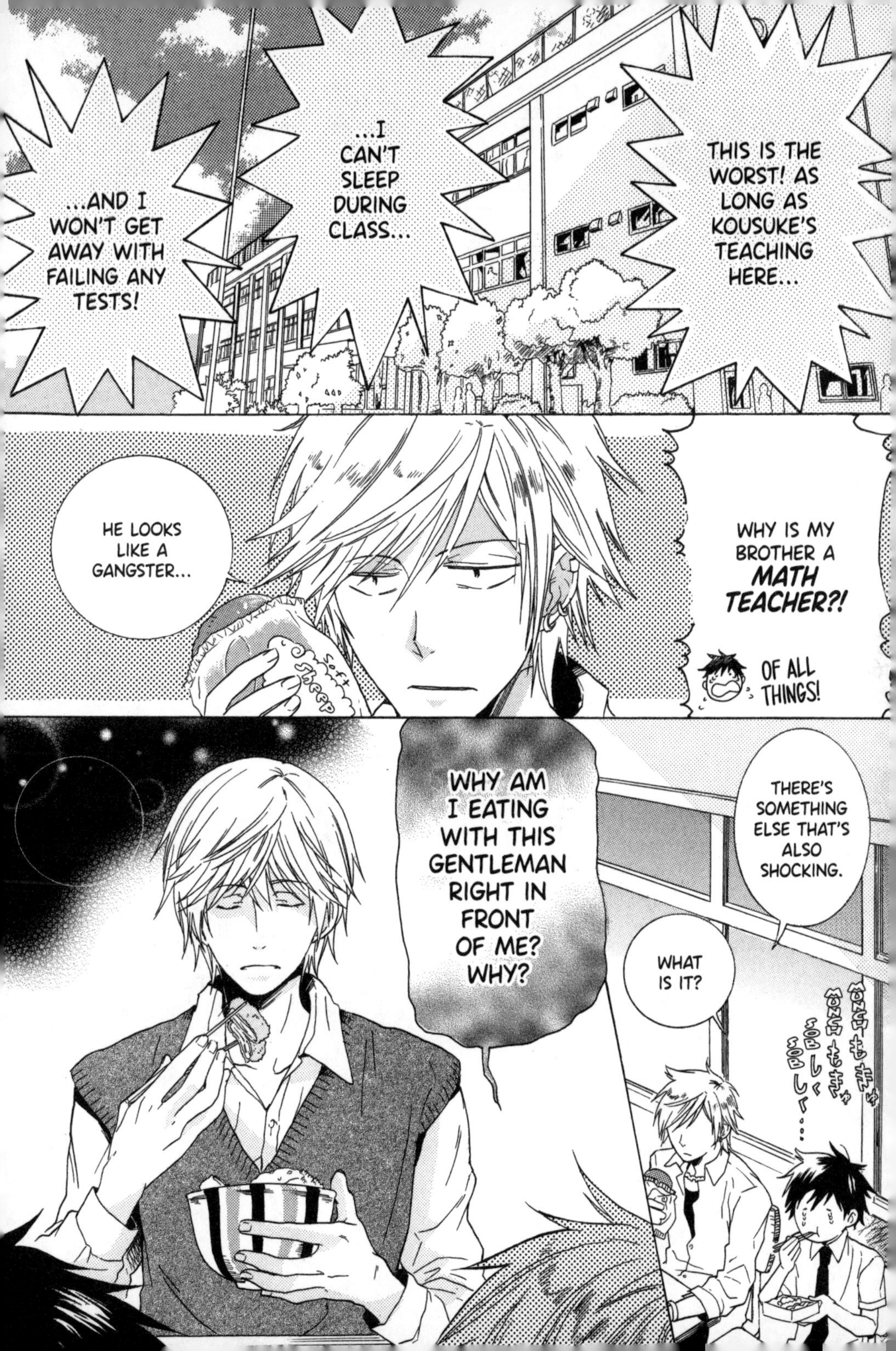
THIS IS THE WORST! AS LONG AS KOUSUKE'S TEACHING HERE...
...I CAN'T SLEEP DURING CLASS...
...AND I WON'T GET AWAY WITH FAILING ANY TESTS!
WHY IS MY BROTHER A ***MATH TEACHER?!***
OF ALL THINGS!
HE LOOKS LIKE A GANGSTER...
Soft Sheep
THERE'S SOMETHING ELSE THAT'S ALSO SHOCKING.
WHAT IS IT?
WHY AM I EATING WITH THIS GENTLEMAN RIGHT IN FRONT OF ME? WHY?

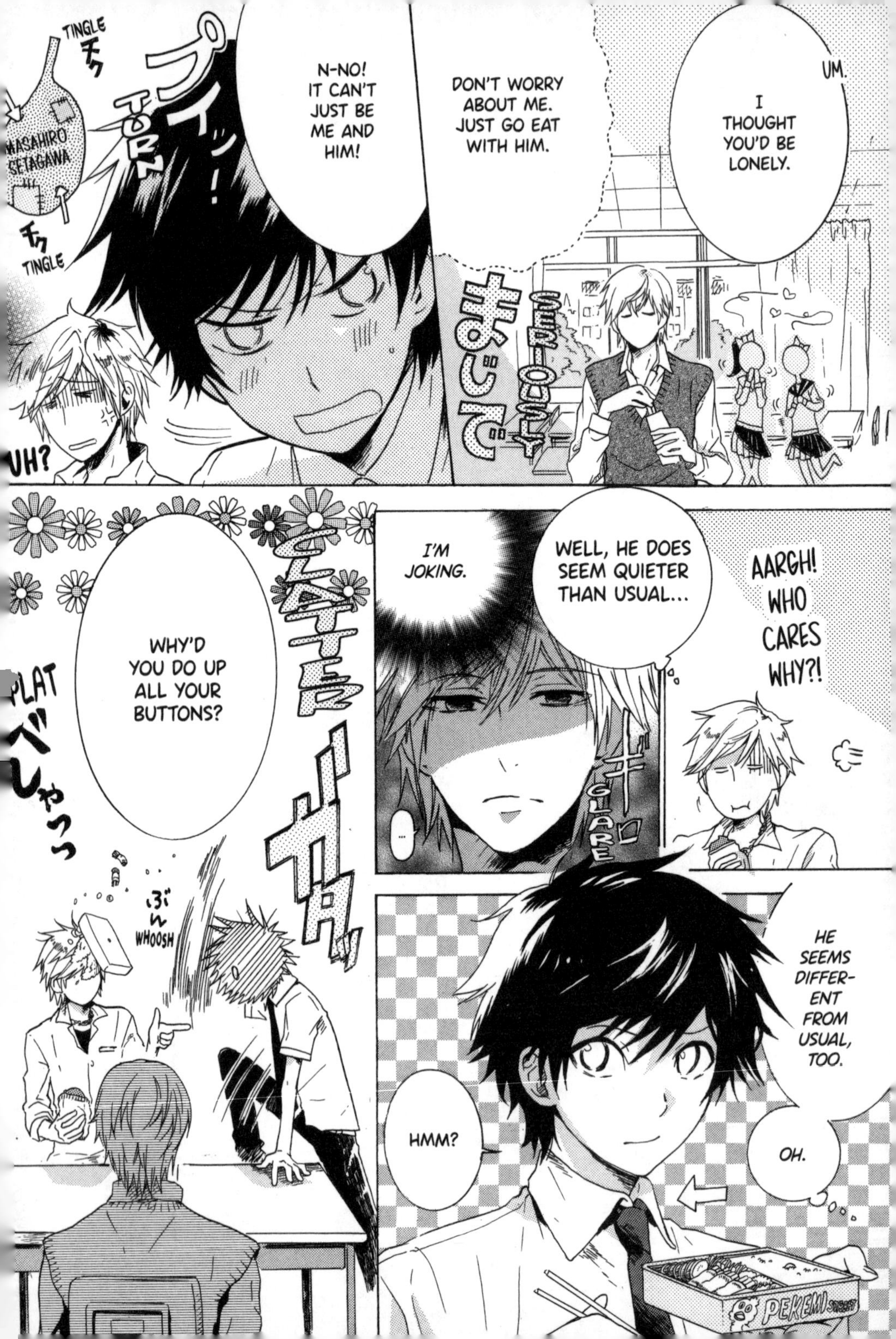
UM.
I THOUGHT YOU'D BE LONELY.
DON'T WORRY ABOUT ME. JUST GO EAT WITH HIM.
SERIOUSLY
N-NO! IT CAN'T JUST BE ME AND HIM!
TORN
TINGLE
MASAHIRO SETAGAWA
TINGLE
UH?
AARGH! WHO CARES WHY?!
WELL, HE DOES SEEM QUIETER THAN USUAL...
I'M JOKING.
GLARE
...
HE SEEMS DIFFER-ENT FROM USUAL, TOO.
OH.
HMM?
PEKEMI
CLATTER
WHY'D YOU DO UP ALL YOUR BUTTONS?
PLAT
WHOOSH

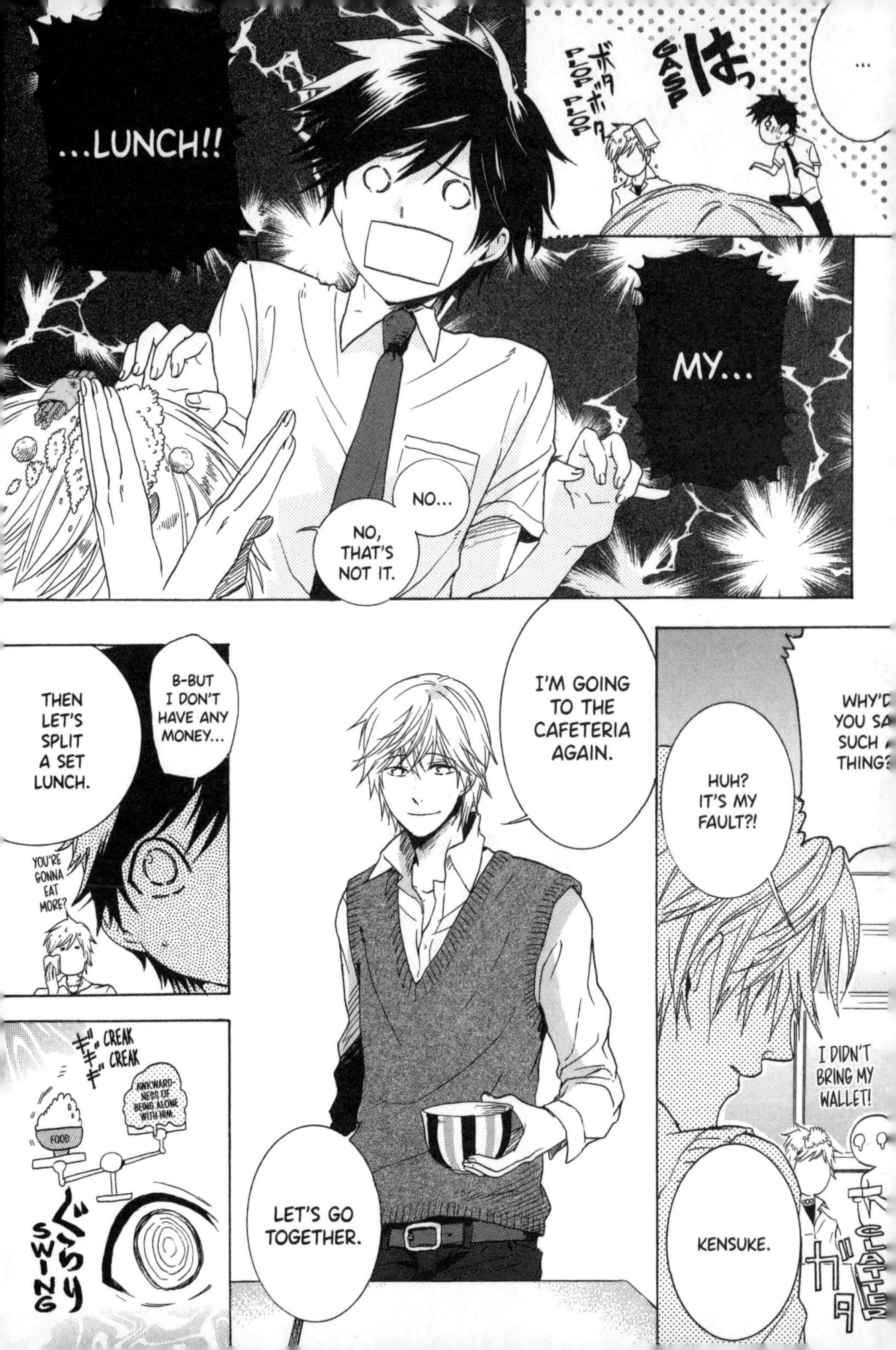

...
はっ GASP
ボタボタ PLOP PLOP
MY...
...LUNCH!!
NO...
NO, THAT'S NOT IT.
WHY'D YOU SA SUCH A THING?
HUH? IT'S MY FAULT?!
I DIDN'T BRING MY WALLET!
KENSUKE.
ガタ CLATTER
I'M GOING TO THE CAFETERIA AGAIN.
LET'S GO TOGETHER.
B-BUT I DON'T HAVE ANY MONEY...
THEN LET'S SPLIT A SET LUNCH.
YOU'RE GONNA EAT MORE?
ギギ CREAK CREAK
AWKWARDNESS OF BEING ALONE WITH HIM.
FOOD
ぐらり SWING

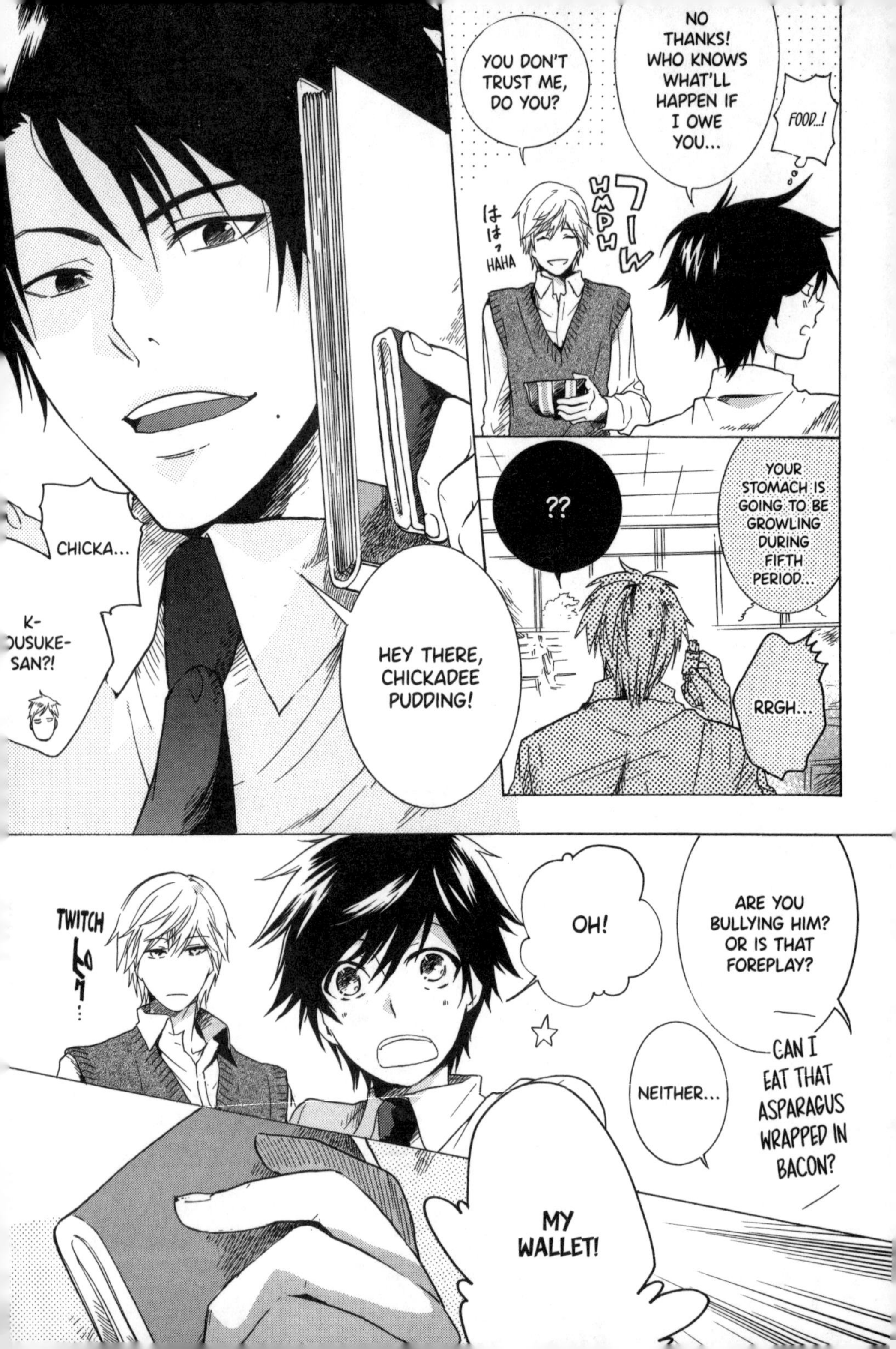
FOOD...!
NO THANKS! WHO KNOWS WHAT'LL HAPPEN IF I OWE YOU...
HMPH
YOU DON'T TRUST ME, DO YOU?
はは HAHA
YOUR STOMACH IS GOING TO BE GROWLING DURING FIFTH PERIOD...
RRGH...
??
HEY THERE, CHICKADEE PUDDING!
CHICKA...
K-OUSUKE-SAN?!
ARE YOU BULLYING HIM? OR IS THAT FOREPLAY?
CAN I EAT THAT ASPARAGUS WRAPPED IN BACON?
NEITHER...
OH!
TWITCH
MY WALLET!

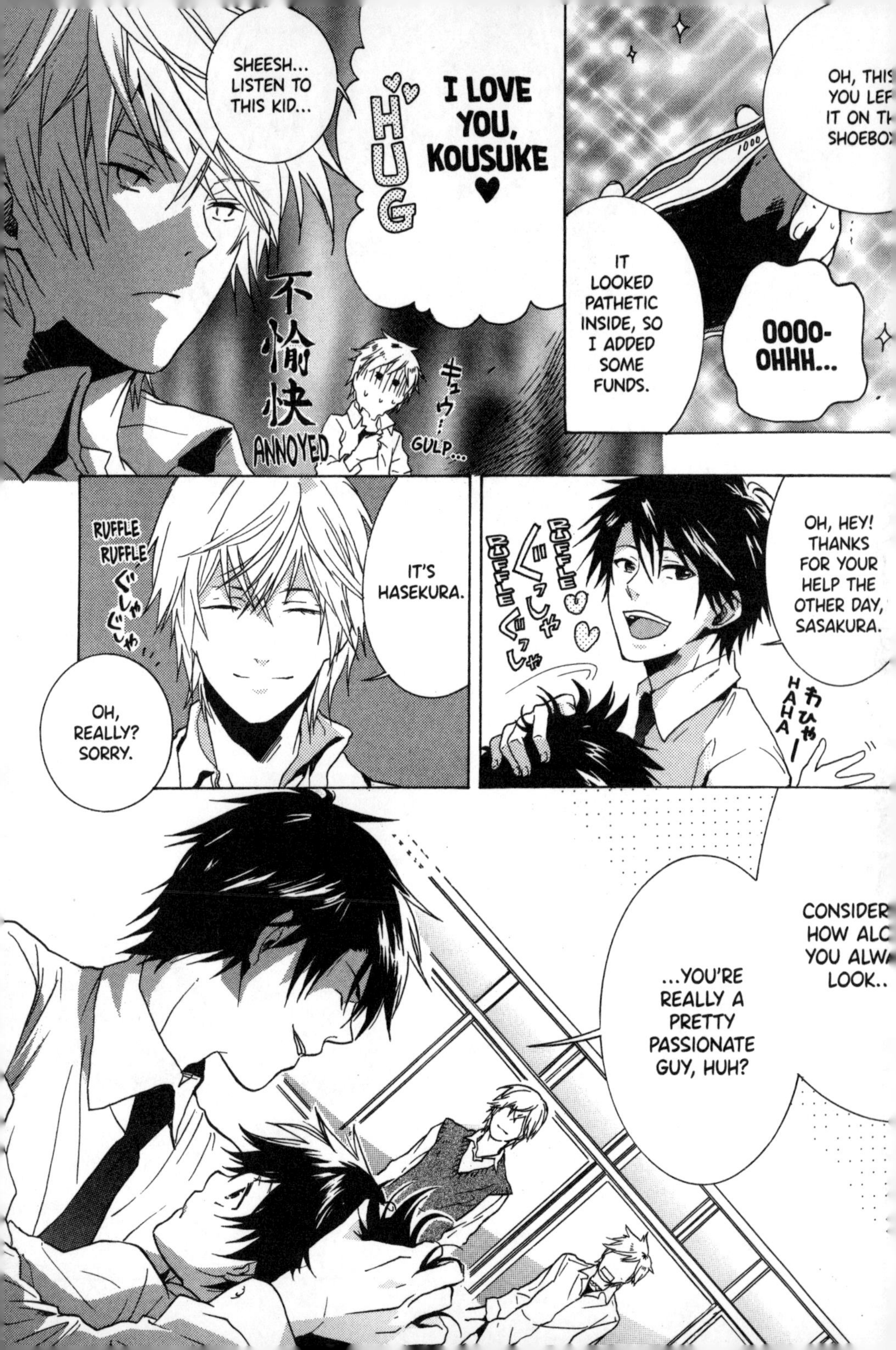

OH, THIS YOU LEF IT ON TH SHOEBO
IT LOOKED PATHETIC INSIDE, SO I ADDED SOME FUNDS.
OOOO-OHHH...
SHEESH... LISTEN TO THIS KID...
I LOVE YOU, KOUSUKE ♥
HUG
不愉快
ANNOYED
キュウ…
GULP...
OH, HEY! THANKS FOR YOUR HELP THE OTHER DAY, SASAKURA.
ぐっしゃ ぐっしゃ
RUFFLE RUFFLE
わひゃー
HAHA
IT'S HASEKURA.
OH, REALLY? SORRY.
RUFFLE RUFFLE
ぐしゃぐしゃ…
CONSIDER HOW ALC YOU ALWA LOOK..
...YOU'RE REALLY A PRETTY PASSIONATE GUY, HUH?

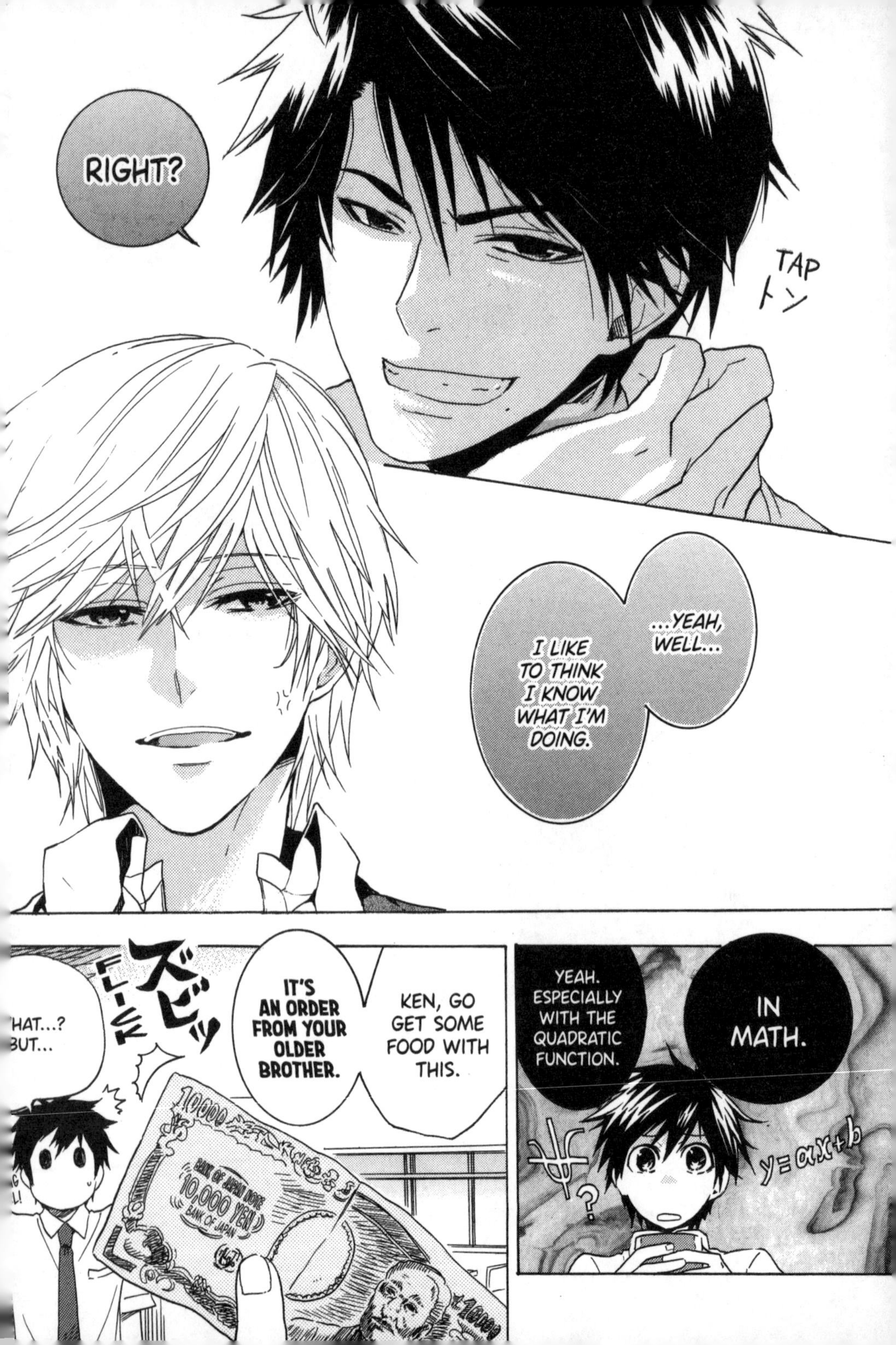
RIGHT?
TAP
トン
...YEAH, WELL...
I LIKE TO THINK I KNOW WHAT I'M DOING.
IN MATH.
YEAH. ESPECIALLY WITH THE QUADRATIC FUNCTION.
y=ax+b
?
KEN, GO GET SOME FOOD WITH THIS.
IT'S AN ORDER FROM YOUR OLDER BROTHER.
ズビッ
FLICK
HAT...? BUT...
BANK OF JAPAN NOTE
10,000 YEN
BANK OF JAPAN

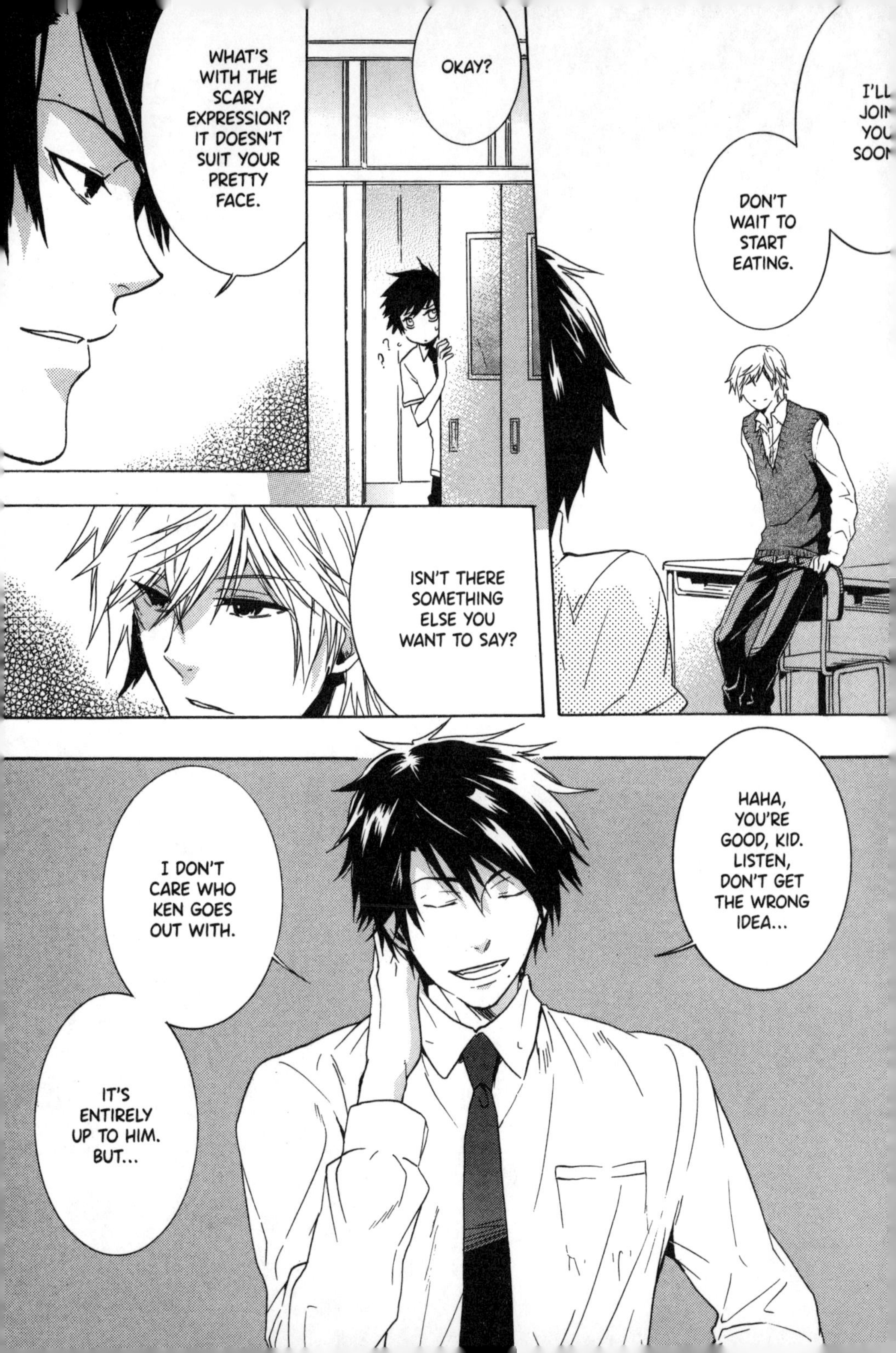

I'LL JOI YOU SOO
DON'T WAIT TO START EATING.
OKAY?
WHAT'S WITH THE SCARY EXPRESSION? IT DOESN'T SUIT YOUR PRETTY FACE.
ISN'T THERE SOMETHING ELSE YOU WANT TO SAY?
HAHA, YOU'RE GOOD, KID. LISTEN, DON'T GET THE WRONG IDEA...
I DON'T CARE WHO KEN GOES OUT WITH.
IT'S ENTIRELY UP TO HIM. BUT...

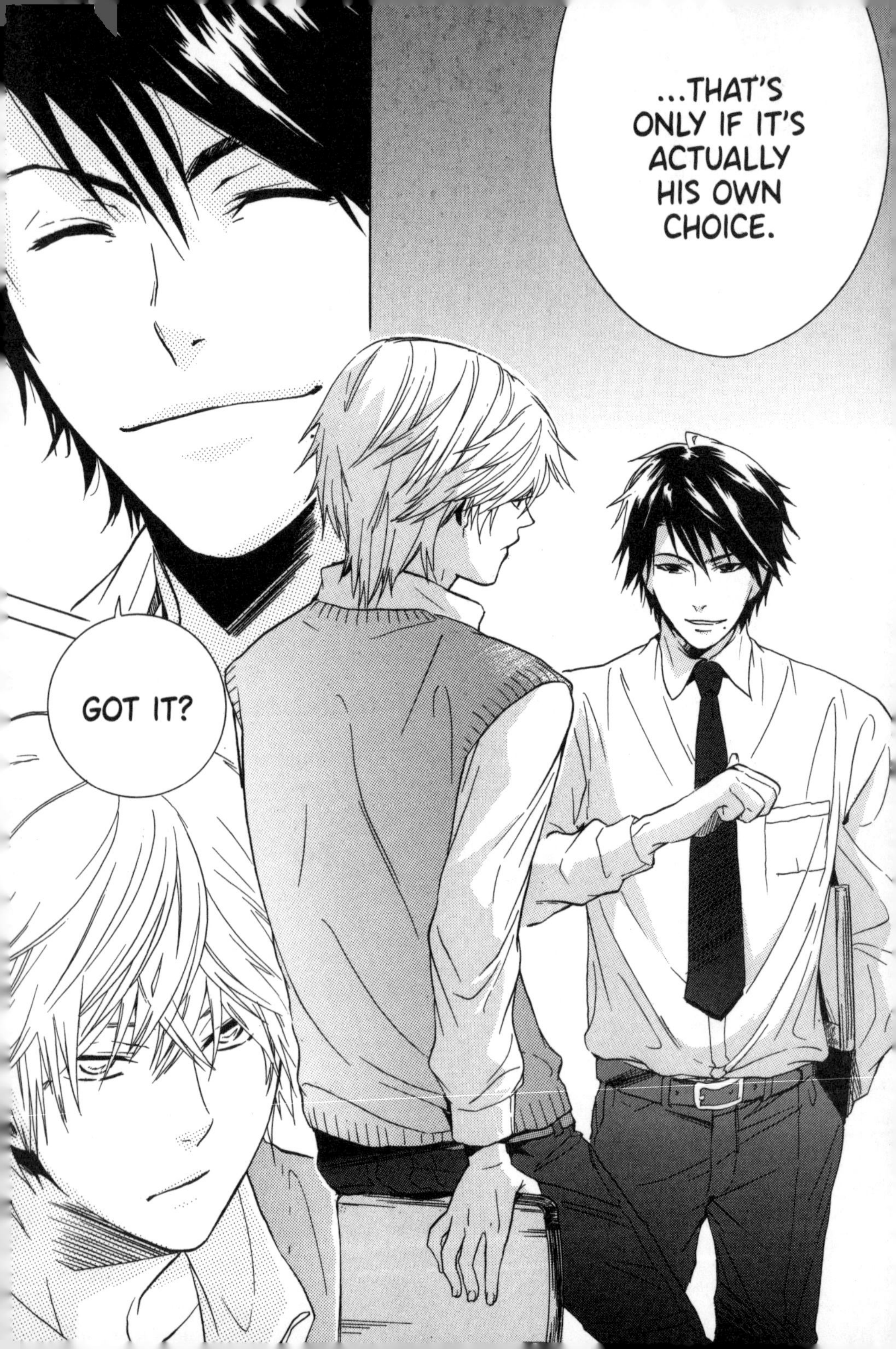
...THAT'S ONLY IF IT'S ACTUALLY HIS OWN CHOICE.
GOT IT?

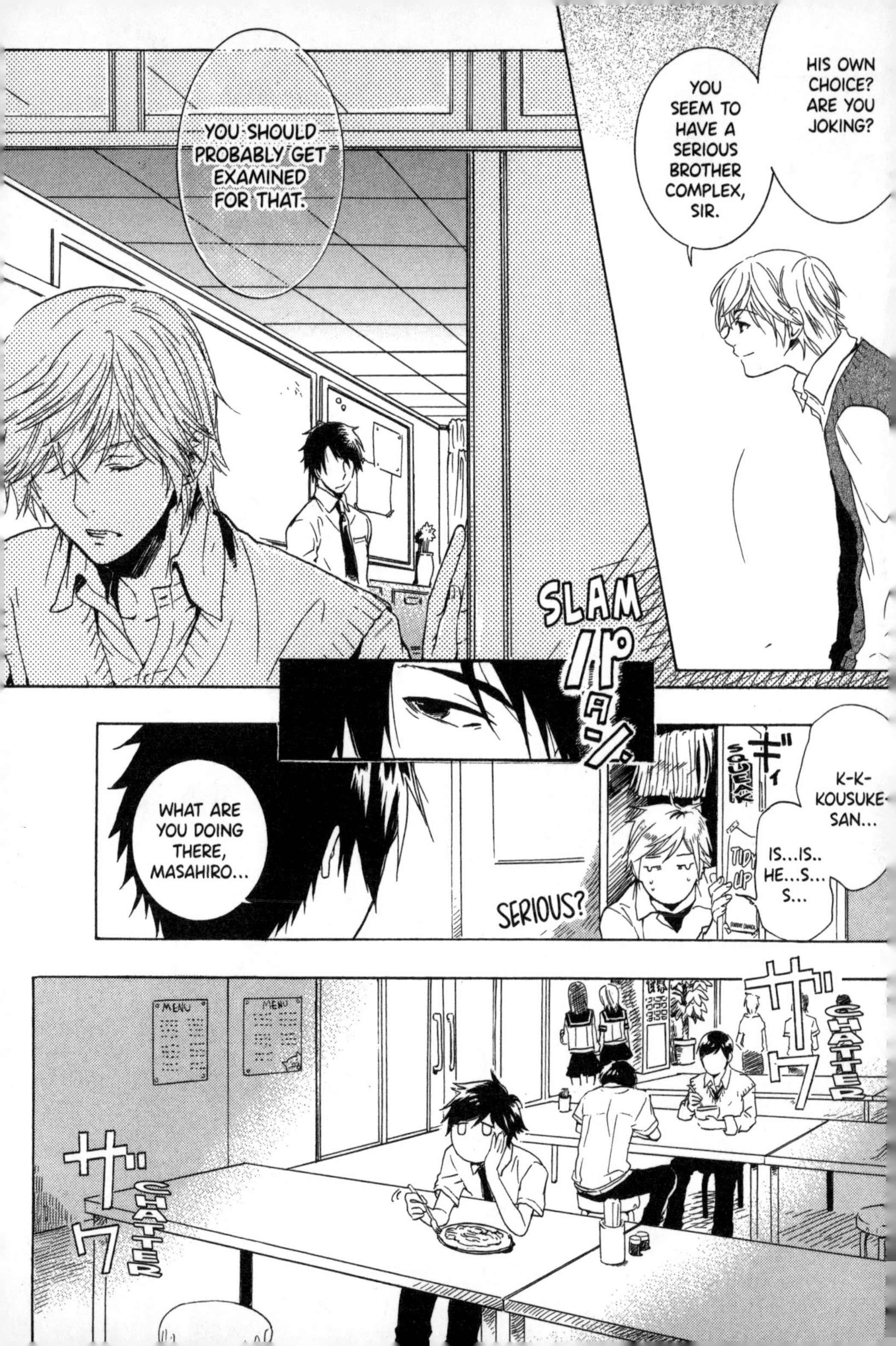
HIS OWN CHOICE? ARE YOU JOKING?
YOU SEEM TO HAVE A SERIOUS BROTHER COMPLEX, SIR.
YOU SHOULD PROBABLY GET EXAMINED FOR THAT.
SLAM
パタン
SQUEAK
ギィ
K-K-KOUSUKE-SAN...
IS...IS.. HE...S... S...
SERIOUS?
TIDY UP
WHAT ARE YOU DOING THERE, MASAHIRO...
CHATTER
MENU
MENU
CHATTER

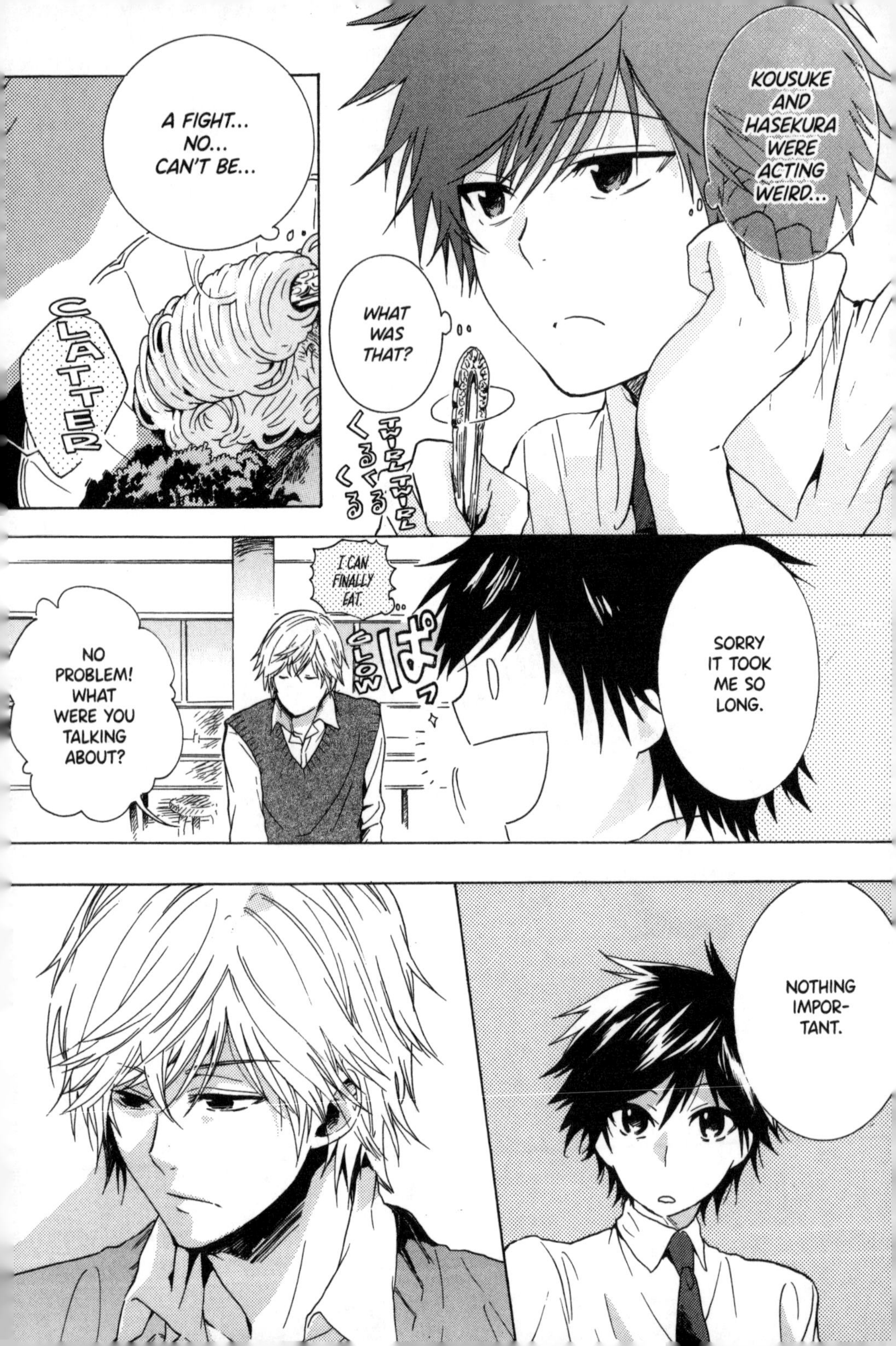
KOUSUKE AND HASEKURA WERE ACTING WEIRD...
WHAT WAS THAT?
TWIRL TWIRL
くるくる
A FIGHT... NO... CAN'T BE...
CLATTER
SORRY IT TOOK ME SO LONG.
GLOW
ぱっ
I CAN FINALLY EAT.
NO PROBLEM! WHAT WERE YOU TALKING ABOUT?
NOTHING IMPOR-TANT.

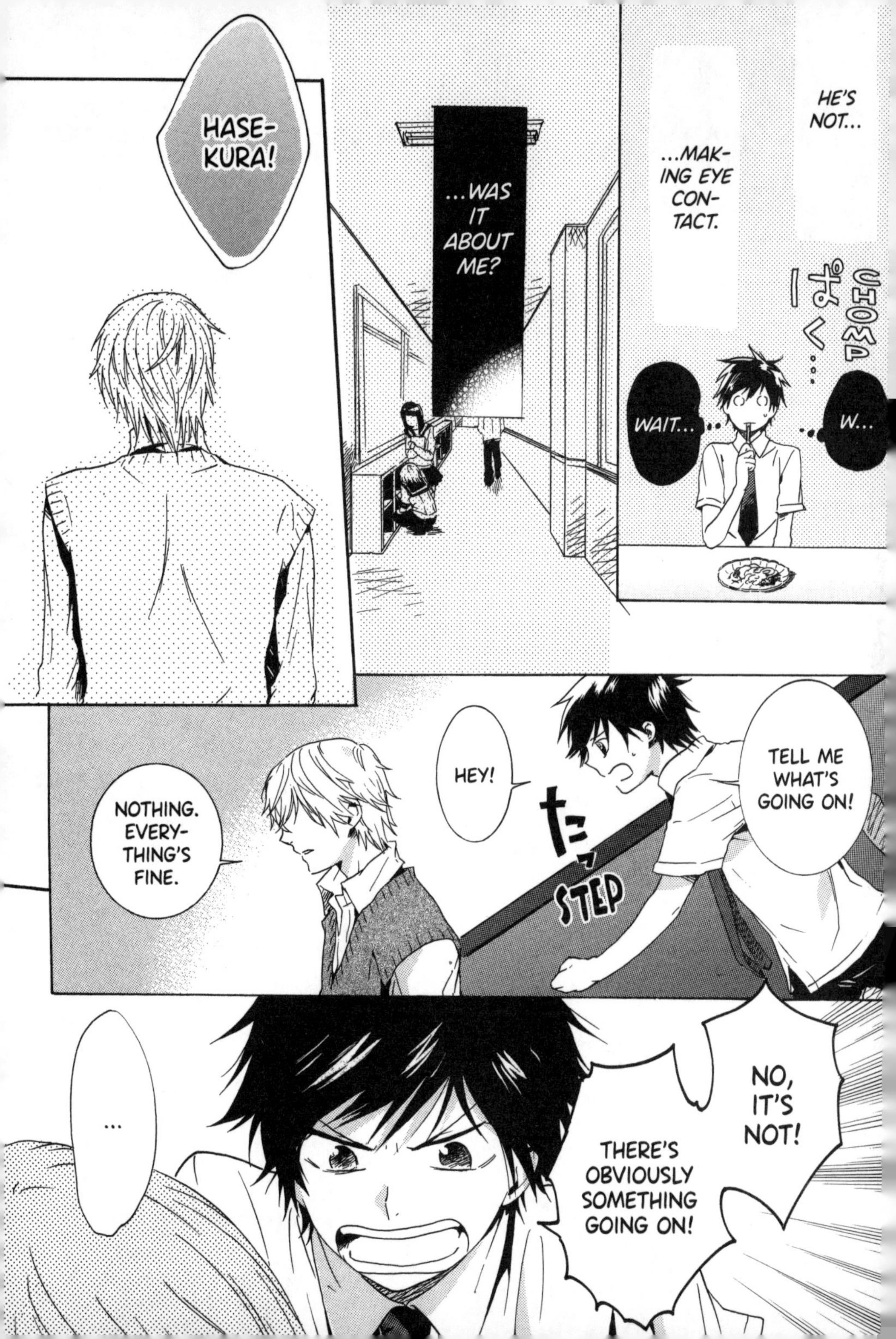

HE'S NOT...
...MAKING EYE CONTACT.
CHOMP
ぱく...
W...
WAIT...
...WAS IT ABOUT ME?
HASE-KURA!
TELL ME WHAT'S GOING ON!
たっ
STEP
HEY!
NOTHING. EVERYTHING'S FINE.
NO, IT'S NOT!
THERE'S OBVIOUSLY SOMETHING GOING ON!
...

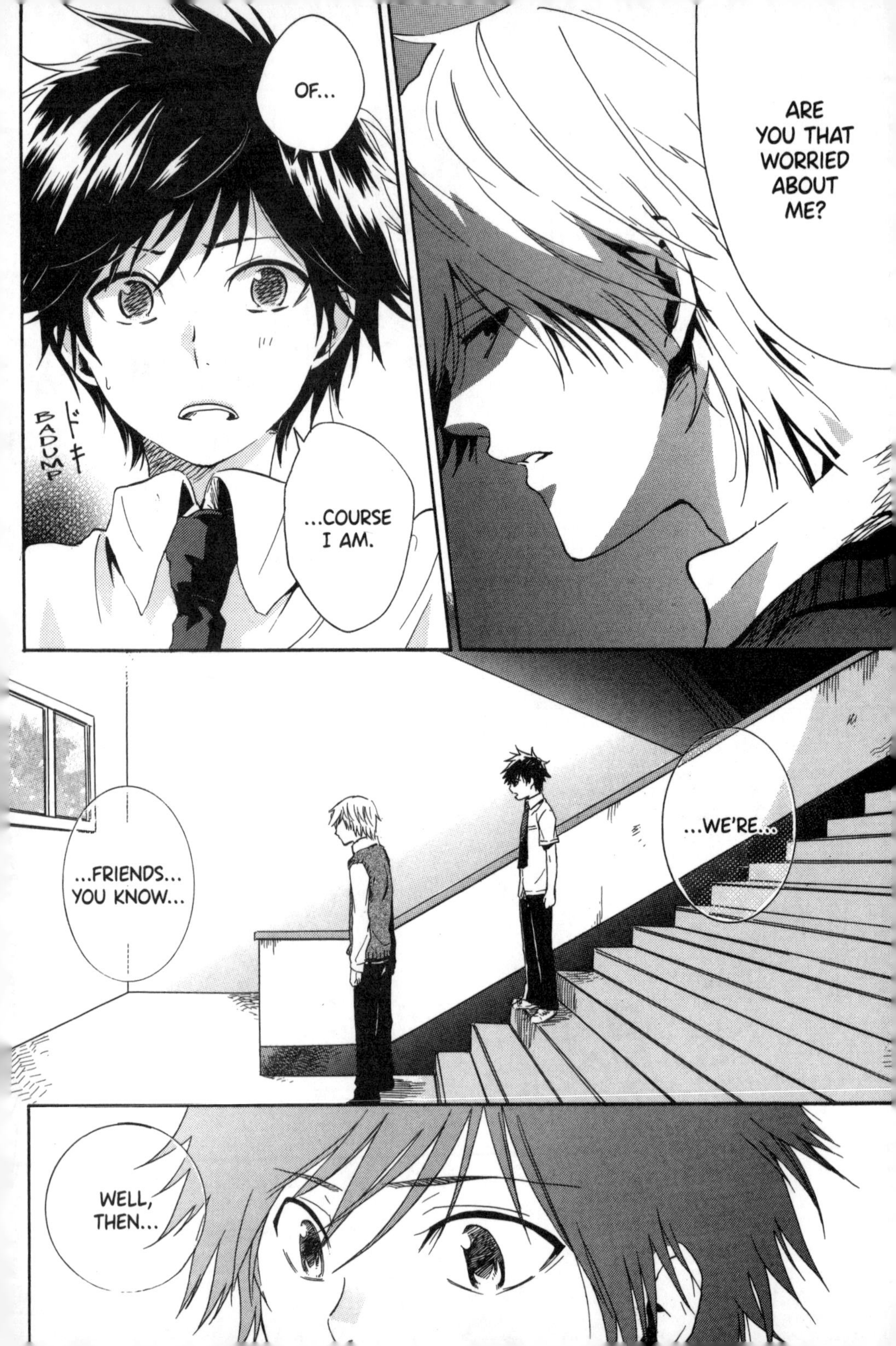
ARE YOU THAT WORRIED ABOUT ME?
OF...
...COURSE I AM.
ドキ
BADUMP
...WE'RE...
...FRIENDS... YOU KNOW...
WELL, THEN...

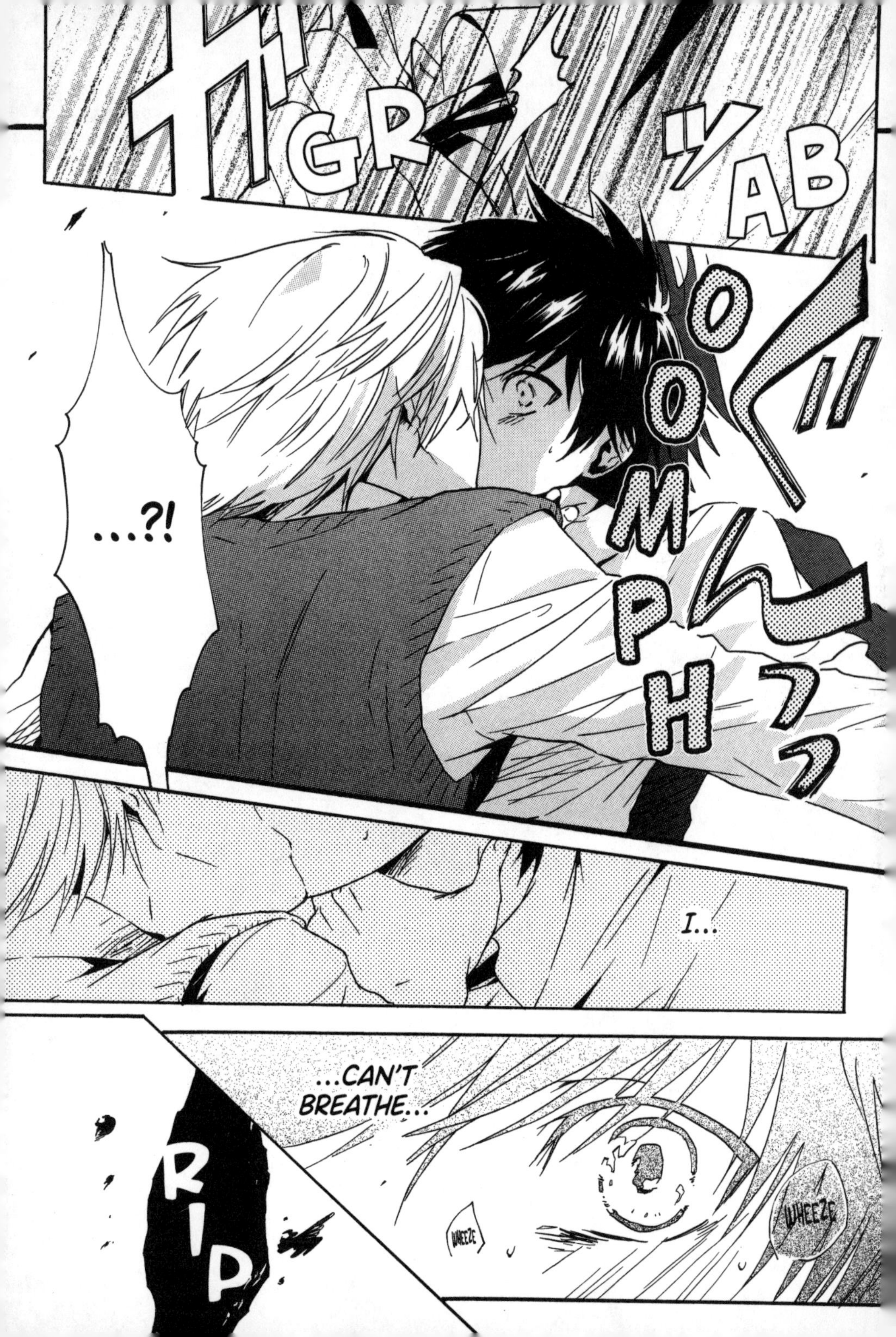

GR
AB
OOOMPH
...?!
I...
...CAN'T BREATHE...
WHEEZE
WHEEZE
RIP

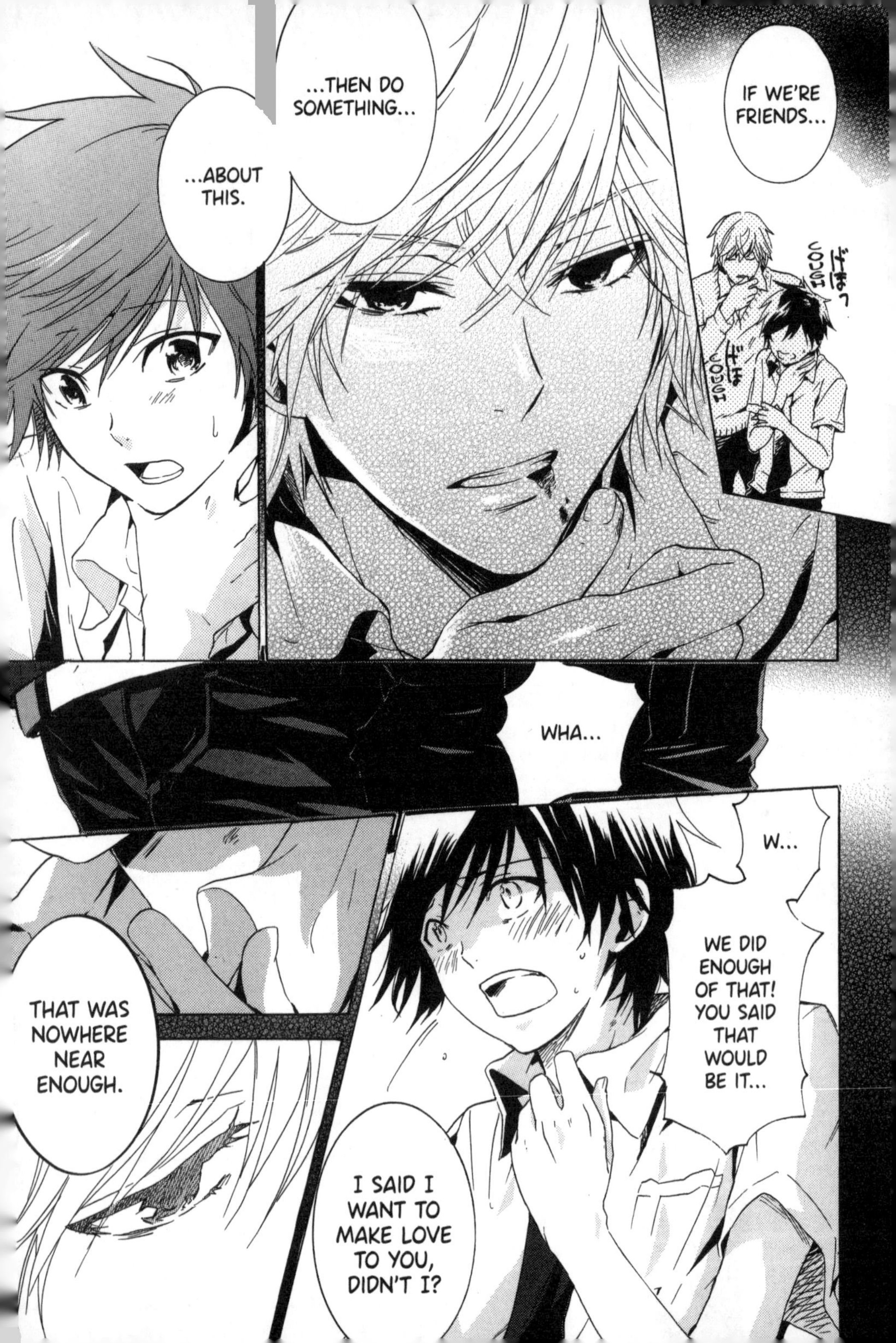
IF WE'RE FRIENDS...
げほっ COUGH
げほ COUGH
...THEN DO SOMETHING...
...ABOUT THIS.
WHA...
W...
WE DID ENOUGH OF THAT! YOU SAID THAT WOULD BE IT...
I SAID I WANT TO MAKE LOVE TO YOU, DIDN'T I?
THAT WAS NOWHERE NEAR ENOUGH.

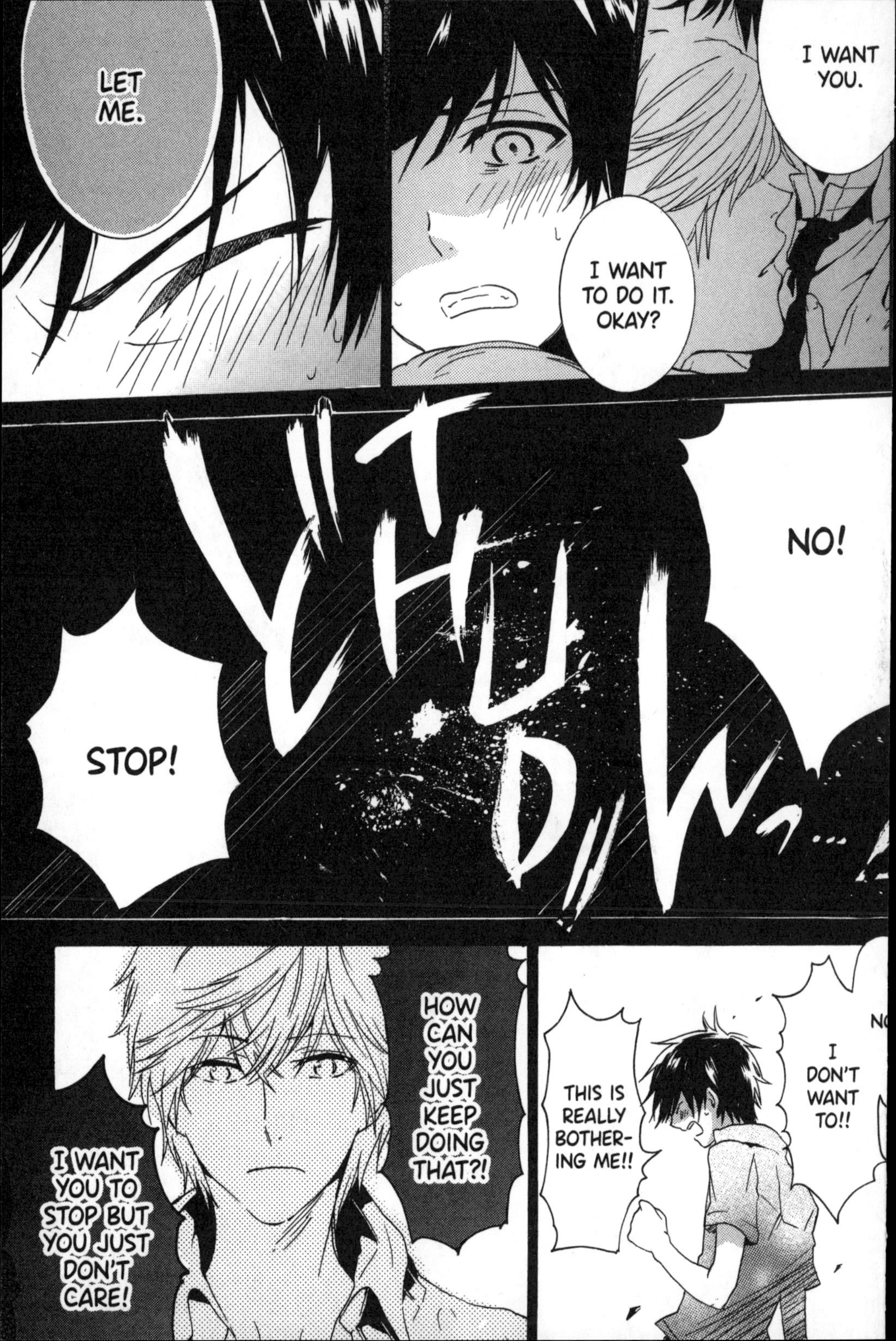

I WANT YOU.
I WANT TO DO IT. OKAY?
LET ME.
NO!
STOP!
I DON'T WANT TO!!
THIS IS REALLY BOTHERING ME!!
HOW CAN YOU JUST KEEP DOING THAT?!
I WANT YOU TO STOP BUT YOU JUST DON'T CARE!

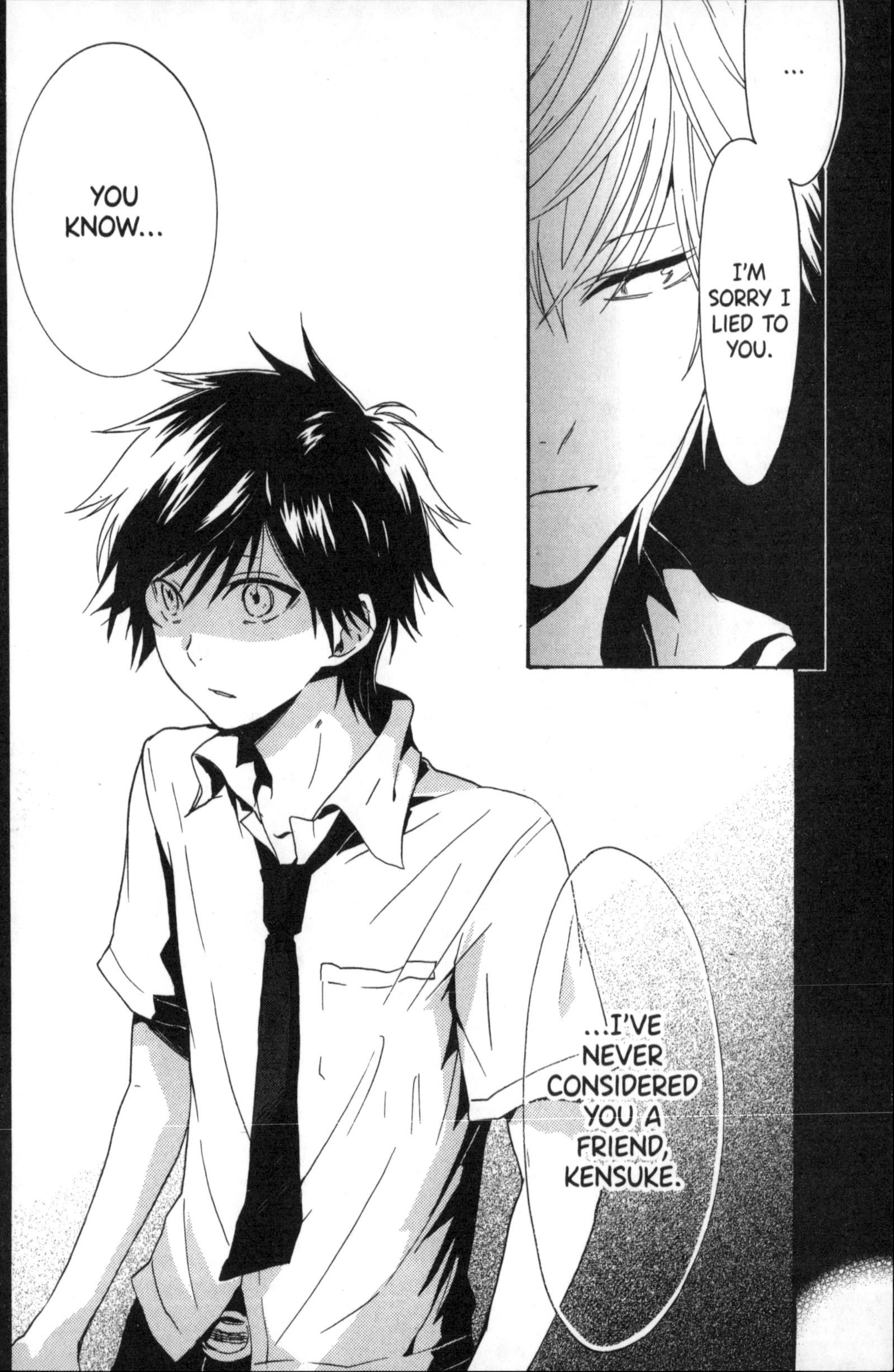
...
I'M SORRY I LIED TO YOU.
YOU KNOW...
...I'VE NEVER CONSIDERED YOU A FRIEND, KENSUKE.

Kousuke Ohshiba
Currently thinking about:
Whether to quit smoking
Personality: Quite meddlesome

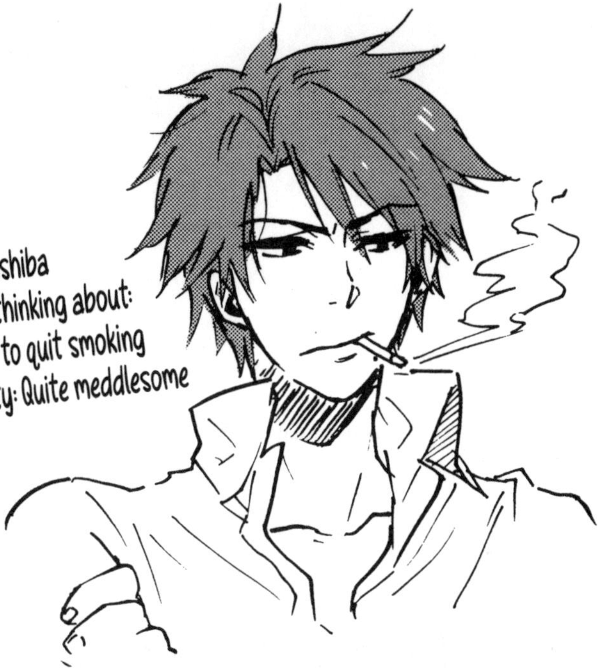

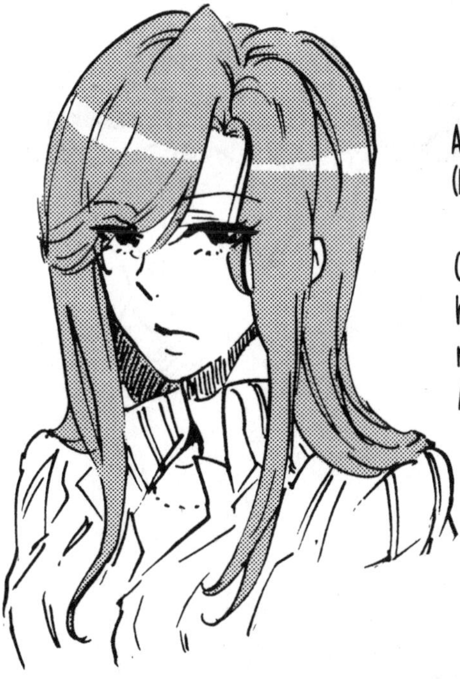

Ayaka Houjou
(Maiden name: Hasekura)

Current concerns: After she got married, her parents got divorced, so she feels responsible for her younger brother
Also, her husband's perverted mannerisms

Hobbies: Road trips

Tsuyoshi Yamabe
Favorite drink: The mouthwash they give you at the hospital

Mitsuru Fukushige
Hobbies: Observing people

Jirou Yoshida
What he wants to be in the
future: ~~Husband to a cute bride~~
Civil servant

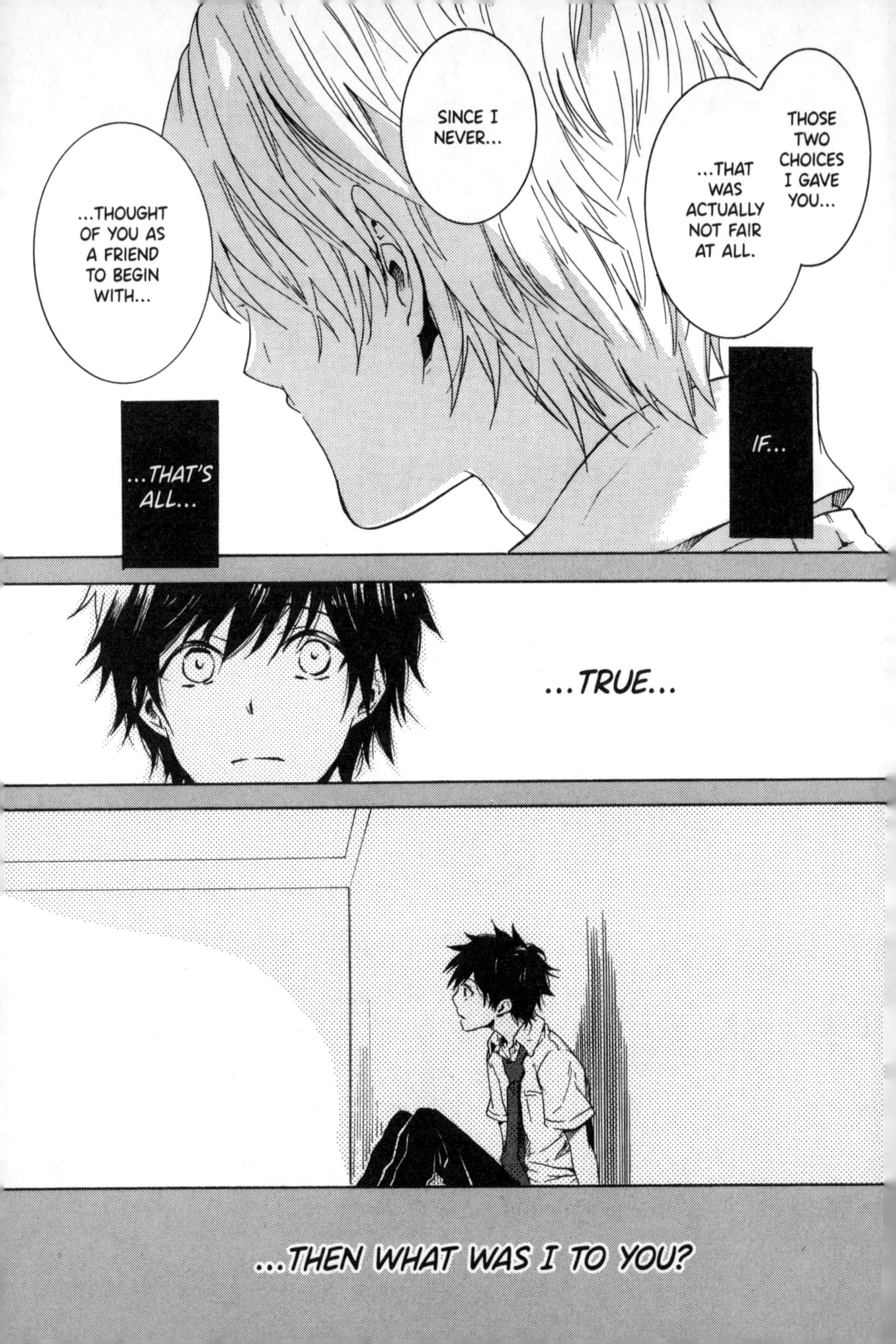
THOSE TWO CHOICES I GAVE YOU...
...THAT WAS ACTUALLY NOT FAIR AT ALL.
SINCE I NEVER...
...THOUGHT OF YOU AS A FRIEND TO BEGIN WITH...
IF...
...THAT'S ALL...
...TRUE...
...THEN WHAT WAS I TO YOU?

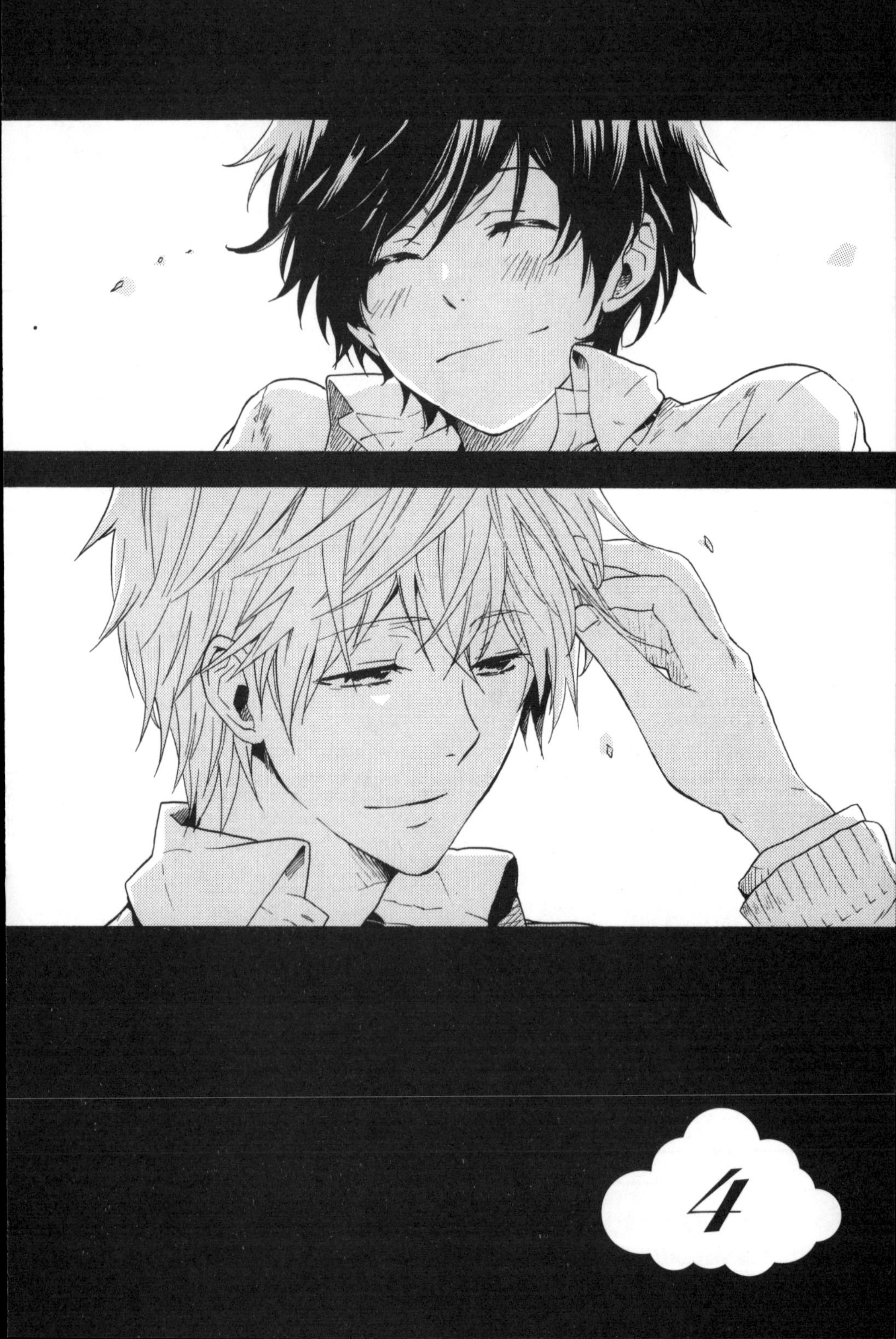
4

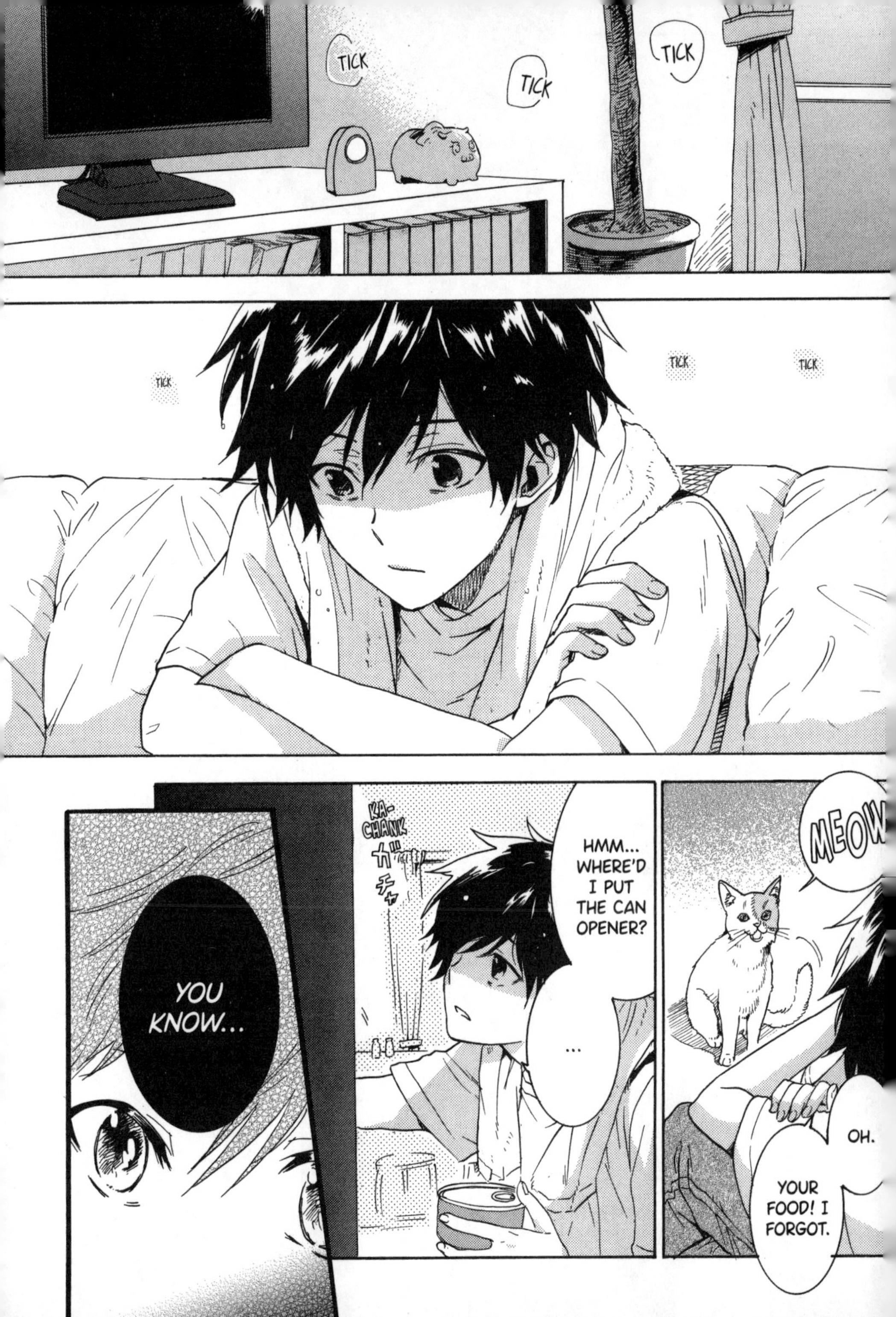
TICK
TICK
TICK
TICK
TICK
TICK
MEOW
OH.
YOUR FOOD! I FORGOT.
KA-CHANK
HMM... WHERE'D I PUT THE CAN OPENER?
...
YOU KNOW...

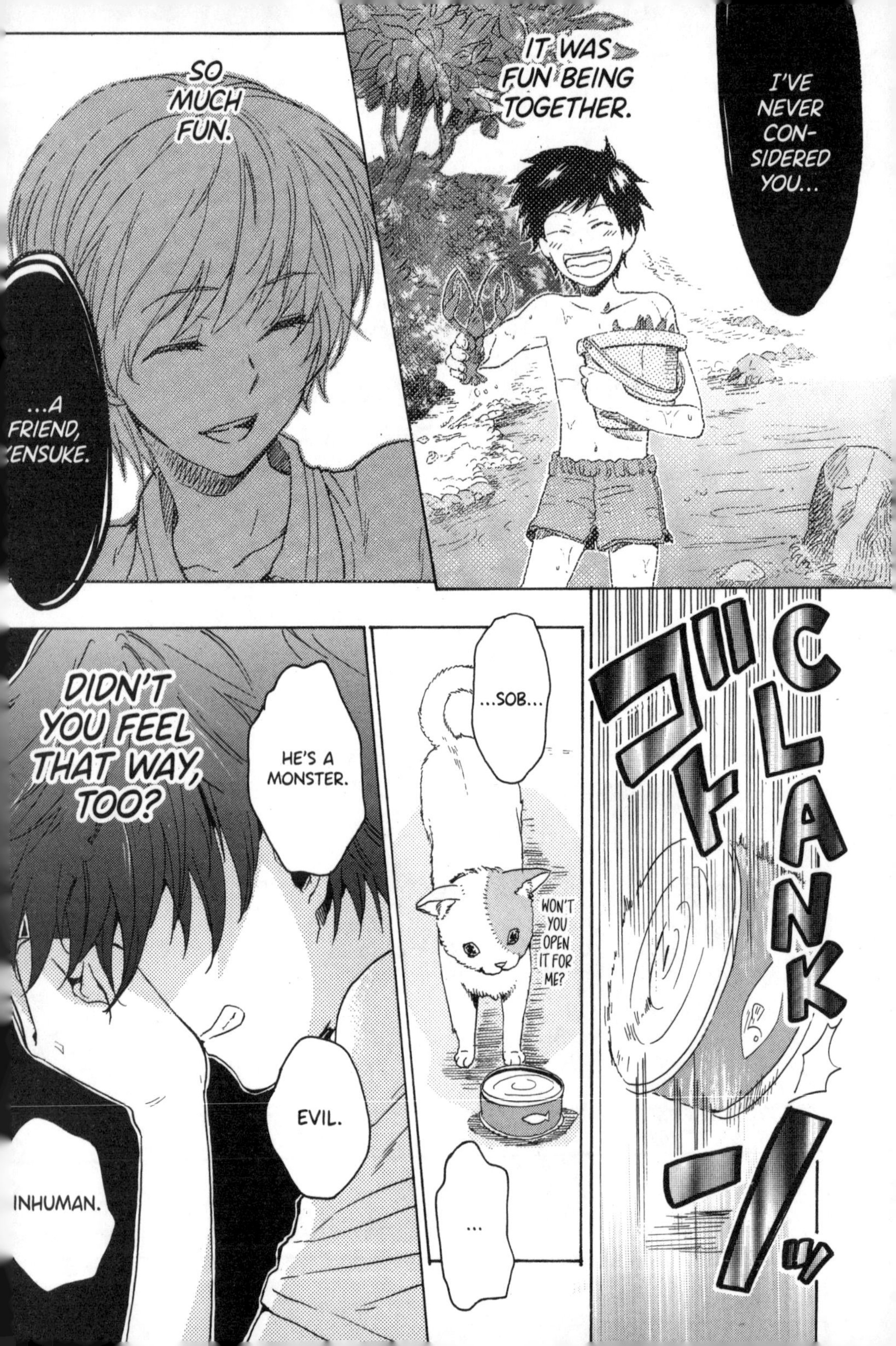
I'VE NEVER CON- SIDERED YOU...
IT WAS FUN BEING TOGETHER.
SO MUCH FUN.
...A FRIEND, KENSUKE.
CLANK
...SOB...
WON'T YOU OPEN IT FOR ME?
...
DIDN'T YOU FEEL THAT WAY, TOO?
HE'S A MONSTER.
EVIL.
INHUMAN.

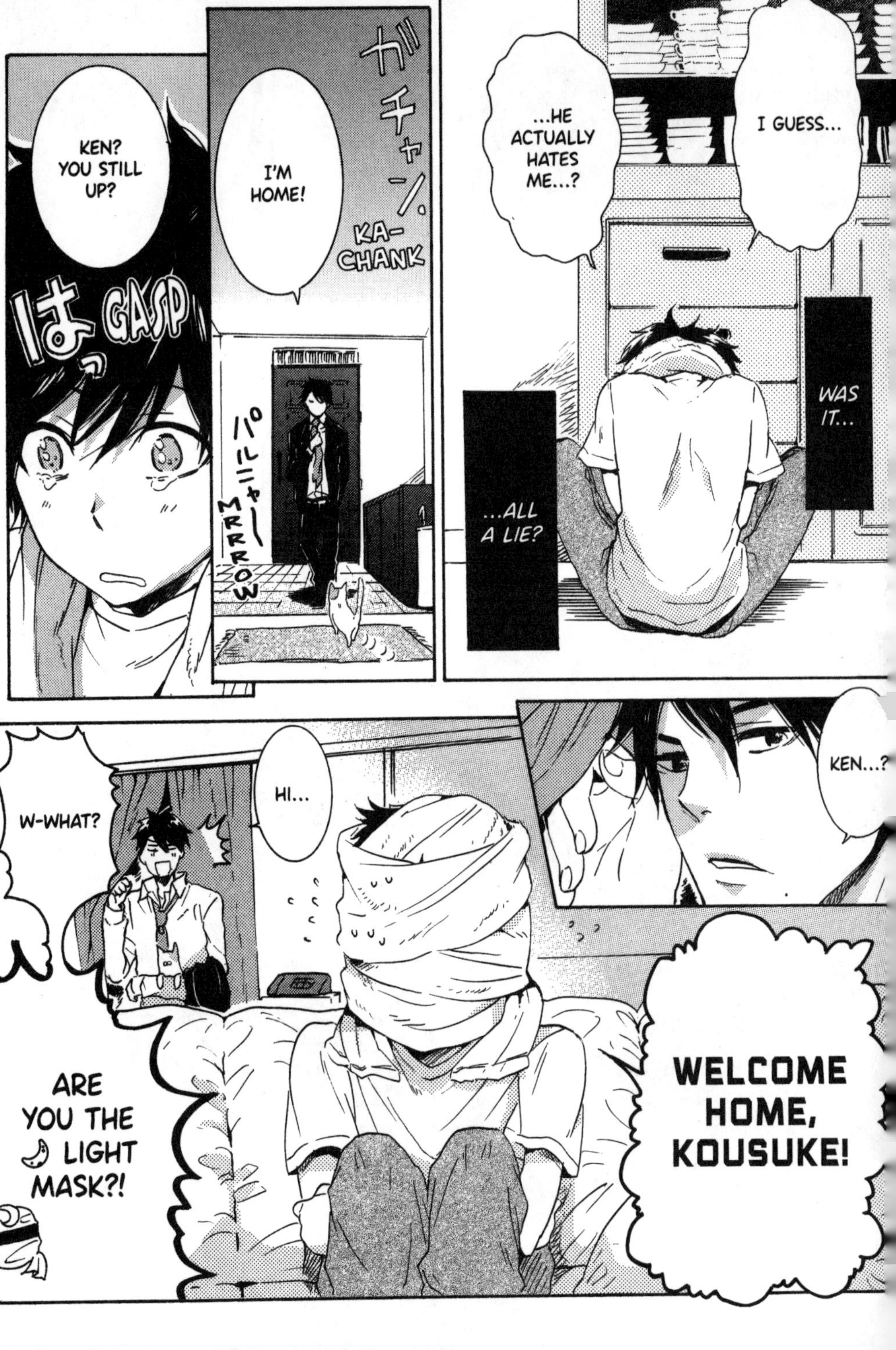

I GUESS...
...HE ACTUALLY HATES ME...?
WAS IT...
...ALL A LIE?
ガチャーン
KA-CHANK
I'M HOME!
パルニャー
MRRROW
KEN? YOU STILL UP?
はっ
GASP
KEN...?
WELCOME HOME, KOUSUKE!
HI...
W-WHAT?
ARE YOU THE LIGHT MASK?!

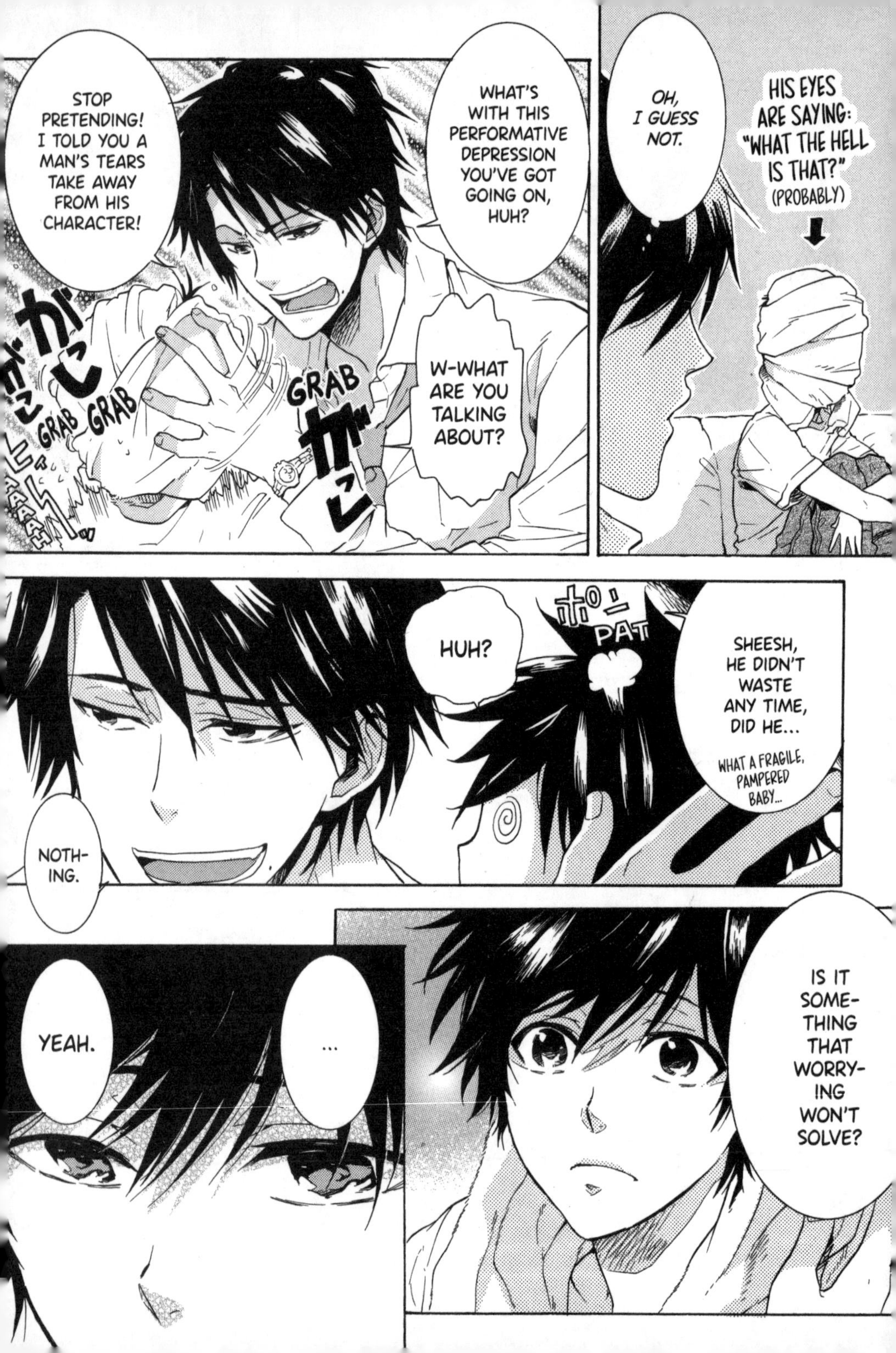
HIS EYES ARE SAYING: "WHAT THE HELL IS THAT?" (PROBABLY)
OH, I GUESS NOT.
WHAT'S WITH THIS PERFORMATIVE DEPRESSION YOU'VE GOT GOING ON, HUH?
STOP PRETENDING! I TOLD YOU A MAN'S TEARS TAKE AWAY FROM HIS CHARACTER!
W-WHAT ARE YOU TALKING ABOUT?
GRAB
GRAB GRAB
SHEESH, HE DIDN'T WASTE ANY TIME, DID HE...
WHAT A FRAGILE, PAMPERED BABY...
PAT
HUH?
NOTH-ING.
IS IT SOME-THING THAT WORRY-ING WON'T SOLVE?
...
YEAH.

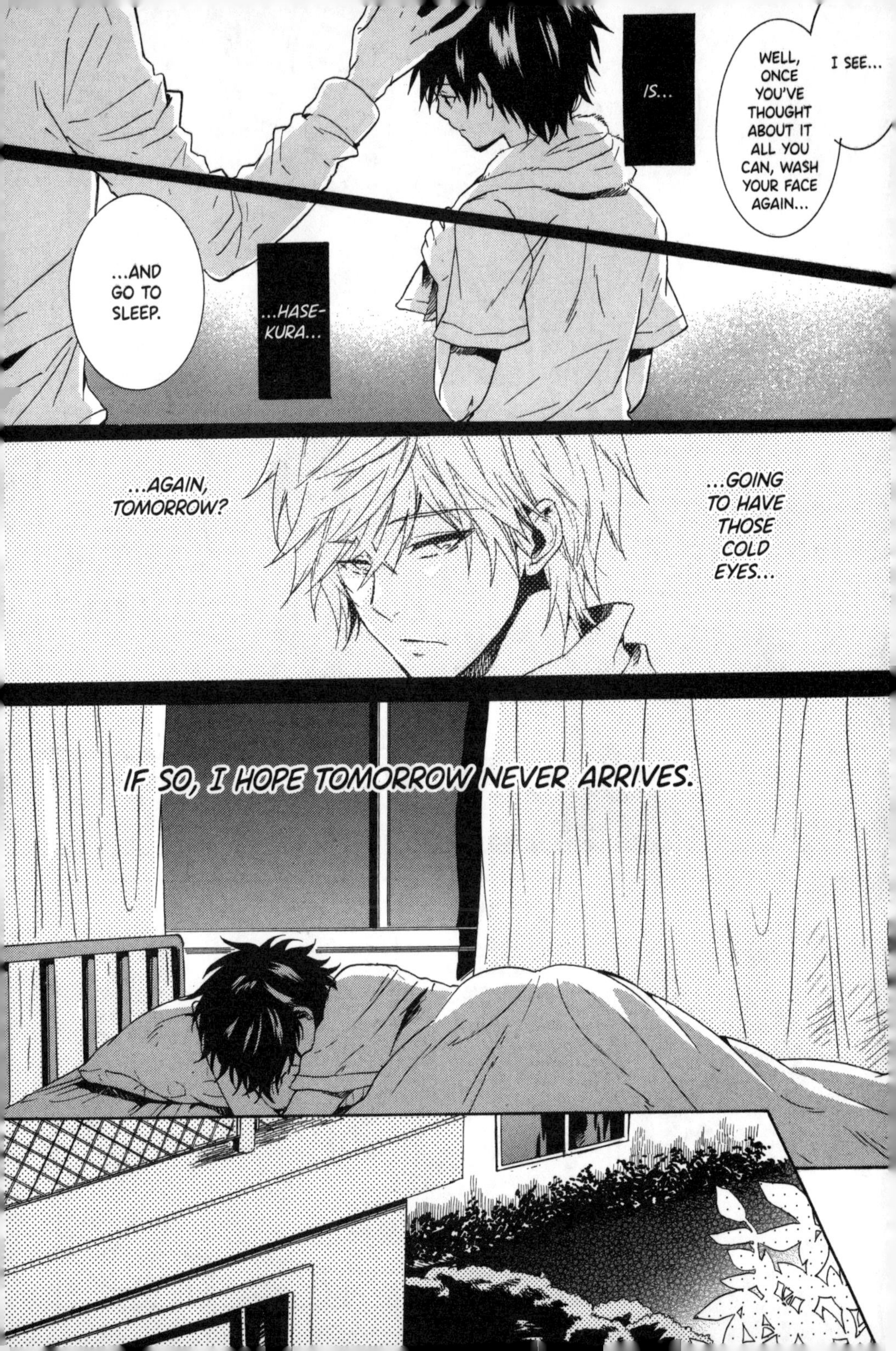
I SEE...
WELL, ONCE YOU'VE THOUGHT ABOUT IT ALL YOU CAN, WASH YOUR FACE AGAIN...
IS...
...HASE-KURA...
...AND GO TO SLEEP.
...GOING TO HAVE THOSE COLD EYES...
...AGAIN, TOMORROW?
IF SO, I HOPE TOMORROW NEVER ARRIVES.

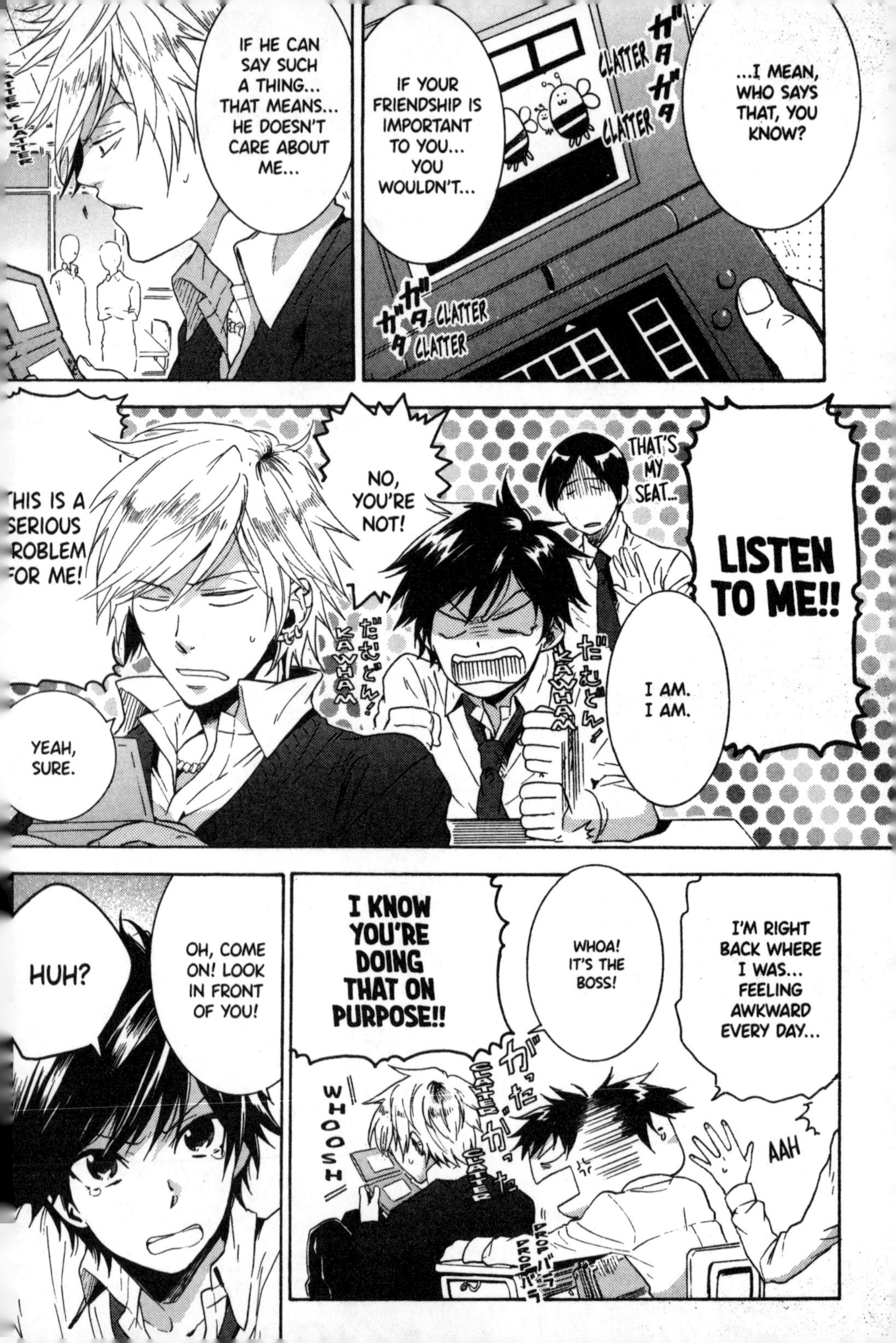

...I MEAN, WHO SAYS THAT, YOU KNOW?
CLATTER ガタガタ CLATTER
IF YOUR FRIENDSHIP IS IMPORTANT TO YOU... YOU WOULDN'T...
ガタガタ CLATTER CLATTER
IF HE CAN SAY SUCH A THING... THAT MEANS... HE DOESN'T CARE ABOUT ME...
CLATTER CLATTER
LISTEN TO ME!!
THAT'S MY SEAT...
I AM. I AM.
だむどん! KAWHAM
NO, YOU'RE NOT!
だむどん! KAWHAM
THIS IS A SERIOUS ROBLEM FOR ME!
YEAH, SURE.
I'M RIGHT BACK WHERE I WAS... FEELING AWKWARD EVERY DAY...
WHOA! IT'S THE BOSS!
I KNOW YOU'RE DOING THAT ON PURPOSE!!
AAH
がたがた CLATTER CLATTER
WHOOSH
DROP DROP
OH, COME ON! LOOK IN FRONT OF YOU!
HUH?

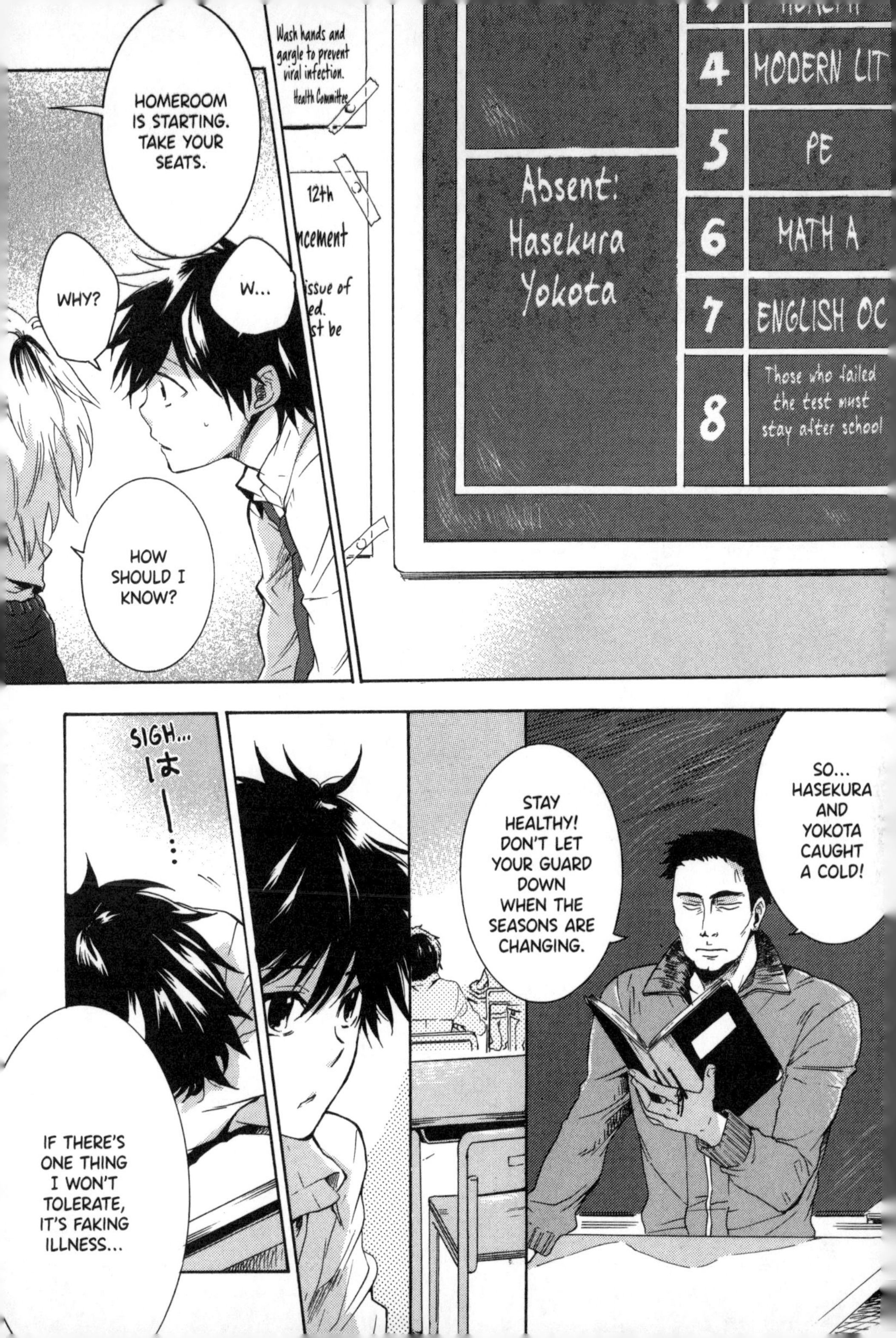
4 MODERN LIT
5 PE
6 MATH A
7 ENGLISH OC
8 Those who failed the test must stay after school
Absent: Hasekura Yokota
Wash hands and gargle to prevent viral infection. Health Committee
12th
HOMEROOM IS STARTING. TAKE YOUR SEATS.
W...
WHY?
HOW SHOULD I KNOW?
SO... HASEKURA AND YOKOTA CAUGHT A COLD!
STAY HEALTHY! DON'T LET YOUR GUARD DOWN WHEN THE SEASONS ARE CHANGING.
SIGH... はー…
IF THERE'S ONE THING I WON'T TOLERATE, IT'S FAKING ILLNESS...

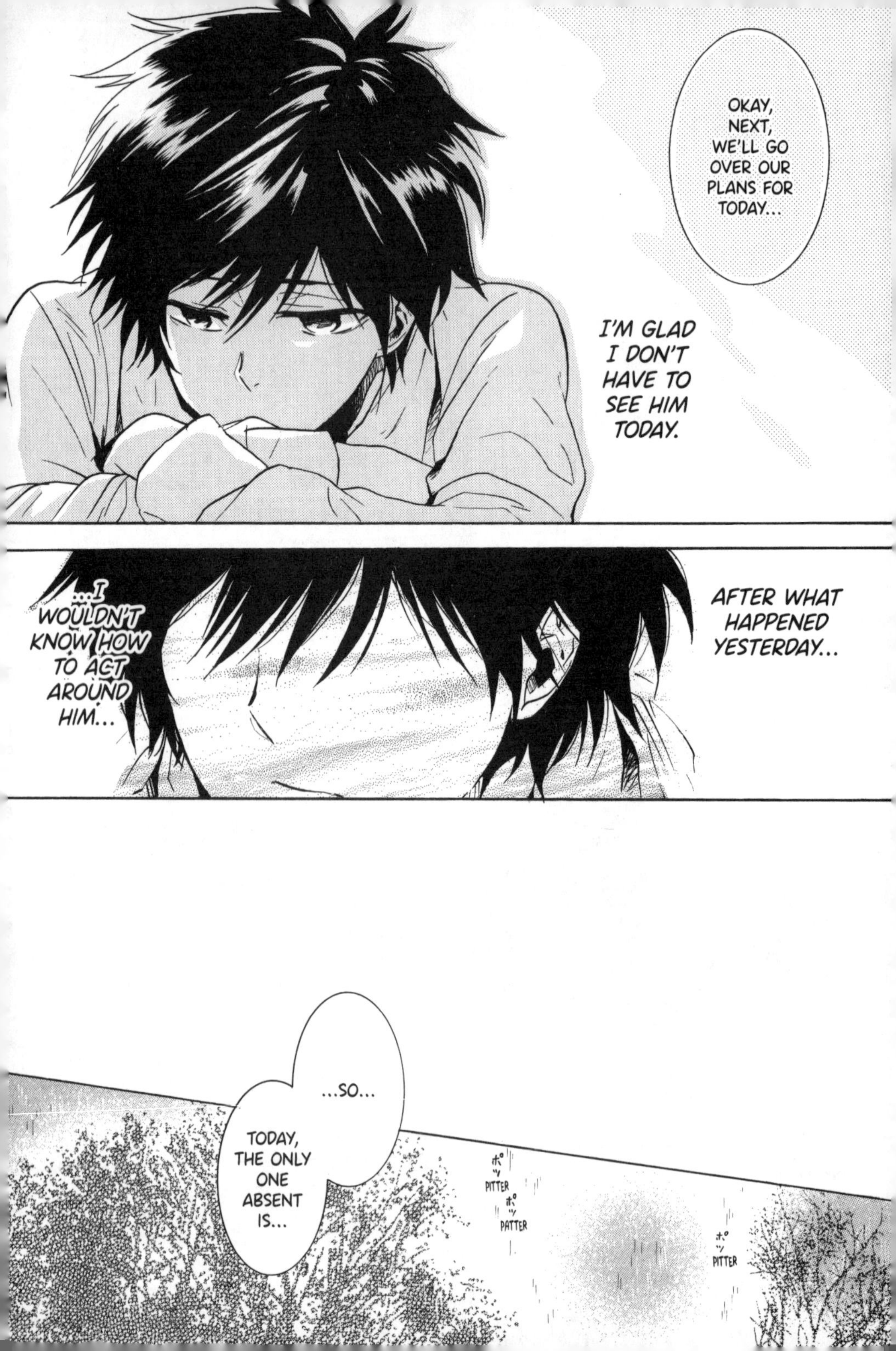
OKAY, NEXT, WE'LL GO OVER OUR PLANS FOR TODAY...
I'M GLAD I DON'T HAVE TO SEE HIM TODAY.
AFTER WHAT HAPPENED YESTERDAY...
...I WOULDN'T KNOW HOW TO ACT AROUND HIM...
...SO...
TODAY, THE ONLY ONE ABSENT IS...
ポツ PITTER
ポツ PATTER
ポツ PITTER

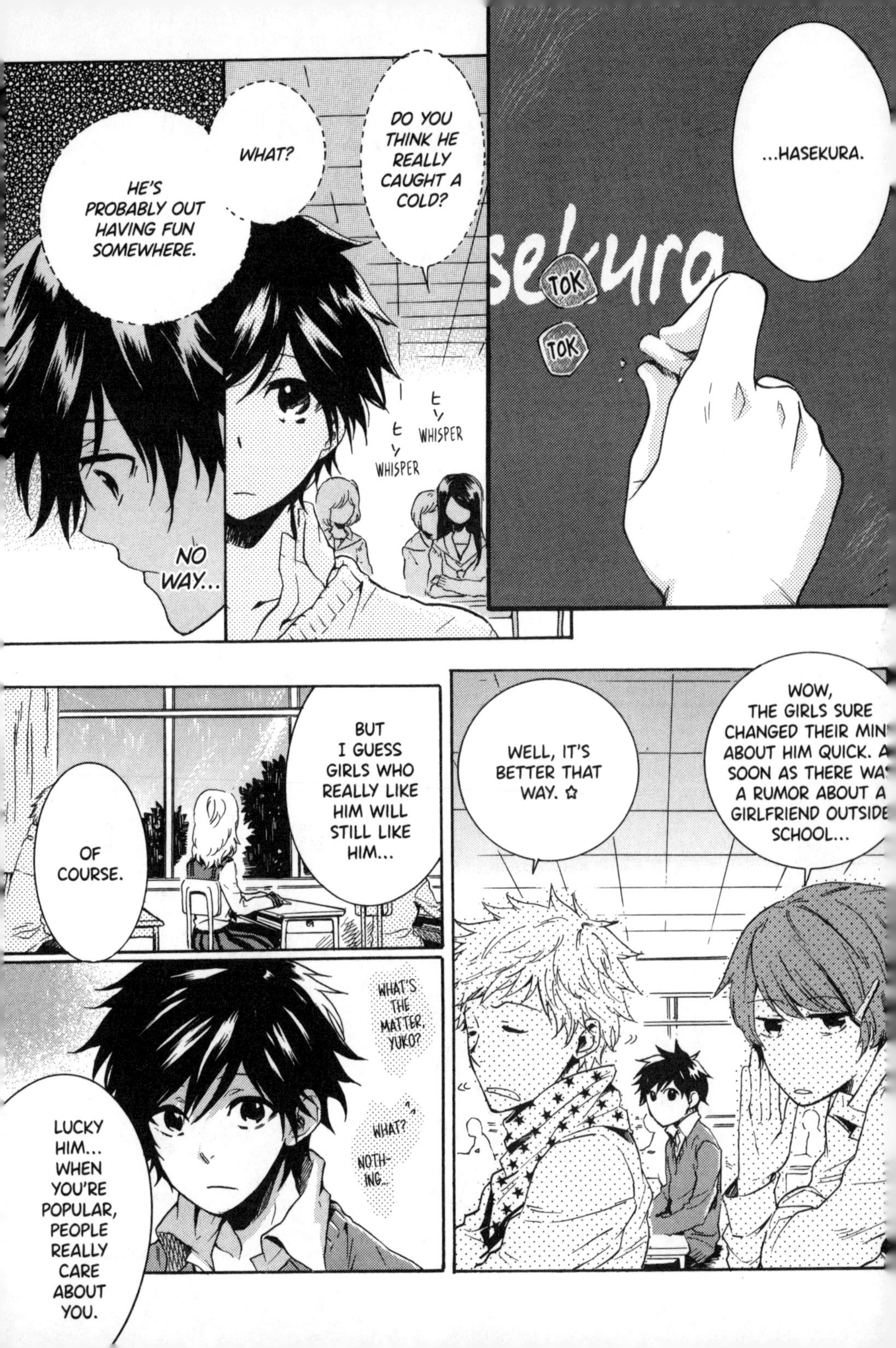

...HASEKURA.
sekura
TOK
TOK
DO YOU THINK HE REALLY CAUGHT A COLD?
WHAT?
HE'S PROBABLY OUT HAVING FUN SOMEWHERE.
WHISPER
WHISPER
NO WAY...
WOW, THE GIRLS SURE CHANGED THEIR MIN ABOUT HIM QUICK. A SOON AS THERE WA A RUMOR ABOUT A GIRLFRIEND OUTSIDE SCHOOL...
WELL, IT'S BETTER THAT WAY. ☆
BUT I GUESS GIRLS WHO REALLY LIKE HIM WILL STILL LIKE HIM...
OF COURSE.
WHAT'S THE MATTER, YUKO?
WHAT?
NOTH-ING...
LUCKY HIM... WHEN YOU'RE POPULAR, PEOPLE REALLY CARE ABOUT YOU.

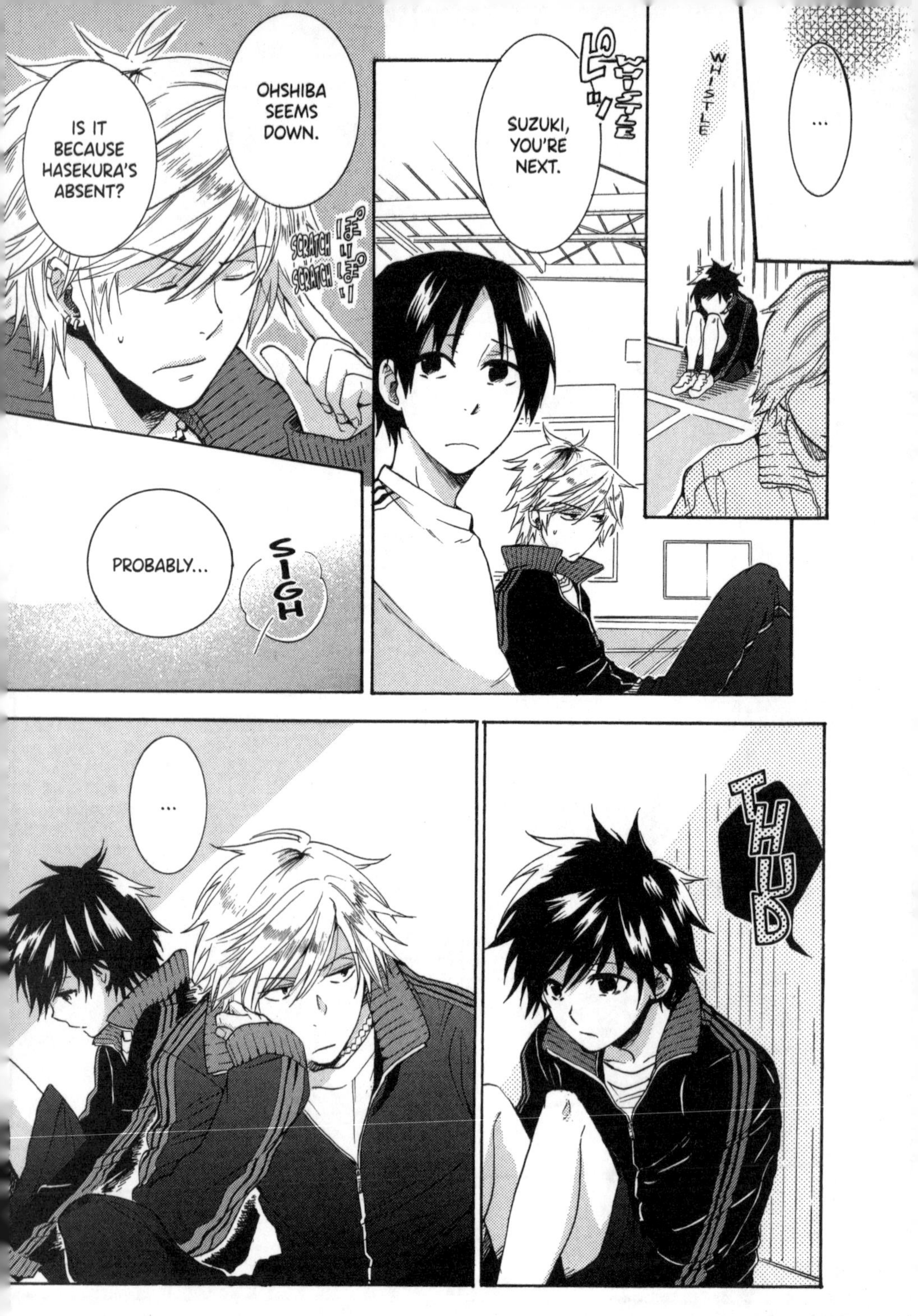
...
WHISTLE
WHISTLE
SUZUKI, YOU'RE NEXT.
OHSHIBA SEEMS DOWN.
IS IT BECAUSE HASEKURA'S ABSENT?
SCRATCH SCRATCH
PROBABLY...
SIGH
THUD
...

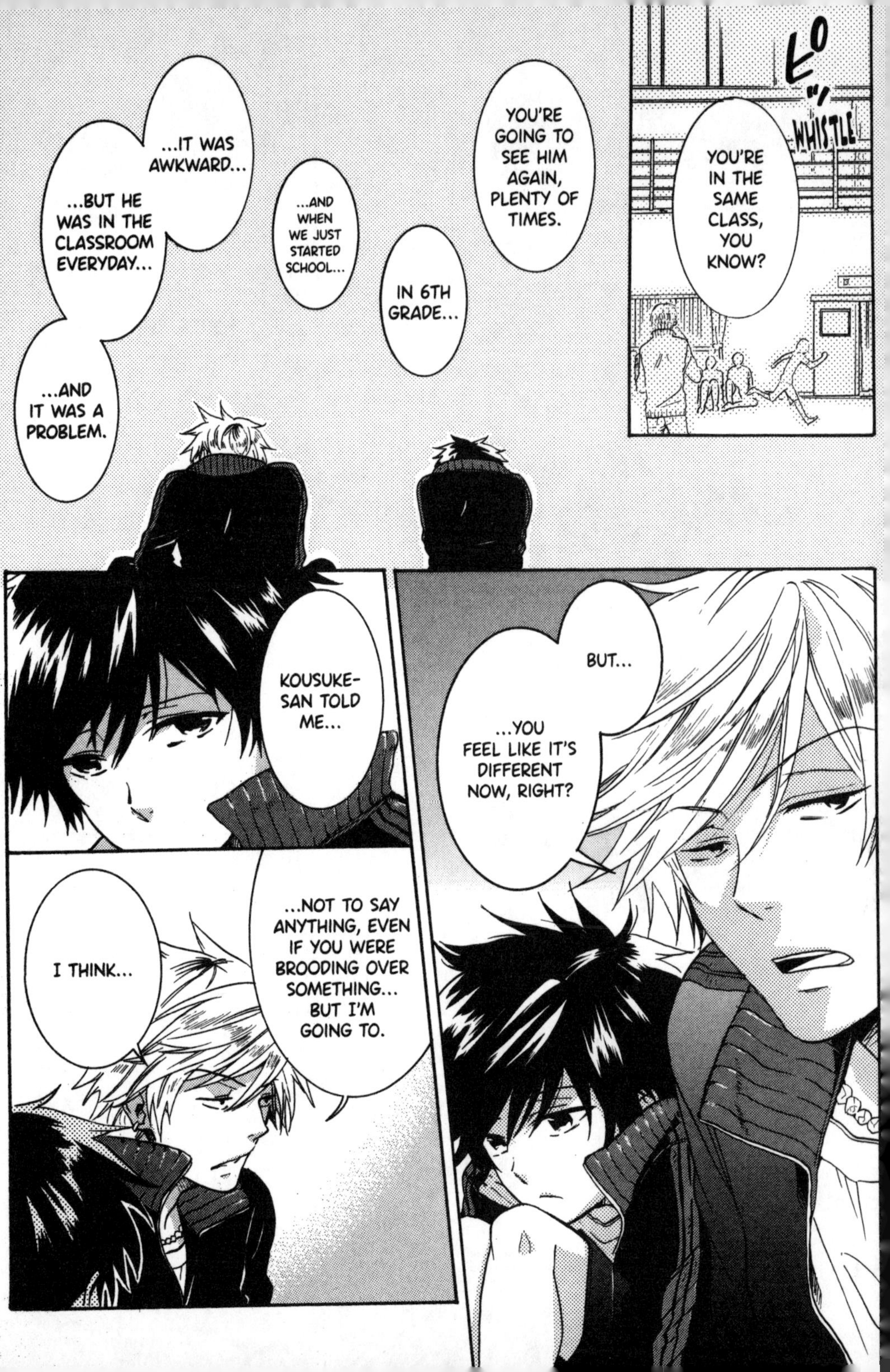
WHISTLE
YOU'RE IN THE SAME CLASS, YOU KNOW?
YOU'RE GOING TO SEE HIM AGAIN, PLENTY OF TIMES.
IN 6TH GRADE...
...AND WHEN WE JUST STARTED SCHOOL...
...IT WAS AWKWARD...
...BUT HE WAS IN THE CLASSROOM EVERYDAY...
...AND IT WAS A PROBLEM.
BUT...
...YOU FEEL LIKE IT'S DIFFERENT NOW, RIGHT?
KOUSUKE-SAN TOLD ME...
...NOT TO SAY ANYTHING, EVEN IF YOU WERE BROODING OVER SOMETHING... BUT I'M GOING TO.
I THINK...

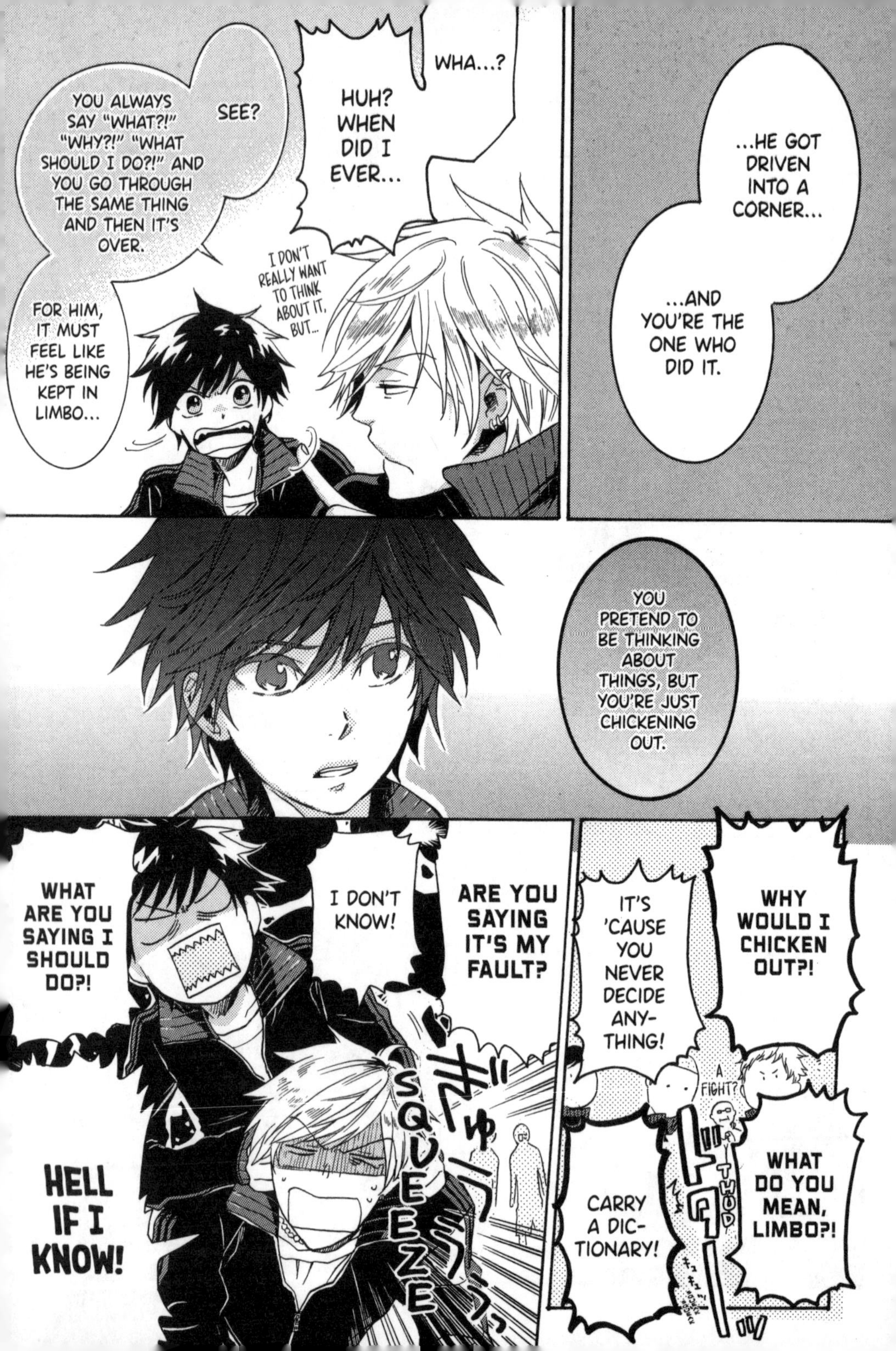
...HE GOT DRIVEN INTO A CORNER...
...AND YOU'RE THE ONE WHO DID IT.
WHA...?
HUH? WHEN DID I EVER...
SEE?
YOU ALWAYS SAY "WHAT?!" "WHY?!" "WHAT SHOULD I DO?!" AND YOU GO THROUGH THE SAME THING AND THEN IT'S OVER.
I DON'T REALLY WANT TO THINK ABOUT IT, BUT...
FOR HIM, IT MUST FEEL LIKE HE'S BEING KEPT IN LIMBO...
YOU PRETEND TO BE THINKING ABOUT THINGS, BUT YOU'RE JUST CHICKENING OUT.
WHY WOULD I CHICKEN OUT?!
IT'S 'CAUSE YOU NEVER DECIDE ANY-THING!
A FIGHT?
THUD
WHAT DO YOU MEAN, LIMBO?!
CARRY A DIC-TIONARY!
ARE YOU SAYING IT'S MY FAULT?
I DON'T KNOW!
WHAT ARE YOU SAYING I SHOULD DO?!
SQUEEZE
HELL IF I KNOW!

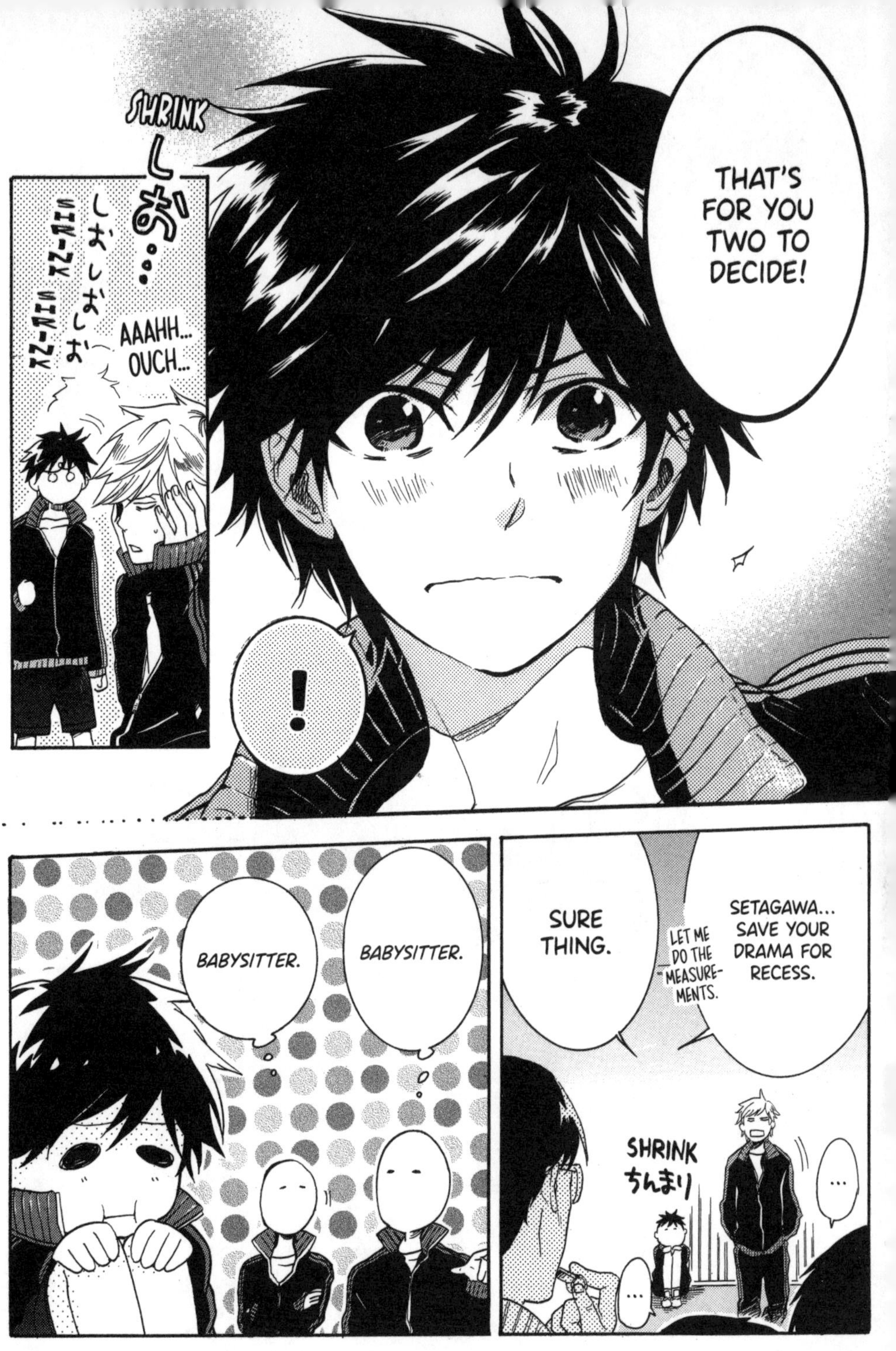
THAT'S FOR YOU TWO TO DECIDE!
!
SHRINK
しお…
しおしおしお
SHRINK SHRINK
AAAHH... OUCH...
SETAGAWA... SAVE YOUR DRAMA FOR RECESS.
LET ME DO THE MEASUREMENTS.
SURE THING.
SHRINK
ちんまり
...
...
BABYSITTER.
BABYSITTER.

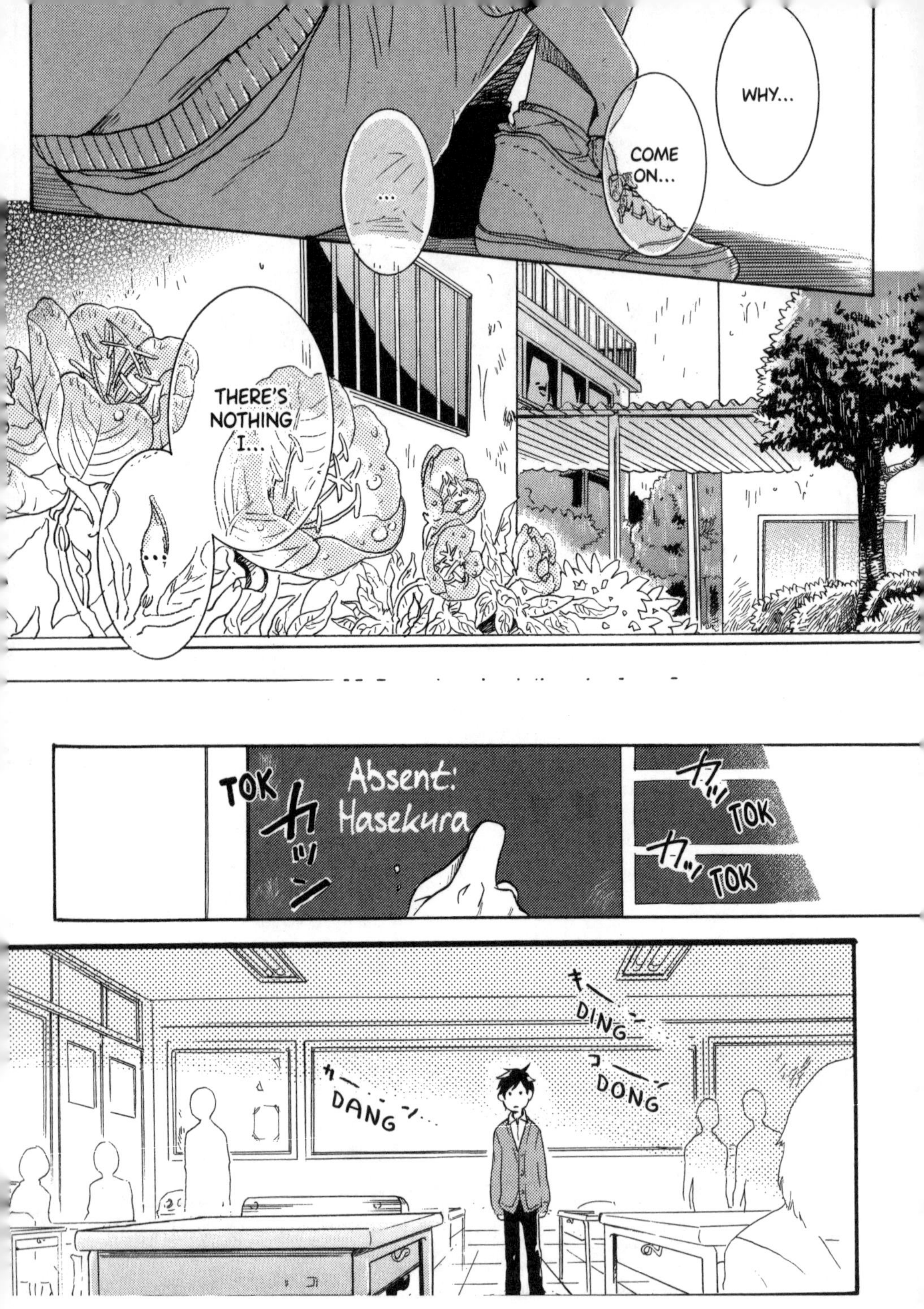
WHY...
COME ON...
...
THERE'S NOTHING I...
...
TOK
TOK
Absent: Hasekura
TOK
DING DONG
DANG

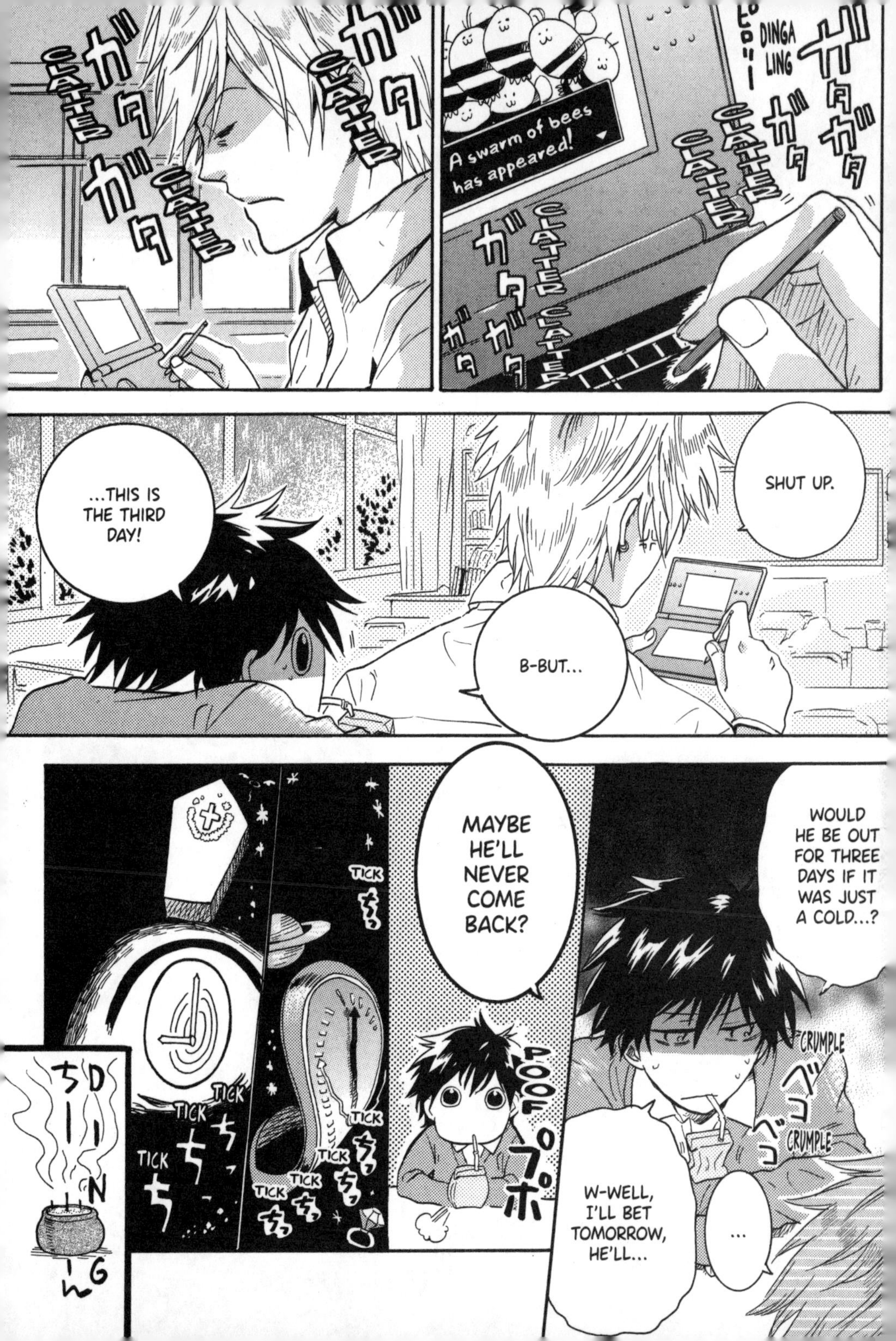
DINGA LING
ピロリーン
ガタガタ
CLATTER
CLATTER
A swarm of bees has appeared!
CLATTER
CLATTER
ガタガタガタ
ガタ
CLATTER
ガタ
CLATTER
SHUT UP.
...THIS IS THE THIRD DAY!
B-BUT...
WOULD HE BE OUT FOR THREE DAYS IF IT WAS JUST A COLD...?
CRUMPLE
ベコ
CRUMPLE
ベコ
...
W-WELL, I'LL BET TOMORROW, HE'LL...
MAYBE HE'LL NEVER COME BACK?
POOF
ポフ
TICK
ちっ
TICK
ちっ
TICK
ちっ
TICK
ちっ
TICK
ち
TICK
ち
TICK
ち
DING
ちーん

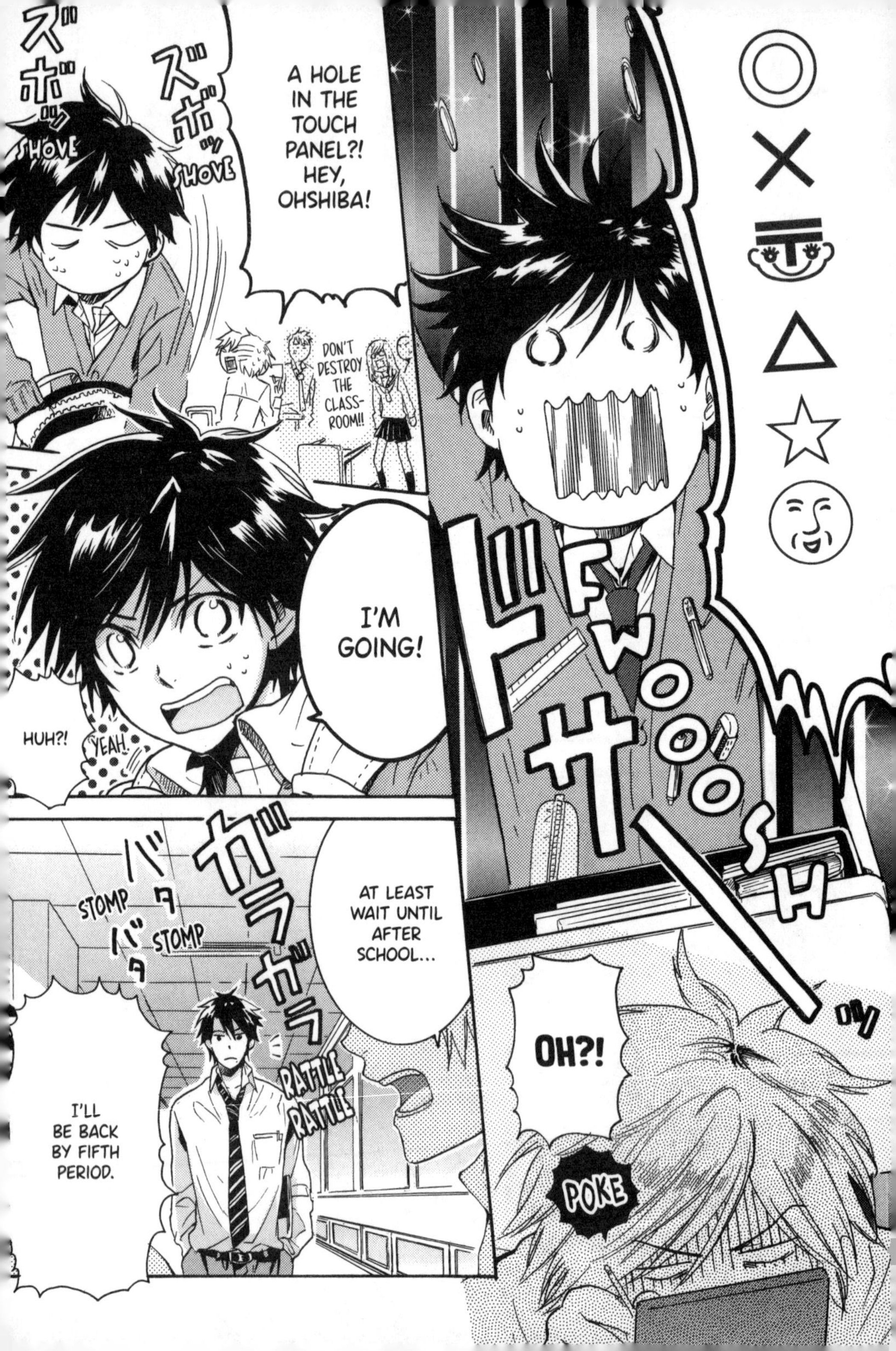

ドサッ
FWOOOSH
OH?!
POKE
A HOLE IN THE TOUCH PANEL?! HEY, OHSHIBA!
ズボッ SHOVE
ズボッ SHOVE
DON'T DESTROY THE CLASSROOM!!
I'M GOING!
YEAH.
HUH?!
AT LEAST WAIT UNTIL AFTER SCHOOL...
ガラガラ RATTLE RATTLE
バタバタ STOMP STOMP
I'LL BE BACK BY FIFTH PERIOD.

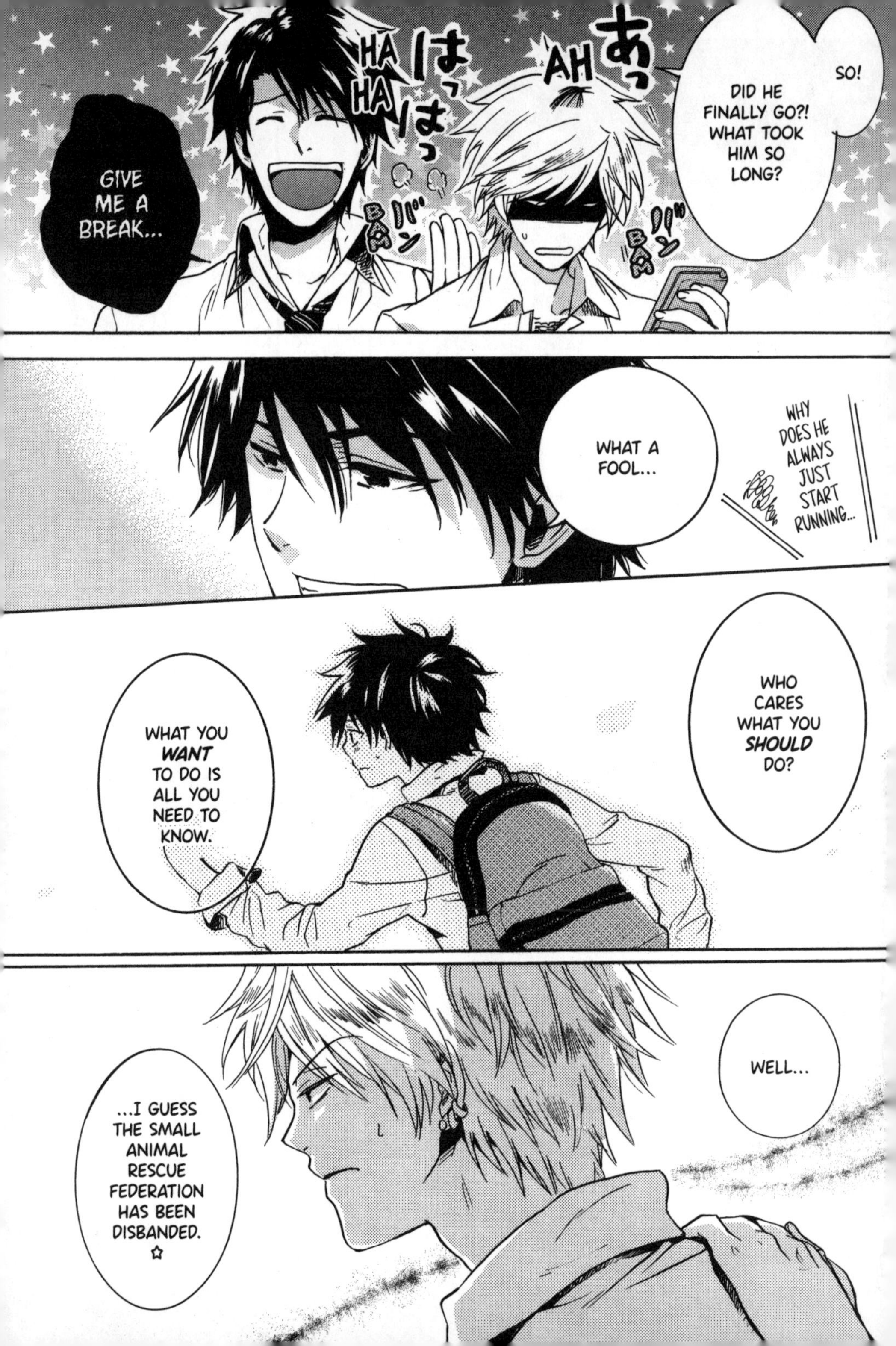
SO!
DID HE FINALLY GO?! WHAT TOOK HIM SO LONG?
AH あっ
BAM バン
HA HA はっはっ
BAM バン
GIVE ME A BREAK...
WHY DOES HE ALWAYS JUST START RUNNING...
WHAT A FOOL...
WHO CARES WHAT YOU **SHOULD** DO?
WHAT YOU **WANT** TO DO IS ALL YOU NEED TO KNOW.
WELL...
...I GUESS THE SMALL ANIMAL RESCUE FEDERATION HAS BEEN DISBANDED. ☆

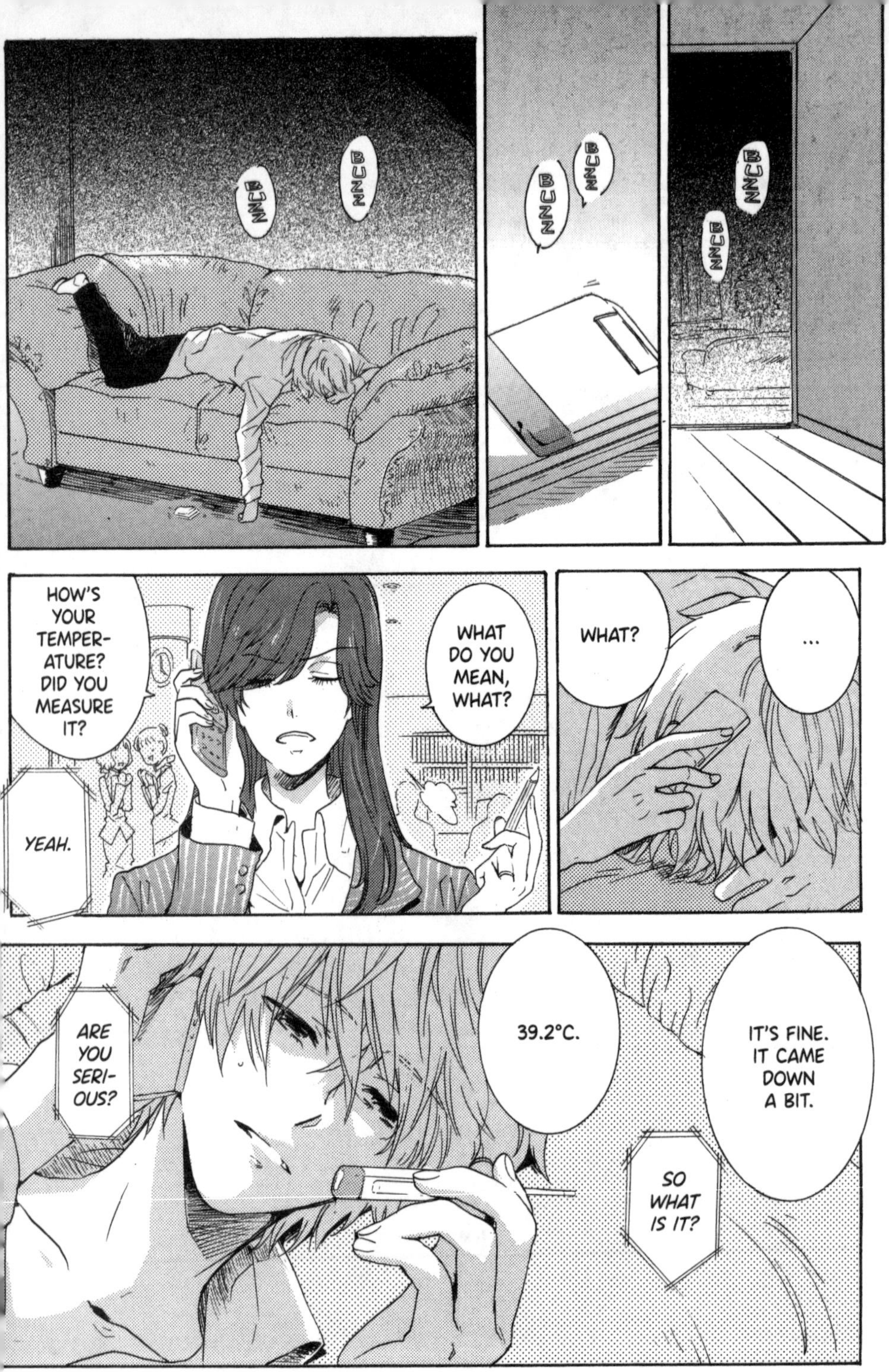
BUZZ
BUZZ
BUZZ
BUZZ
BUZZ
BUZZ
...
WHAT?
WHAT DO YOU MEAN, WHAT?
HOW'S YOUR TEMPERATURE? DID YOU MEASURE IT?
YEAH.
IT'S FINE. IT CAME DOWN A BIT.
39.2°C.
SO WHAT IS IT?
ARE YOU SERIOUS?

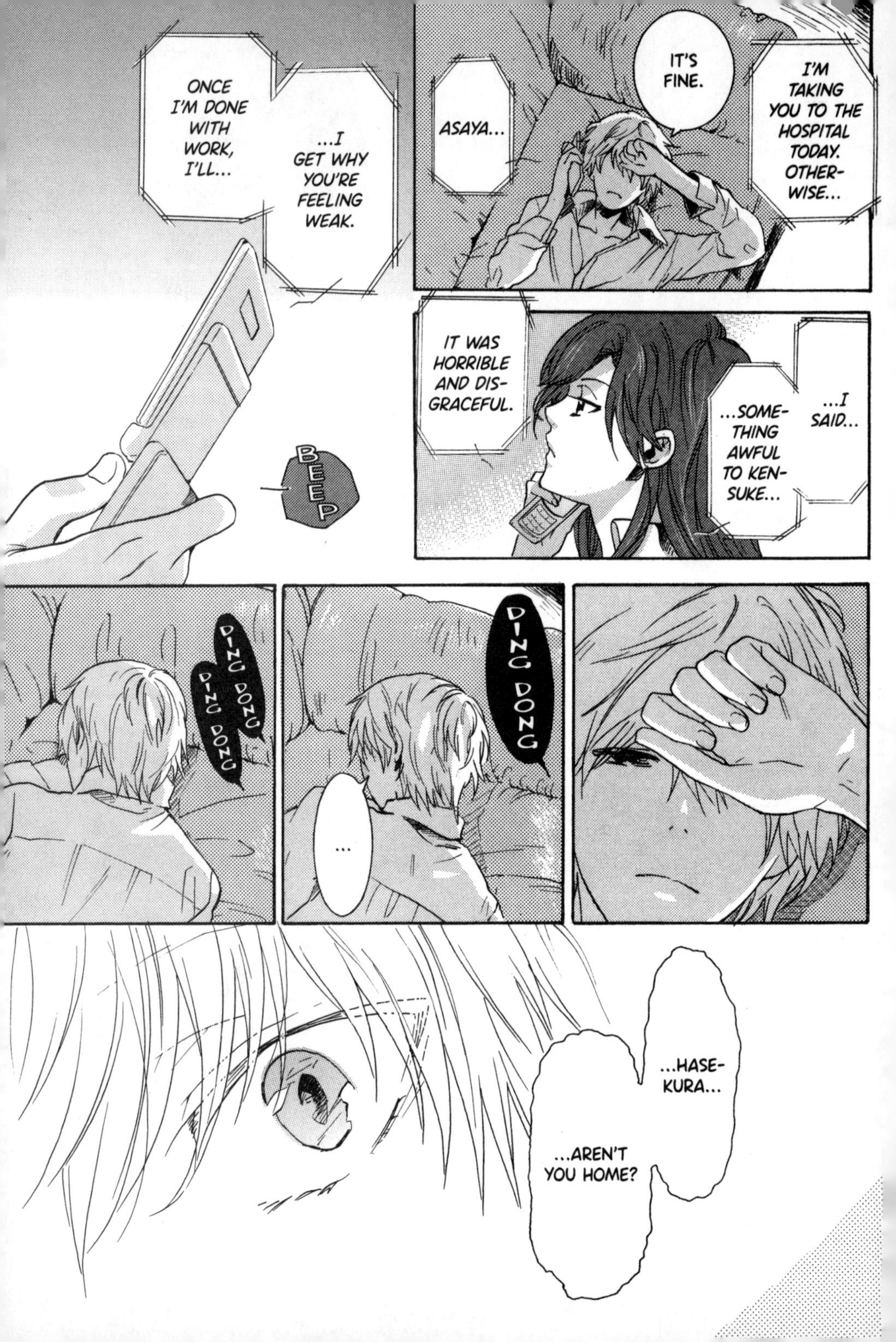
I'M TAKING YOU TO THE HOSPITAL TODAY. OTHER-WISE...
IT'S FINE.
ASAYA...
...I GET WHY YOU'RE FEELING WEAK.
ONCE I'M DONE WITH WORK, I'LL...
...I SAID...
...SOME-THING AWFUL TO KEN-SUKE...
IT WAS HORRIBLE AND DIS-GRACEFUL.
BEEP
DING DONG
...
DING DONG
DING DONG
...HASE-KURA...
...AREN'T YOU HOME?

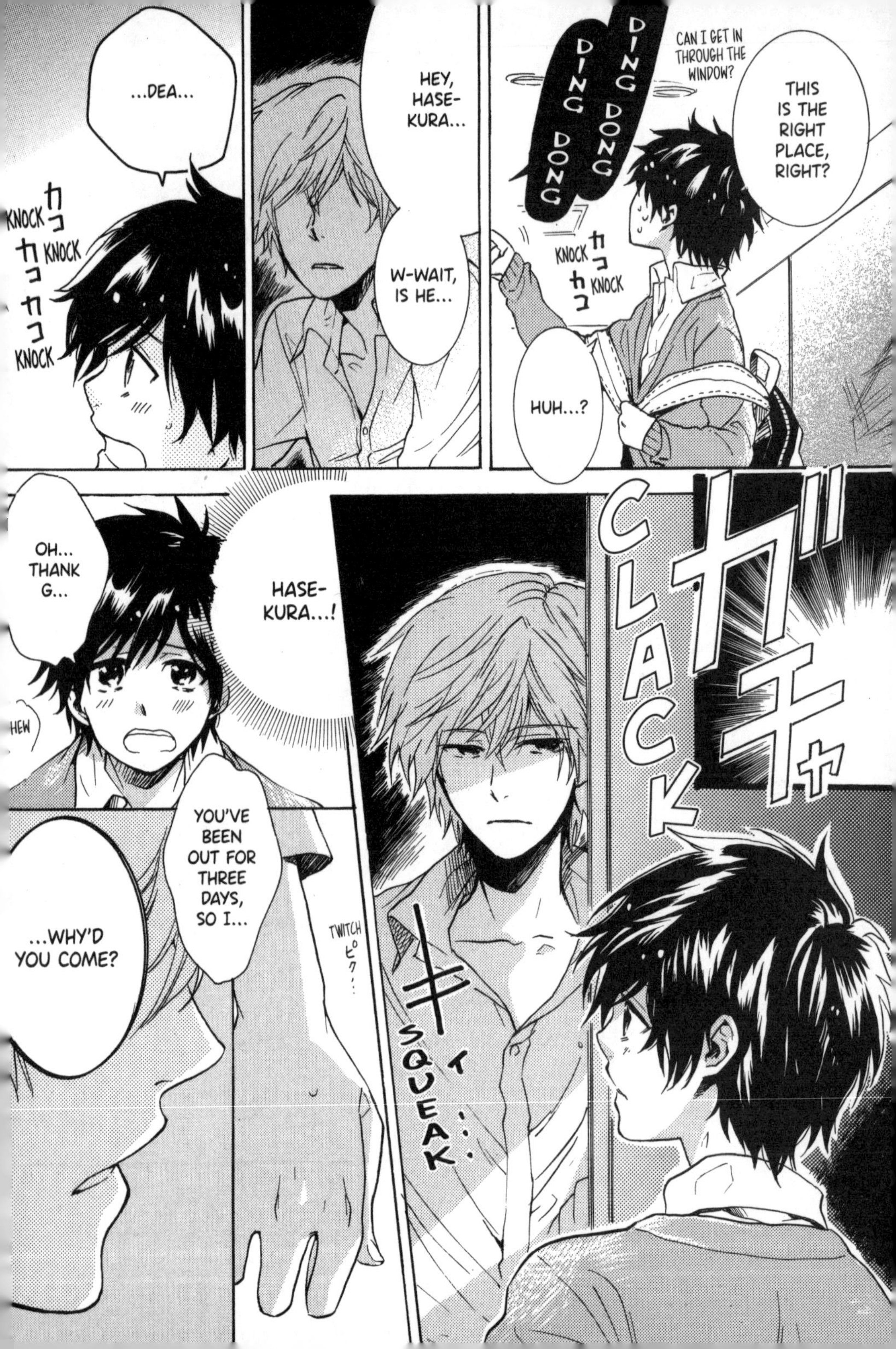
THIS IS THE RIGHT PLACE, RIGHT?
CAN I GET IN THROUGH THE WINDOW?
DING DONG DING DONG
KNOCK カコ カコ KNOCK
HUH...?
HEY, HASE-KURA...
W-WAIT, IS HE...
...DEA...
KNOCK カコ カコ カコ KNOCK
ガチャ CLACK
ギィ SQUEAK
TWITCH ピク...
HASE-KURA...!
OH... THANK G...
HEW
YOU'VE BEEN OUT FOR THREE DAYS, SO I...
...WHY'D YOU COME?

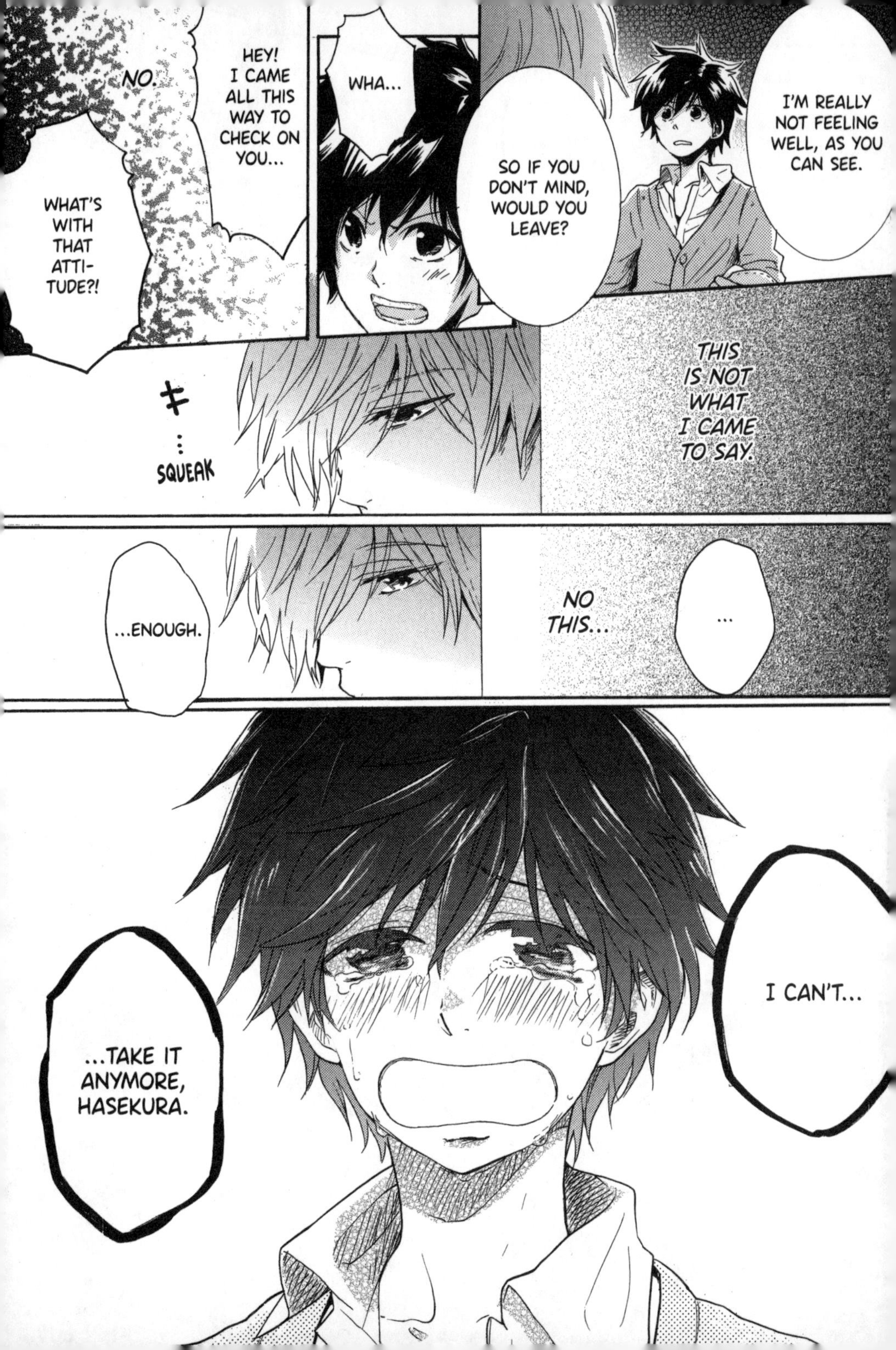
I'M REALLY NOT FEELING WELL, AS YOU CAN SEE.
SO IF YOU DON'T MIND, WOULD YOU LEAVE?
WHA...
HEY! I CAME ALL THIS WAY TO CHECK ON YOU...
NO.
WHAT'S WITH THAT ATTITUDE?!
THIS IS NOT WHAT I CAME TO SAY.
キ…
SQUEAK
...
NO THIS...
...ENOUGH.
I CAN'T...
...TAKE IT ANYMORE, HASEKURA.

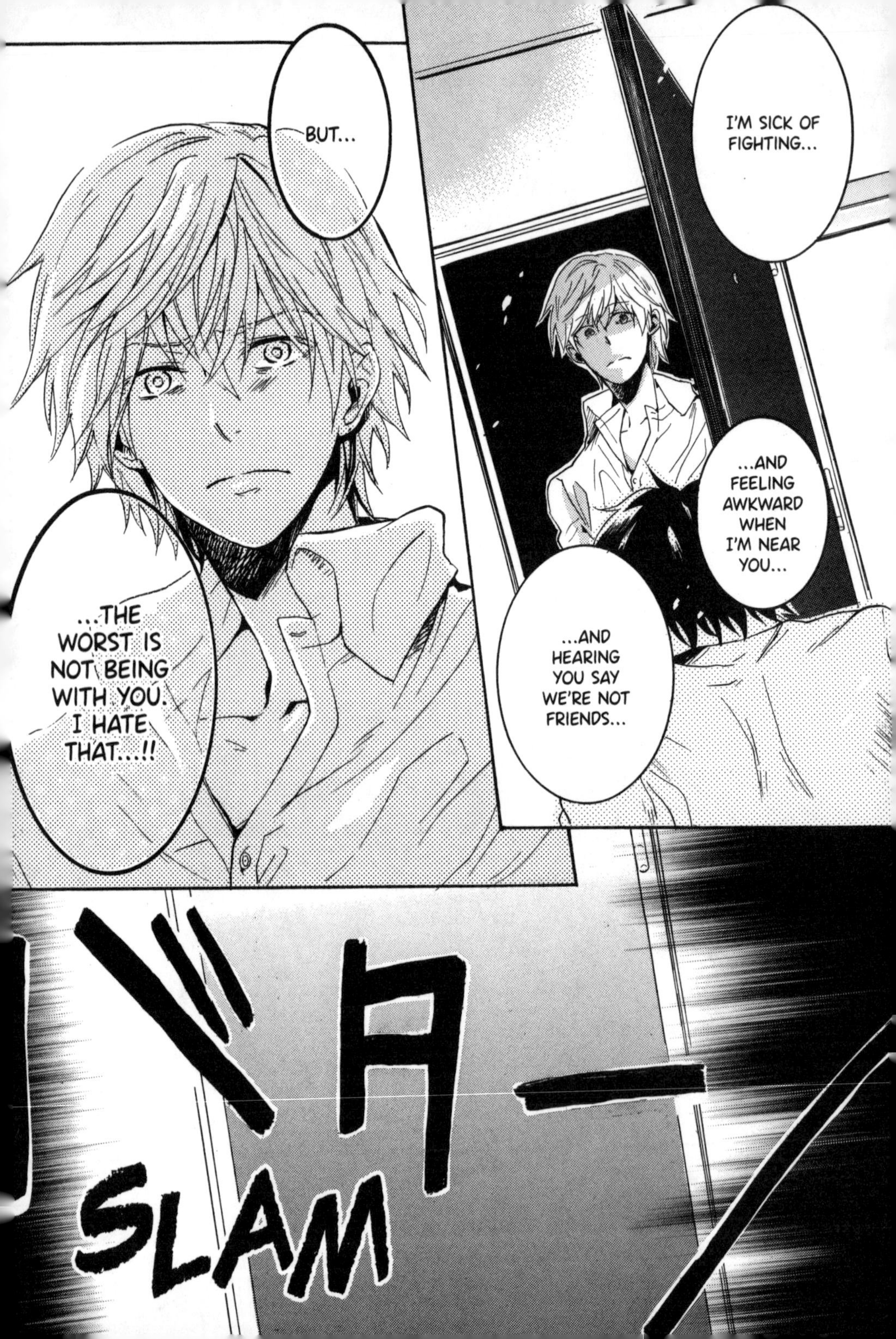
I'M SICK OF FIGHTING...
...AND FEELING AWKWARD WHEN I'M NEAR YOU...
...AND HEARING YOU SAY WE'RE NOT FRIENDS...
BUT...
...THE WORST IS NOT BEING WITH YOU. I HATE THAT...!!
SLAM

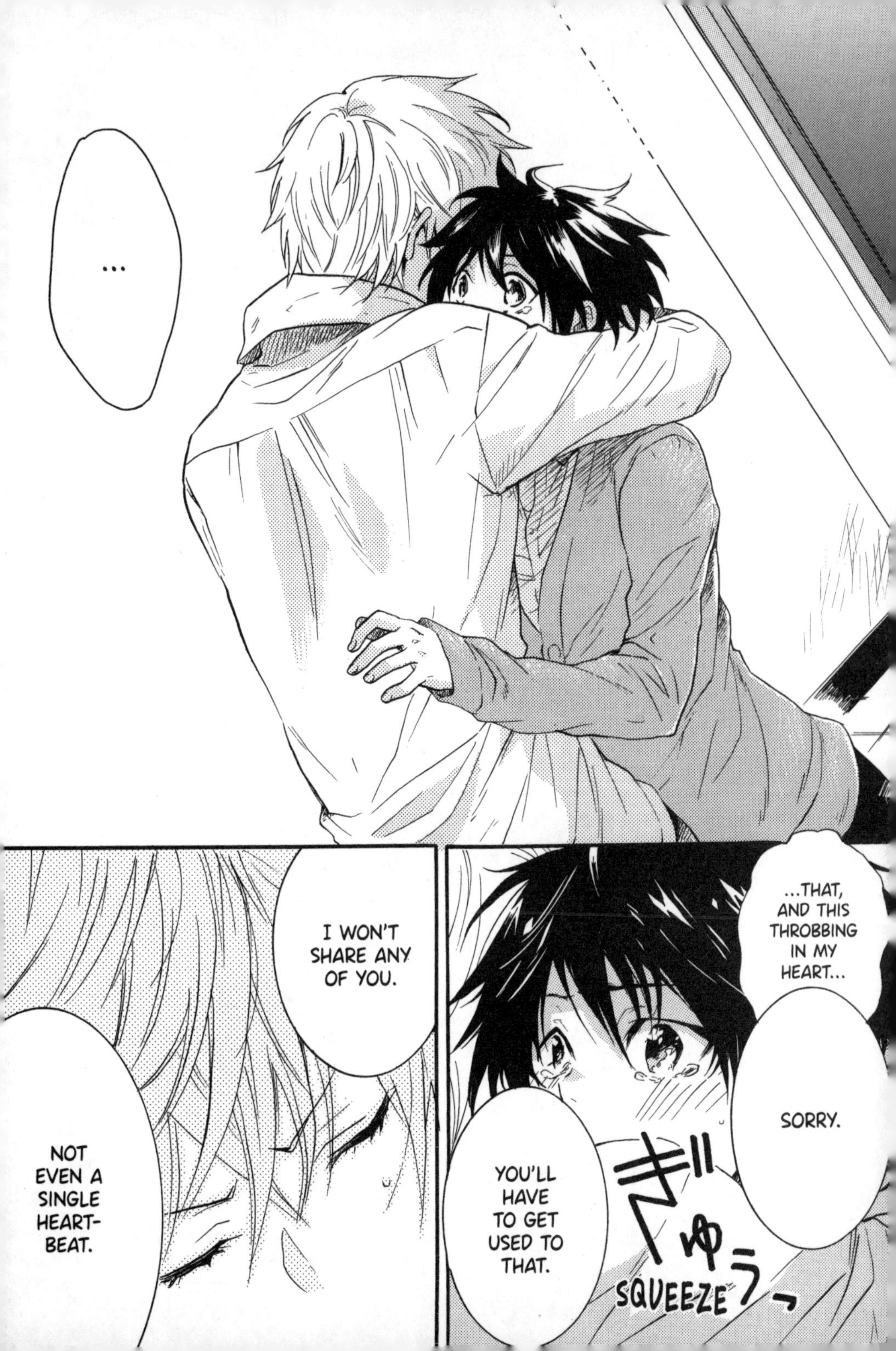
...
...THAT, AND THIS THROBBING IN MY HEART...
SORRY.
YOU'LL HAVE TO GET USED TO THAT.
ぎゅう
SQUEEZE
I WON'T SHARE ANY OF YOU.
NOT EVEN A SINGLE HEART-BEAT.

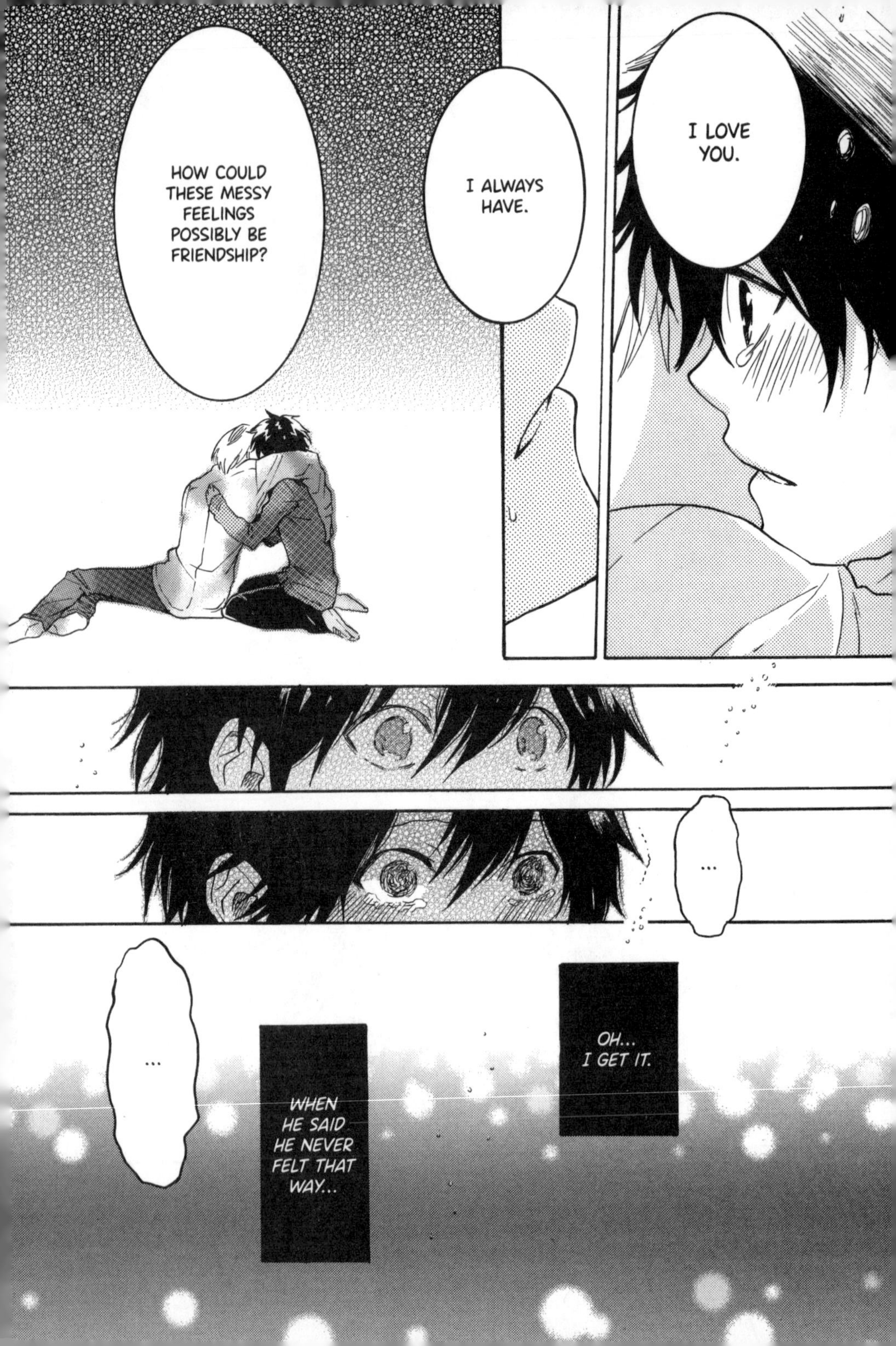
I LOVE YOU.
I ALWAYS HAVE.
HOW COULD THESE MESSY FEELINGS POSSIBLY BE FRIENDSHIP?
...
OH... I GET IT.
WHEN HE SAID HE NEVER FELT THAT WAY...
...

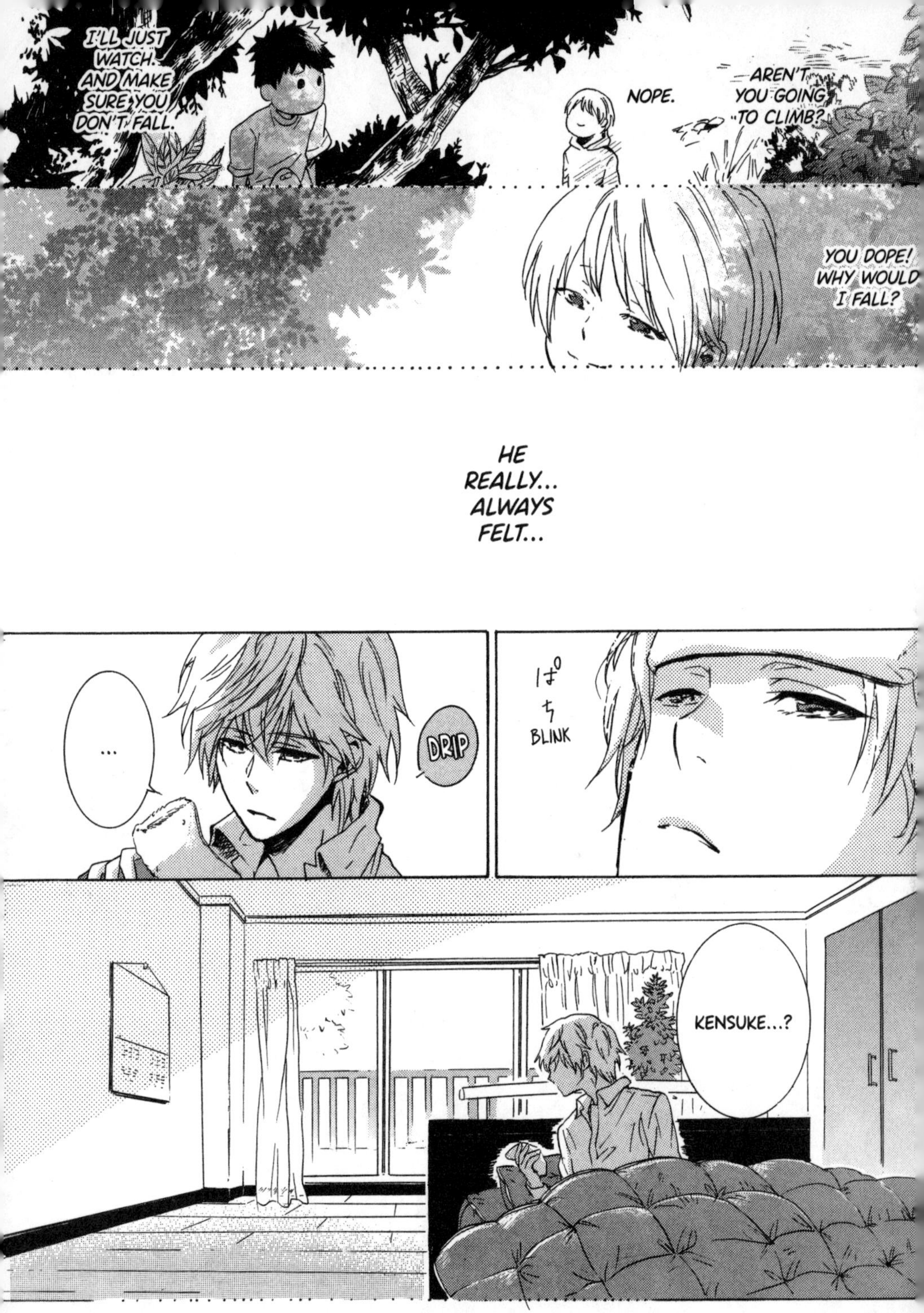
AREN'T YOU GOING TO CLIMB?
NOPE.
I'LL JUST WATCH. AND MAKE SURE YOU DON'T FALL.
YOU DOPE! WHY WOULD I FALL?
HE REALLY... ALWAYS FELT...
ぱち
BLINK
DRIP
...
KENSUKE...?

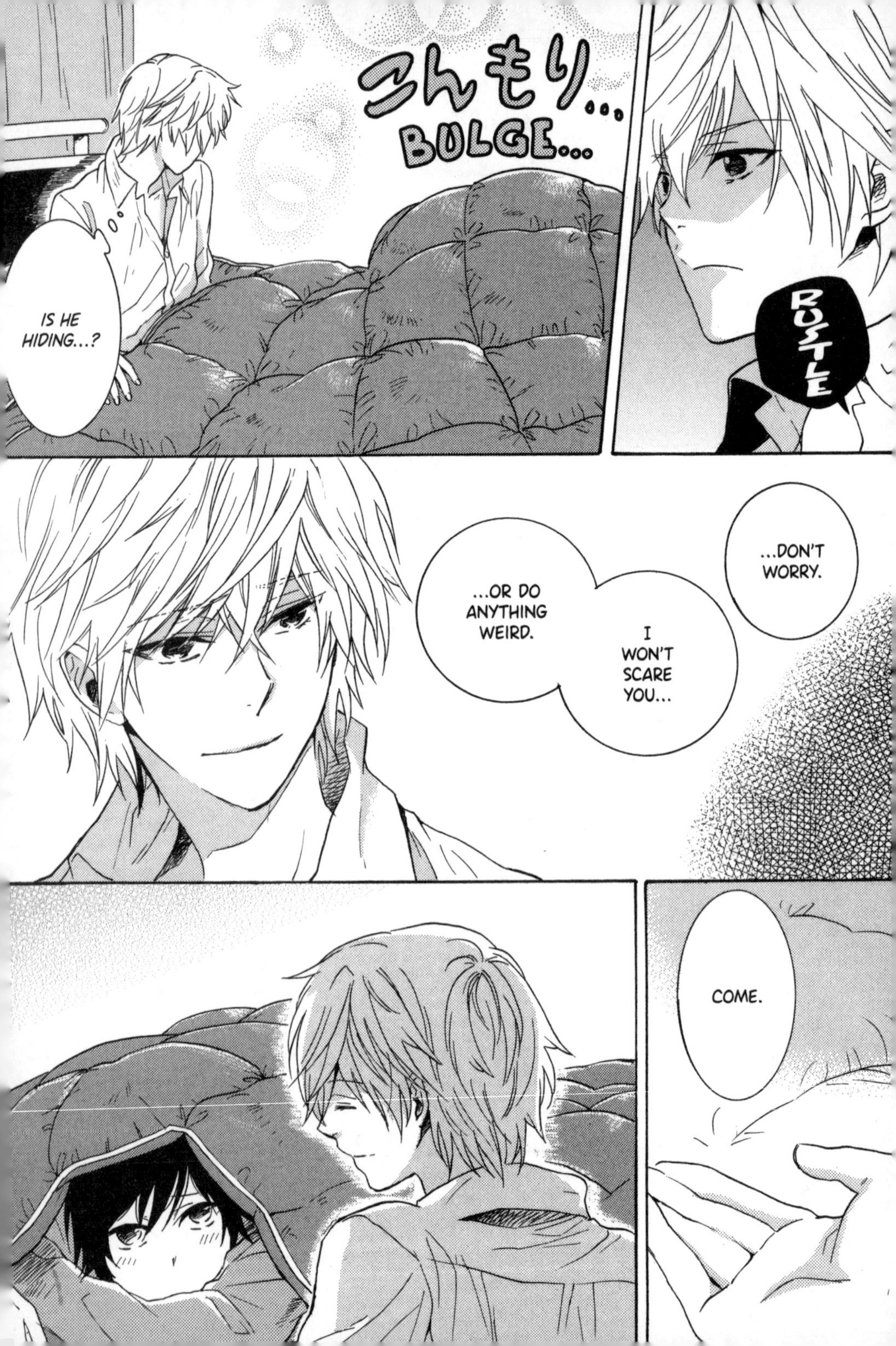
RUSTLE
こんもり…
BULGE…
IS HE HIDING…?
…DON'T WORRY.
I WON'T SCARE YOU…
…OR DO ANYTHING WEIRD.
COME.

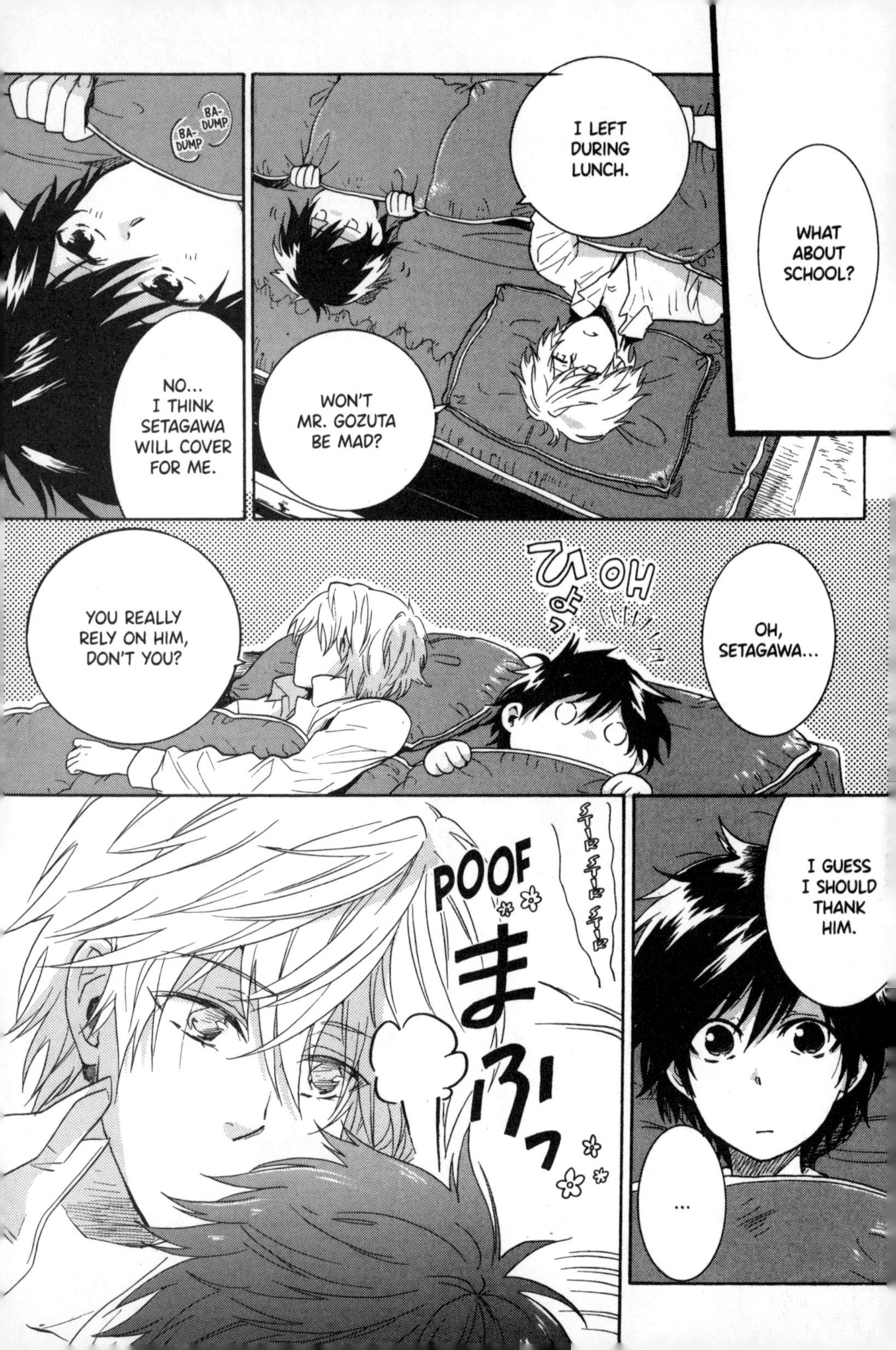
WHAT ABOUT SCHOOL?
I LEFT DURING LUNCH.
WON'T MR. GOZUTA BE MAD?
BA-DUMP BA-DUMP
NO... I THINK SETAGAWA WILL COVER FOR ME.
OH, SETAGAWA...
ひょっ OH
YOU REALLY RELY ON HIM, DON'T YOU?
I GUESS I SHOULD THANK HIM.
...
STIR STIR STIR
POOF
まふっ

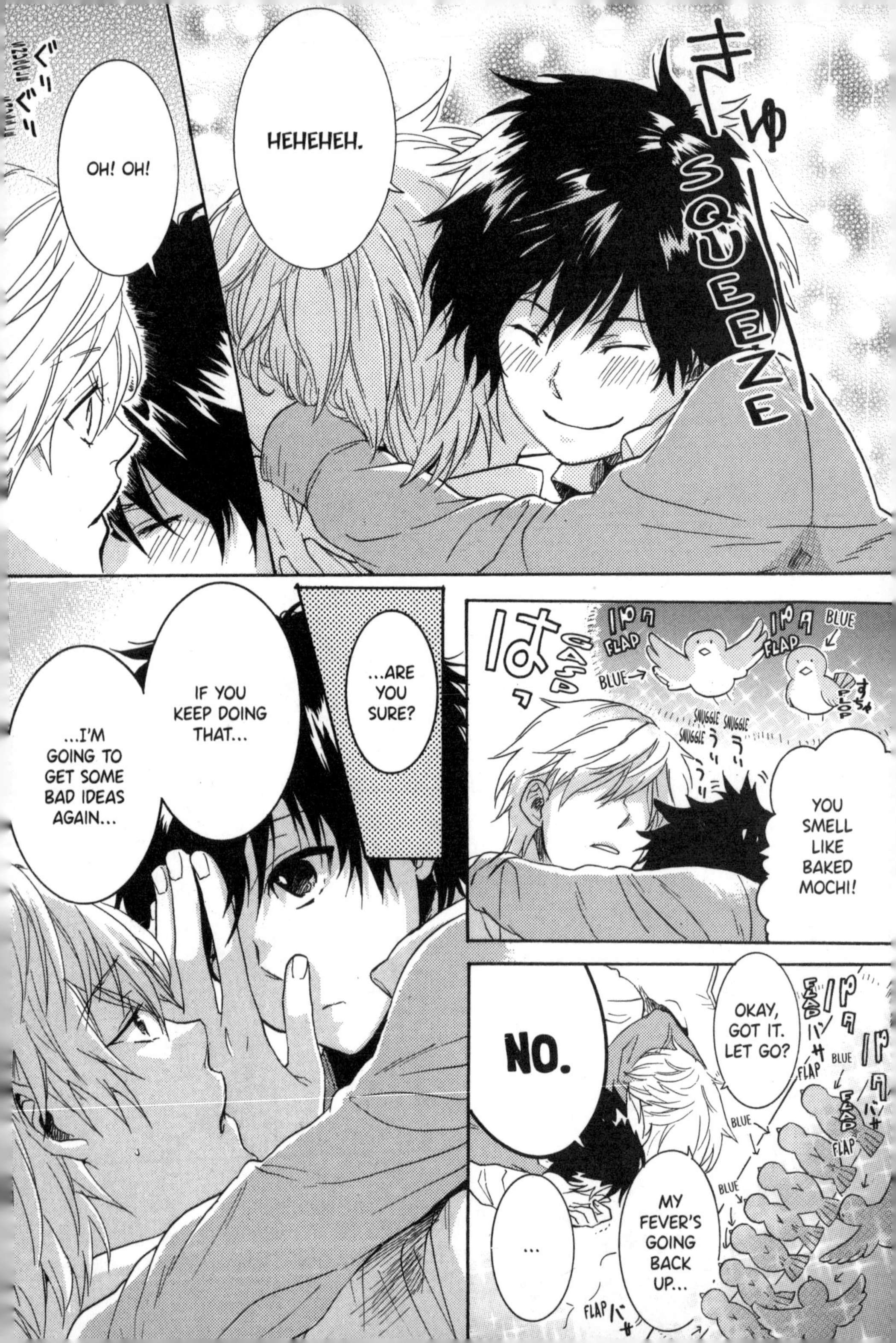
きゅ
SQUEEZE
HEHEHEH.
OH! OH!
ぐりぐり
パタ FLAP
パタ FLAP
BLUE
BLUE
は GASP
すちゃ FLOP
SNUGGLE SNUGGLE SNUGGLE
YOU SMELL LIKE BAKED MOCHI!
OKAY, GOT IT. LET GO?
パタ バサ FLAP
BLUE
FLAP
NO.
...
MY FEVER'S GOING BACK UP...
FLAP バサ
...ARE YOU SURE?
IF YOU KEEP DOING THAT...
...I'M GOING TO GET SOME BAD IDEAS AGAIN...

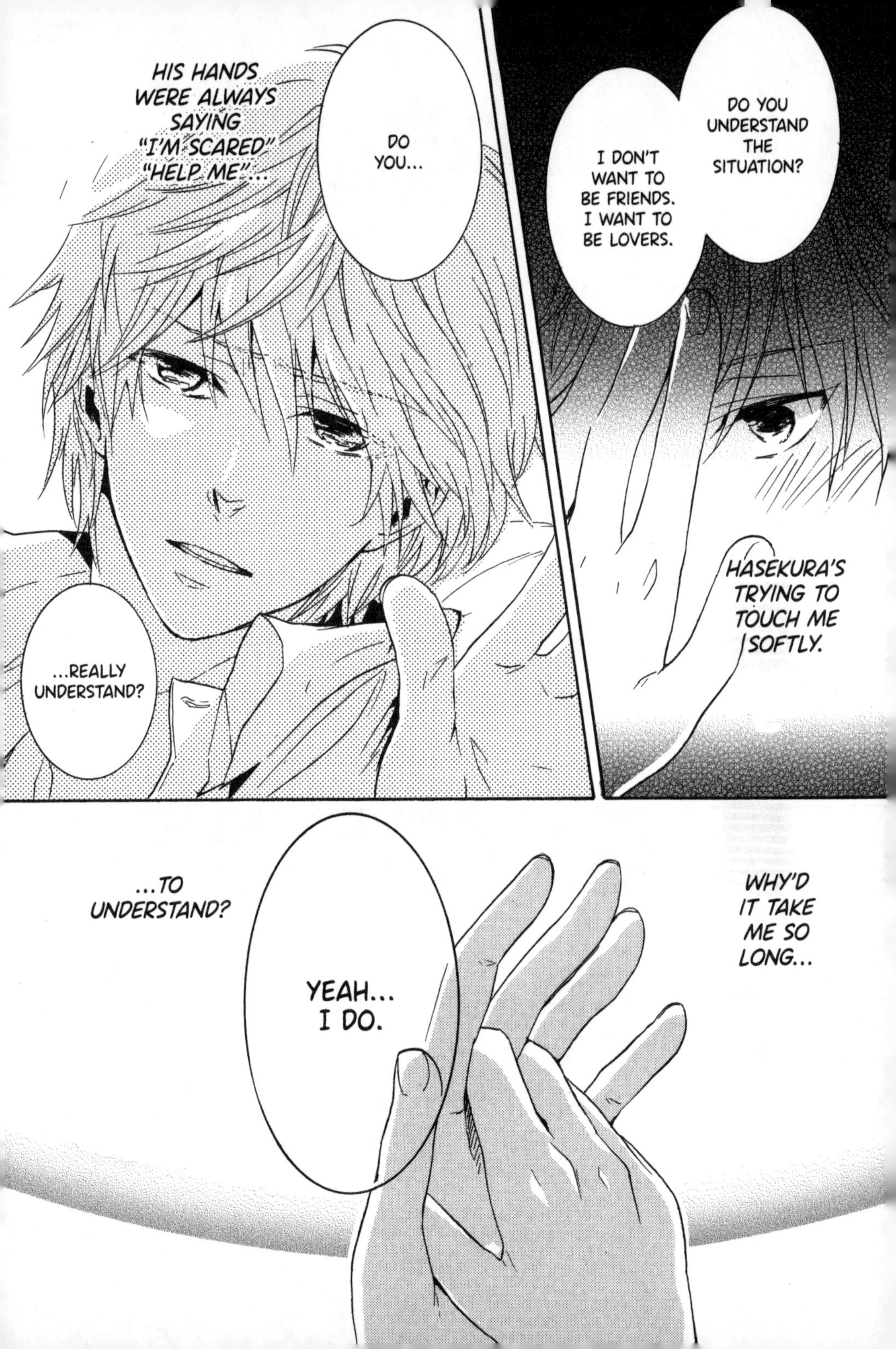
DO YOU UNDERSTAND THE SITUATION?
I DON'T WANT TO BE FRIENDS. I WANT TO BE LOVERS.
HASEKURA'S TRYING TO TOUCH ME SOFTLY.
DO YOU...
HIS HANDS WERE ALWAYS SAYING "I'M SCARED" "HELP ME"...
...REALLY UNDERSTAND?
WHY'D IT TAKE ME SO LONG...
YEAH... I DO.
...TO UNDERSTAND?

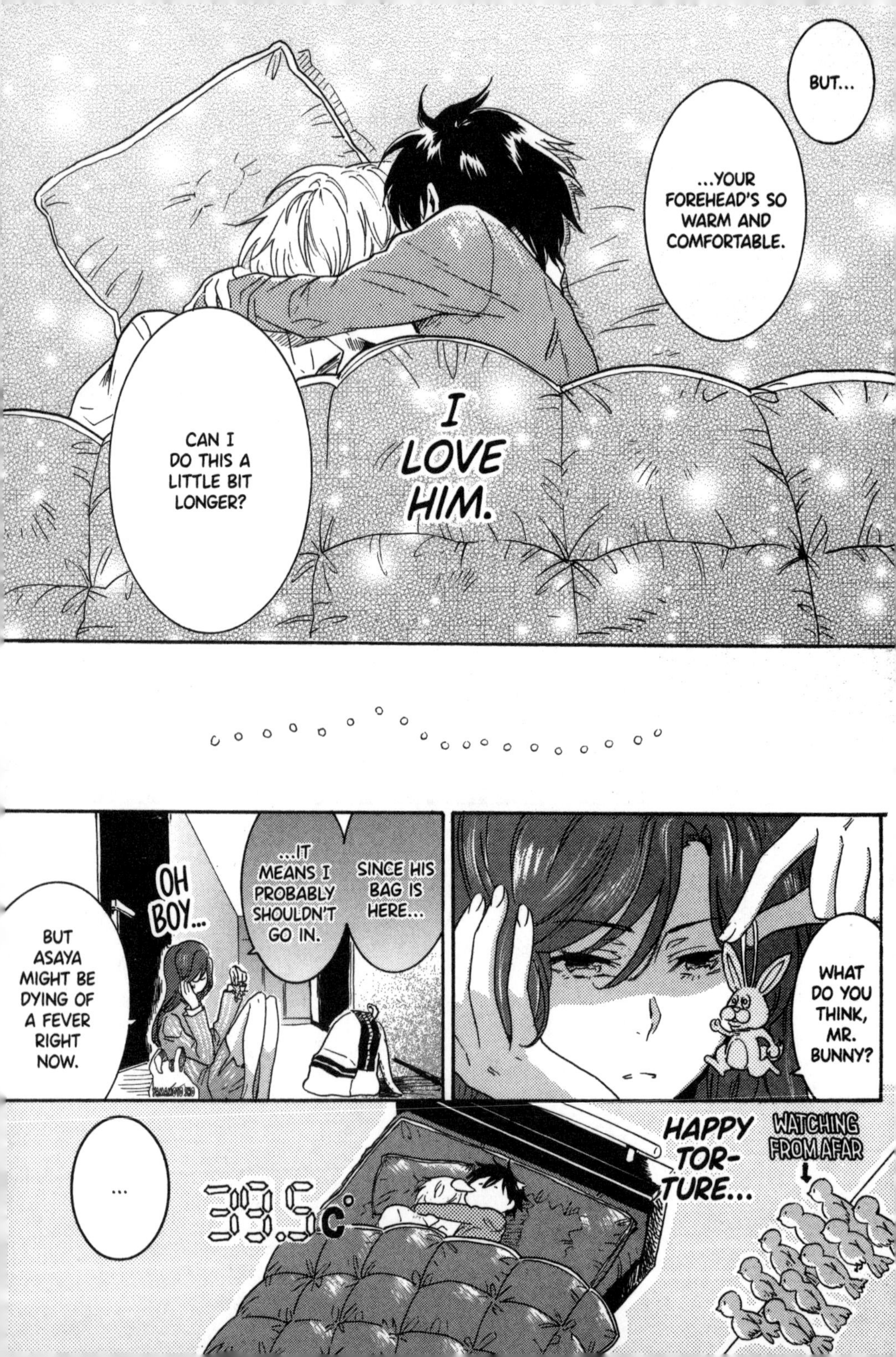
BUT...
...YOUR FOREHEAD'S SO WARM AND COMFORTABLE.
I LOVE HIM.
CAN I DO THIS A LITTLE BIT LONGER?
WHAT DO YOU THINK, MR. BUNNY?
SINCE HIS BAG IS HERE...
...IT MEANS I PROBABLY SHOULDN'T GO IN.
OH BOY...
BUT ASAYA MIGHT BE DYING OF A FEVER RIGHT NOW.
WATCHING FROM AFAR
HAPPY TOR-TURE...
39.5°C
...

Asaya Hasekura
Height: 180 cm
Special skill: Doesn't put on weight no matter how much he eats
Animal he's actually afraid of: Cats (because they stretch a lot)

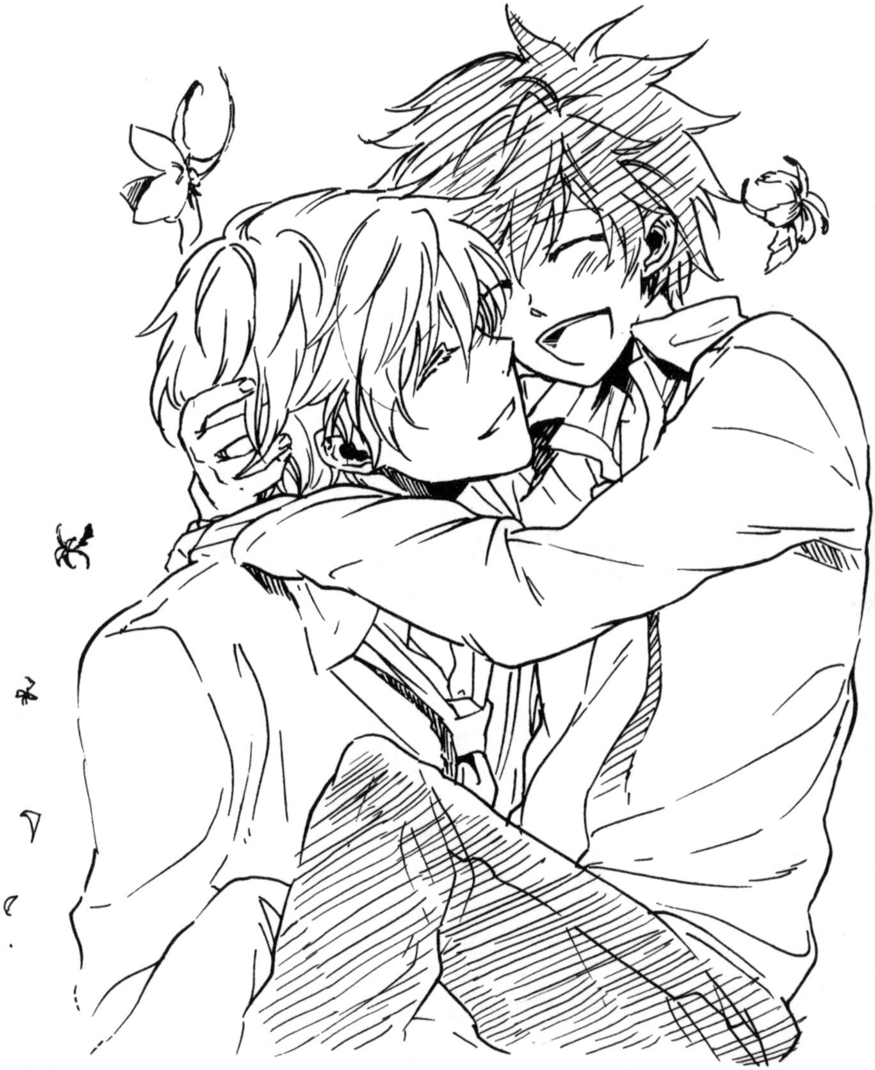

HITORIJIME BOYFRIEND

PRESENTED BY MEMECO ARII

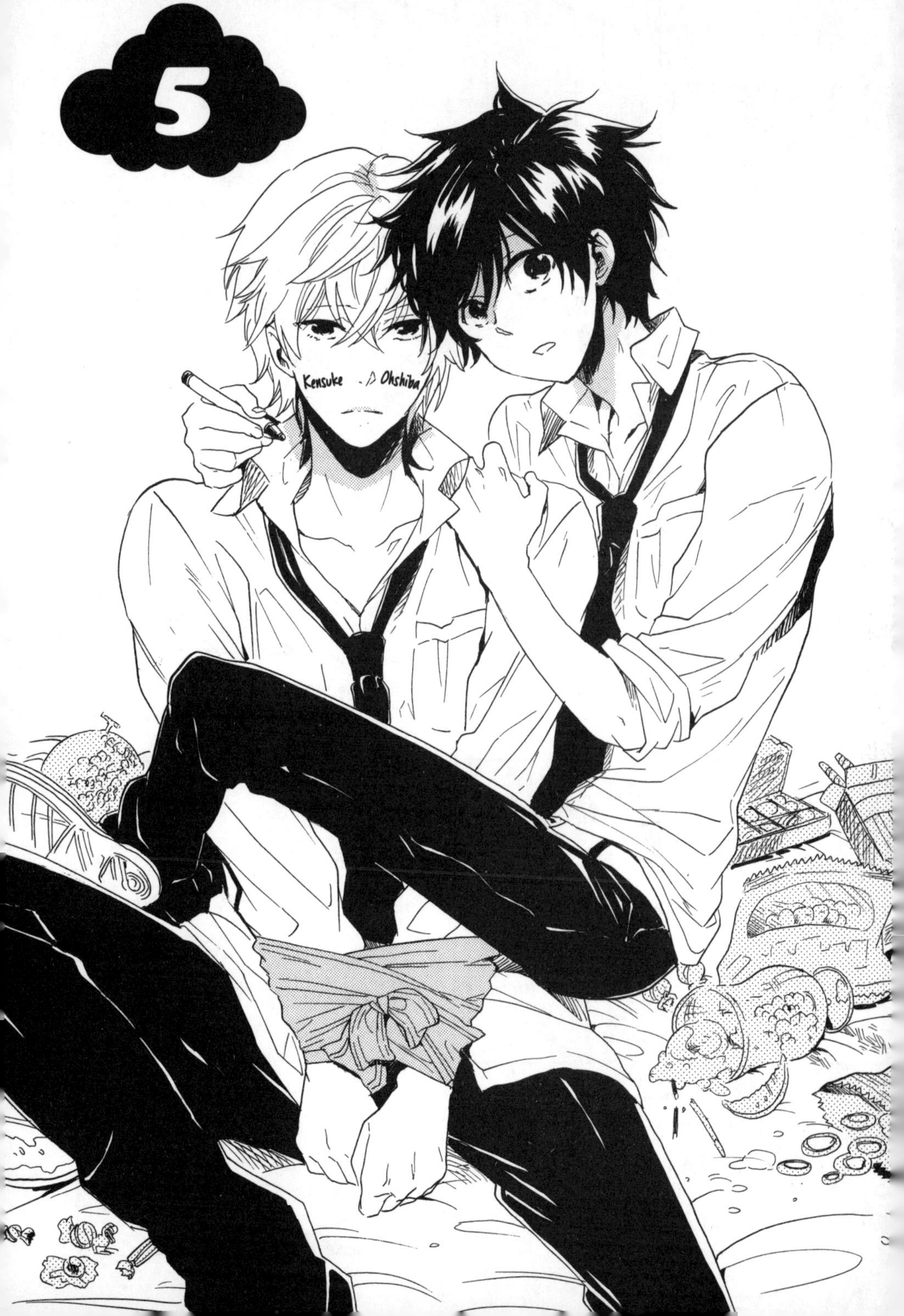
5
Kensuke
Ohshiba

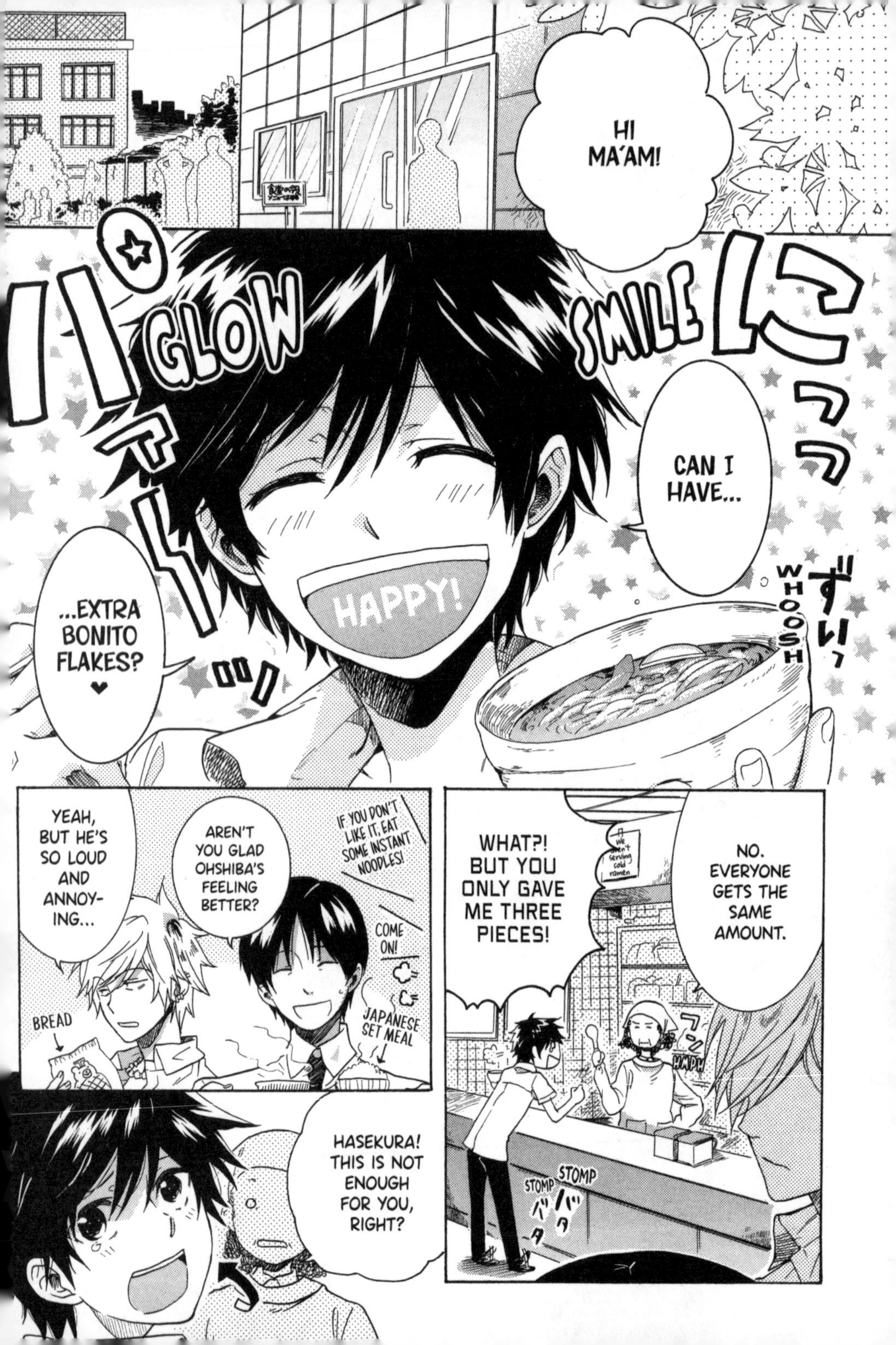
HI MA'AM!
SMILE
にこっ
CAN I HAVE...
WHOOSH
ずいっ
HAPPY!
GLOW
パァ
...EXTRA BONITO FLAKES? ❤
NO. EVERYONE GETS THE SAME AMOUNT.
We aren't serving cold ramen
WHAT?! BUT YOU ONLY GAVE ME THREE PIECES!
フン
HMPH
STOMP
バタ
STOMP
バタ
IF YOU DON'T LIKE IT, EAT SOME INSTANT NOODLES!
COME ON!
AREN'T YOU GLAD OHSHIBA'S FEELING BETTER?
YEAH, BUT HE'S SO LOUD AND ANNOY-ING...
JAPANESE SET MEAL
BREAD
HASEKURA! THIS IS NOT ENOUGH FOR YOU, RIGHT?

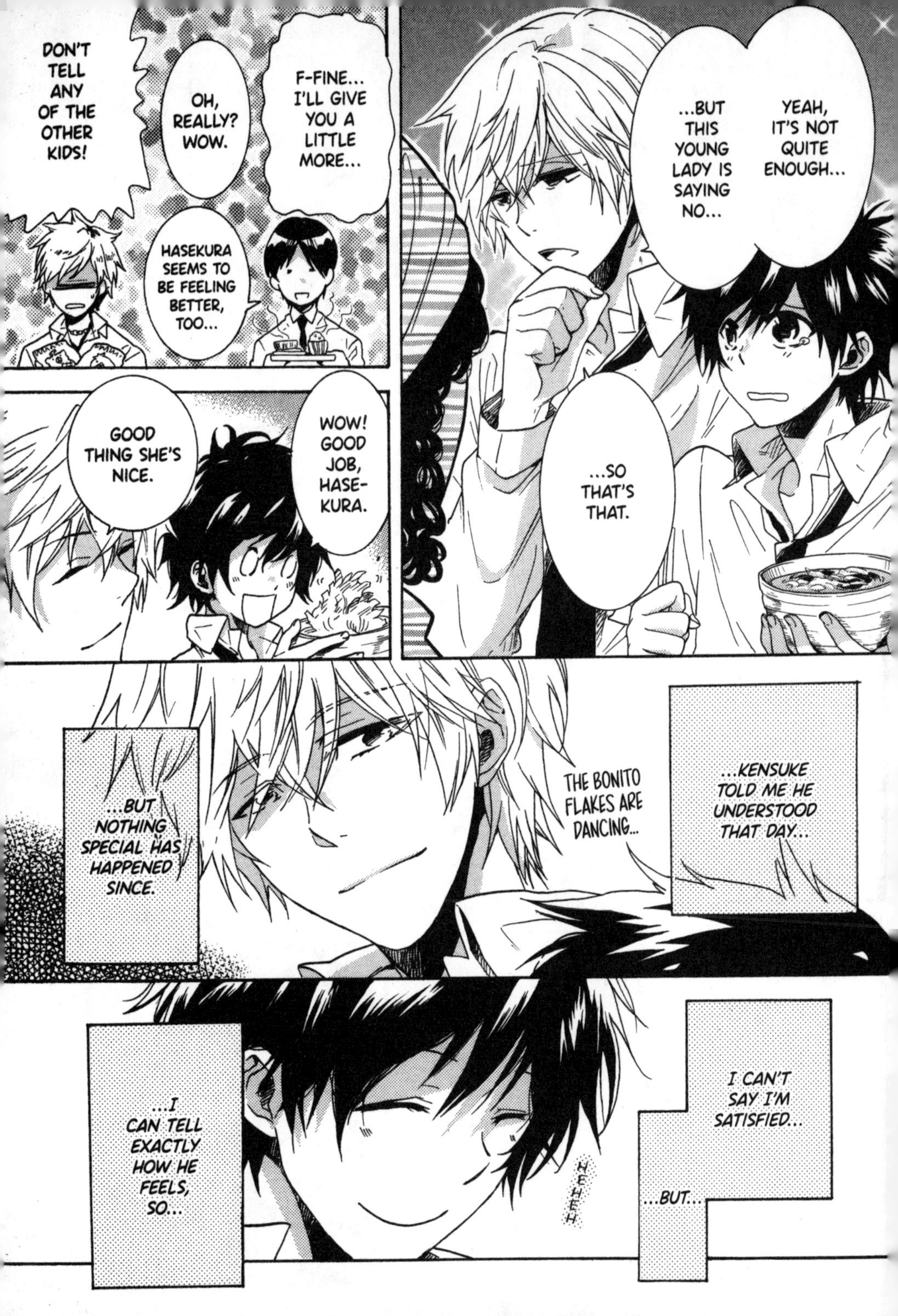
YEAH, IT'S NOT QUITE ENOUGH...
...BUT THIS YOUNG LADY IS SAYING NO...
...SO THAT'S THAT.
F-FINE... I'LL GIVE YOU A LITTLE MORE...
OH, REALLY? WOW.
DON'T TELL ANY OF THE OTHER KIDS!
HASEKURA SEEMS TO BE FEELING BETTER, TOO...
WOW! GOOD JOB, HASE-KURA.
GOOD THING SHE'S NICE.
...KENSUKE TOLD ME HE UNDERSTOOD THAT DAY...
THE BONITO FLAKES ARE DANCING...
...BUT NOTHING SPECIAL HAS HAPPENED SINCE.
I CAN'T SAY I'M SATISFIED...
...BUT...
HEHEH
...I CAN TELL EXACTLY HOW HE FEELS, SO...

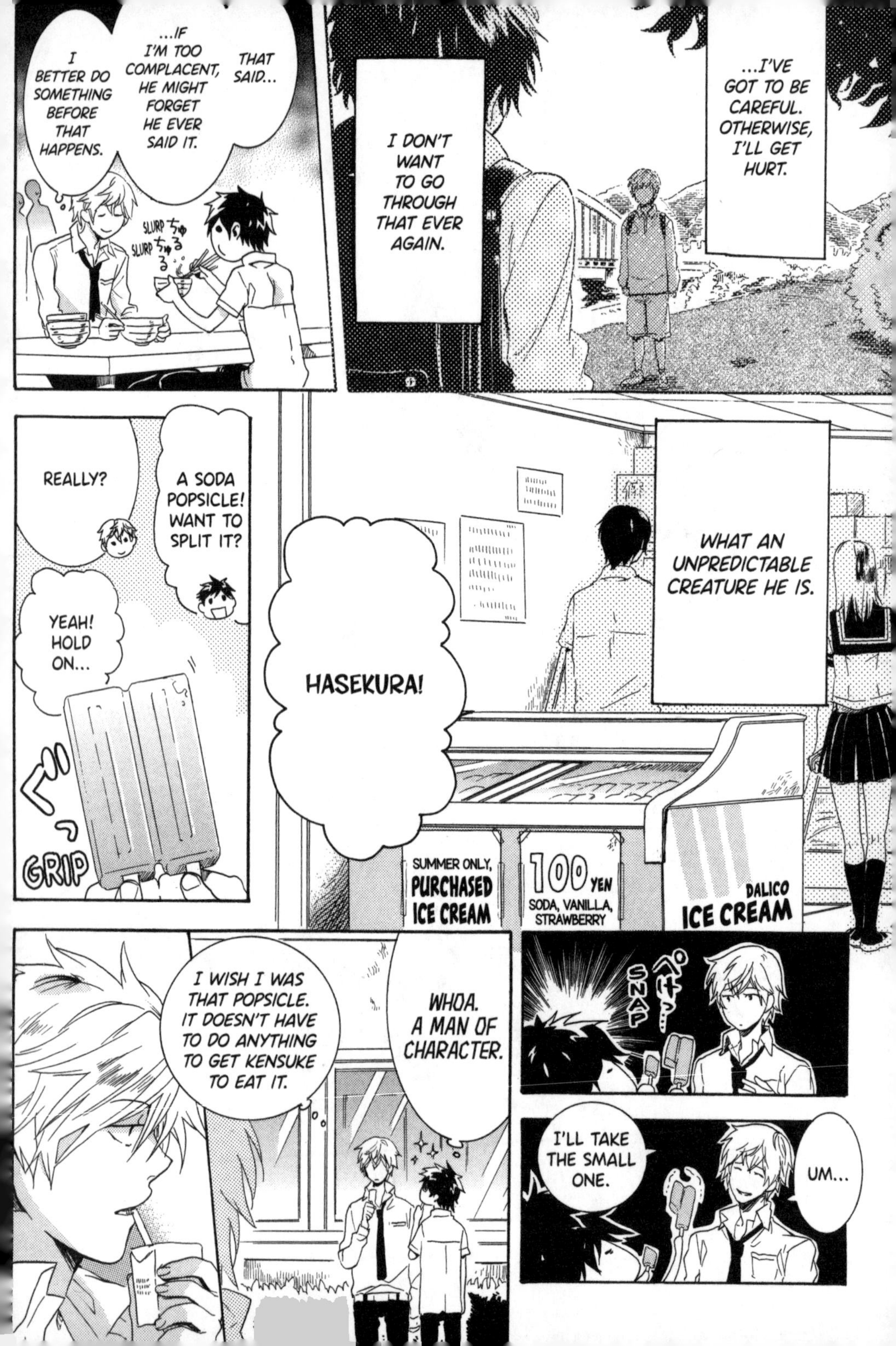

...I'VE GOT TO BE CAREFUL. OTHERWISE, I'LL GET HURT.
I DON'T WANT TO GO THROUGH THAT EVER AGAIN.
THAT SAID...
...IF I'M TOO COMPLACENT, HE MIGHT FORGET HE EVER SAID IT.
I BETTER DO SOMETHING BEFORE THAT HAPPENS.
SLURP
SLURP
WHAT AN UNPREDICTABLE CREATURE HE IS.
HASEKURA!
DALICO ICE CREAM
100 YEN
SODA, VANILLA, STRAWBERRY
SUMMER ONLY, PURCHASED ICE CREAM
A SODA POPSICLE! WANT TO SPLIT IT?
REALLY?
YEAH! HOLD ON...
GRIP
SNAP
UM...
I'LL TAKE THE SMALL ONE.
WHOA. A MAN OF CHARACTER.
I WISH I WAS THAT POPSICLE. IT DOESN'T HAVE TO DO ANYTHING TO GET KENSUKE TO EAT IT.

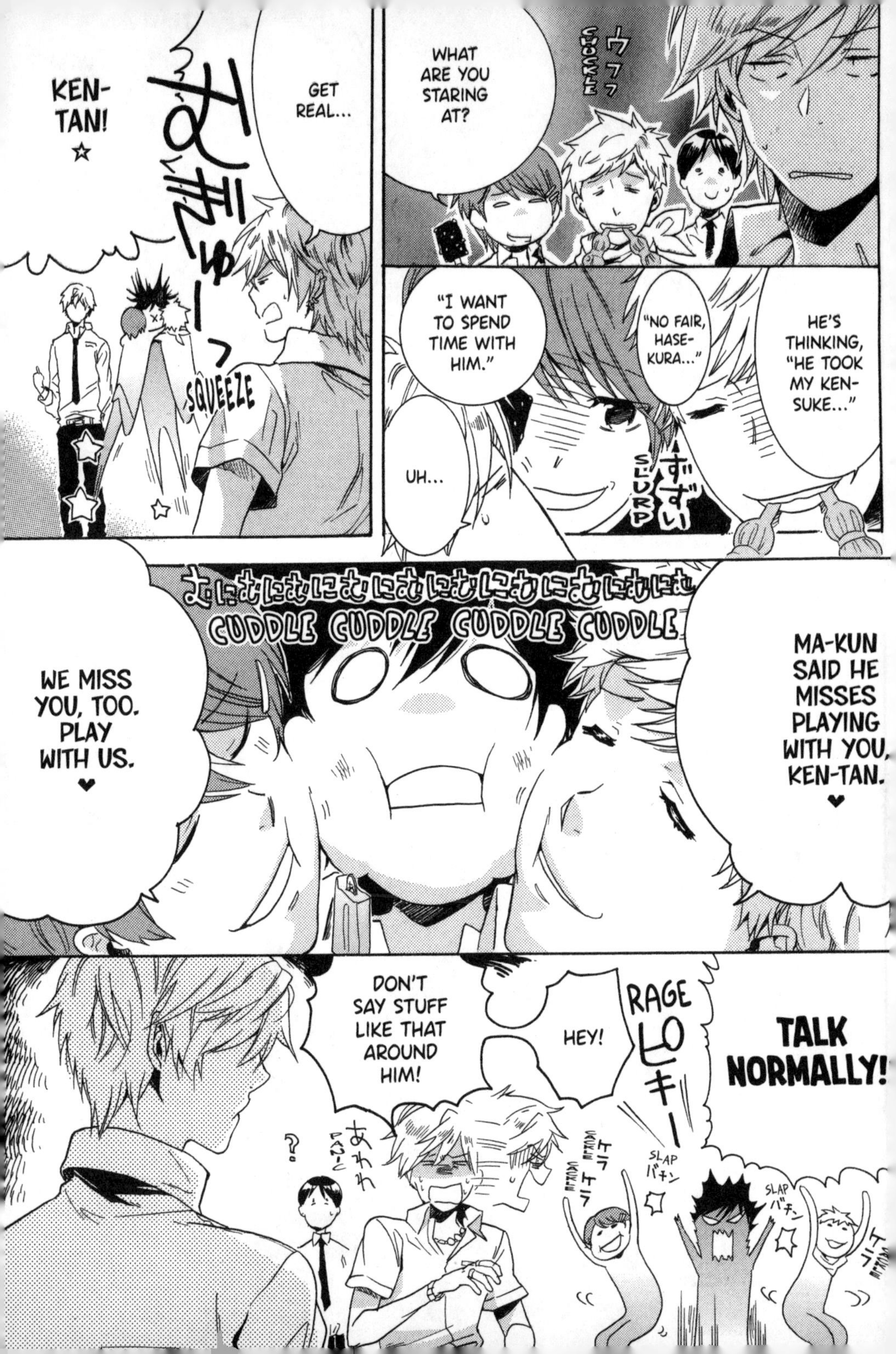
ウフフ
CHUCKLE
WHAT ARE YOU STARING AT?
HE'S THINKING, "HE TOOK MY KEN-SUKE..."
"NO FAIR, HASE-KURA..."
"I WANT TO SPEND TIME WITH HIM."
ずずい
SLURP
UH...
GET REAL...
KEN-TAN! ☆
SQUEEZE
MA-KUN SAID HE MISSES PLAYING WITH YOU, KEN-TAN. ❤
CUDDLE CUDDLE CUDDLE CUDDLE
WE MISS YOU, TOO. PLAY WITH US. ❤
TALK NORMALLY!
RAGE
ピキー
HEY!
DON'T SAY STUFF LIKE THAT AROUND HIM!
SLAP
バチン
SLAP
バチン
ケラ
ケラ
あれ
?

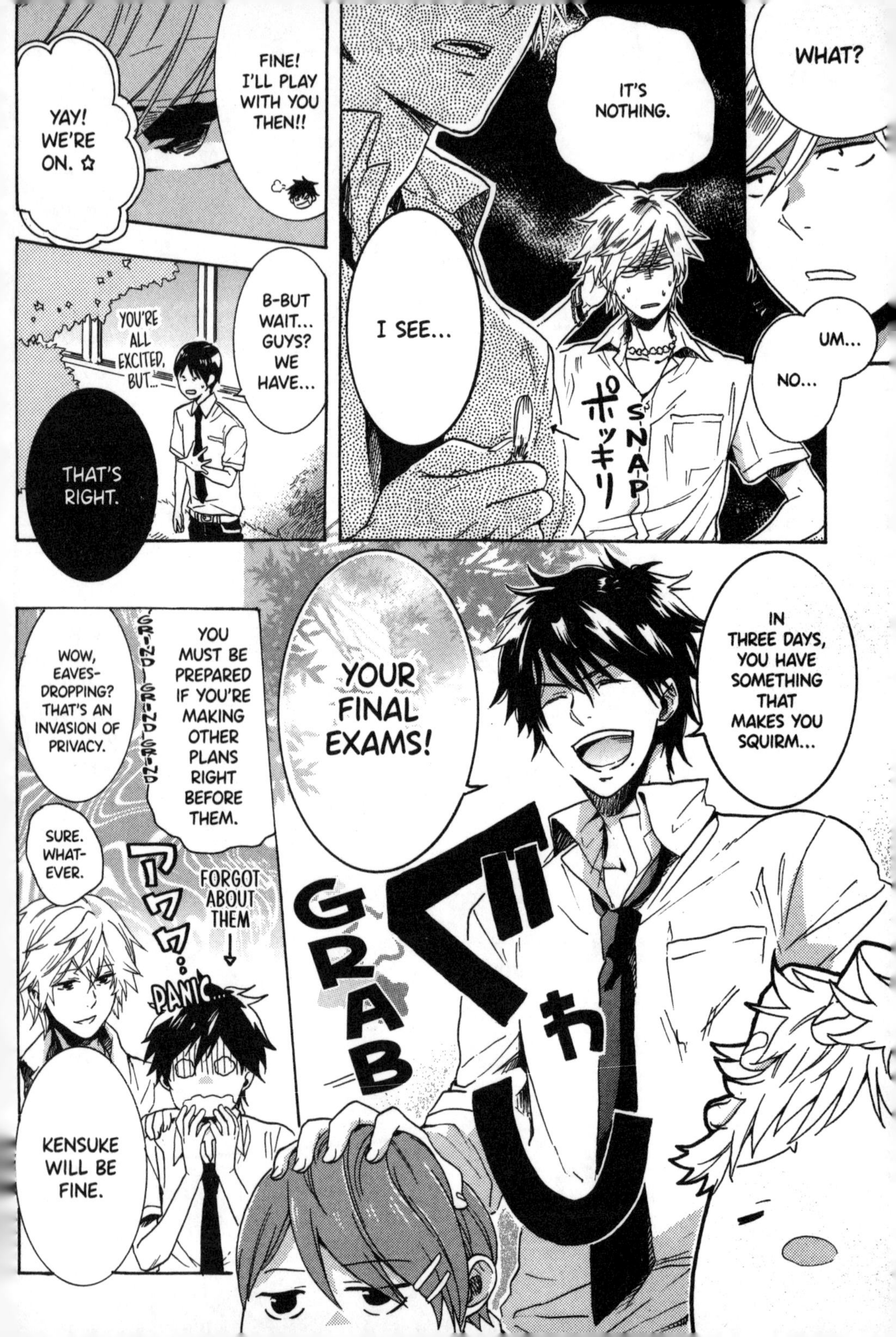
WHAT?
UM... NO...
IT'S NOTHING.
I SEE...
ポッキリ SNAP
FINE! I'LL PLAY WITH YOU THEN!!
YAY! WE'RE ON. ✩
B-BUT WAIT... GUYS? WE HAVE...
YOU'RE ALL EXCITED, BUT...
THAT'S RIGHT.
IN THREE DAYS, YOU HAVE SOMETHING THAT MAKES YOU SQUIRM...
YOUR FINAL EXAMS!
GRAB
YOU MUST BE PREPARED IF YOU'RE MAKING OTHER PLANS RIGHT BEFORE THEM.
GRIND GRIND GRIND GRIND
WOW, EAVES-DROPPING? THAT'S AN INVASION OF PRIVACY.
SURE. WHAT-EVER.
FORGOT ABOUT THEM
アワワ.. PANIC...
KENSUKE WILL BE FINE.

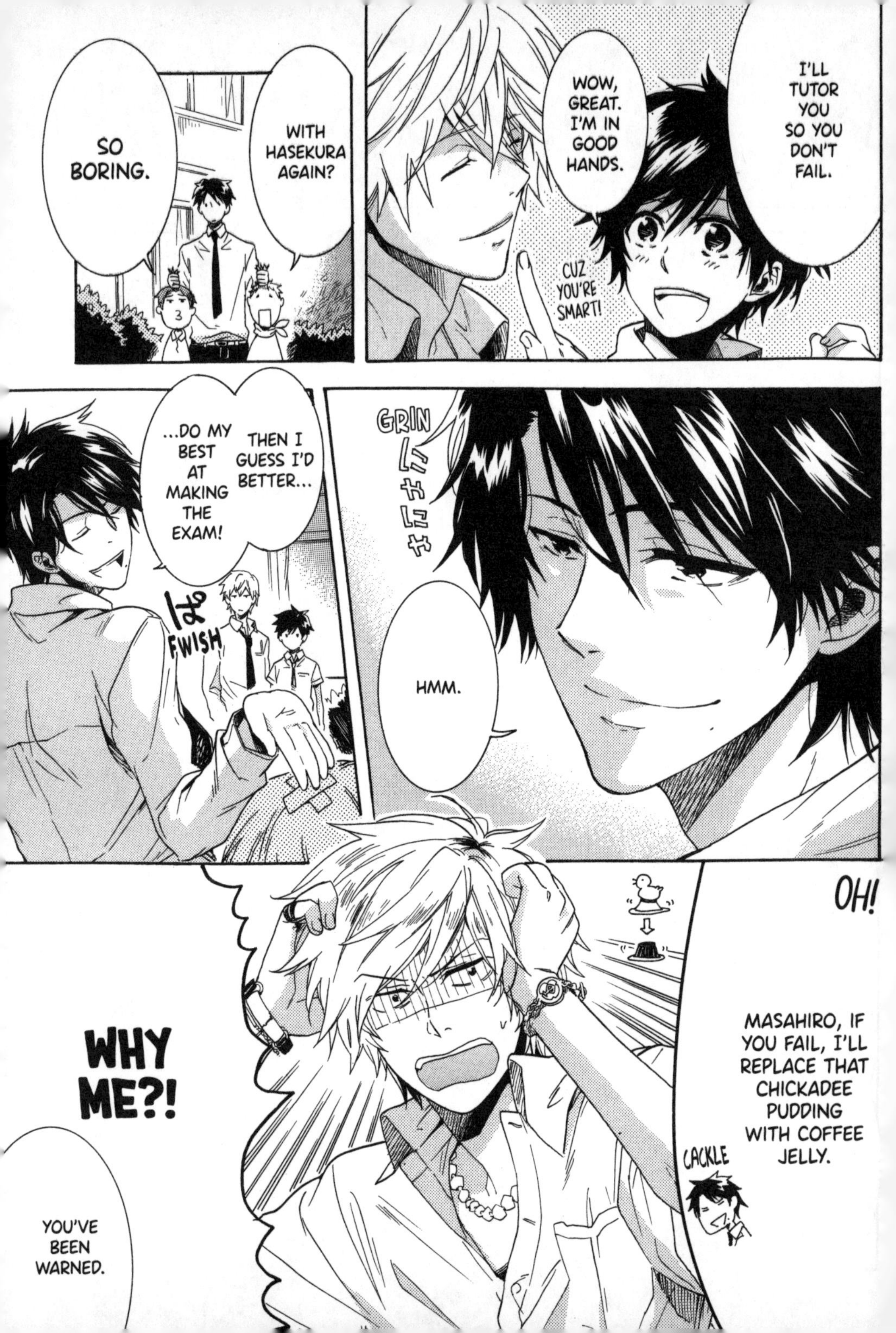
I'LL TUTOR YOU SO YOU DON'T FAIL.
WOW, GREAT. I'M IN GOOD HANDS.
CUZ YOU'RE SMART!
WITH HASEKURA AGAIN?
SO BORING.
GRIN
にやにや
HMM.
THEN I GUESS I'D BETTER...
...DO MY BEST AT MAKING THE EXAM!
ぱ
FWISH
OH!
MASAHIRO, IF YOU FAIL, I'LL REPLACE THAT CHICKADEE PUDDING WITH COFFEE JELLY.
CACKLE
WHY ME?!
YOU'VE BEEN WARNED.

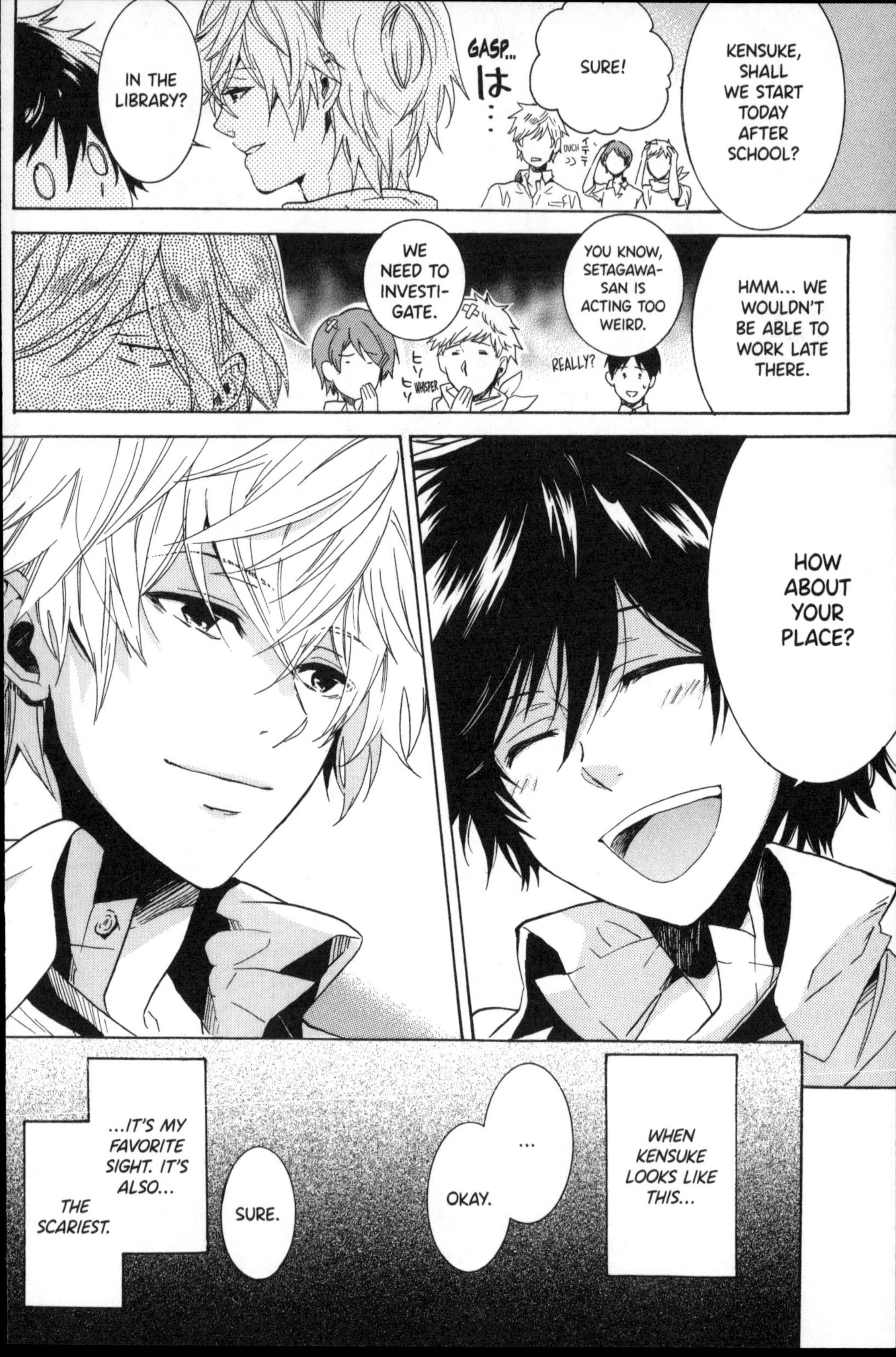
KENSUKE, SHALL WE START TODAY AFTER SCHOOL?
SURE!
GASP... は...
OUCH
IN THE LIBRARY?
HMM... WE WOULDN'T BE ABLE TO WORK LATE THERE.
YOU KNOW, SETAGAWA-SAN IS ACTING TOO WEIRD.
REALLY?
WE NEED TO INVESTI-GATE.
WHISPER
HOW ABOUT YOUR PLACE?
WHEN KENSUKE LOOKS LIKE THIS...
... OKAY.
SURE.
...IT'S MY FAVORITE SIGHT. IT'S ALSO... THE SCARIEST.

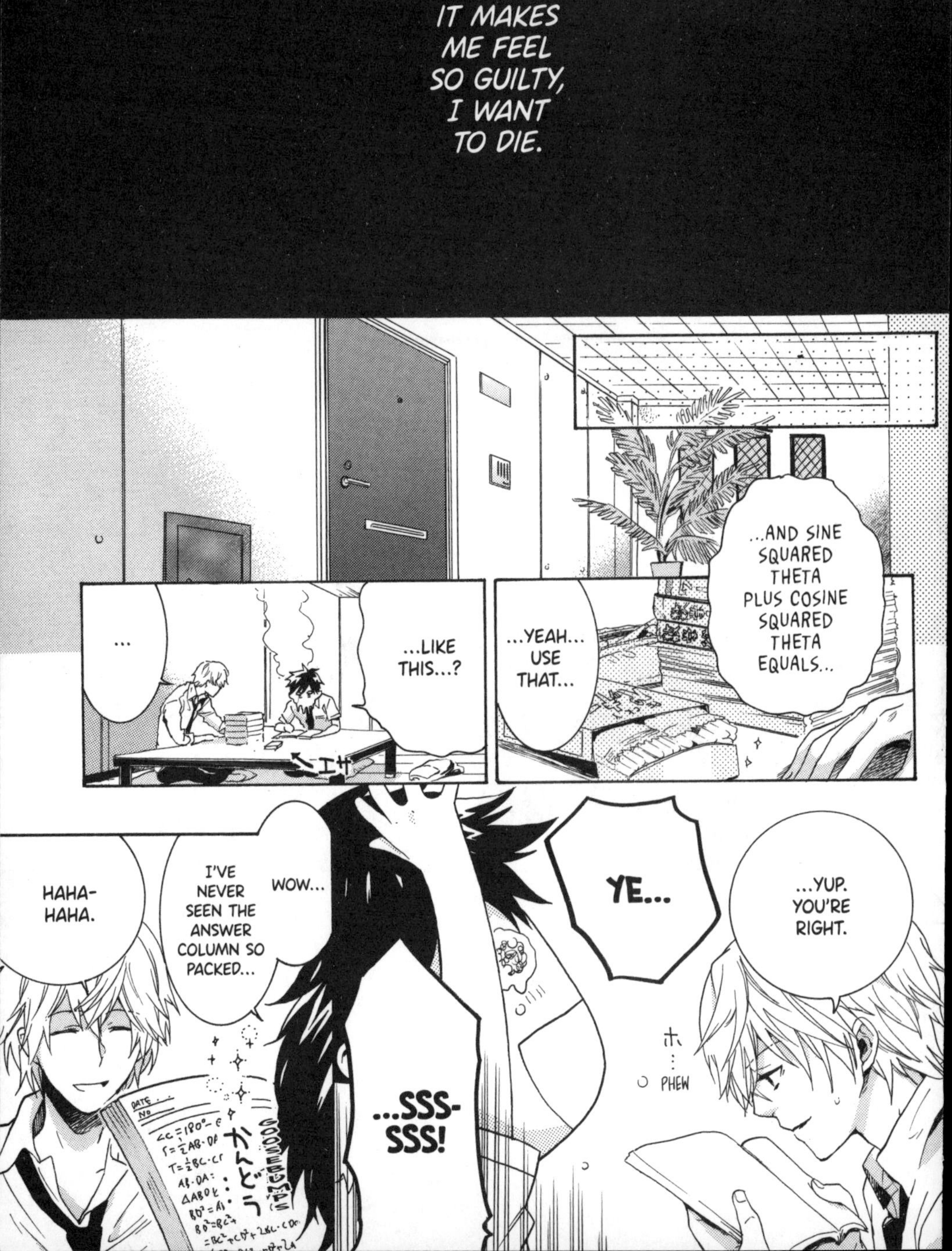
IT MAKES ME FEEL SO GUILTY, I WANT TO DIE.
...AND SINE SQUARED THETA PLUS COSINE SQUARED THETA EQUALS...
...YEAH... USE THAT...
...LIKE THIS...?
...
...YUP. YOU'RE RIGHT.
PHEW
YE...
...SSS-SSS!
WOW...
I'VE NEVER SEEN THE ANSWER COLUMN SO PACKED...
HAHA-HAHA.
GOOSEBUMPS

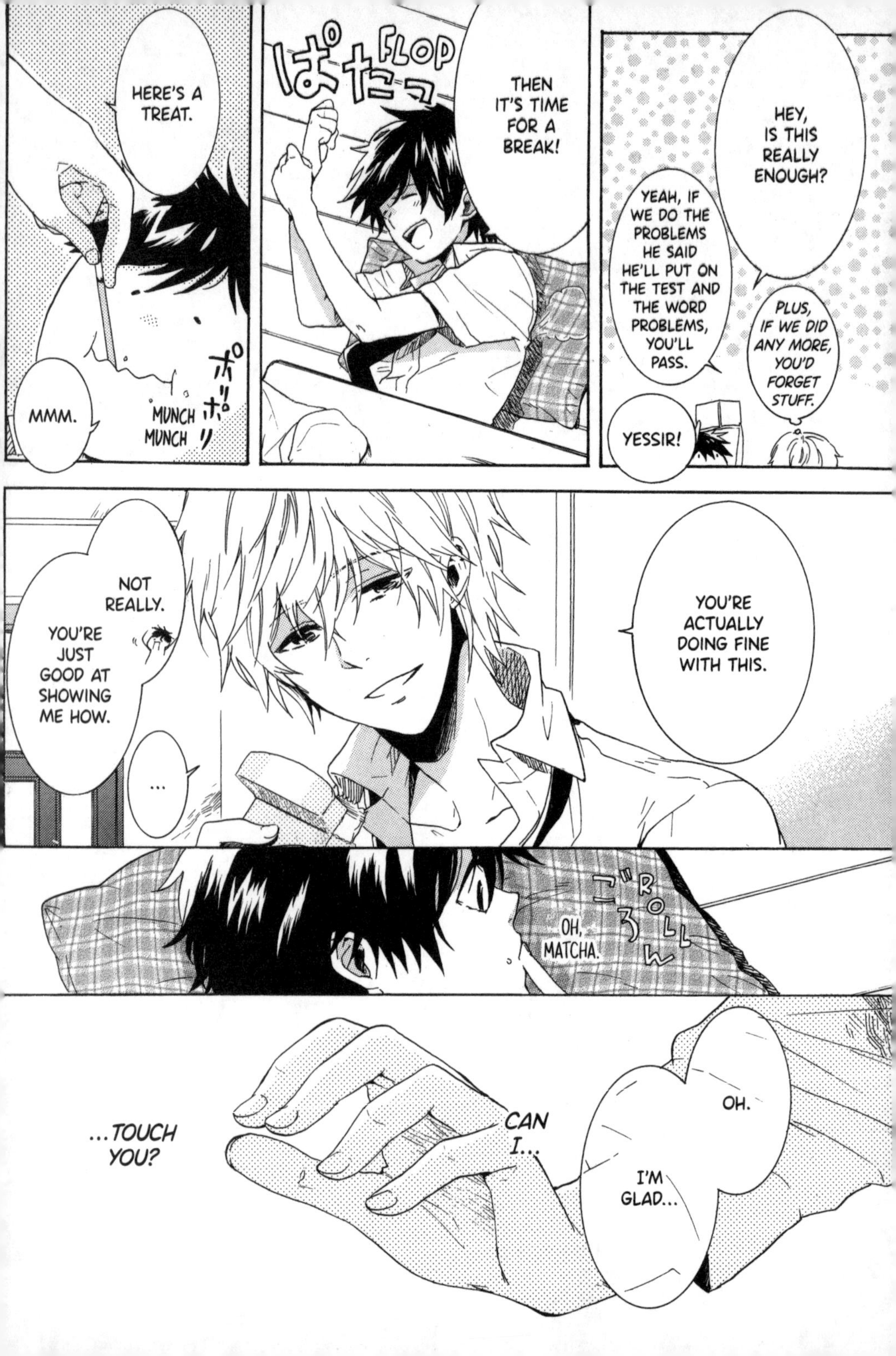
HEY, IS THIS REALLY ENOUGH?
YEAH, IF WE DO THE PROBLEMS HE SAID HE'LL PUT ON THE TEST AND THE WORD PROBLEMS, YOU'LL PASS.
PLUS, IF WE DID ANY MORE, YOU'D FORGET STUFF.
YESSIR!
ぱたっ FLOP
THEN IT'S TIME FOR A BREAK!
HERE'S A TREAT.
ポリポリ MUNCH MUNCH
MMM.
YOU'RE ACTUALLY DOING FINE WITH THIS.
NOT REALLY. YOU'RE JUST GOOD AT SHOWING ME HOW.
...
ごろ ROLL
OH, MATCHA.
OH.
I'M GLAD...
CAN I...
...TOUCH YOU?

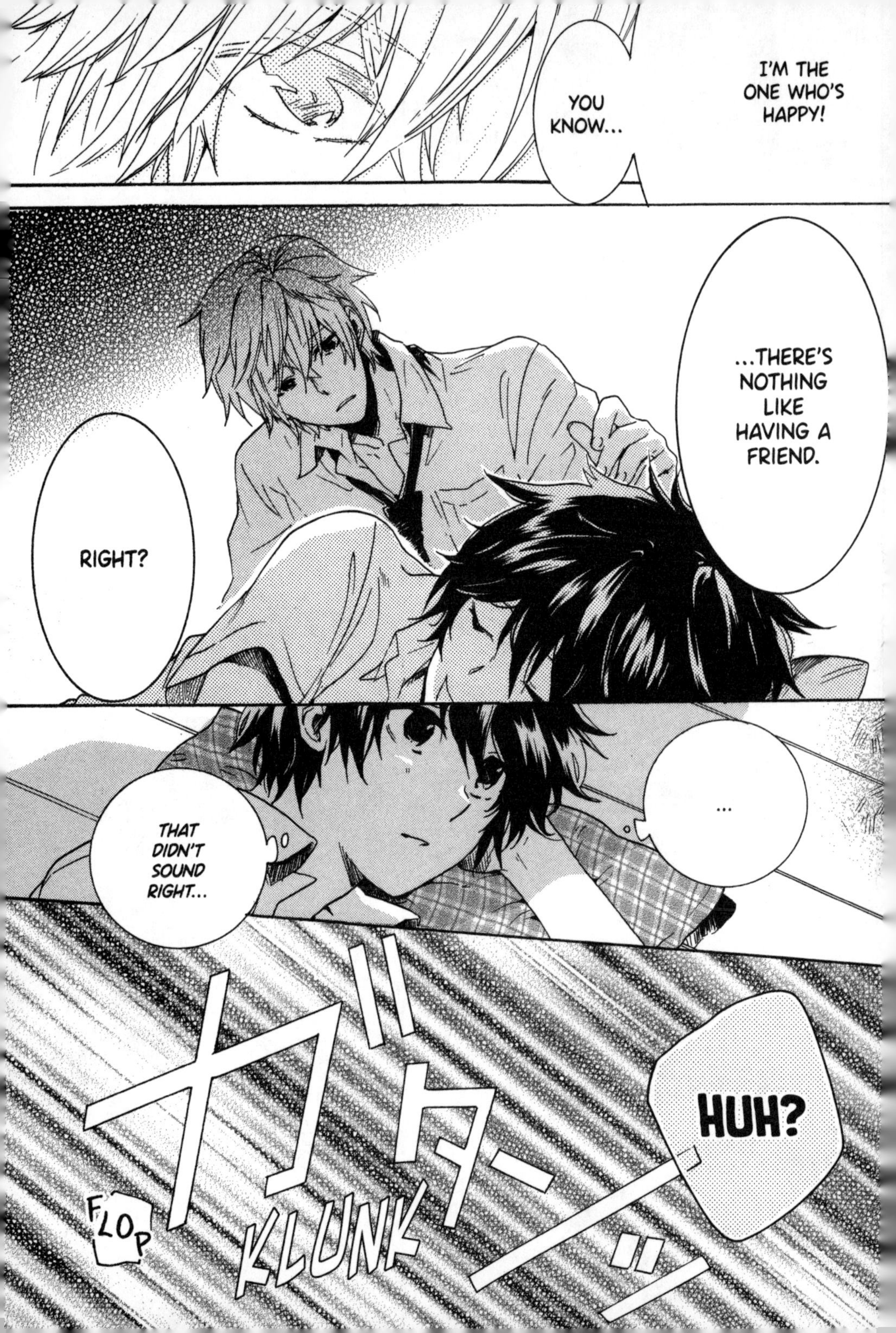
I'M THE ONE WHO'S HAPPY!
YOU KNOW...
...THERE'S NOTHING LIKE HAVING A FRIEND.
RIGHT?
...
THAT DIDN'T SOUND RIGHT...
HUH?
KLUNK
FLOP

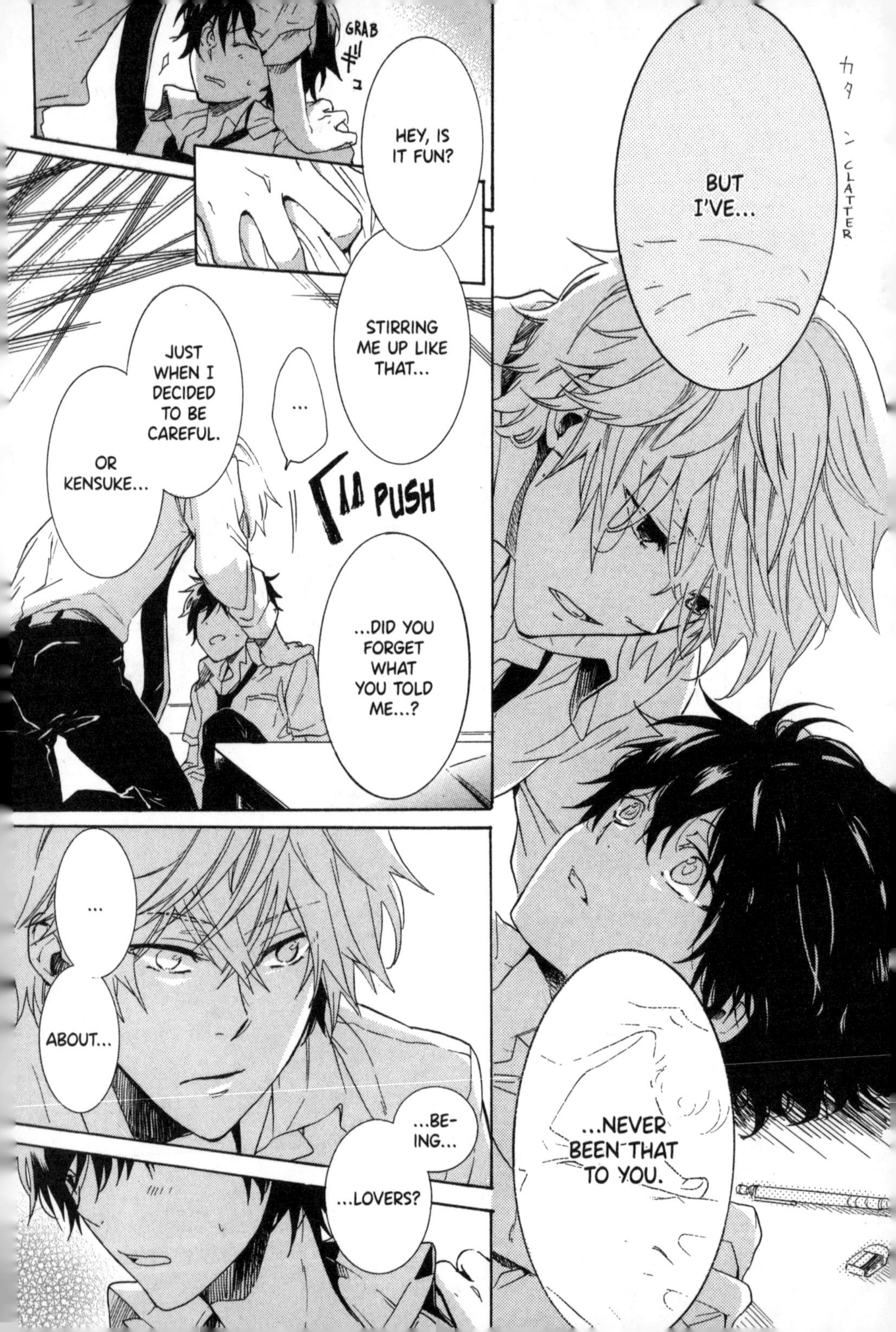

カタン CLATTER
BUT I'VE...
...NEVER BEEN THAT TO YOU.
GRAB ギュ
HEY, IS IT FUN?
STIRRING ME UP LIKE THAT...
...
JUST WHEN I DECIDED TO BE CAREFUL.
OR KENSUKE...
PUSH
...DID YOU FORGET WHAT YOU TOLD ME...?
...
ABOUT...
...BE-ING...
...LOVERS?

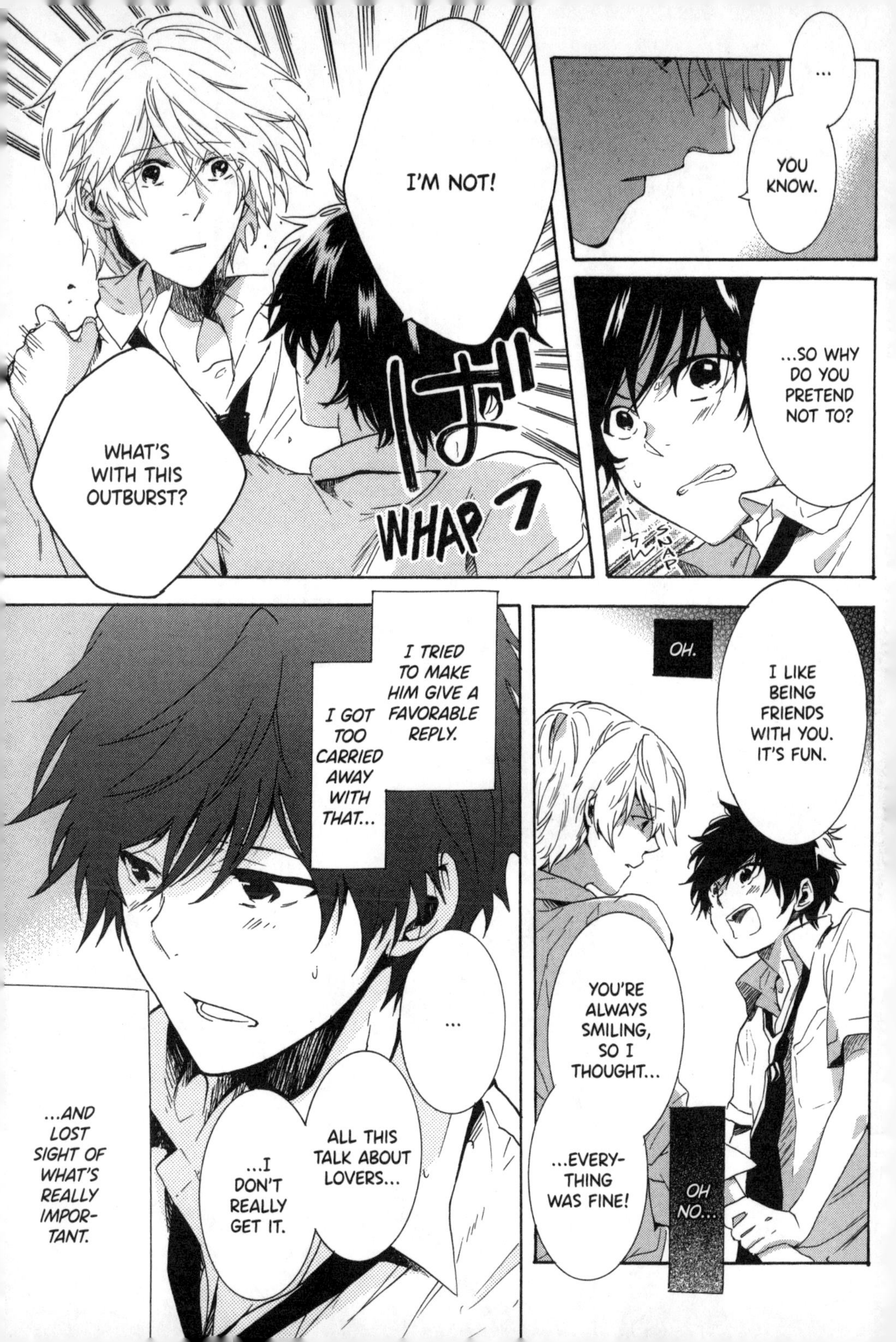
...
YOU KNOW.
...SO WHY DO YOU PRETEND NOT TO?
SNAP
I'M NOT!
WHAP
WHAT'S WITH THIS OUTBURST?
OH.
I LIKE BEING FRIENDS WITH YOU. IT'S FUN.
YOU'RE ALWAYS SMILING, SO I THOUGHT...
...EVERY-THING WAS FINE!
OH NO...
I TRIED TO MAKE HIM GIVE A FAVORABLE REPLY.
I GOT TOO CARRIED AWAY WITH THAT...
...
ALL THIS TALK ABOUT LOVERS...
...I DON'T REALLY GET IT.
...AND LOST SIGHT OF WHAT'S REALLY IMPOR-TANT.

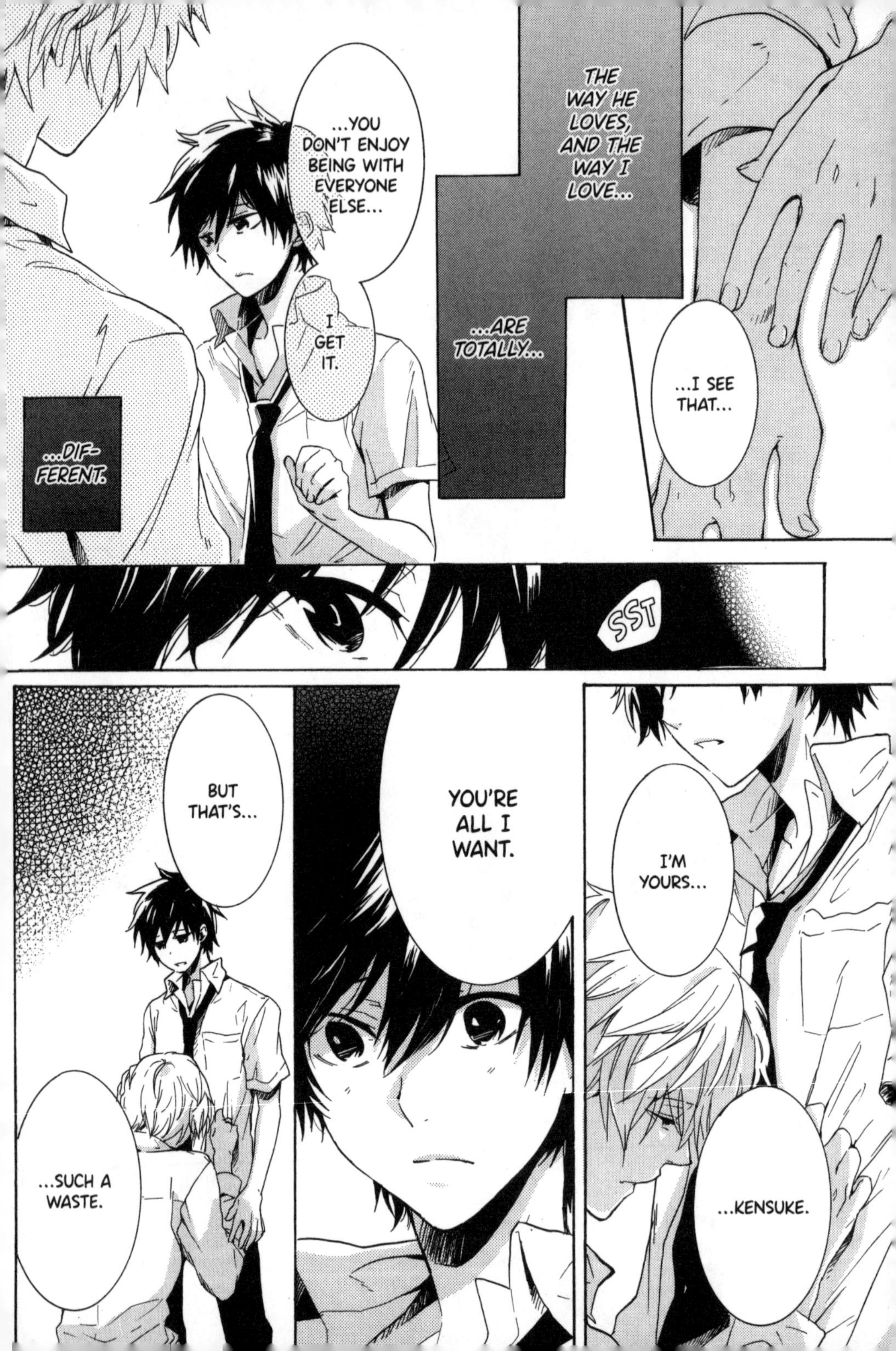
THE WAY HE LOVES, AND THE WAY I LOVE...
...I SEE THAT...
...ARE TOTALLY...
...YOU DON'T ENJOY BEING WITH EVERYONE ELSE...
I GET IT.
...DIF-FERENT.
SST
I'M YOURS...
...KENSUKE.
YOU'RE ALL I WANT.
BUT THAT'S...
...SUCH A WASTE.

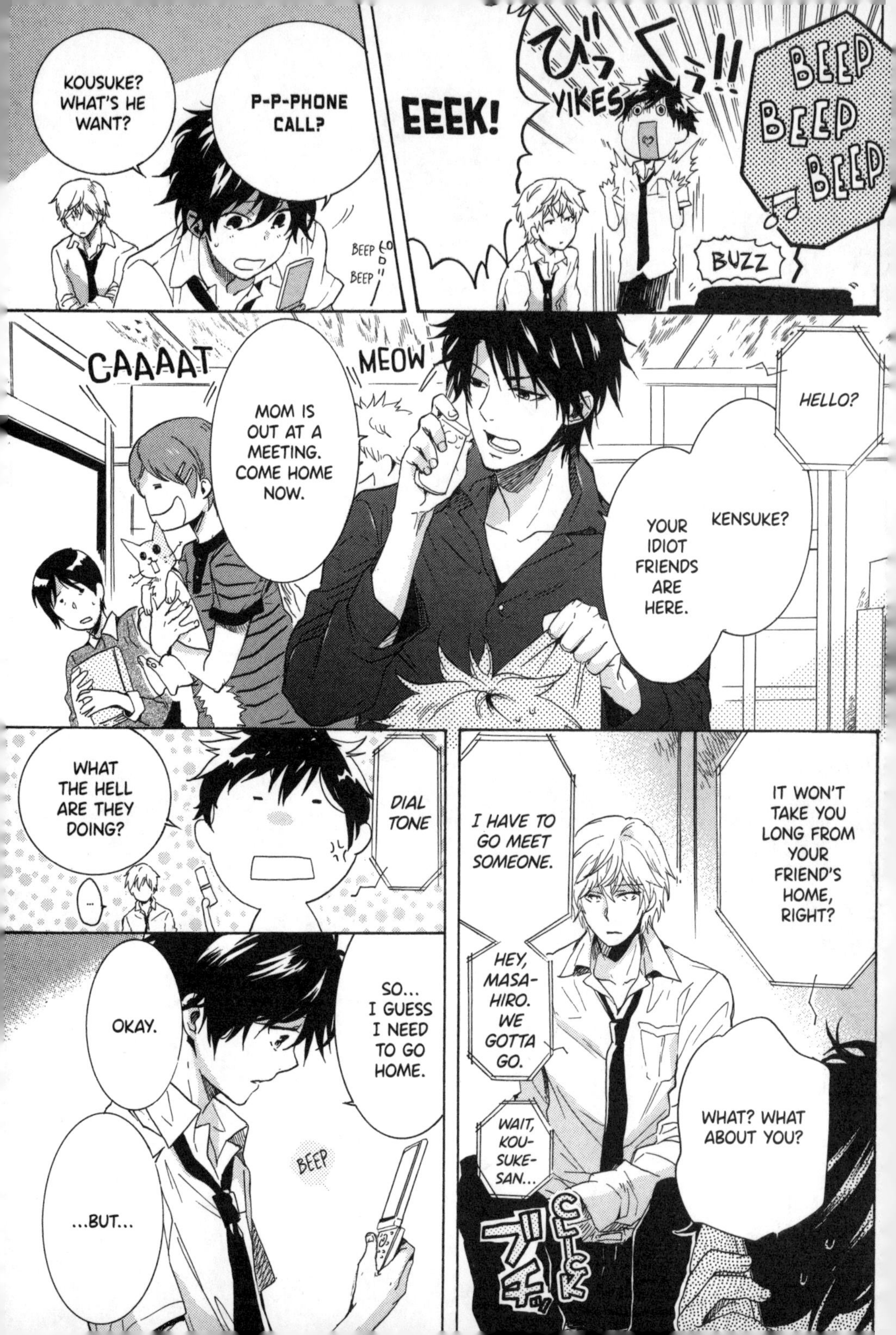
BEEP BEEP BEEP
BUZZ
びっくぅ!!
YIKES
EEEK!
P-P-PHONE CALL?
KOUSUKE? WHAT'S HE WANT?
BEEP BEEP
HELLO?
KENSUKE?
YOUR IDIOT FRIENDS ARE HERE.
MEOW
MOM IS OUT AT A MEETING. COME HOME NOW.
CAAAAT
IT WON'T TAKE YOU LONG FROM YOUR FRIEND'S HOME, RIGHT?
I HAVE TO GO MEET SOMEONE.
HEY, MASA-HIRO. WE GOTTA GO.
WHAT? WHAT ABOUT YOU?
WAIT, KOU-SUKE-SAN...
CLICK
ブチッ
DIAL TONE
WHAT THE HELL ARE THEY DOING?
...
SO... I GUESS I NEED TO GO HOME.
OKAY.
BEEP
...BUT...

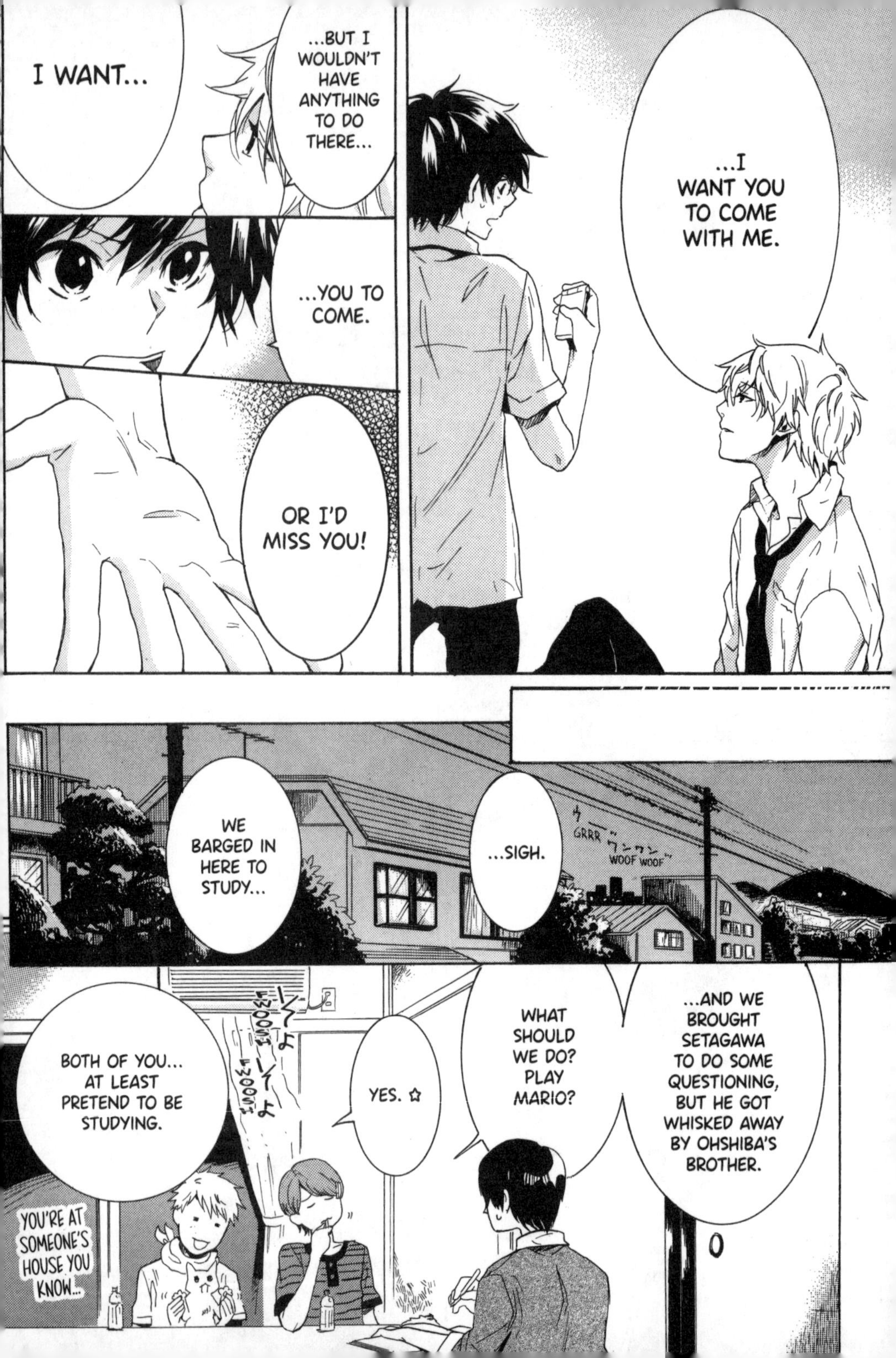
...I WANT YOU TO COME WITH ME.
...BUT I WOULDN'T HAVE ANYTHING TO DO THERE...
I WANT...
...YOU TO COME.
OR I'D MISS YOU!
WOOF WOOF
GRRR
...SIGH.
WE BARGED IN HERE TO STUDY...
...AND WE BROUGHT SETAGAWA TO DO SOME QUESTIONING, BUT HE GOT WHISKED AWAY BY OHSHIBA'S BROTHER.
WHAT SHOULD WE DO? PLAY MARIO?
YES. ☆
FWOOSH
FWOOSH
BOTH OF YOU... AT LEAST PRETEND TO BE STUDYING.
YOU'RE AT SOMEONE'S HOUSE YOU KNOW...

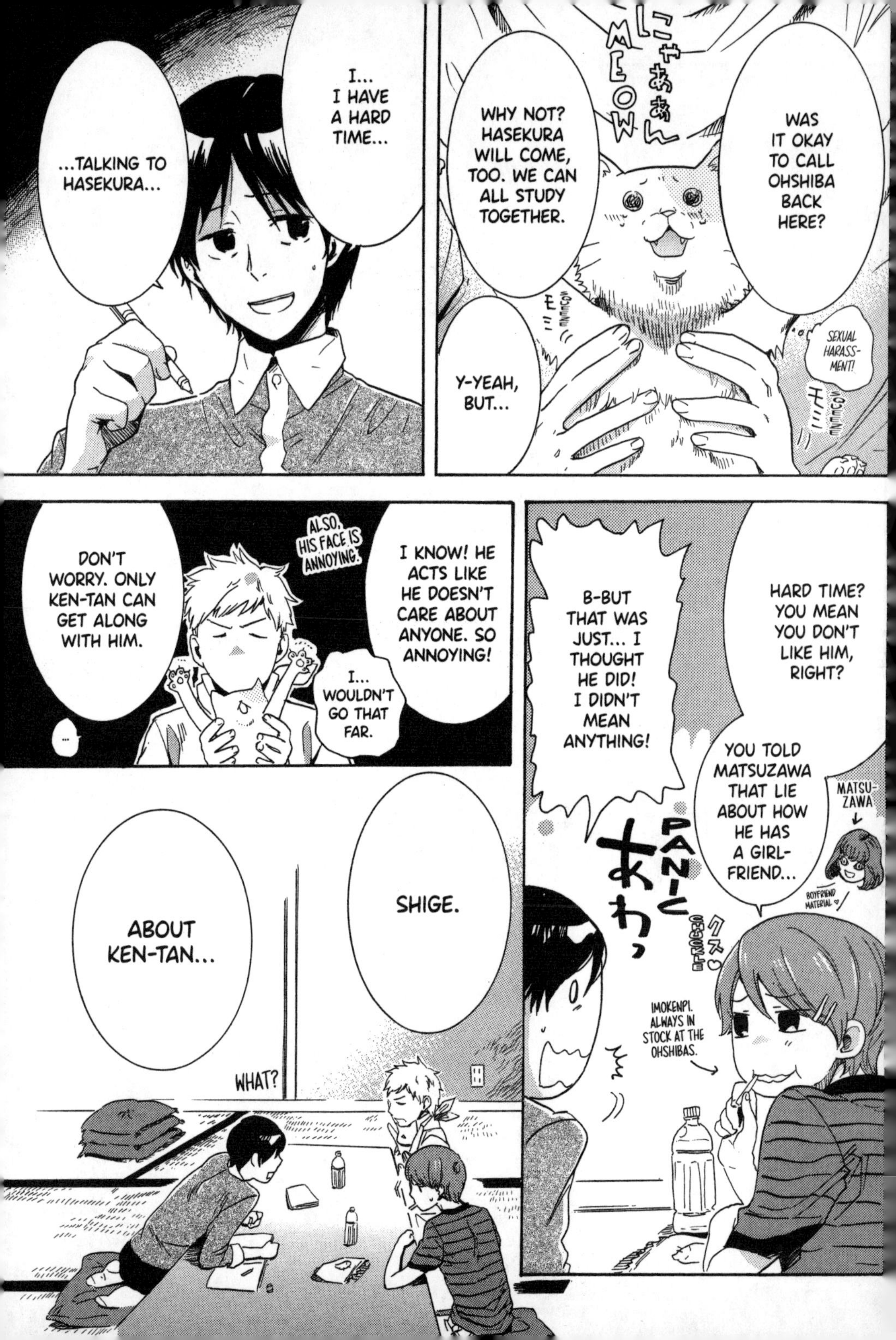
WAS IT OKAY TO CALL OHSHIBA BACK HERE?
にゃあぁん MEOW
WHY NOT? HASEKURA WILL COME, TOO. WE CAN ALL STUDY TOGETHER.
SEXUAL HARASS-MENT!
モミ SQUEEZE
モミ SQUEEZE
Y-YEAH, BUT...
I... I HAVE A HARD TIME...
...TALKING TO HASEKURA...
HARD TIME? YOU MEAN YOU DON'T LIKE HIM, RIGHT?
B-BUT THAT WAS JUST... I THOUGHT HE DID! I DIDN'T MEAN ANYTHING!
YOU TOLD MATSUZAWA THAT LIE ABOUT HOW HE HAS A GIRL-FRIEND...
MATSU-ZAWA
BOYFRIEND MATERIAL ♡
あわっ PANIC
クス♡ CHUCKLE
IMOKENPI. ALWAYS IN STOCK AT THE OHSHIBAS.
I KNOW! HE ACTS LIKE HE DOESN'T CARE ABOUT ANYONE. SO ANNOYING!
ALSO, HIS FACE IS ANNOYING.
I... WOULDN'T GO THAT FAR.
DON'T WORRY. ONLY KEN-TAN CAN GET ALONG WITH HIM.
...
SHIGE.
ABOUT KEN-TAN...
WHAT?

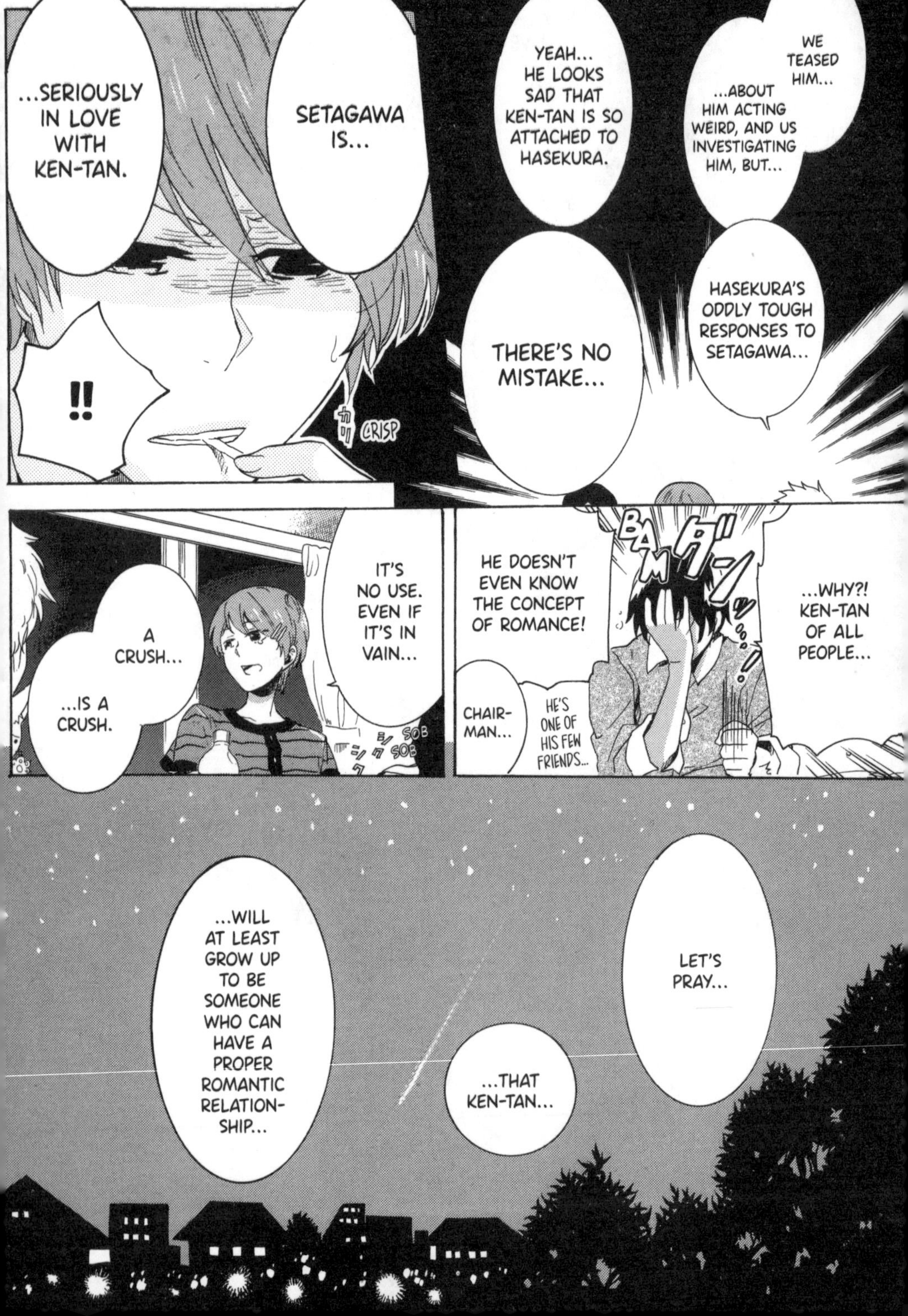
WE TEASED HIM...
...ABOUT HIM ACTING WEIRD, AND US INVESTIGATING HIM, BUT...
HASEKURA'S ODDLY TOUGH RESPONSES TO SETAGAWA...
YEAH... HE LOOKS SAD THAT KEN-TAN IS SO ATTACHED TO HASEKURA.
THERE'S NO MISTAKE...
SETAGAWA IS...
...SERIOUSLY IN LOVE WITH KEN-TAN.
!!
CRISP
...WHY?! KEN-TAN OF ALL PEOPLE...
BAM
HE DOESN'T EVEN KNOW THE CONCEPT OF ROMANCE!
HE'S ONE OF HIS FEW FRIENDS...
CHAIR-MAN...
IT'S NO USE. EVEN IF IT'S IN VAIN...
A CRUSH...
...IS A CRUSH.
SOB SOB
LET'S PRAY...
...THAT KEN-TAN...
...WILL AT LEAST GROW UP TO BE SOMEONE WHO CAN HAVE A PROPER ROMANTIC RELATION-SHIP...

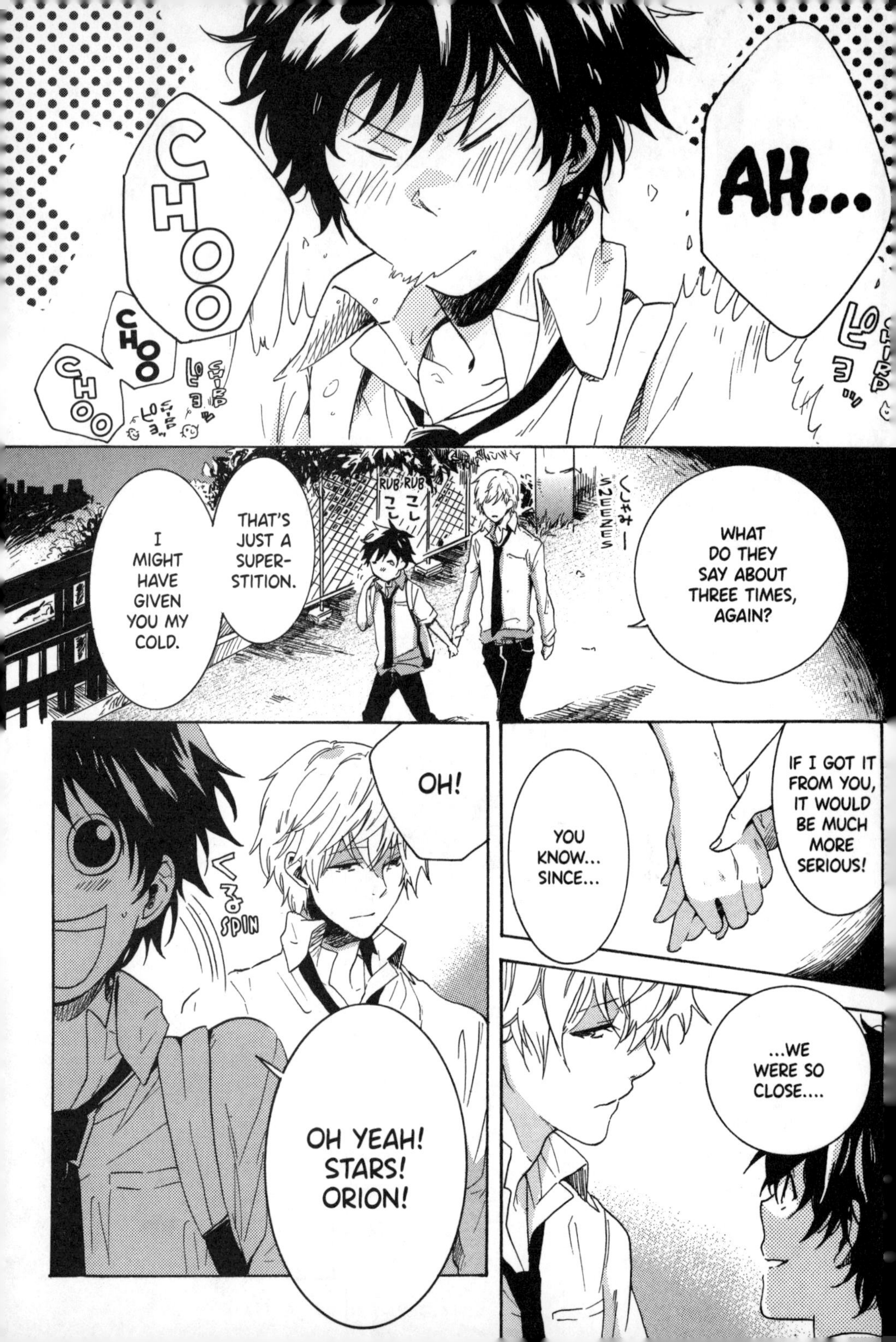
AH...
SHIRP
CHOO
CHOO
CHOO
SHIRP
WHAT DO THEY SAY ABOUT THREE TIMES, AGAIN?
SNEEZE
RUB RUB
こし こし
THAT'S JUST A SUPERSTITION.
I MIGHT HAVE GIVEN YOU MY COLD.
IF I GOT IT FROM YOU, IT WOULD BE MUCH MORE SERIOUS!
YOU KNOW... SINCE...
...WE WERE SO CLOSE....
OH!
SPIN
OH YEAH! STARS! ORION!

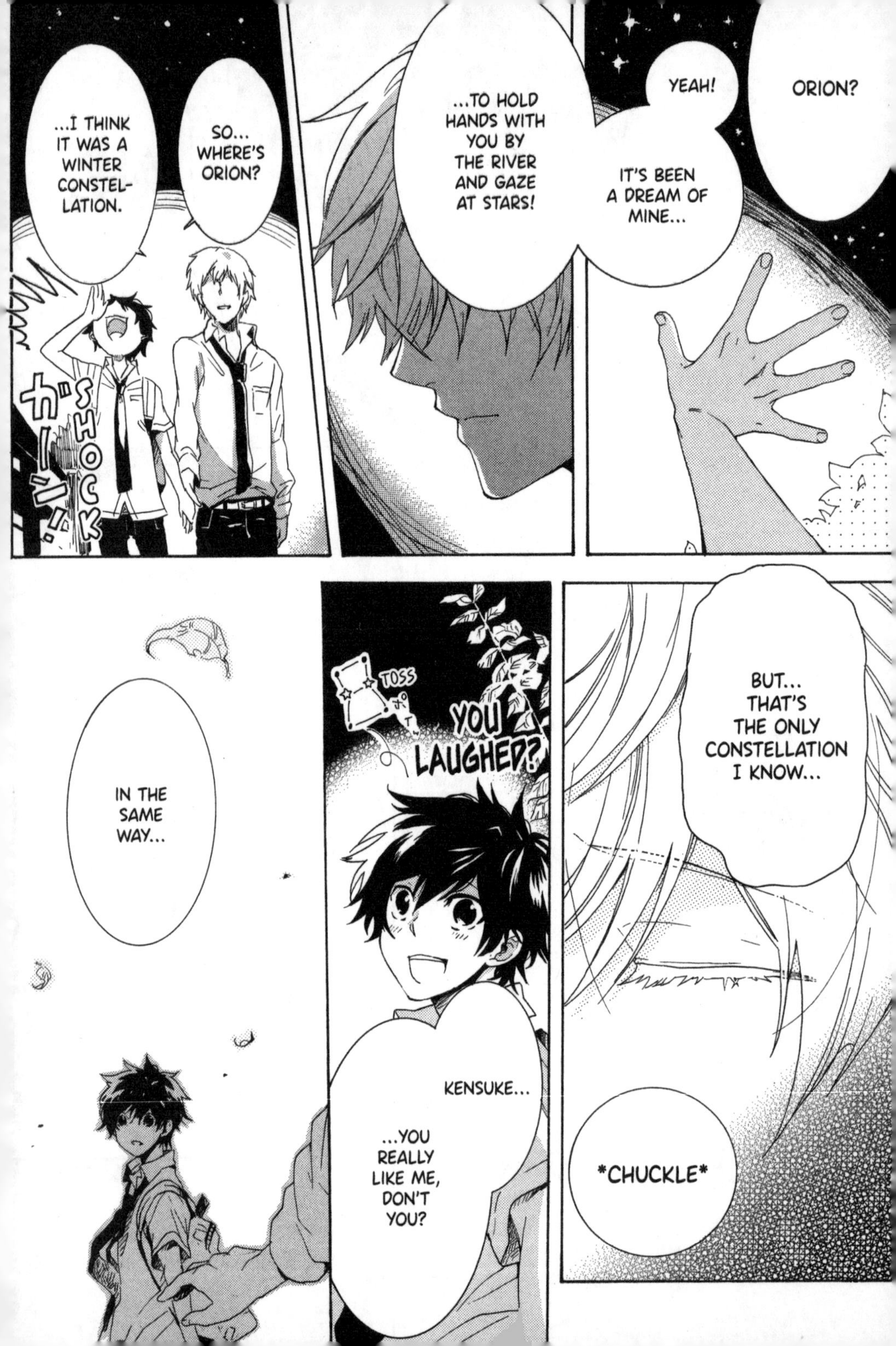
ORION?
YEAH!
IT'S BEEN A DREAM OF MINE...
...TO HOLD HANDS WITH YOU BY THE RIVER AND GAZE AT STARS!
SO... WHERE'S ORION?
...I THINK IT WAS A WINTER CONSTEL-LATION.
SHOCK
BUT... THAT'S THE ONLY CONSTELLATION I KNOW...
CHUCKLE
TOSS
YOU LAUGHED?
KENSUKE...
...YOU REALLY LIKE ME, DON'T YOU?
IN THE SAME WAY...

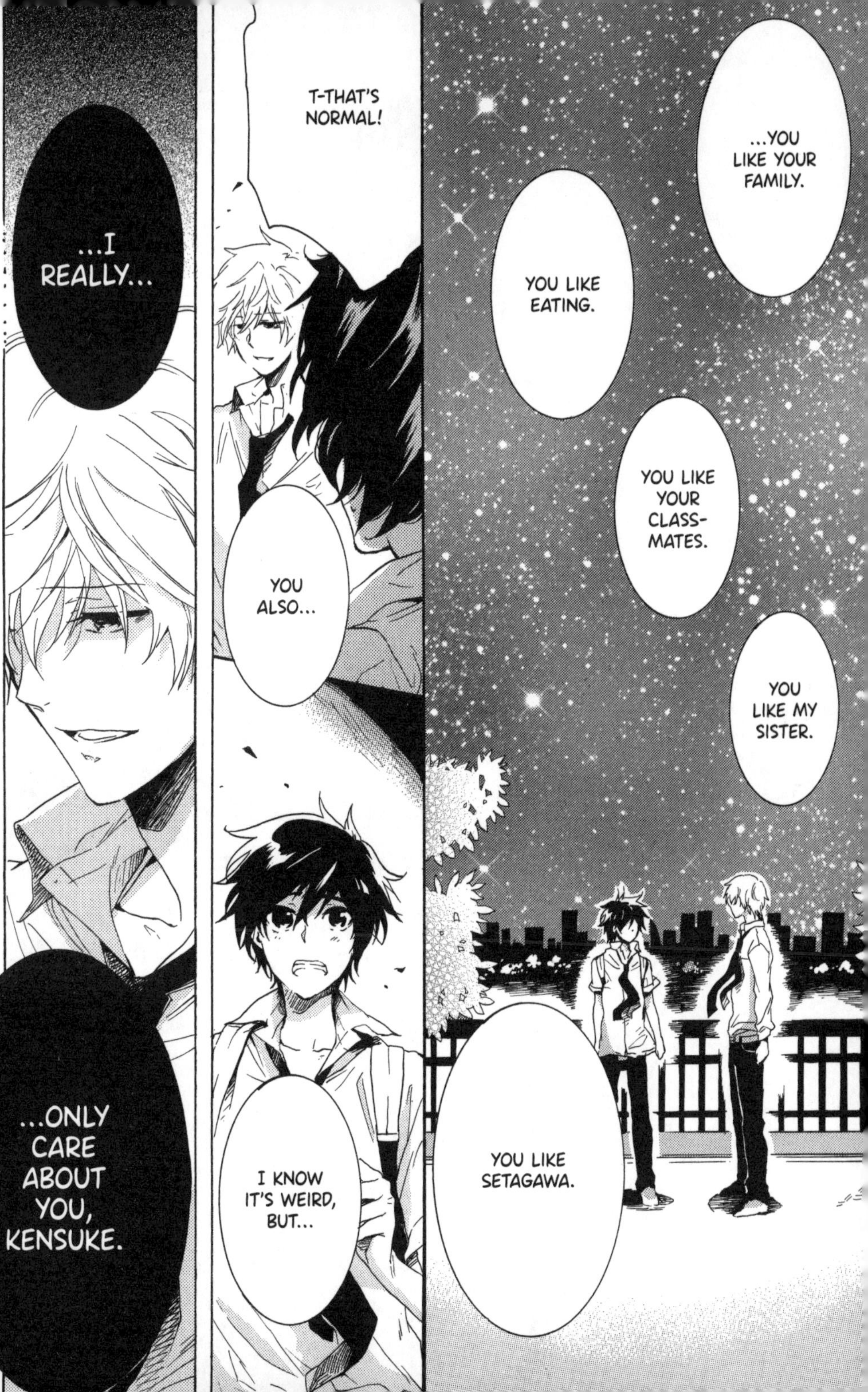
...YOU LIKE YOUR FAMILY.
YOU LIKE EATING.
YOU LIKE YOUR CLASS-MATES.
YOU LIKE MY SISTER.
YOU LIKE SETAGAWA.
T-THAT'S NORMAL!
YOU ALSO...
I KNOW IT'S WEIRD, BUT...
...I REALLY...
...ONLY CARE ABOUT YOU, KENSUKE.

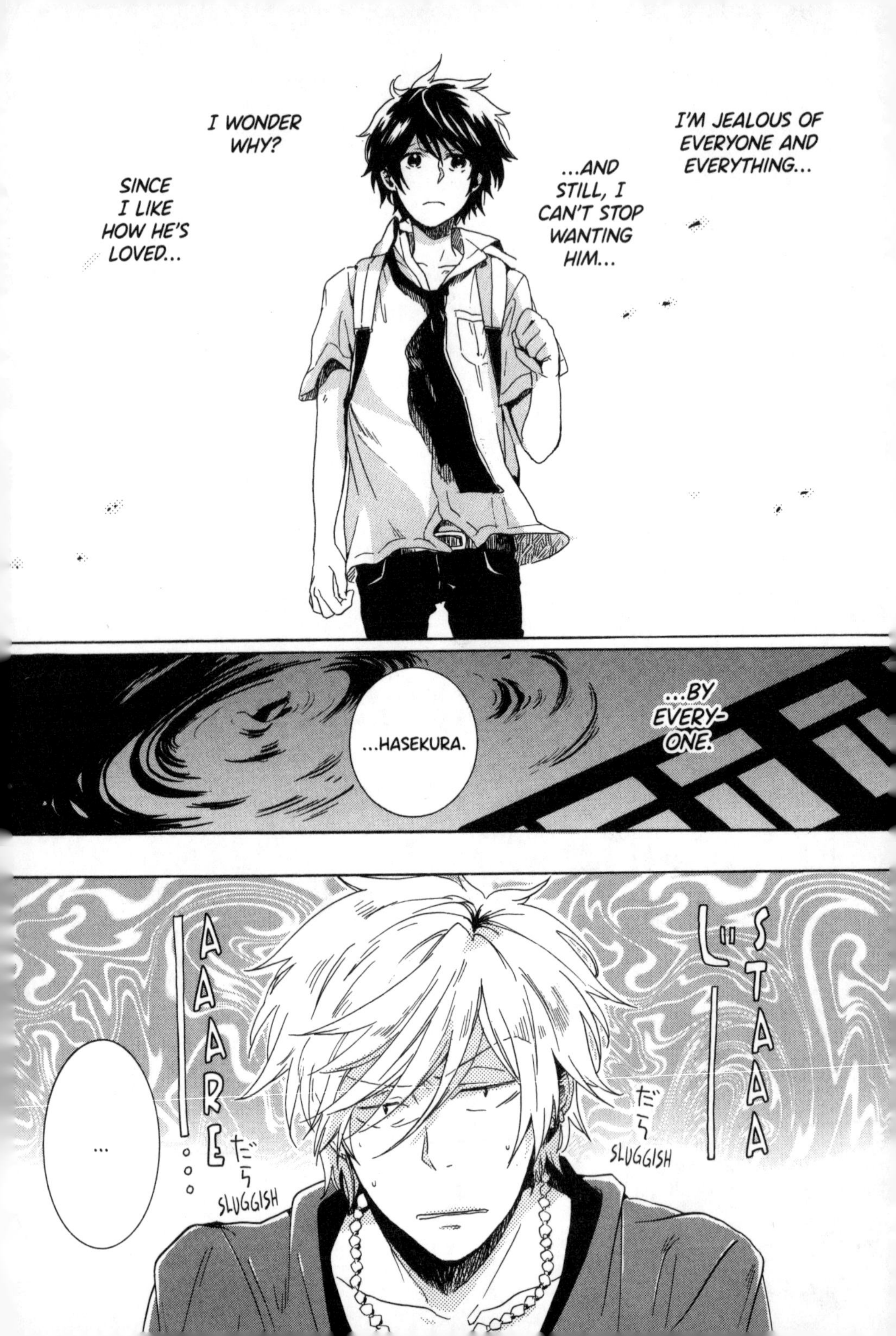

I'M JEALOUS OF EVERYONE AND EVERYTHING...
...AND STILL, I CAN'T STOP WANTING HIM...
I WONDER WHY?
SINCE I LIKE HOW HE'S LOVED...
...BY EVERY-ONE.
...HASEKURA.
STAAA
じー
だら
SLUGGISH
AAARE
だら
SLUGGISH
...

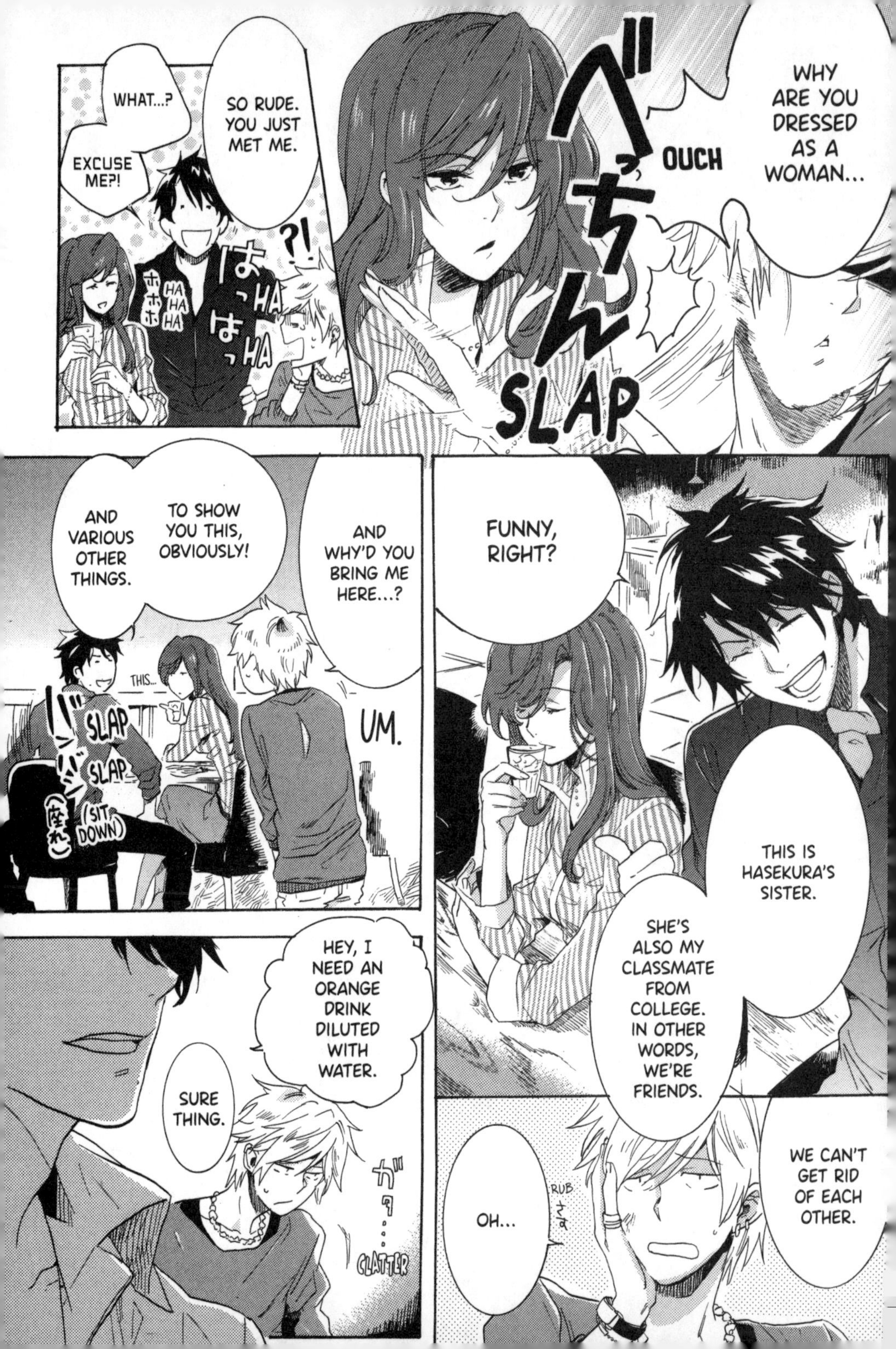
WHY ARE YOU DRESSED AS A WOMAN...
OUCH
べちん
SLAP
SO RUDE. YOU JUST MET ME.
WHAT...?
EXCUSE ME?!
?!
はっはっ
HA HA
ほほほ
HA HA HA
FUNNY, RIGHT?
THIS IS HASEKURA'S SISTER.
SHE'S ALSO MY CLASSMATE FROM COLLEGE. IN OTHER WORDS, WE'RE FRIENDS.
AND WHY'D YOU BRING ME HERE...?
TO SHOW YOU THIS, OBVIOUSLY!
AND VARIOUS OTHER THINGS.
THIS...
UM.
バンバン
SLAP
SLAP
(座れ)
(SIT DOWN)
WE CAN'T GET RID OF EACH OTHER.
OH...
さす
RUB
HEY, I NEED AN ORANGE DRINK DILUTED WITH WATER.
SURE THING.
ガタ...
CLATTER

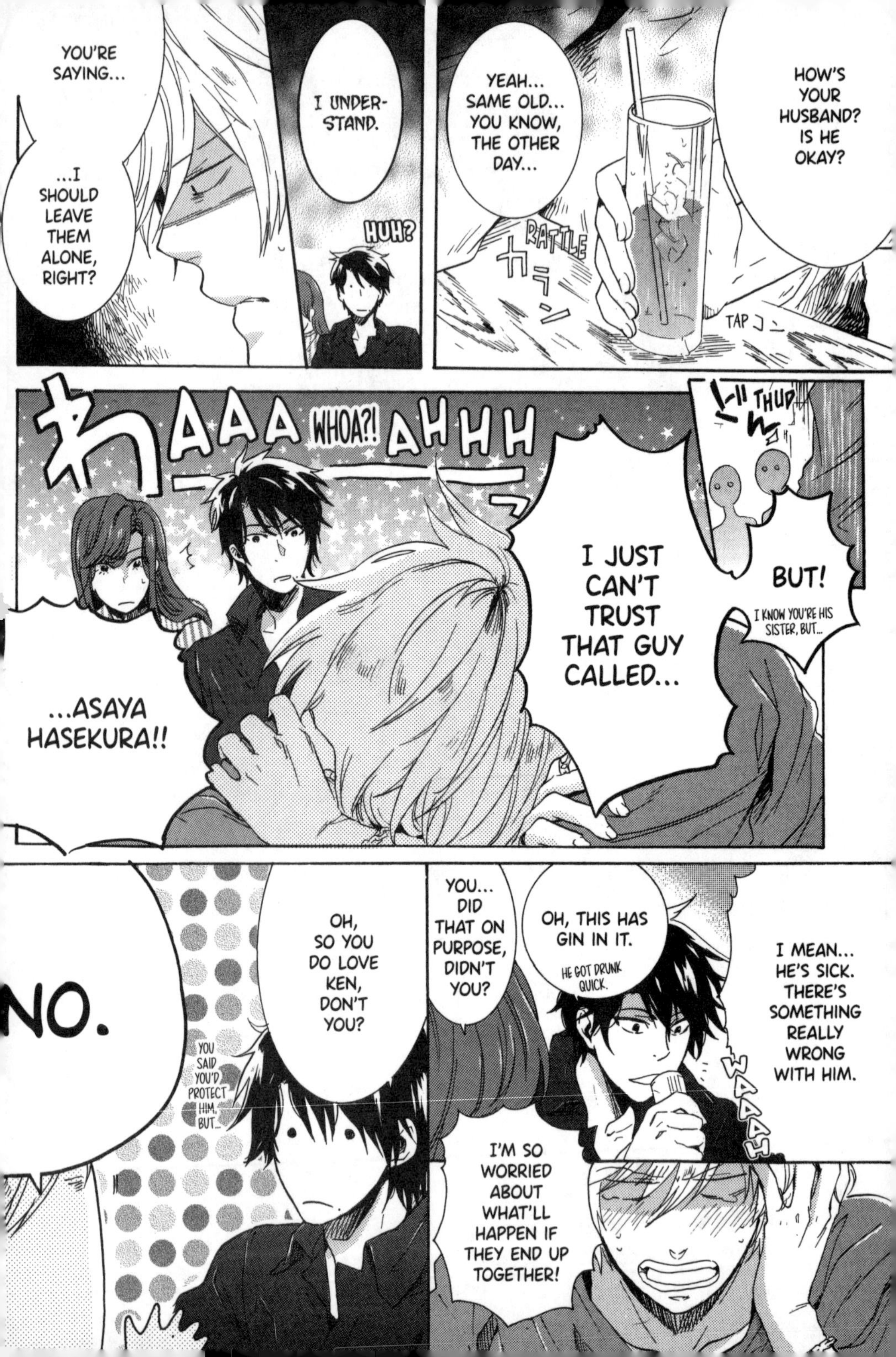
HOW'S YOUR HUSBAND? IS HE OKAY?
YEAH... SAME OLD... YOU KNOW, THE OTHER DAY...
RATTLE カラン
TAP コン
I UNDER-STAND.
HUH?
YOU'RE SAYING...
...I SHOULD LEAVE THEM ALONE, RIGHT?
THUD
BUT!
I KNOW YOU'RE HIS SISTER, BUT...
I JUST CAN'T TRUST THAT GUY CALLED...
わAAA WHOA?! AHHH
...ASAYA HASEKURA!!
I MEAN... HE'S SICK. THERE'S SOMETHING REALLY WRONG WITH HIM.
WAAAAH
OH, THIS HAS GIN IN IT.
HE GOT DRUNK QUICK.
YOU... DID THAT ON PURPOSE, DIDN'T YOU?
I'M SO WORRIED ABOUT WHAT'LL HAPPEN IF THEY END UP TOGETHER!
OH, SO YOU DO LOVE KEN, DON'T YOU?
YOU SAID YOU'D PROTECT HIM, BUT...
NO.

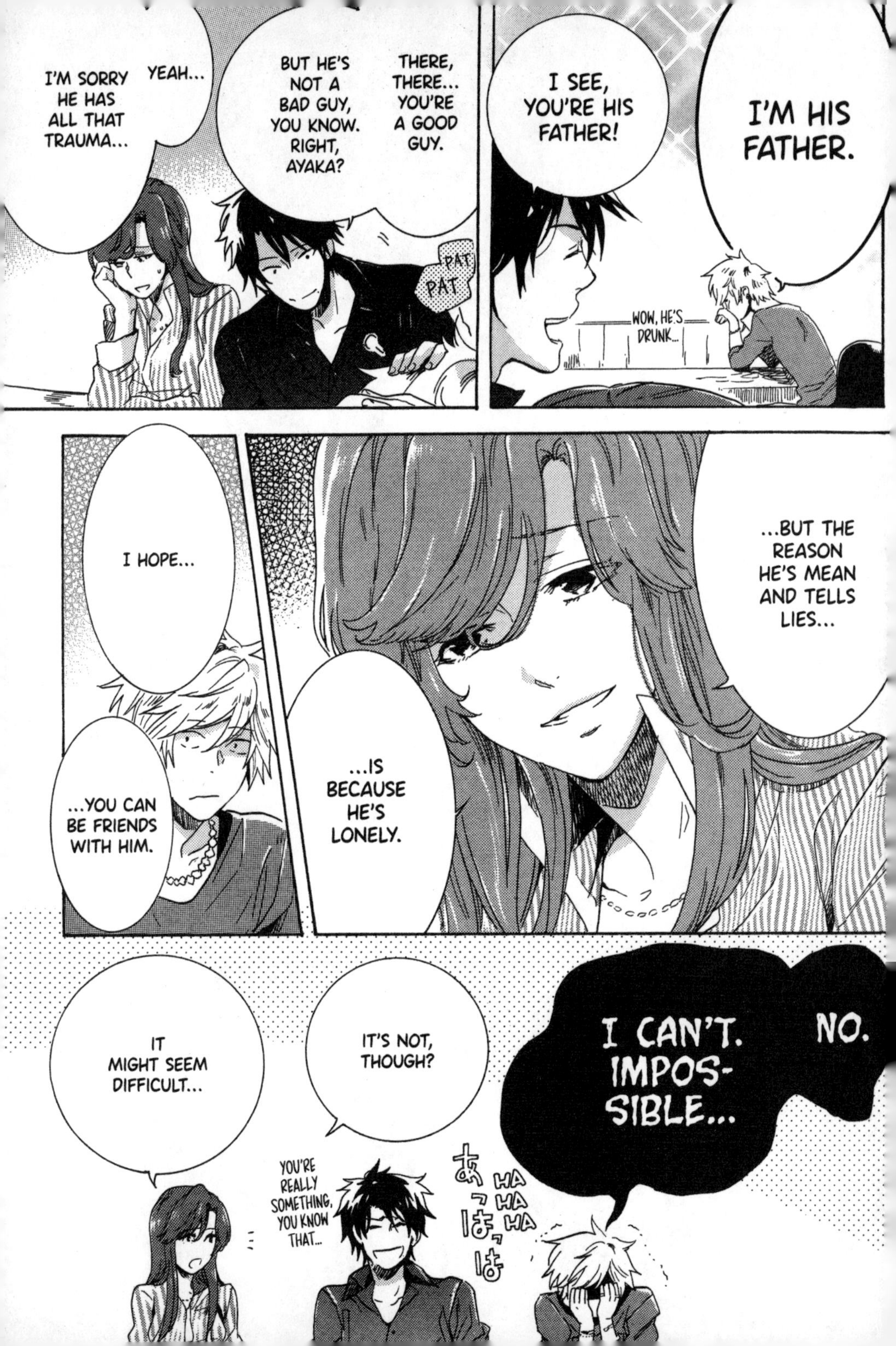
I'M HIS FATHER.
I SEE, YOU'RE HIS FATHER!
WOW, HE'S DRUNK...
THERE, THERE... YOU'RE A GOOD GUY.
PAT PAT
BUT HE'S NOT A BAD GUY, YOU KNOW. RIGHT, AYAKA?
YEAH...
I'M SORRY HE HAS ALL THAT TRAUMA...
...BUT THE REASON HE'S MEAN AND TELLS LIES...
...IS BECAUSE HE'S LONELY.
I HOPE...
...YOU CAN BE FRIENDS WITH HIM.
NO.
I CAN'T. IMPOS-SIBLE...
HA HA HA
あっはっは
IT'S NOT, THOUGH?
YOU'RE REALLY SOMETHING, YOU KNOW THAT...
IT MIGHT SEEM DIFFICULT...

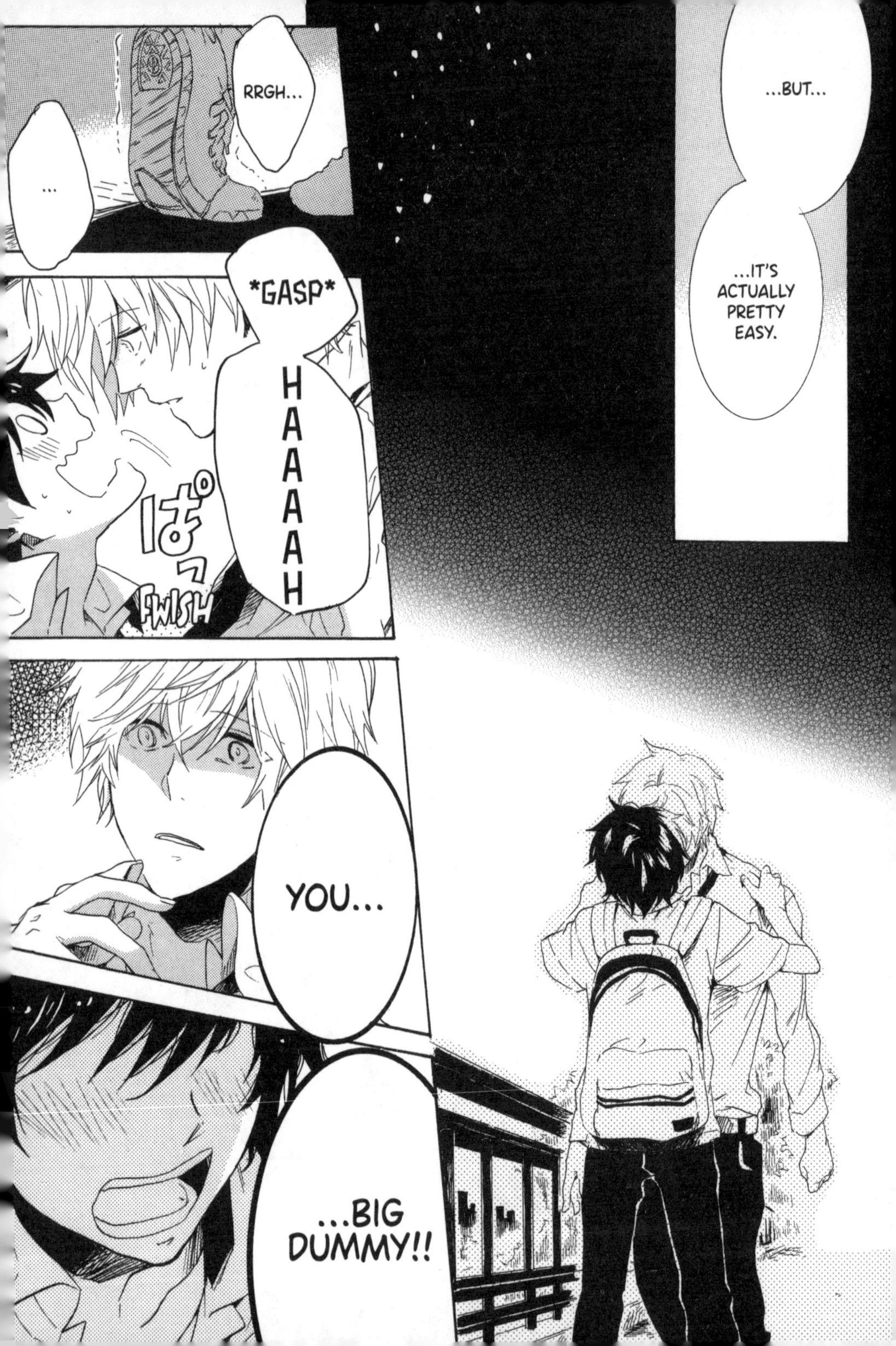
...BUT...
...IT'S ACTUALLY PRETTY EASY.
RRGH...
...
GASP
HAAAAAH
ぱっ
FWISH
YOU...
...BIG DUMMY!!

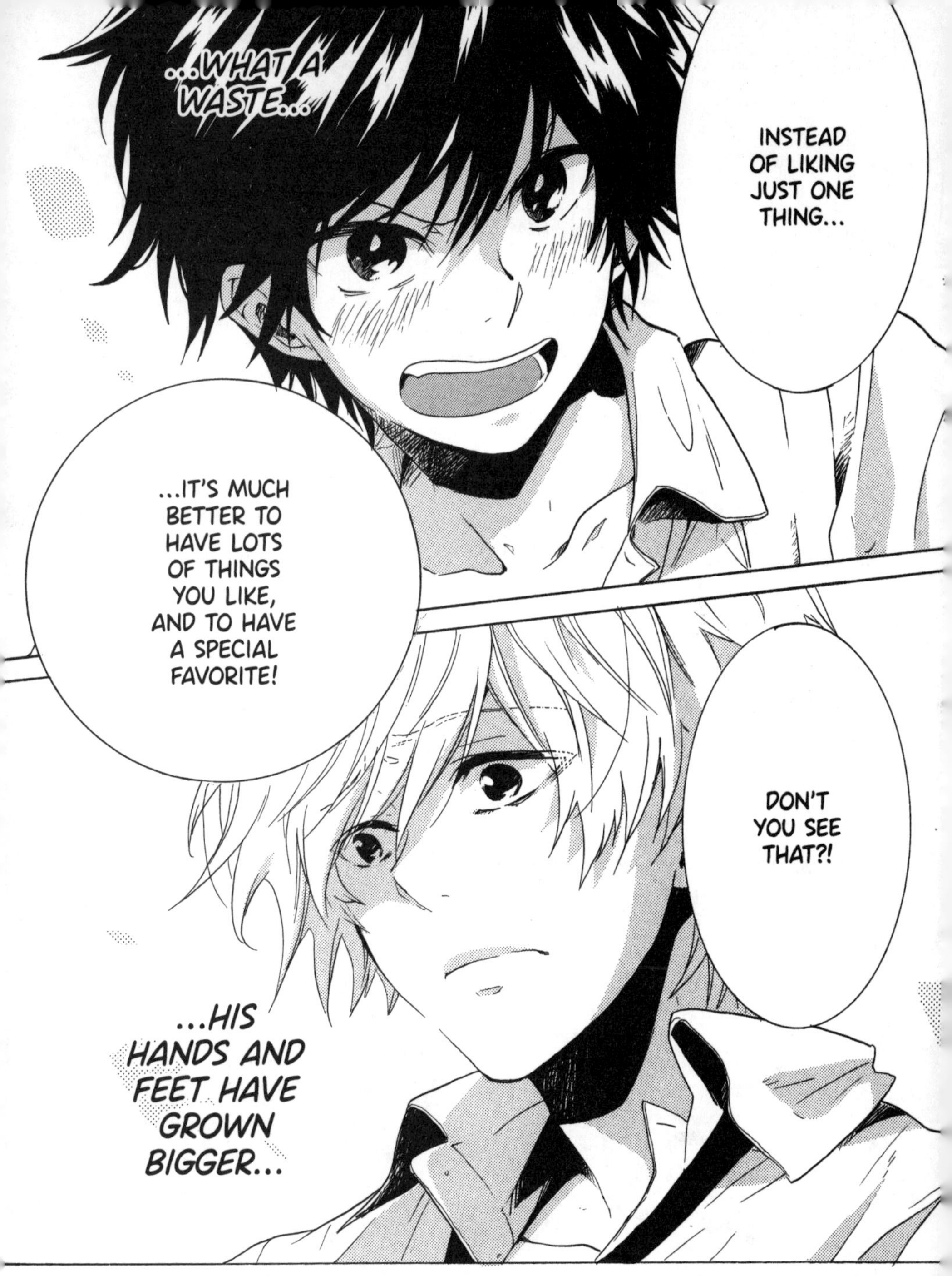

INSTEAD OF LIKING JUST ONE THING...
...WHAT A WASTE...
...IT'S MUCH BETTER TO HAVE LOTS OF THINGS YOU LIKE, AND TO HAVE A SPECIAL FAVORITE!
DON'T YOU SEE THAT?!
...HIS HANDS AND FEET HAVE GROWN BIGGER...

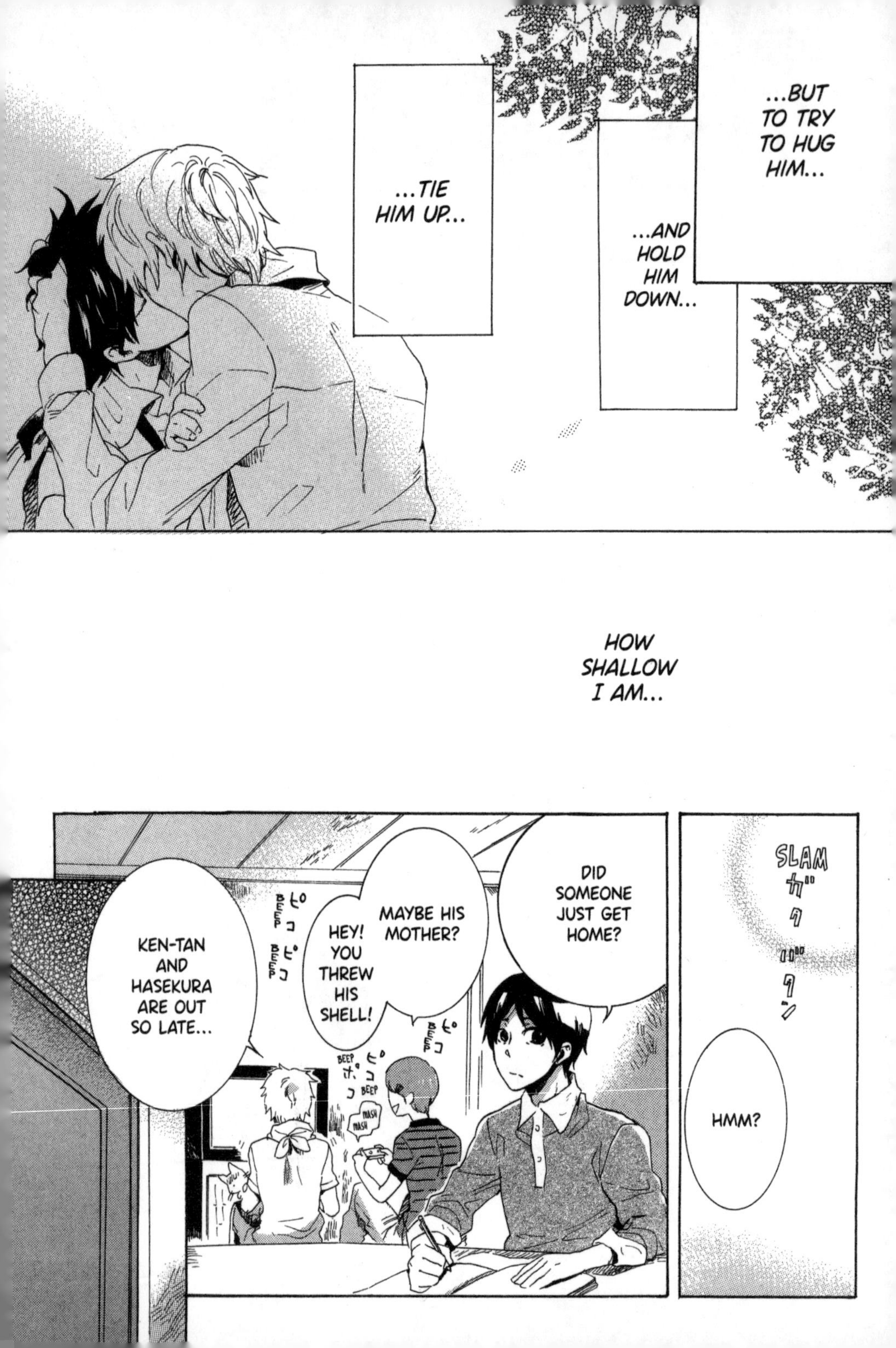
...BUT TO TRY TO HUG HIM...
...AND HOLD HIM DOWN...
...TIE HIM UP...
HOW SHALLOW I AM...
SLAM
HMM?
DID SOMEONE JUST GET HOME?
MAYBE HIS MOTHER?
BEEP
HEY! YOU THREW HIS SHELL!
BEEP
BEEP
MASH MASH
KEN-TAN AND HASEKURA ARE OUT SO LATE...
BEEP
BEEP

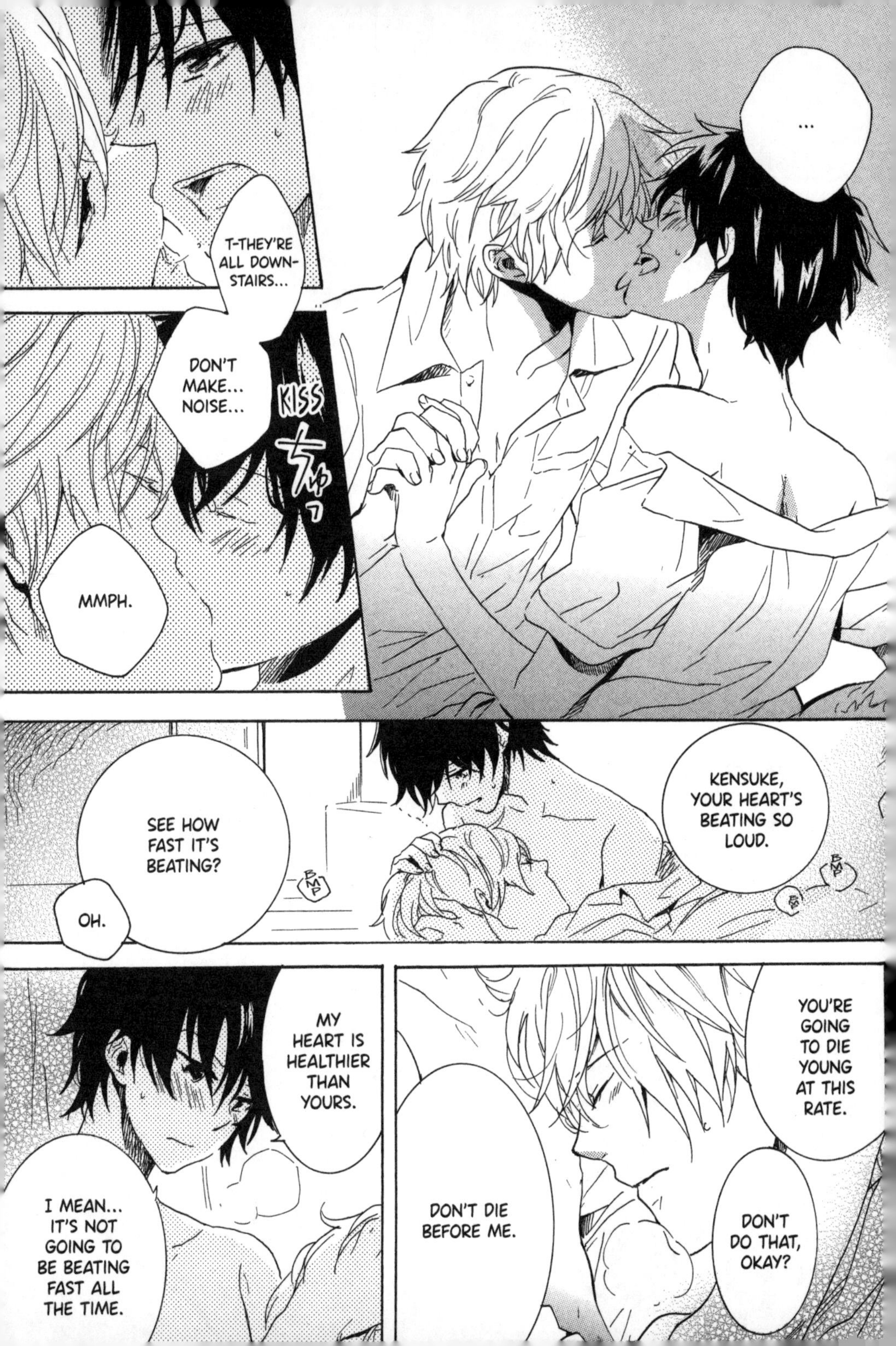
...
T-THEY'RE ALL DOWN-STAIRS...
DON'T MAKE... NOISE...
KISS
MMPH.
KENSUKE, YOUR HEART'S BEATING SO LOUD.
BMP
BMP
SEE HOW FAST IT'S BEATING?
OH.
YOU'RE GOING TO DIE YOUNG AT THIS RATE.
DON'T DO THAT, OKAY?
DON'T DIE BEFORE ME.
MY HEART IS HEALTHIER THAN YOURS.
I MEAN... IT'S NOT GOING TO BE BEATING FAST ALL THE TIME.

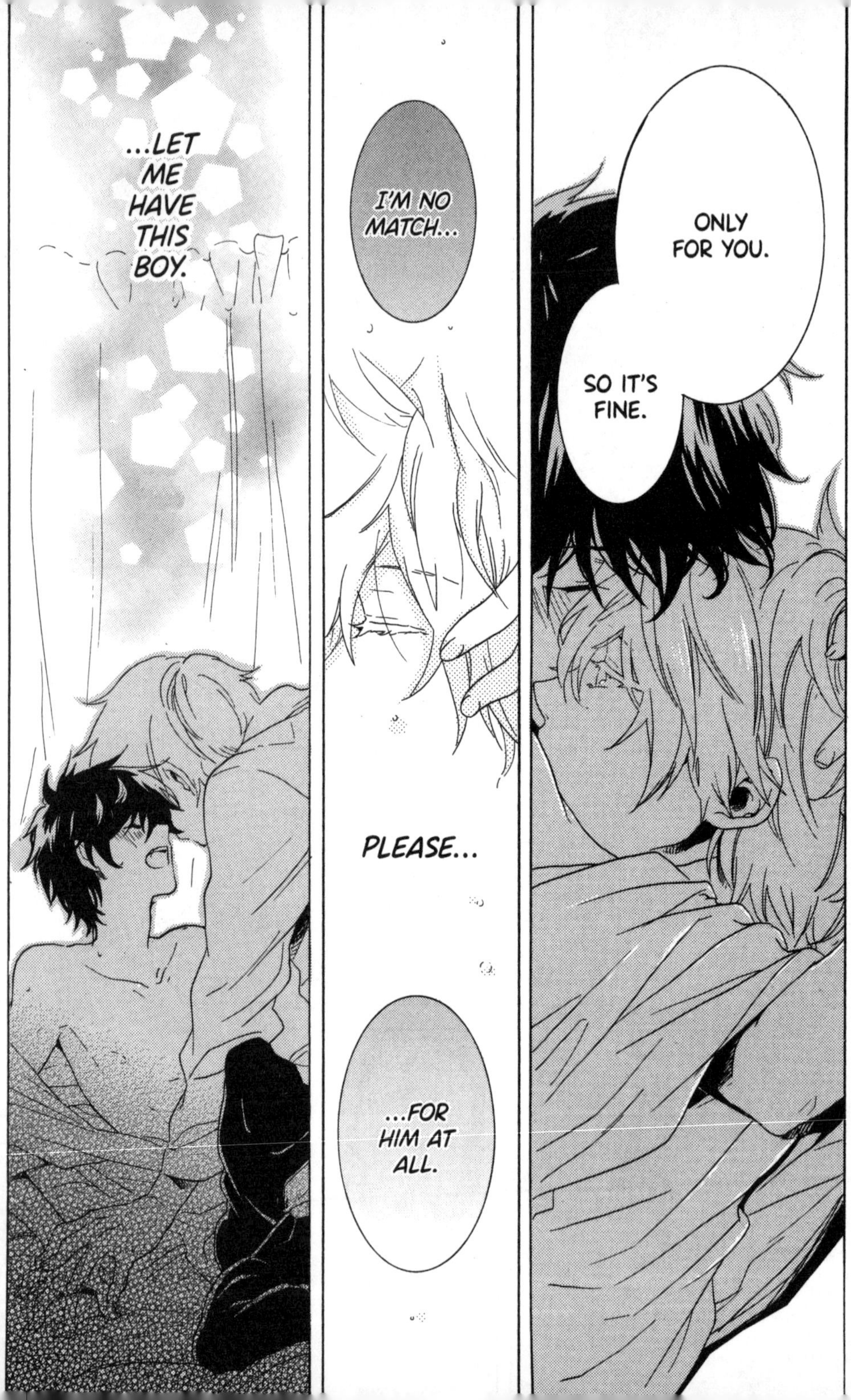

ONLY FOR YOU.
SO IT'S FINE.
I'M NO MATCH...
PLEASE...
...FOR HIM AT ALL.
...LET ME HAVE THIS BOY.

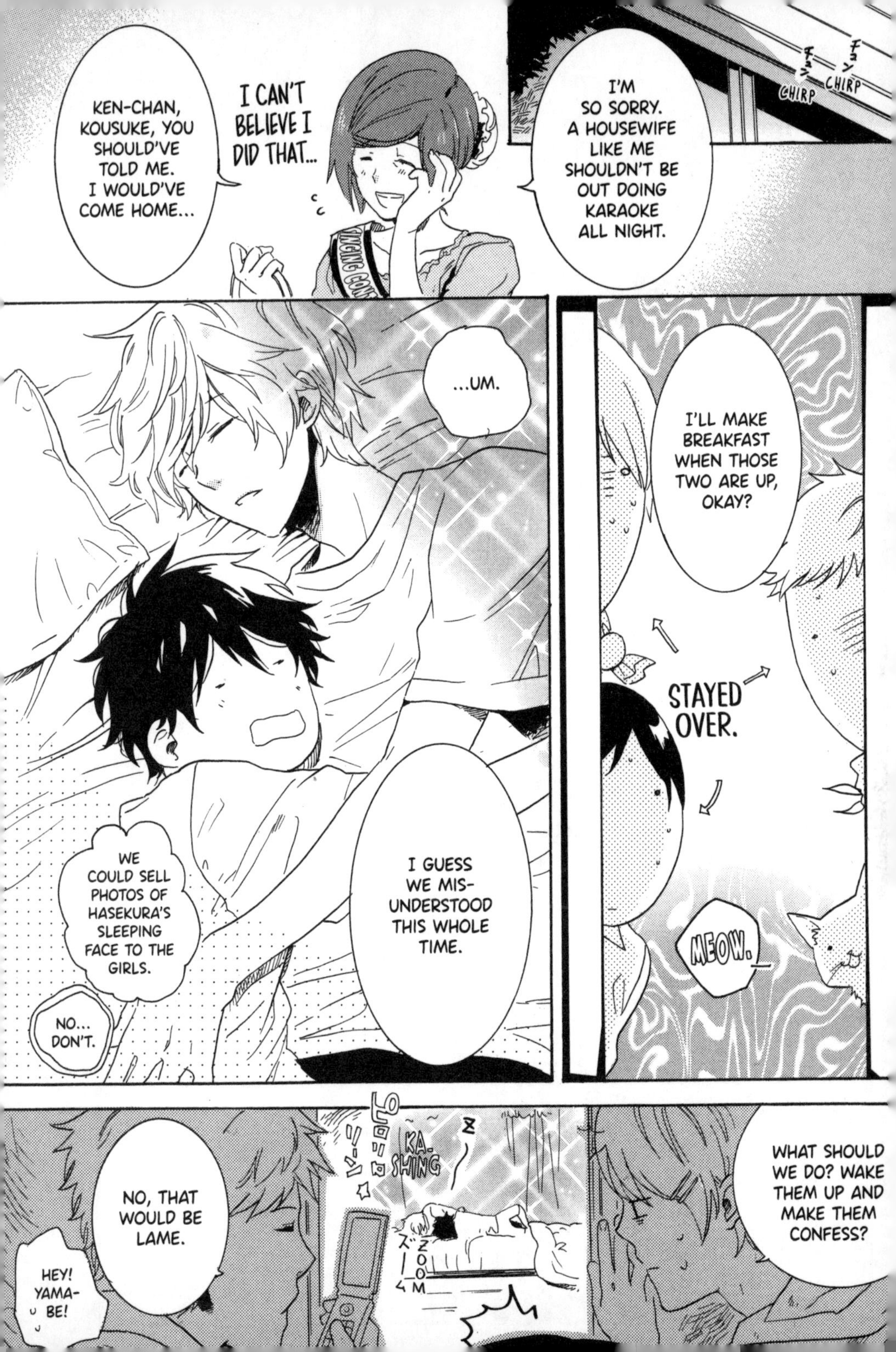
チュン チュン
CHIRP CHIRP
I'M SO SORRY. A HOUSEWIFE LIKE ME SHOULDN'T BE OUT DOING KARAOKE ALL NIGHT.
I CAN'T BELIEVE I DID THAT...
KEN-CHAN, KOUSUKE, YOU SHOULD'VE TOLD ME. I WOULD'VE COME HOME...
I'LL MAKE BREAKFAST WHEN THOSE TWO ARE UP, OKAY?
STAYED OVER.
MEOW.
...UM.
I GUESS WE MIS-UNDERSTOOD THIS WHOLE TIME.
WE COULD SELL PHOTOS OF HASEKURA'S SLEEPING FACE TO THE GIRLS.
NO... DON'T.
WHAT SHOULD WE DO? WAKE THEM UP AND MAKE THEM CONFESS?
KA-SHING
Z
ZOOM
NO, THAT WOULD BE LAME.
HEY! YAMA-BE!

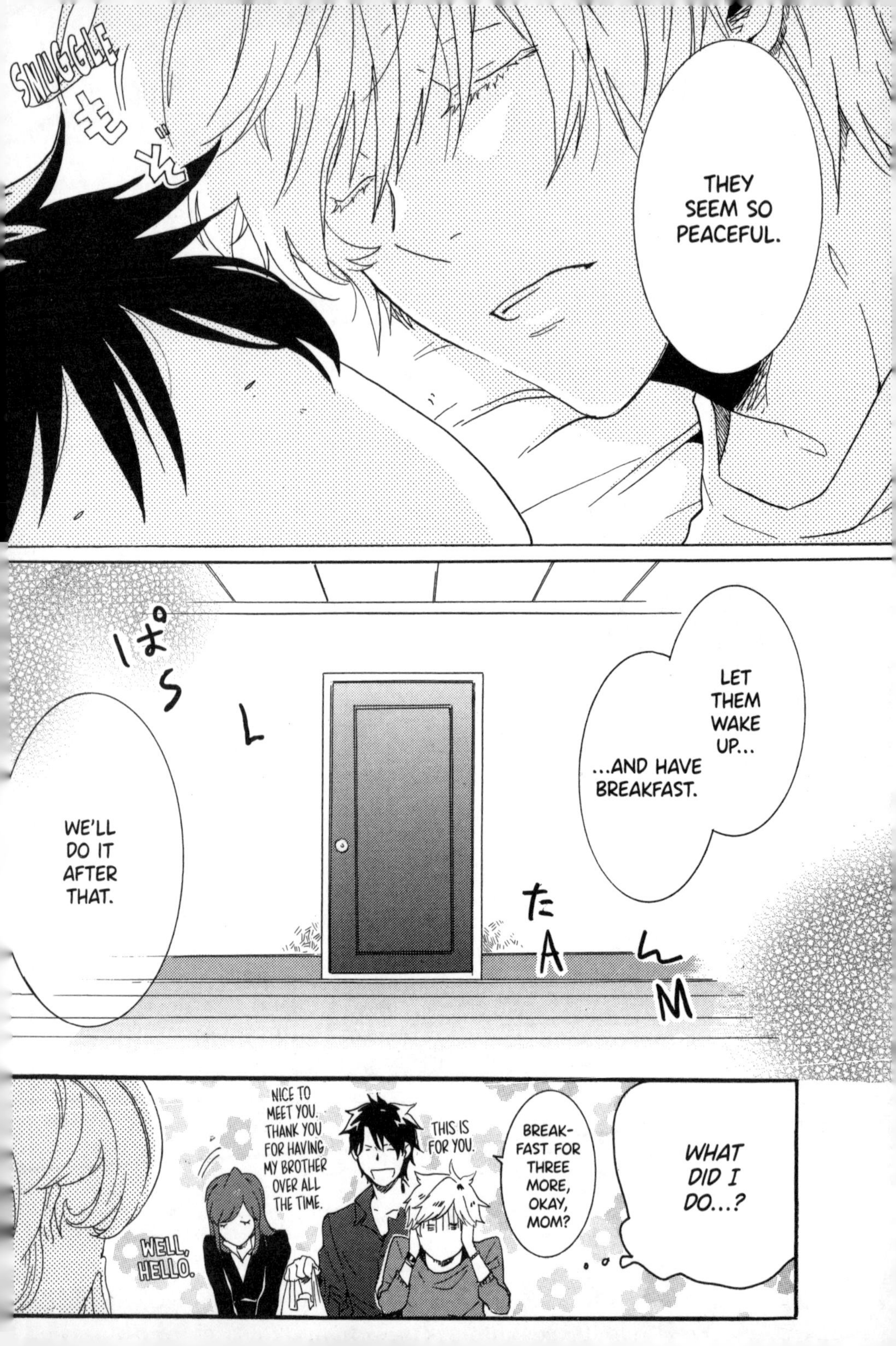
THEY SEEM SO PEACEFUL.
SNUGGLE
もぞ
LET THEM WAKE UP...
...AND HAVE BREAKFAST.
た A ん M
ぱ S L
WE'LL DO IT AFTER THAT.
WHAT DID I DO...?
BREAK-FAST FOR THREE MORE, OKAY, MOM?
THIS IS FOR YOU.
NICE TO MEET YOU. THANK YOU FOR HAVING MY BROTHER OVER ALL THE TIME.
WELL, HELLO.

NEWLY WRITTEN CHAPTER

Their Future

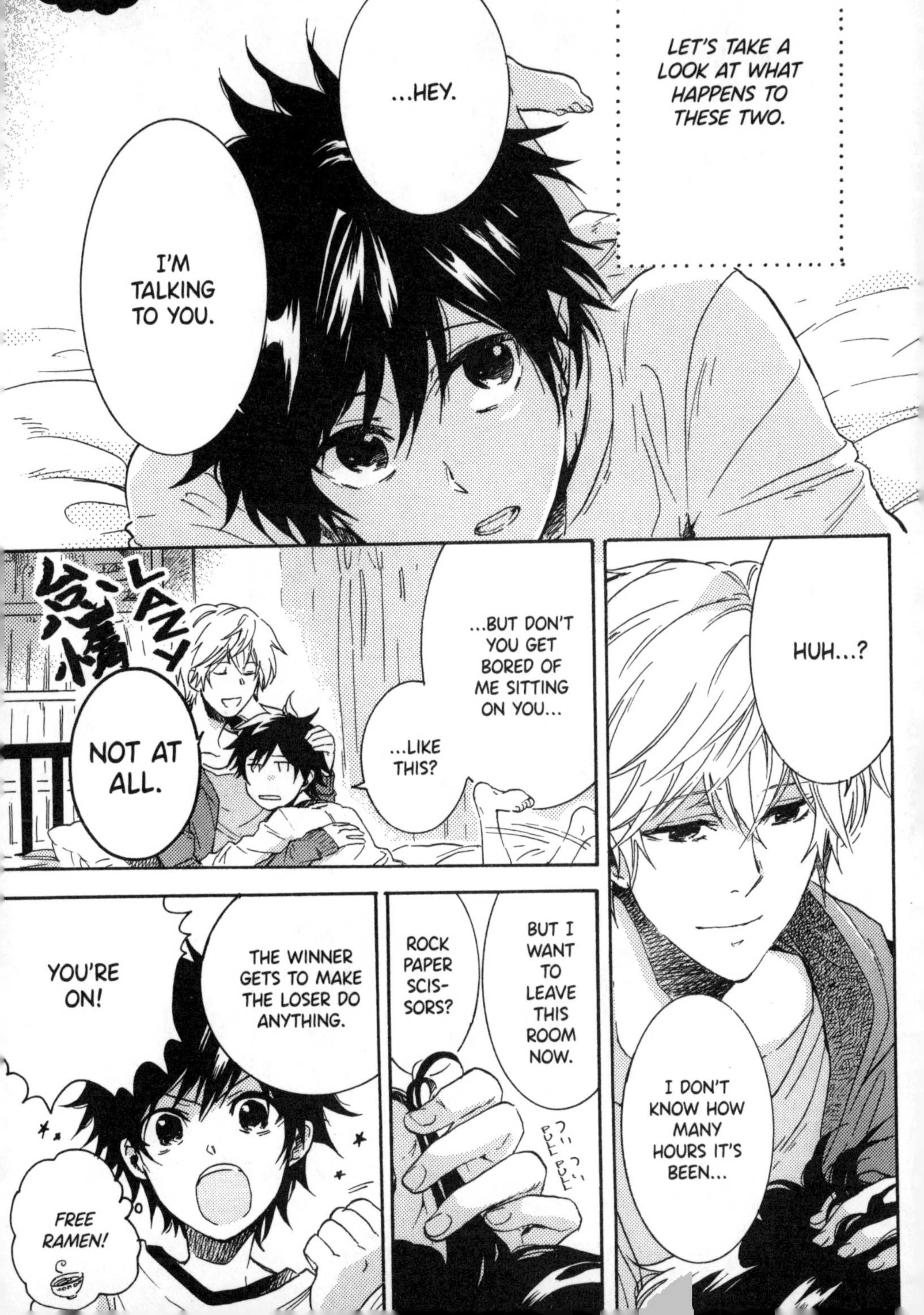
LET'S TAKE A LOOK AT WHAT HAPPENS TO THESE TWO.
...HEY.
I'M TALKING TO YOU.
HUH...?
I DON'T KNOW HOW MANY HOURS IT'S BEEN...
...BUT DON'T YOU GET BORED OF ME SITTING ON YOU...
...LIKE THIS?
LAZY
NOT AT ALL.
BUT I WANT TO LEAVE THIS ROOM NOW.
ROCK PAPER SCIS-SORS?
PULL PULL
THE WINNER GETS TO MAKE THE LOSER DO ANYTHING.
YOU'RE ON!
FREE RAMEN!

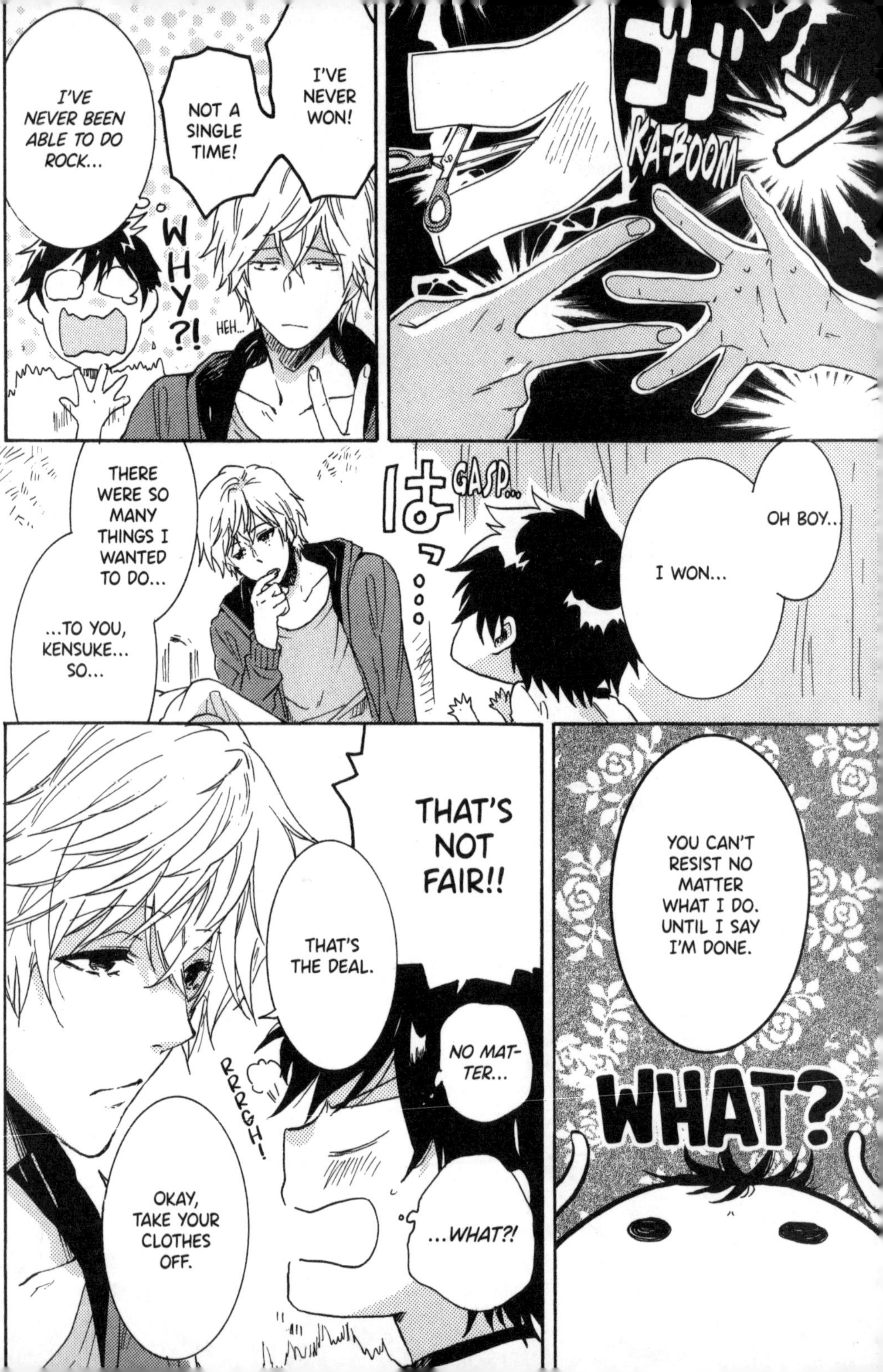

KA-BOOM
I'VE NEVER WON!
NOT A SINGLE TIME!
I'VE NEVER BEEN ABLE TO DO ROCK...
WHY?!
HEH...
OH BOY...
I WON...
は
GASP...
THERE WERE SO MANY THINGS I WANTED TO DO...
...TO YOU, KENSUKE... SO...
YOU CAN'T RESIST NO MATTER WHAT I DO. UNTIL I SAY I'M DONE.
WHAT?
THAT'S NOT FAIR!!
THAT'S THE DEAL.
NO MAT- TER...
RRRGH!
...WHAT?!
OKAY, TAKE YOUR CLOTHES OFF.

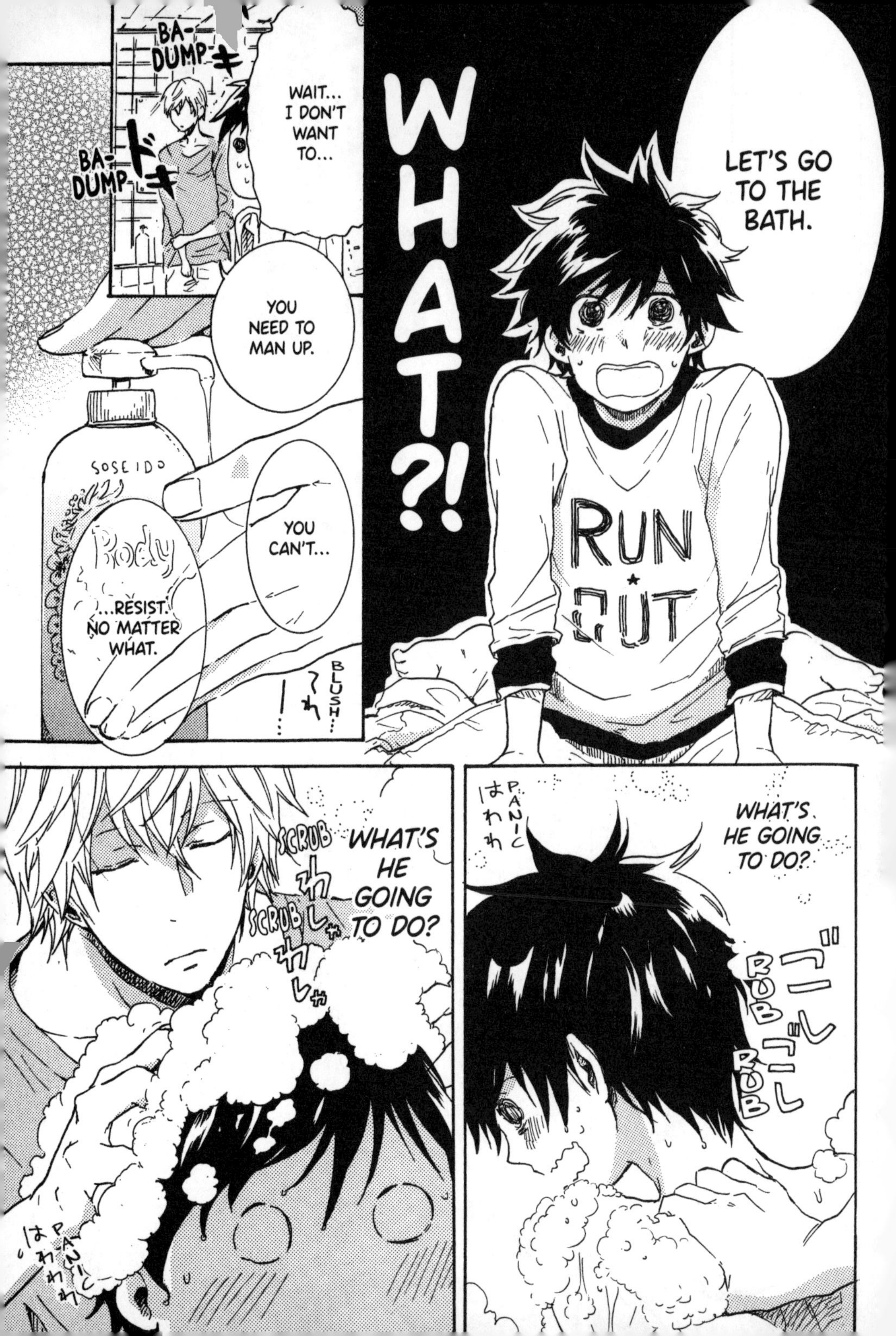
LET'S GO TO THE BATH.
WHAT?!
BA-DUMP ドキ
BA-DUMP ドキ
WAIT... I DON'T WANT TO...
YOU NEED TO MAN UP.
YOU CAN'T...
...RESIST. NO MATTER WHAT.
BLUSH... てれ
SOSEIDO
Body
PANIC はわわ
WHAT'S HE GOING TO DO?
RUB ゴシ
RUB ゴシ
SCRUB わしゃ
SCRUB わしゃ
WHAT'S HE GOING TO DO?
PANIC はわわわ
RUN ★ OUT

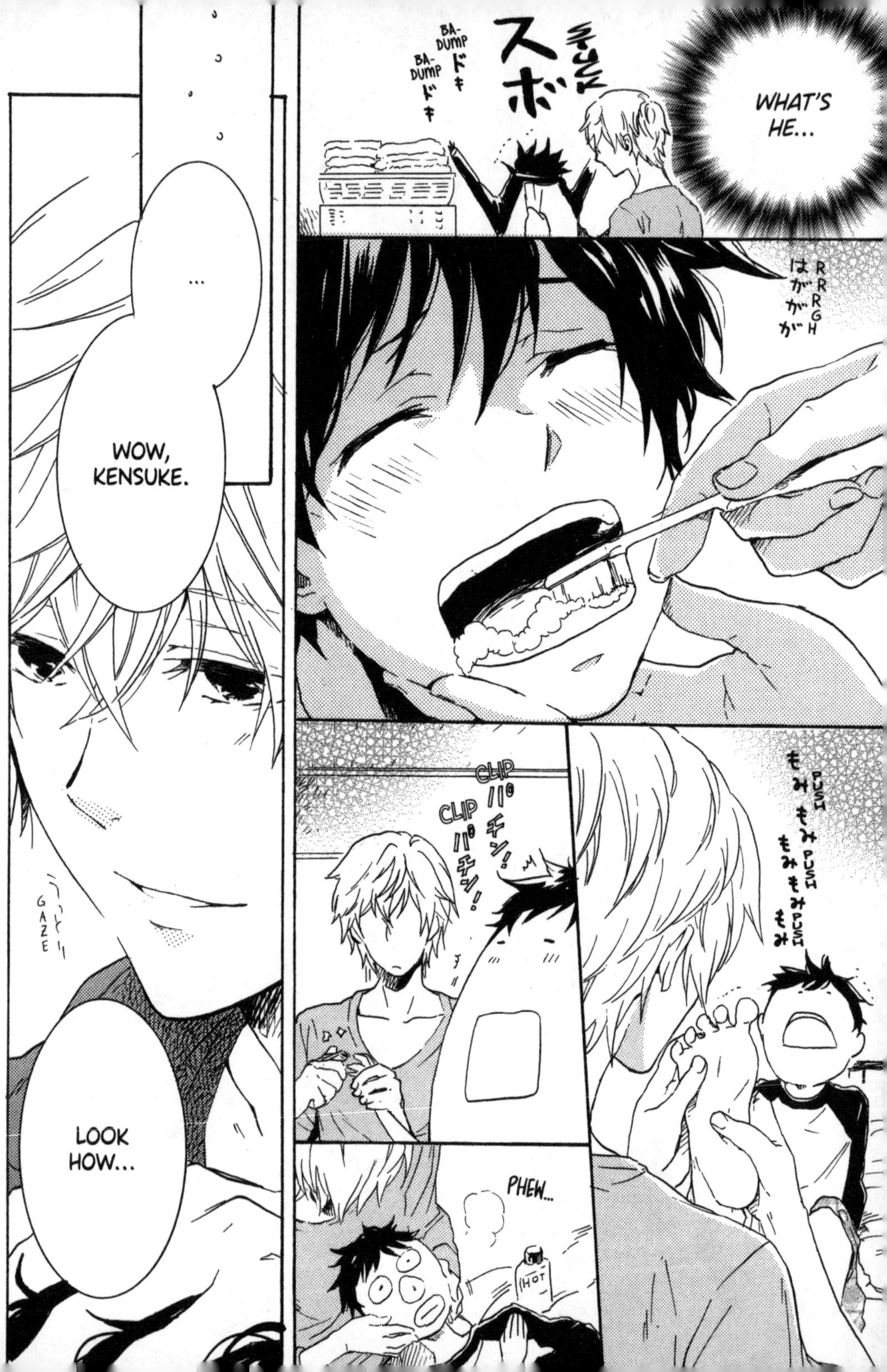

WHAT'S HE...
スポ
BA-DUMP ドキ
BA-DUMP ドキ
RRRGH はがが
もみもみ PUSH もみもみ PUSH もみもみ PUSH
CLIP パチン!
CLIP パチン!
PHEW...
...
WOW, KENSUKE.
GAZE
LOOK HOW...

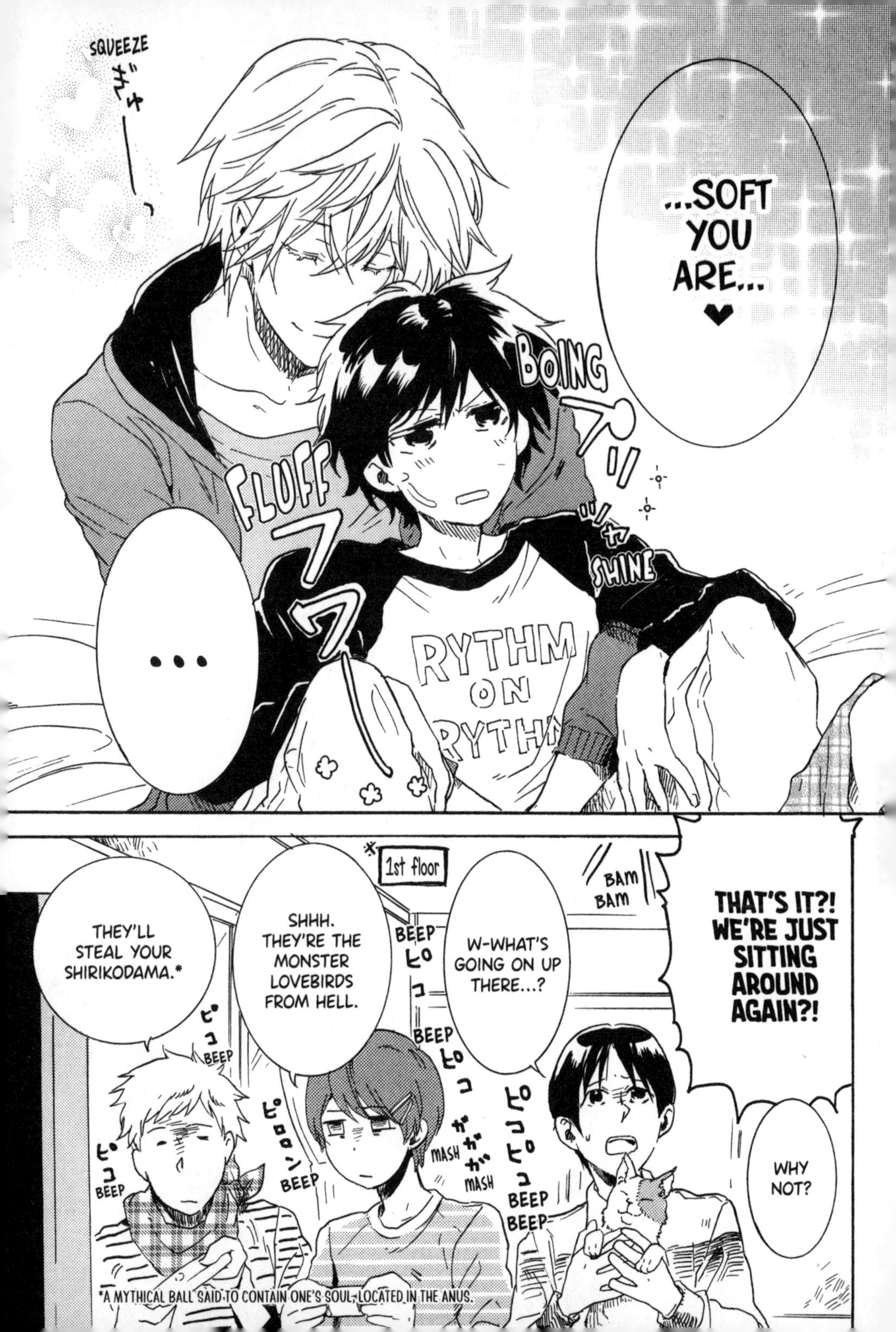
...SOFT YOU ARE... ❤
BOING
SHINE
FLUFF
SQUEEZE
...
THAT'S IT?! WE'RE JUST SITTING AROUND AGAIN?!
WHY NOT?
BAM BAM
W-WHAT'S GOING ON UP THERE...?
BEEP BEEP
MASH MASH
BEEP
BEEP
1st floor
SHHH. THEY'RE THE MONSTER LOVEBIRDS FROM HELL.
BEEP
THEY'LL STEAL YOUR SHIRIKODAMA.*
BEEP
BEEP

*A MYTHICAL BALL SAID TO CONTAIN ONE'S SOUL, LOCATED IN THE ANUS.

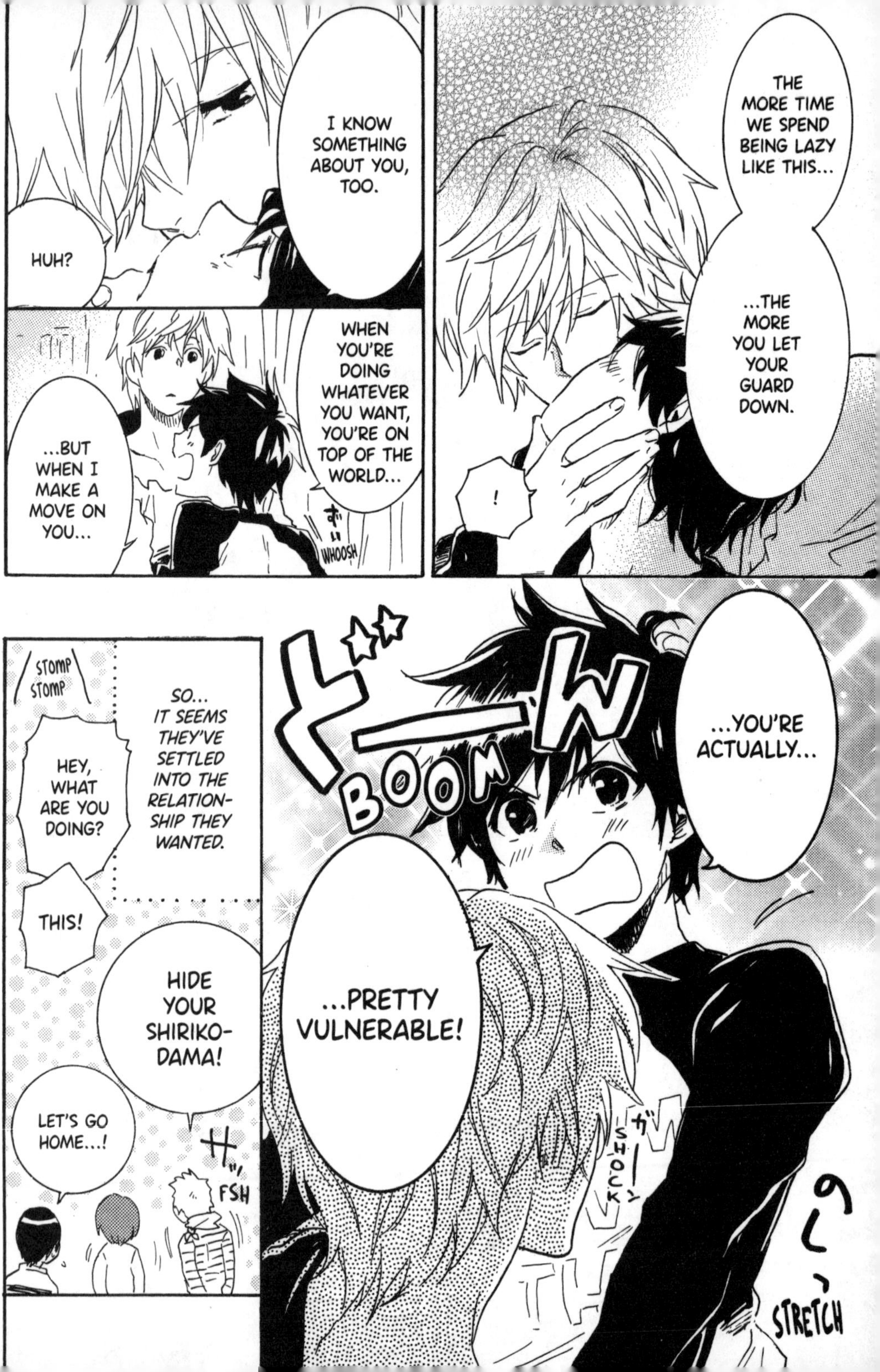
THE MORE TIME WE SPEND BEING LAZY LIKE THIS...
...THE MORE YOU LET YOUR GUARD DOWN.
!
I KNOW SOMETHING ABOUT YOU, TOO.
HUH?
WHEN YOU'RE DOING WHATEVER YOU WANT, YOU'RE ON TOP OF THE WORLD...
ずい
WHOOSH
...BUT WHEN I MAKE A MOVE ON YOU...
...YOU'RE ACTUALLY...
ド—ン
BOOM
...PRETTY VULNERABLE!
ガーン
SHOCK
のし
STRETCH
STOMP STOMP
SO... IT SEEMS THEY'VE SETTLED INTO THE RELATION-SHIP THEY WANTED.
HEY, WHAT ARE YOU DOING?
THIS!
HIDE YOUR SHIRIKO-DAMA!
LET'S GO HOME...!
サッ
FSH

THE IDEAL

- FOR SOME REASON, THIS PART ONLY HAS GIRLS IN IT -

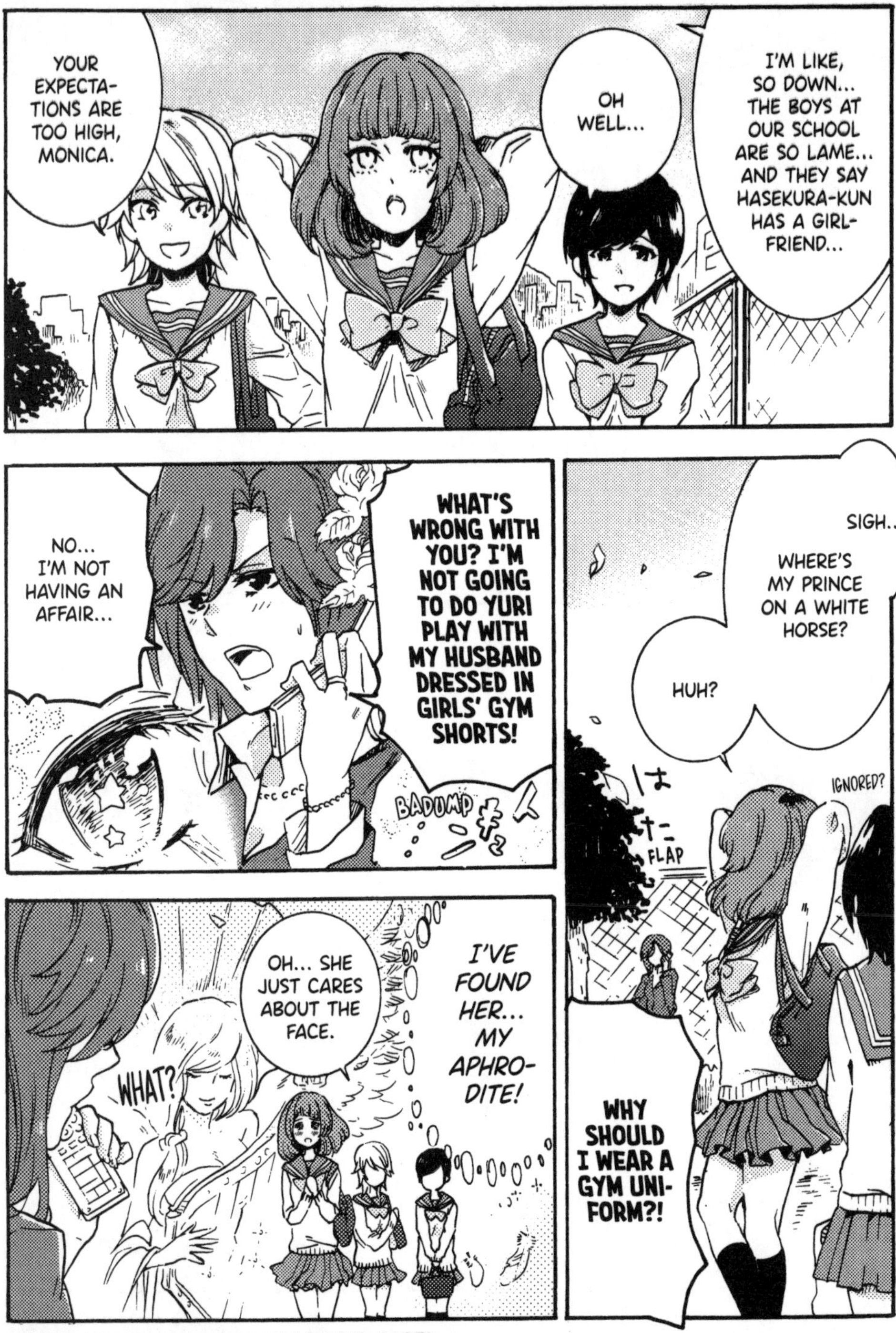

I'M LIKE, SO DOWN... THE BOYS AT OUR SCHOOL ARE SO LAME... AND THEY SAY HASEKURA-KUN HAS A GIRLFRIEND...
OH WELL...
YOUR EXPECTATIONS ARE TOO HIGH, MONICA.
SIGH...
WHERE'S MY PRINCE ON A WHITE HORSE?
HUH?
IGNORED?
FLAP
WHY SHOULD I WEAR A GYM UNIFORM?!
WHAT'S WRONG WITH YOU? I'M NOT GOING TO DO YURI PLAY WITH MY HUSBAND DRESSED IN GIRLS' GYM SHORTS!
NO... I'M NOT HAVING AN AFFAIR...
BADUMP
I'VE FOUND HER... MY APHRODITE!
OH... SHE JUST CARES ABOUT THE FACE.
WHAT?

TO BE CONTINUED IN YURI HIME! (NOT)

FLAGS

- SET UP AS MANY AS POSSIBLE -

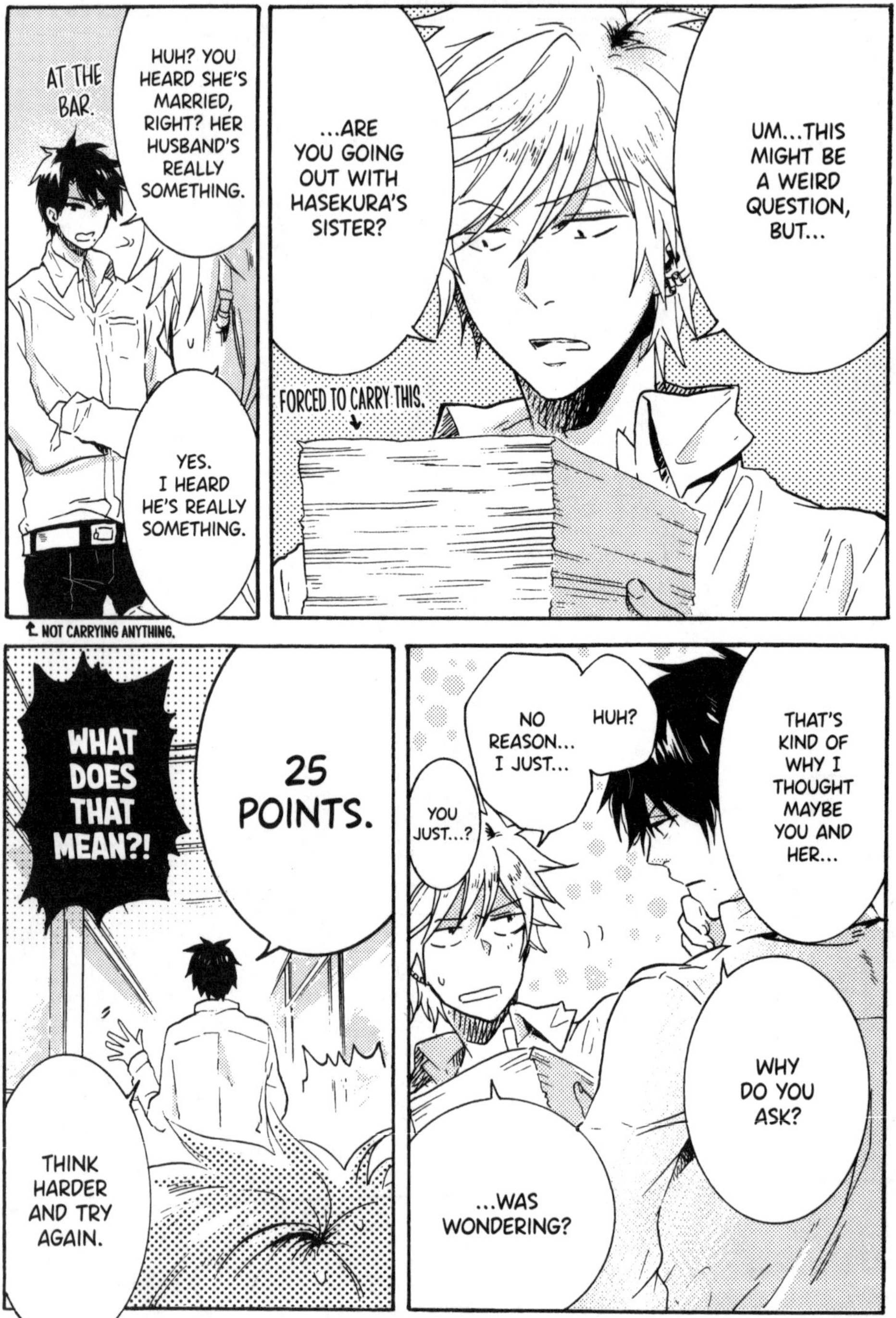
UM...THIS MIGHT BE A WEIRD QUESTION, BUT...
...ARE YOU GOING OUT WITH HASEKURA'S SISTER?
FORCED TO CARRY THIS.
AT THE BAR.
HUH? YOU HEARD SHE'S MARRIED, RIGHT? HER HUSBAND'S REALLY SOMETHING.
YES. I HEARD HE'S REALLY SOMETHING.
NOT CARRYING ANYTHING.
THAT'S KIND OF WHY I THOUGHT MAYBE YOU AND HER...
HUH?
NO REASON... I JUST...
YOU JUST...?
WHY DO YOU ASK?
...WAS WONDERING?
25 POINTS.
WHAT DOES THAT MEAN?!
THINK HARDER AND TRY AGAIN.

A HEARTFUL AFTERWORD

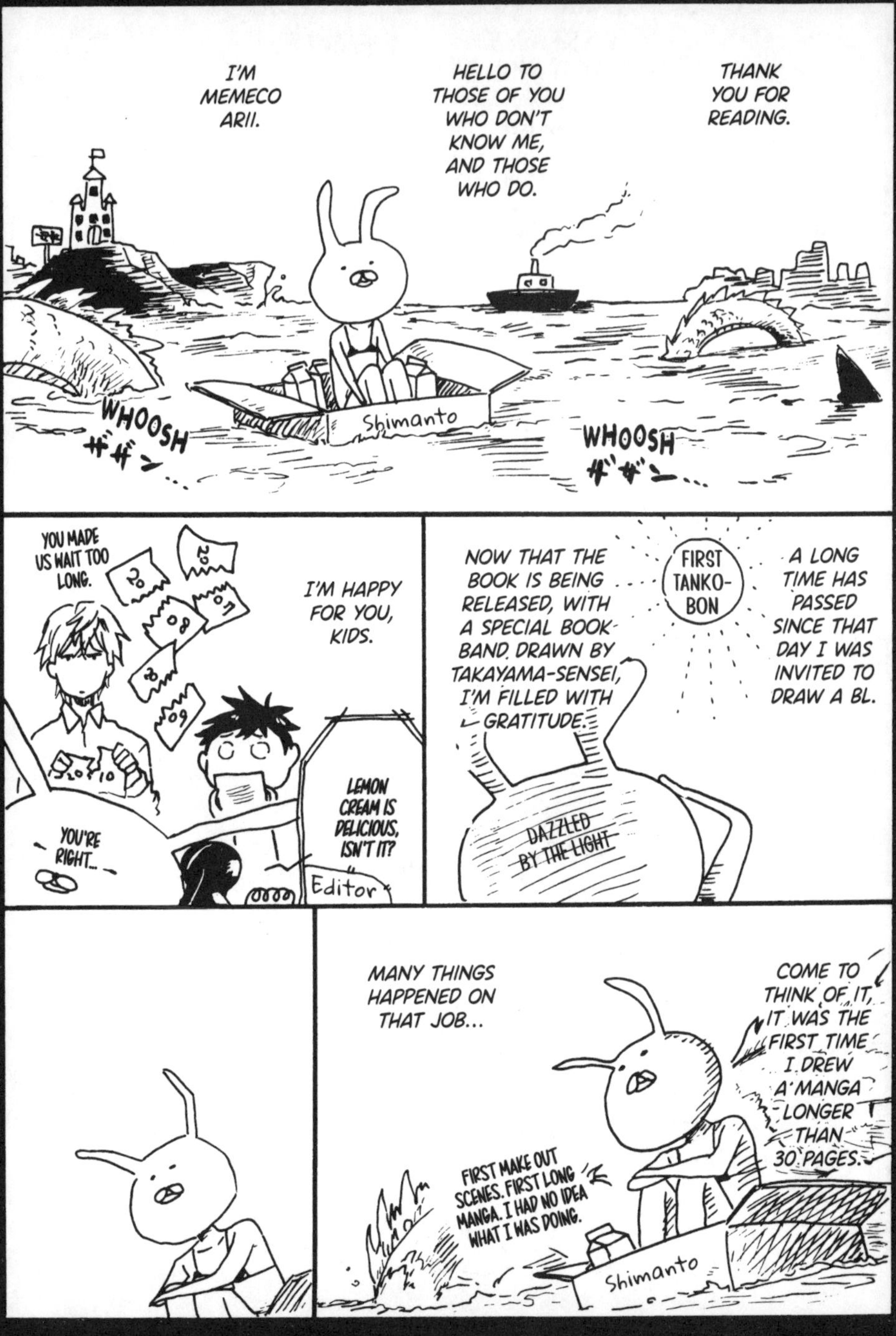
THANK YOU FOR READING.
HELLO TO THOSE OF YOU WHO DON'T KNOW ME, AND THOSE WHO DO.
I'M MEMECO ARII.
Shimanto
WHOOSH
WHOOSH
A LONG TIME HAS PASSED SINCE THAT DAY I WAS INVITED TO DRAW A BL.
FIRST TANKO-BON
NOW THAT THE BOOK IS BEING RELEASED, WITH A SPECIAL BOOK BAND DRAWN BY TAKAYAMA-SENSEI, I'M FILLED WITH GRATITUDE.
DAZZLED BY THE LIGHT
I'M HAPPY FOR YOU, KIDS.
YOU MADE US WAIT TOO LONG.
LEMON CREAM IS DELICIOUS, ISN'T IT?
YOU'RE RIGHT...
Editor
COME TO THINK OF IT, IT WAS THE FIRST TIME I DREW A MANGA LONGER THAN 30 PAGES.
MANY THINGS HAPPENED ON THAT JOB...
FIRST MAKE OUT SCENES. FIRST LONG MANGA. I HAD NO IDEA WHAT I WAS DOING.
Shimanto

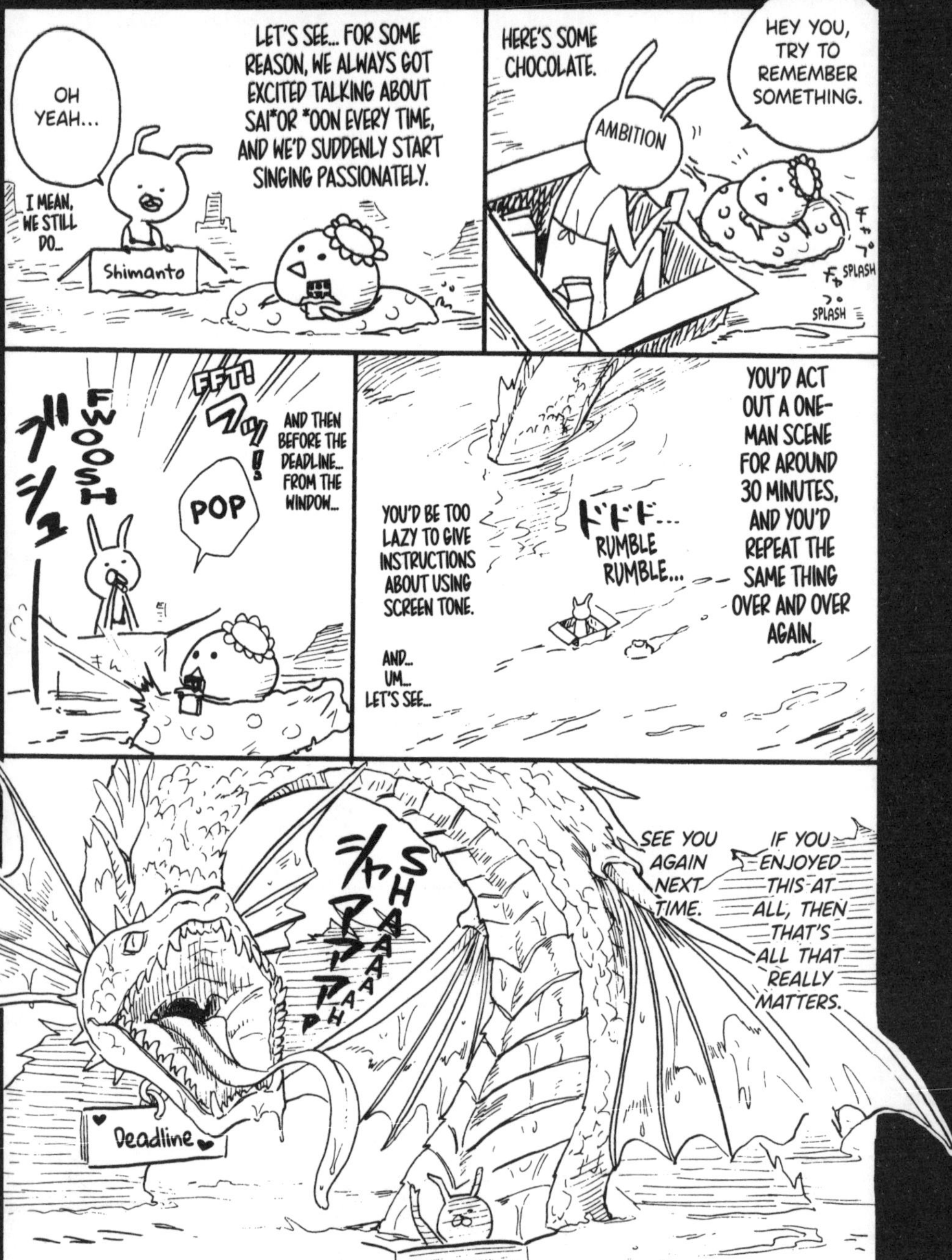
HEY YOU, TRY TO REMEMBER SOMETHING.
HERE'S SOME CHOCOLATE.
AMBITION
SPLASH
SPLASH
LET'S SEE... FOR SOME REASON, WE ALWAYS GOT EXCITED TALKING ABOUT SAI*OR *OON EVERY TIME, AND WE'D SUDDENLY START SINGING PASSIONATELY.
OH YEAH...
I MEAN, WE STILL DO...
Shimanto
YOU'D ACT OUT A ONE-MAN SCENE FOR AROUND 30 MINUTES, AND YOU'D REPEAT THE SAME THING OVER AND OVER AGAIN.
ドドド...
RUMBLE RUMBLE...
YOU'D BE TOO LAZY TO GIVE INSTRUCTIONS ABOUT USING SCREEN TONE.
AND... UM... LET'S SEE...
AND THEN BEFORE THE DEADLINE... FROM THE WINDOW...
FFT!
POP
FWOOSH
IF YOU ENJOYED THIS AT ALL, THEN THAT'S ALL THAT REALLY MATTERS.
SEE YOU AGAIN NEXT TIME.
SHAAAAAAAH
Deadline

TO MY BELOVED FRIENDS, ACQUAINTANCES, FAMILY, DESIGNERS, EDITOR, TAKAYAMA-SENSEI (TOTALLY SADISTIC), AND EVERYONE WHO READ THIS BOOK. THANK YOU!

HITORIJIME BOYFRIEND

PRESENTED BY MEMECO ARII

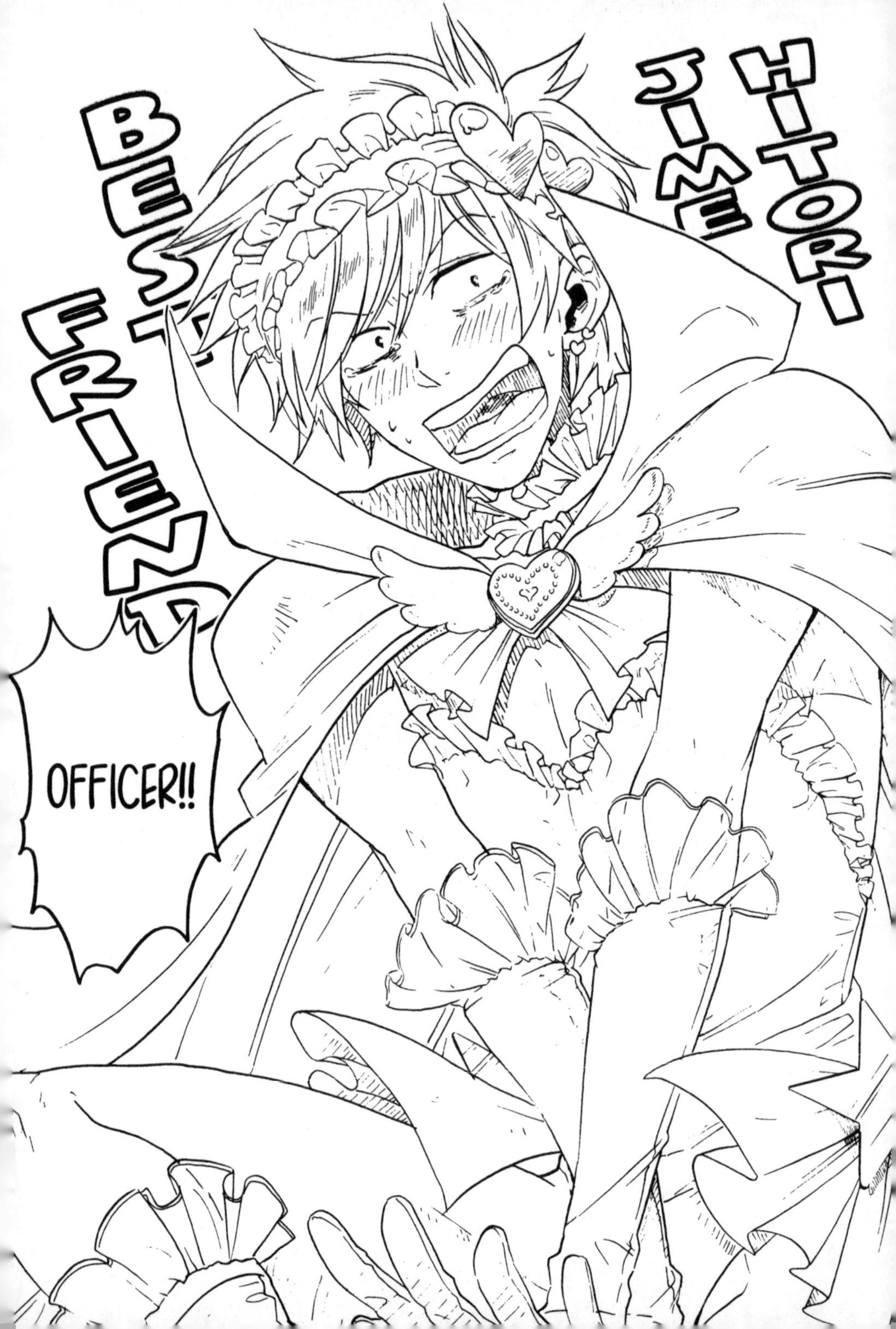
HITORI-JIME
BEST FRIEND
OFFICER!!

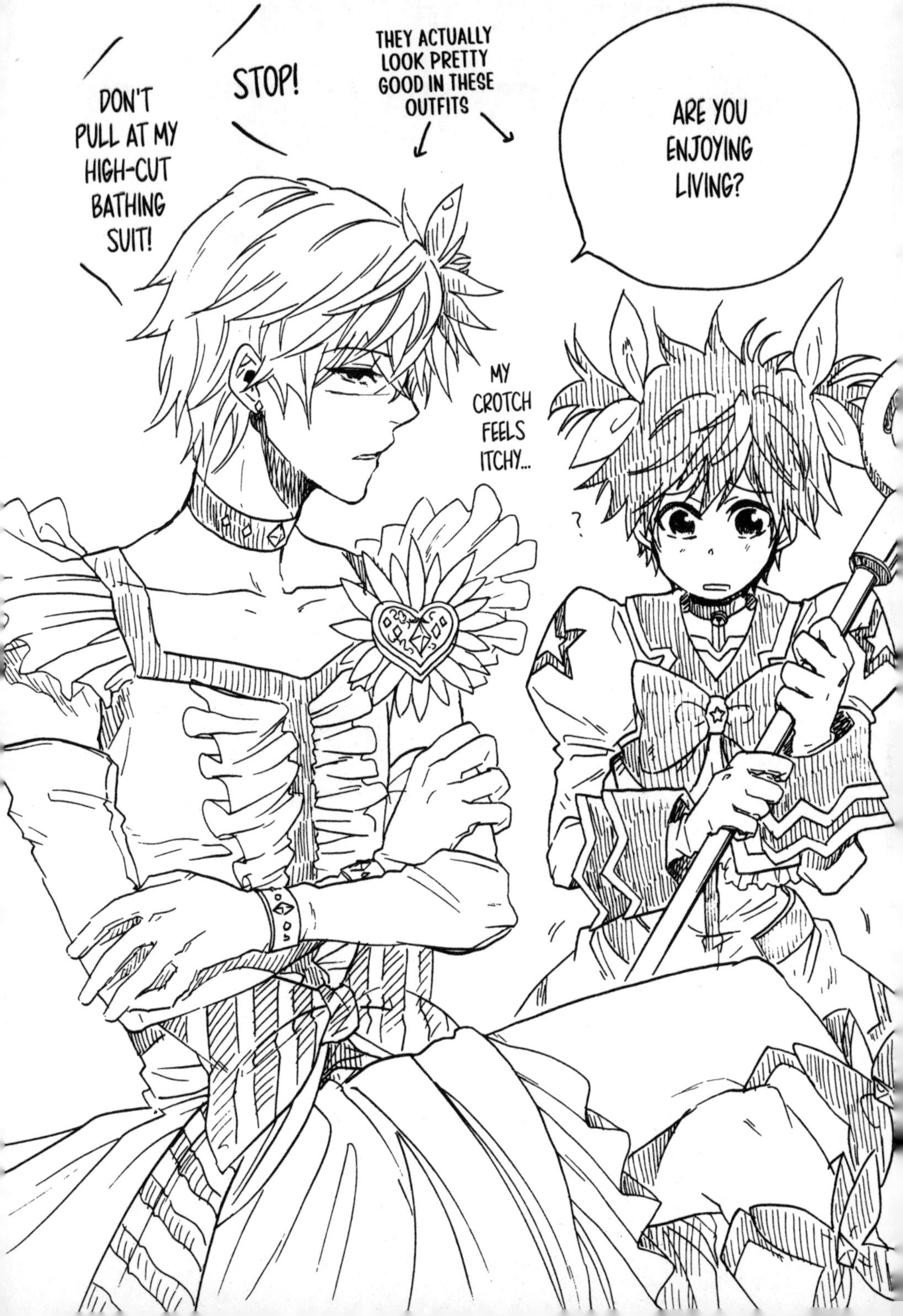

ARE YOU ENJOYING LIVING?
THEY ACTUALLY LOOK PRETTY GOOD IN THESE OUTFITS
STOP!
DON'T PULL AT MY HIGH-CUT BATHING SUIT!
MY CROTCH FEELS ITCHY...
?

Translation Notes

Chickadee pudding, page 88
When someone dyes their hair brown or blonde but lets enough time pass that the natural color of their roots starts to show, they are sometimes said to have a case of "pudding head," due to its resemblance to Japanese pudding (which is an egg custard similar to flan).

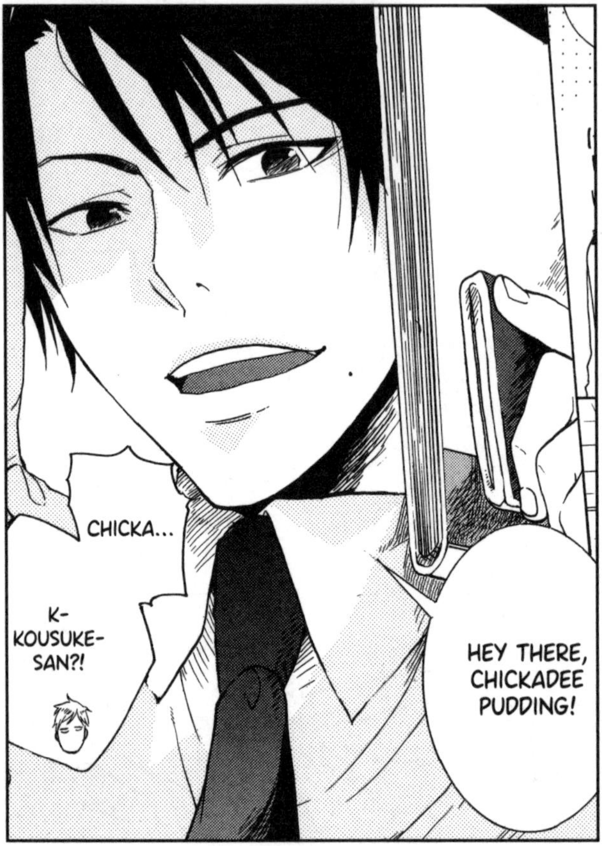
HEY THERE, CHICKADEE PUDDING!
CHICKA...
K-KOUSUKE-SAN?!

One of CLAMP's biggest hits returns in this definitive, premium, hardcover 20th anniversary collector's edition!

"A wonderfully entertaining story that would be a great installment in anybody's manga collection."
— Anime News Network

"CLAMP is an all-female manga-creating team whose feminine touch shows in this entertaining, sci-fi soap opera."
— Publishers Weekly

Poor college student Hideki is down on his luck. All he wants is a good job, a girlfriend, and his very own "persocom"—the latest and greatest in humanoid computer technology. Hideki's luck changes one night when he finds Chi—a persocom thrown out in a pile of trash. But Hideki soon discovers that there's much more to his cute new persocom than meets the eye.

KC
KODANSHA
COMICS

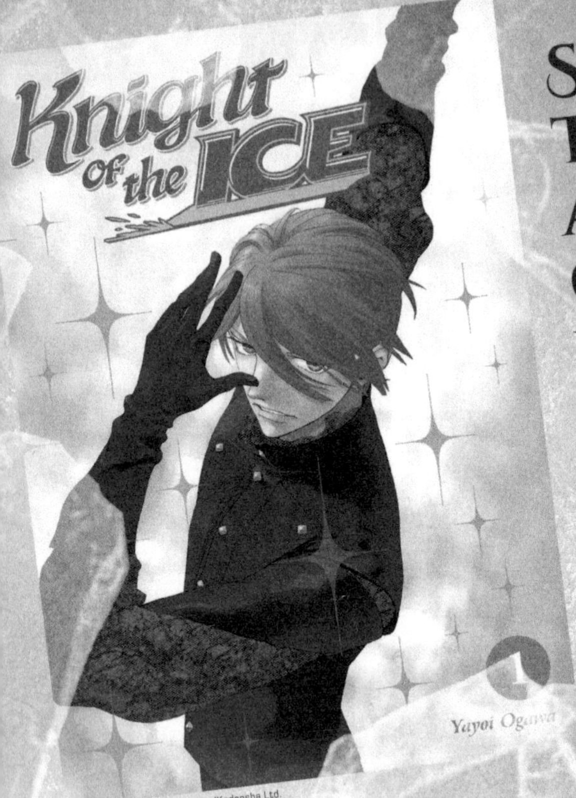
Knight of the ICE
1
Yayoi Ogawa

Knight of the Ice ©Yayoi Ogawa/Kodansha Ltd.

SKATING THRILLS AND ICY CHILLS WITH THIS NEW TINGLY ROMANCE SERIES!

A rom-com on ice, perfect for fans of *Princess Jellyfish* and *Wotakoi*. Kokoro is the talk of the figure-skating world, winning trophies and hearts. But little do they know... he's actually a huge nerd! From the beloved creator of *You're My Pet* (*Tramps Like Us*).

Chitose is a serious young woman, working for the health magazine *SASSO*. Or at least, she would be, if she wasn't constantly getting distracted by her childhood friend, international figure skating star Kokoro Kijinami! In the public eye and on the ice, Kokoro is a gallant, flawless knight, but behind his glittery costumes and breathtaking spins lies a secret: He's actually a hopelessly romantic otaku, who can only land his quad jumps when Chitose is on hand to recite a spell from his favorite magical girl anime!

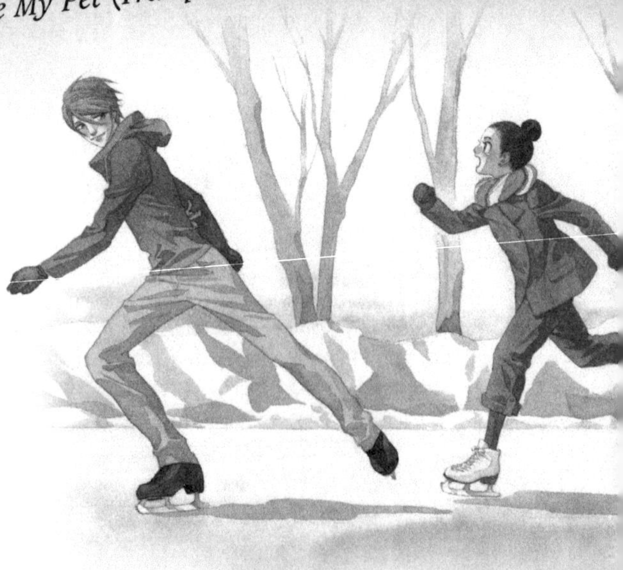

KC KODANSHA COMICS

A SMART, NEW ROMANTIC COMEDY FOR FANS OF *SHORTCAKE CAKE* AND *TERRACE HOUSE*!

Living-Room Matsunaga-san © Keiko Iwashita / Kodansha Ltd.

A romance manga starring high school girl Meeko, who learns to live on her own in a boarding house whose living room is home to the odd (but handsome) Matsunaga-san. She begins to adjust to her new life away from her parents, but Meeko soon learns that no matter how far away from home she is, she's still a young girl at heart — especially when she finds herself falling for Matsunaga-san.

PERFECT WORLD

Rie Aruga

A TOUCHING
NEW SERIES
ABOUT LOVE AND
COPING WITH
DISABILITY

An office party reunites Tsugumi with her high school crush Itsuki. He's realized his dream of becoming an architect, but along the way, he experienced a spinal injury that put him in a wheelchair. Now Tsugumi's rekindled feelings will butt up against prejudices she never considered — and Itsuki will have to decide if he's ready to let someone into his heart...

"Depicts with great delicacy and courage the difficulties some with disabilities experience getting involved in romantic relationships... Rie Aruga refuses to romanticize, pushing her heroine to face the reality of disability. She invites her readers to the same tasks of empathy, knowledge and recognition."
—Slate.fr

"An important entry [in manga romance]... The emotional core of both plot and characters indicates thoughtfulness... [Aruga's] research is readily apparent in the text and artwork, making this feel like a real story."
—Anime News Network

KC
KODANSHA
COMICS

The boys are back, in 400-page hardcovers that are as pretty and badass as they are!

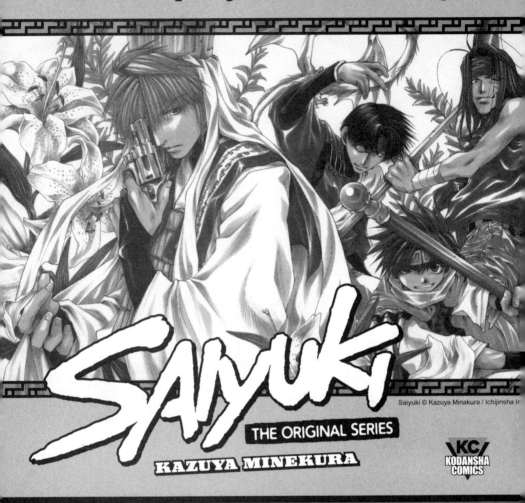

Saiyuki © Kazuya Minakura / Ichijinsha In

SAIYUKI

THE ORIGINAL SERIES

KAZUYA MINEKURA

"AN EDGY COMIC LOOK AT AN ANCIENT CHINESE TALE." —YALSA

Genjo Sanzo is a Buddhist priest in the city of Togenkyo, which is being ravaged by yokai spirits that have fallen out of balance with the natural order. His superiors send him on a journey far to the west to discover why this is happening and how to stop it. His companions are three yokai with human souls. But this is no day trip — the four will encounter many discoveries and horrors on the way.

FEATURES NEW TRANSLATION, COLOR PAGES, AND BEAUTIFUL WRAPAROUND COVER ART!

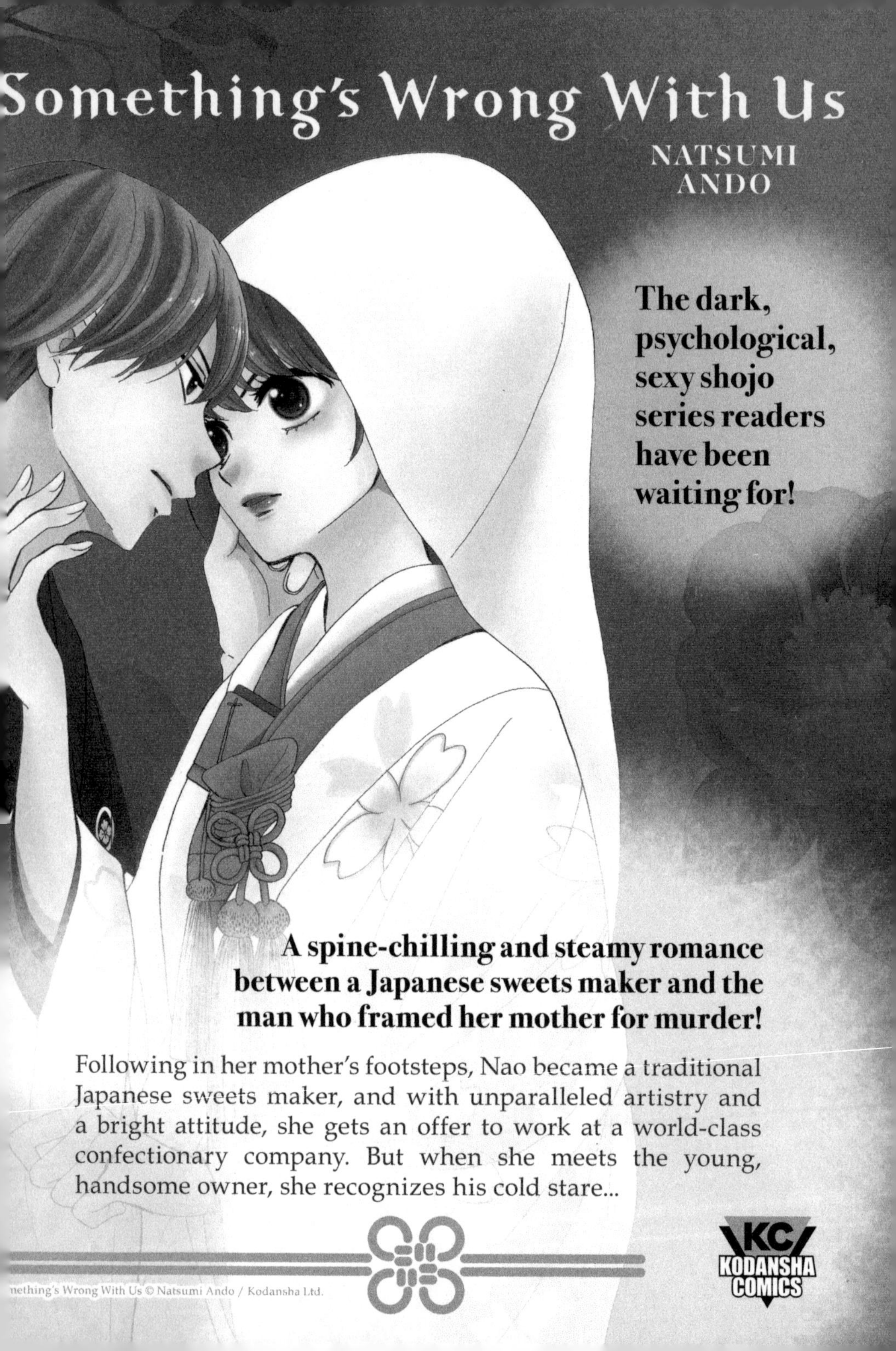
Something's Wrong With Us
NATSUMI ANDO
The dark, psychological, sexy shojo series readers have been waiting for!
A spine-chilling and steamy romance between a Japanese sweets maker and the man who framed her mother for murder!
Following in her mother's footsteps, Nao became a traditional Japanese sweets maker, and with unparalleled artistry and a bright attitude, she gets an offer to work at a world-class confectionary company. But when she meets the young, handsome owner, she recognizes his cold stare...
KC KODANSHA COMICS
nething's Wrong With Us © Natsumi Ando / Kodansha Ltd.

The adorable new odd-couple cat comedy manga from the creator of the beloved *Chi's Sweet Home*, in full color!

Praise for Chi's Sweet Home

"Nearly impossible to turn away... a true all-ages title that anyone, young or old, cat lover or not, will enjoy. The stories will bring a smile to your face and warm your heart."

—School Library Journal

Sue & Tai-chan

Konami Kanata

Sue is an aging housecat who's looking forward to living out her life in peace... but her plans change when the mischievous black tomcat Tai-chan enters the picture! Hey! Sue never signed up to be a catsitter! *Sue & Tai-chan* is the latest from the reigning meow-narch of cute kitty comics, Konami Kanata.

KC
KODANSHA
COMICS

THE SWEET SCENT OF LOVE IS IN THE AIR! FOR FANS OF OFFBEAT ROMANCES LIKE *WOTAKOI*

Sweat and Soap © Kintetsu Yamada / Kodansha Ltd.

In an office romance, there's a fine line between sexy and awkward... and that line is where Asako — a woman who sweats copiously — meets Koutarou — a perfume developer who can't get enough of Asako's, er, scent. Don't miss a romcom manga like no other!

KC
KODANSHA
COMICS

CUTE ANIMALS AND LIFE LESSONS,
PERFECT FOR ASPIRING PET VETS OF ALL AGES!

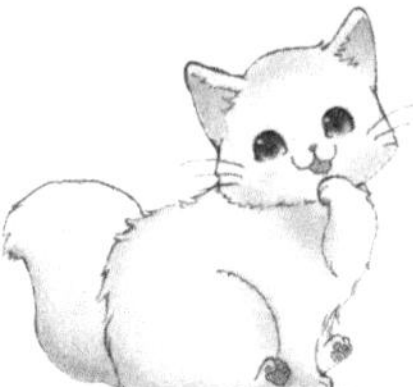

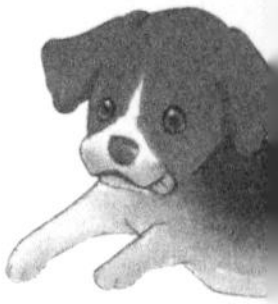

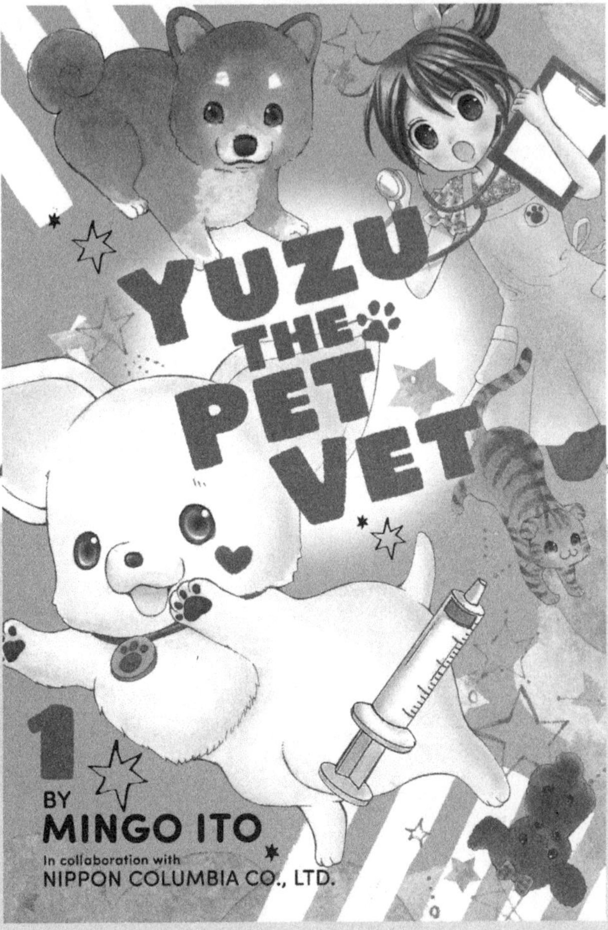

YUZU THE PET VET
1
BY
MINGO ITO
In collaboration with
NIPPON COLUMBIA CO., LTD.

For an 11-year-old, Yuzu has a lot on her plate. When her mom gets sick and has to be hospitalized, Yuzu goes to live with her uncle who runs the local veterinary clinic. Yuzu's always been scared of animals, but she tries to help out. Through all the tough moments in her life, Yuzu realizes that she can help make things all right with a little help from her animal pals, peers, and kind grown-ups.

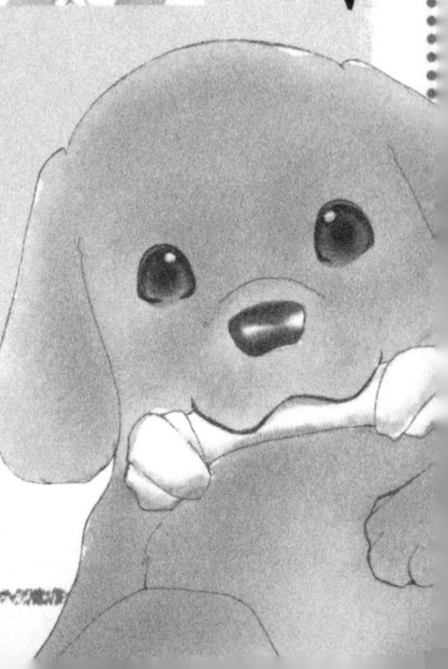

Every new patient is a furry friend in the making!

Young characters and steampunk setting, like *Howl's Moving Castle* and *Battle Angel Alita*

Beyond the Clouds © 2018 Nicke / Ki-oon

A boy with a talent for machines and a mysterious girl whose wings he's fixed will take you beyond the clouds! In the tradition of the high-flying, resonant adventure stories of Studio Ghibli comes a gorgeous tale about the longing of young hearts for adventure and friendship!

THE WORLD OF CLAMP!

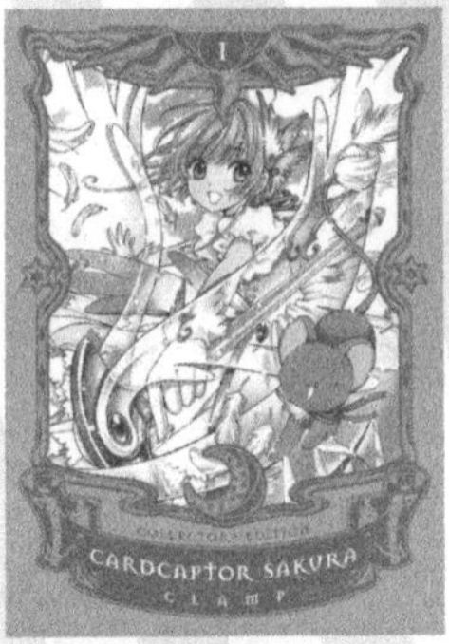
CARDCAPTOR SAKURA
CLAMP

Cardcaptor Sakura
Collector's Edition

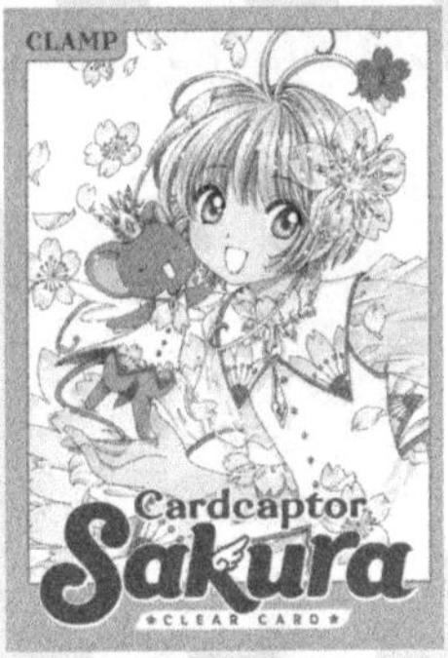
CLAMP
Cardcaptor
Sakura
CLEAR CARD

Cardcaptor Sakura:
Clear Card

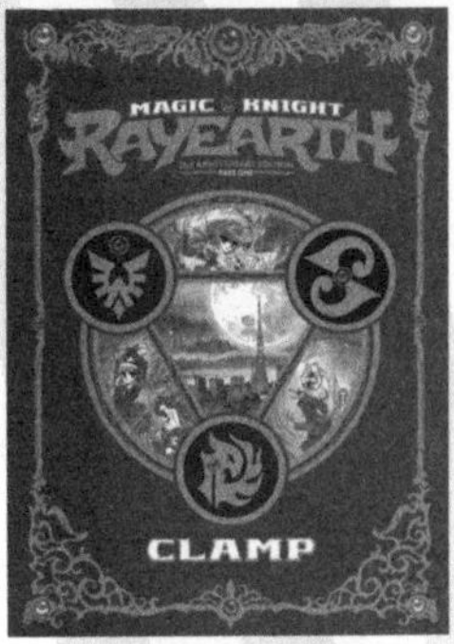
MAGIC KNIGHT
RAYEARTH
CLAMP

Magic Knight Rayearth
25th Anniversary Box Set

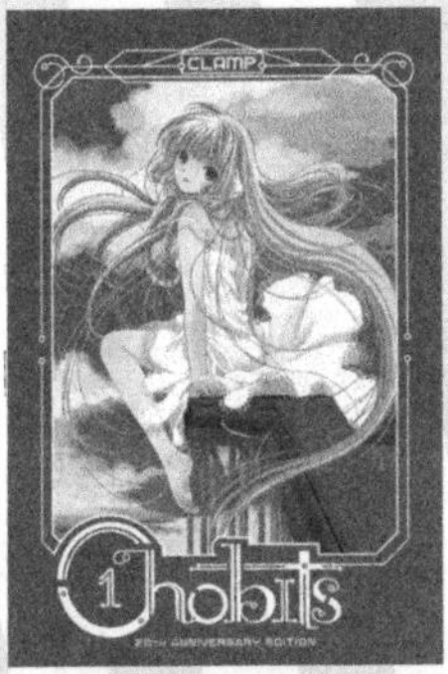
CLAMP
Chobits
1

Chobits

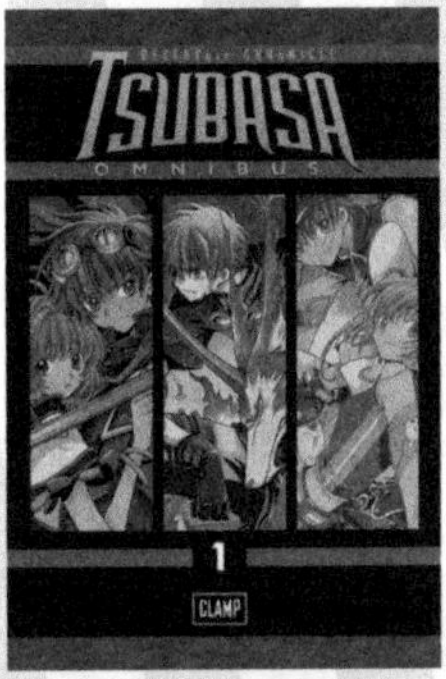
TSUBASA
OMNIBUS
1
CLAMP

TSUBASA Omnibus

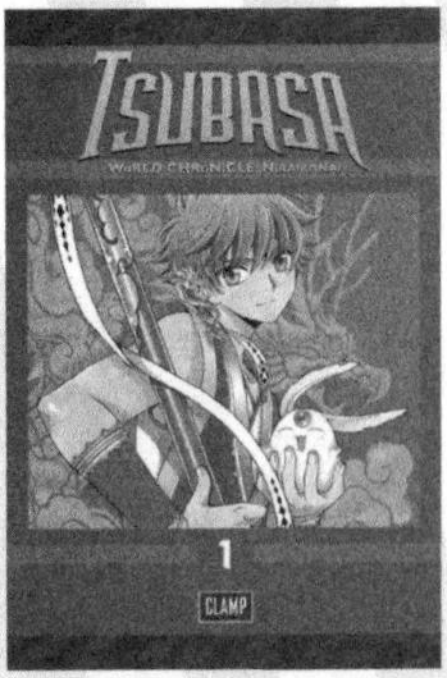
TSUBASA
1
CLAMP

TSUBASA WoRLD CHRoNiCLE

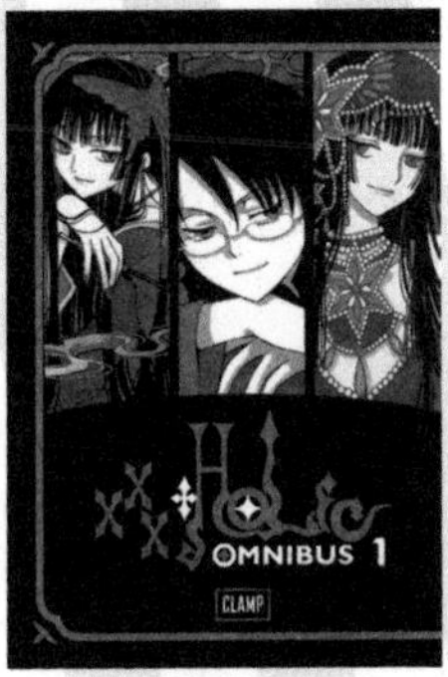
xxxHOLiC
OMNIBUS 1
CLAMP

xxxHOLiC Omnibus

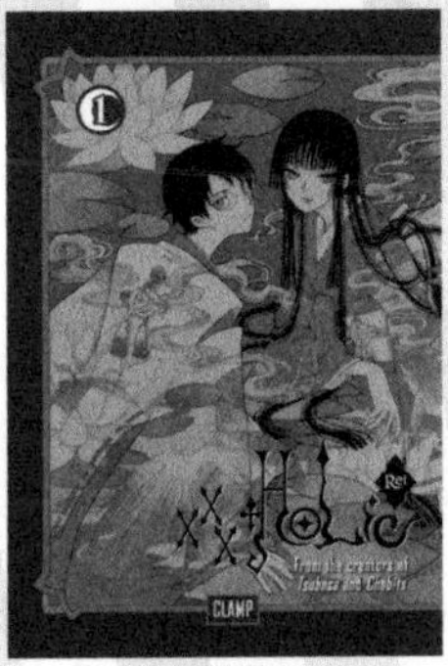
1
xxxHOLiC
Rei
CLAMP

xxxHOLiC Rei

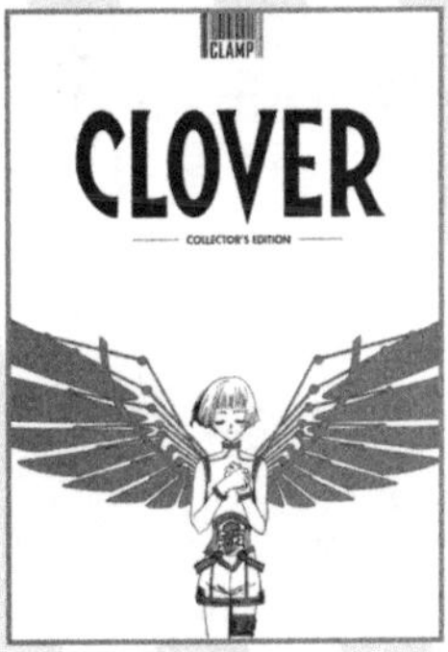
CLAMP
CLOVER
COLLECTOR'S EDITION

CLOVER Collector's Edition

Kodansha Comics welcomes you to explore the expansive world of CLAMP, the all-female artist collective that has produced some of the most acclaimed manga of the century. Our growing catalog includes icons like *Cardcaptor Sakura* and *Magic Knight Rayearth*, each crafted with CLAMP's one-of-a-kind style and characters!

The beloved characters from *Cardcaptor Sakura* return in a brand new, reimagined fantasy adventure!

RESERVoir CHRoNiCLE
TSUBASA
OMNIBUS
1
CLAMP

TSUBASA
WoRLD CHRoNiCLE: NIRAIKANAI
1
CLAMP

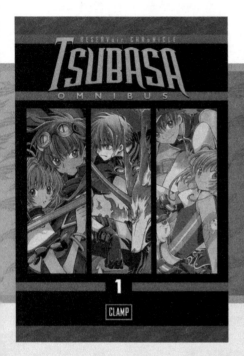

"[*Tsubasa*] takes readers on a fantastic ride that only gets more exhilarating with each successive chapter." –Anime News Network

In the Kingdom of Clow, an archaeological dig unleashes an incredible power, causing Princess Sakura to lose her memories. To save her, her childhood friend Syaoran must follow the orders of the Dimension Witch and travel alongside Kurogane, an unrivaled warrior; Fai, a powerful magician; and Mokona, a curiously strange creature, to retrieve Sakura's dispersed memories!

KC
KODANSHA COMICS

"Clever, sassy, and original....*xxxHOLiC* has the inherent hallmarks of a runaway hit."
—NewType magazine

Beautifully seductive artwork and uniquely Japanese depictions of the supernatural will hypnotize CLAMP fans!

Kimihiro Watanuki is haunted by visions of ghosts and spirits. He seeks help from a mysterious woman named Yuko, who claims she can help. However, Watanuki must work for Yuko in order to pay for her aid. Soon Watanuki finds himself employed in Yuko's shop, where he sees things and meets customers that are stranger than anything he could have ever imagined.

A Kodansha Comics Trade Paperback Original
Hitorijime Boyfriend copyright © 2010 Memeco Arii
English translation copyright © 2021 Memeco Arii

Published in the United States by Kodansha Comics, an imprint of Kodansha USA Publishing, LLC, New York.

Publication rights for this English edition arranged through Kodansha Ltd., Tokyo.

First published in Japan in 2010 by Ichijinsha Inc., Tokyo.

ISBN 978-1-63236-933-8

Printed in the United States of America.

www.kodansha.us

9 8 7 6 5 4 3 2 1
Translation: Iyasu Nagata
Lettering: Michael Martin
Editing: Greg Moore
Kodansha USA Publishing edition cover design by My Truong

Publisher: Kiichiro Sugawara

Director of publishing services: Ben Applegate
Associate director of operations: Stephen Pakula
Publishing services managing editors: Madison Salters, Alanna Ruse
Production managers: Emi Lotto, Angela Zurlo
Logo and character art ©Kodansha USA Publishing, LLC